Global Issues Series

General Editor: **Jim Whitman**

This exciting new series encompasses three principal themes: the interaction of human and natural systems; cooperation and conflict; and the enactment of values. The series as a whole places an emphasis on the examination of complex systems and causal relations in political decision-making; problems of knowledge; authority, control and accountability in issues of scale; and the reconciliation of conflicting values and competing claims. Throughout the series the concentration is on an integration of existing disciplines towards the clarification of political possibility as well as impending crises.

Titles include:

Alexander Kelle, Kathryn Nixdorff and Malcolm Dando
CONTROLLING BIOCHEMICAL WEAPONS
Adapting Multilateral Arms Control for the 21st Century

W. Andy Knight
A CHANGING UNITED NATIONS
Multilateral Evolution and the Quest for Global Governance

W. Andy Knight (*editor*)
ADAPTING THE UNITED NATIONS TO A POSTMODERN ERA
Lessons Learned

Kelley Lee (*editor*)
HEALTH IMPACTS OF GLOBALIZATION
Towards Global Governance
GLOBALIZATION AND HEALTH
An Introduction

Nicholas Low and Brendan Gleeson (*editors*)
MAKING URBAN TRANSPORT SUSTAINABLE

Catherine Lu
JUST AND UNJUST INTERVENTIONS IN WORLD POLITICS
Public and Private

Robert L. Ostergard Jr. (*editor*)
HIV, AIDS AND THE THREAT TO NATIONAL AND INTERNATIONAL SECURITY

Graham S. Pearson
THE UNSCOM SAGA
Chemical and Biological Weapons Non-Proliferation
THE SEARCH FOR IRAQ'S WEAPONS OF MASS DESTRUCTION
Inspection, Verification and Non-Proliferation

Andrew T. Price-Smith (*editor*)
PLAGUES AND POLITICS
Infectious Disease and International Policy

Michael Pugh (*editor*)
REGENERATION OF WAR-TORN SOCIETIES

David Scott
'THE CHINESE CENTURY'?
The Challenge to Global Order

Marco Verweij and Michael Thompson (*editors*)
CLUMSY SOLUTIONS FOR A COMPLEX WORLD
Governance, Politics and Plural Perceptions

Bhaskar Vira and Roger Jeffery (*editors*)
ANALYTICAL ISSUES IN PARTICIPATORY NATURAL RESOURCE MANAGEMENT

Simon M. Whitby
BIOLOGICAL WARFARE AGAINST CROPS

Global Issues Series
Series Standing Order ISBN 978–0–333–79483–8
(*outside North America only*)

You can receive future titles in this series as they are published by placing a standing order. Please contact your bookseller or, in case of difficulty, write to us at the address below with your name and address, the title of the series and the ISBN quoted above.

Customer Services Department, Macmillan Distribution Ltd, Houndmills, Basingstoke, Hampshire RG21 6XS, England

The Role of Business in Global Governance

Corporations as Norm-Entrepreneurs

Annegret Flohr
Research Associate, Department of Political Science,
Technische Universität Darmstadt, Germany

Lothar Rieth
Research Associate, Department of Political Science,
Technische Universität Darmstadt, Germany

Sandra Schwindenhammer
Research Associate, Department of International Politics,
FernUniversität in Hagen, Germany

and

Klaus Dieter Wolf
Professor for International Relations at Technische Universität Darmstadt and
Deputy Director of the Peace Research Institute Frankfurt (PRIF), Germany

First published 2010 by
PALGRAVE MACMILLAN

Palgrave Macmillan in the UK is an imprint of Macmillan Publishers Limited,
registered in England, company number 785998, of Houndmills, Basingstoke,
Hampshire RG21 6XS.

Palgrave Macmillan in the US is a division of St Martin's Press LLC,
175 Fifth Avenue, New York, NY 10010.

Palgrave Macmillan is the global academic imprint of the above companies
and has companies and representatives throughout the world.

Palgrave® and Macmillan® are registered trademarks in the United States,
the United Kingdom, Europe and other countries.

ISBN: 978–0–230–24397–2

This book is printed on paper suitable for recycling and made from fully
managed and sustained forest sources. Logging, pulping and manufacturing
processes are expected to conform to the environmental regulations of the
country of origin.

A catalogue record for this book is available from the British Library.

A catalog record for this book is available from the Library of Congress.

Printed and bound in Great Britain by
CPI Antony Rowe, Chippenham and Eastbourne

Contents

Part III   Evaluating Corporate Norm-entrepreneurship

Illustrations

Tables

Figures

Foreword

In this book the new political role of corporations in the execution of transnational governance functions is analyzed. Governance beyond the state faces considerable challenges since economic globalization has exceeded the capabilities of any single state and even of intergovernmental governance systems to provide public goods effectively. Against this background, new forms of self-regulation, notably in the socioeconomic and environmental fields, are emerging in which business corporations participate in norm setting. There is a shift in the division of labor between the public and the private sector in the provision of governance functions.

By conceptualizing this role change of business actors as corporate norm-entrepreneurship and employing a coherent set of criteria for its evaluation this book examines to what extent the contributions by private norm-entrepreneurs to global governance can be meaningful supplements or even substitutes for public regulation. We believe that the results of our research will contribute to a better understanding of the potential and the limits of private self-regulatory arrangements as components of a future global governance architecture. We take stock of private contributions to transnational governance, investigate under what conditions which kinds of contributions can be expected, and evaluate their implications for the effectiveness and legitimacy of governance beyond the state.

Acknowledgments

This volume results from a research project directed by Klaus Dieter Wolf, Thomas Conzelmann, and Helmut Breitmeier at Technische Universität Darmstadt, Germany. We are extremely grateful to the German Research Foundation (DFG) for the generous financial support that we have received since October 2005.

We also want to thank the numerous representatives of companies and self-regulatory initiatives for the valuable insights they have contributed as interview partners. Without their cooperation and frankness this research would not have been possible. We cannot do justice to all colleagues whose valuable comments we received at various occasions. The inspiring intellectual exchange with the Research Centers 'Governance in Areas of Limited Statehood' in Berlin and 'Transformations of the State' in Bremen were particularly valuable. Moreover, we benefited tremendously from the regular exchanges with our colleagues Moira Feil, Susanne Fischer, Andreas Haidvogl and Melanie Zimmer at the Peace Research Institute Frankfurt. In addition, we are grateful to a number of individual colleagues, including A. Claire Cutler, Nicole Deitelhoff, Virginia Haufler, and Andreas Georg Scherer, for their continuous intellectual and personal support since the very beginning of this project. We also like to thank the series' editor Jim Whitman and our publisher Alexandra C. Webster for their enthusiasm and the reviewers for their encouraging comments.

Finally, the authors wish to thank Martina Borusewitsch, Julia Ebling, Kristian Lempa, Florian Ringer, Iman Sakkaki, Svenja Schuchmann, Samuil Simeonov, and Linda Wallbott for their research assistance, Stefanie Herr for editorial assistance, and Larissa Moore for language editing.

DARMSTADT, July 2009

Notes on the Authors

Klaus Dieter Wolf holds the Chair for International Relations at Technische Universität Darmstadt, Germany. He is also the Deputy Director of the Peace Research Institute Frankfurt (PRIF) and one of the Principal Investigators of the Cluster of Excellence 'Formation of Normative Orders'. He was president of the German Political Science Association (DVPW) from 2003 to 2006 and has been Non-North American Member of the Governing Council of the International Studies Association (ISA) from 2008 to 2009. His research areas include international political theory, transnational private governance, and peace and conflict studies.

Annegret Flohr is a Research Associate at the Chair of International Relations, and a Ph.D. candidate at Technische Universität Darmstadt, Germany. She completed her B.A. in International Relations at Dresden University of Technology, Germany, in 2004 and her M.A. in Human Rights and Democratization at the University of Malta in 2006. Her research interests revolve around global governance, international law and the role of nonstate actors in international politics. Her dissertation analyzes the impact of self-regulation on international legalization in the banking sector and features case studies of the Wolfsberg and the Equator Principles.

Lothar Rieth works as a Research Associate at the Department of Political Science, Technische Universität Darmstadt. He holds M.A.s in Political Science (Rutgers University, NJ, the United States) and Public Policy & Management (Universität Konstanz, Germany). His doctoral dissertation focused on 'Global Governance and Corporate Social Responsibility' and the effectiveness of self-regulatory initiatives. He has published a number of articles on the role of nonstate actors and new modes of governance. Moreover, he is interested in new teaching methodologies, linking theory and practice. As an expert in the field of corporate social responsibility he provides policy advice to international and national institutions.

Sandra Schwindenhammer is a Research Associate at the Department of International Politics, FernUniversität in Hagen, Germany. From 2005 to 2008 she worked at the Department for International Relations at Technische Universität Darmstadt on the research project 'Corporations as Norm-entrepreneurs?'. She holds a Master's degree and graduated in political science, sociology, and law from Technische Universität Darmstadt in 2005. Her research focus lies on global governance, corporate social responsibility (CSR), and sustainability reporting. In her Ph.D. dissertation, she is analyzing the impact of home state conditions on corporate contributions to governance in the Global Reporting Initiative.

Abbreviations

AML	AntiMoney Laundering
ASEAN	Association of Southeast Asian Nations
B2B	Business to Business
B2C	Business to Consumer
BBC	British Broadcast Corporation
BMZ	German Federal Ministry for Economic Cooperation and Development
BPCB	Business Principles for Countering Bribery
BRIC	Brazil, Russia, India, China
BSCI	Business Social Compliance Initiative
CBI	Confederation of British Industry
CEE	Central and Eastern European States
CEO	Chief Executive Officer
CERES	Coalition for Environmentally Responsible Economics
CFP	Corporate Financial Performance
CIS	Chartered Institute of Secretaries and Administrators
CoP	Communication on Progress
CSR	Corporate Social Responsibility
DIHR	Danish Institute for Human Rights
ECOSOC	UN Economic and Social Council
ECOWAS	Economic Community of West African States
EEA	European Economic Area
EITI	Extractive Industries Transparency Initiative
EMAS	Eco-Management and Audit Scheme
ERRI	Environmental Regulatory Regime Index
ESG	Environmental, Social and Governance Performance
ETNO	European Telecommunications Network Operators Association
EU	European Union
EVA	Economic Value Added
FATF	Financial Action Task Force on Money Laundering
FLO	Fairtrade Labelling Organization International
FSC	Forest Stewardship Council
FTA	Foreign Trade Association
GC	Global Compact
GCI	Global Competitiveness Index
GCR	Global Competitiveness Report
GRI	Global Reporting Initiative
GRPP	Global and Regional Partnership Program

GTZ	Deutsche Gesellschaft für Technische Zusammenarbeit
IEG	Independent Evaluation Group
IFOAM	International Federation of Organic Agriculture Movements
ILO	International Labour Organization
IoD	Institute of Directors
IPE	International Political Economy
IR	International Relations
ISEAL	International Social and Environmental Accreditation and Labelling
IUCN	International Union for Conservation of Nature
JSE	Johannesburg Stock Exchange
MERCOSUR	Mercado Común del Sur or Common Market of the South
MROS	Money Laundering Reporting Office Switzerland
NAFTA	North American Free-Trade Agreement
NGOs	Non-Governmental Organization
OECD	Organisation for Economic Co-operation and Development
OFAC	Office for Foreign Assets Control in the United States Department of the Treasury
PEP	Politically Exposed Persons
PPP	Public Private Partnership
RTA	Regional Trade Areas
SA 8000	Social Accountability 8000
SAAS	Social Accountability Accreditation Services
SACOB	South African Chamber of Business
SAI	Social Accountability International
SAIBE	South African Institute of Business Ethics
SAICA	South African Institute of Chartered Accountants
SAN	Sustainable Agriculture Network
SASA	Social Accountability in Sustainable Agriculture
SDT	Special and Different Treatment (WTO)
SFP	Structured Feedback Process (GRI)
SME	Small and Medium Enterprises
SRI	Socially Responsible Investment
TI	Transparency International
TNCs	Transnational Corporations
UN	United Nations
UNCTAD	United Nations Conference on Trade and Development
UNEP	United Nations Environmental Programme
VoC	Varieties of Capitalism
WTO	World Trade Organization

Part I
The Research Context

International Relations research is facing an increasing involvement of the business sector in transnational norm setting and norm development. The aim of this book is to explore the conditions under which corporations can be expected to make meaningful contributions to global governance. Part I provides the conceptual background for a better understanding of the new interplay among the state, the business sector, and civil society in the co-performance of governance in the transnational sphere. It outlines basic concepts and assumptions for the study of corporate norm-entrepreneurship. Chapter 1 deals with a still underconceptualized role shift: Companies are re-inventing themselves as political actors in an increasing number of self-regulatory arrangements. The chapter reflects the political and analytical challenges that are provoked by assigning regulatory functions to profit driven, self-interested market actors. Chapter 2 introduces the core concept of this study: corporate norm-entrepreneurship. Based on this concept, a representative sample of ten companies is selected that contains particularly proactive norm-entrepreneurs. These ten companies are at the center of the empirical analysis of the conditions under which corporate norm-entrepreneurship is likely to occur. Chapter 2 ends with identifying three clusters of potential explanatory factors for corporate norm-entrepreneurship that are put to the test in Part II: the social and political environment, certain characteristics of the corporations themselves, and the institutional design of self-regulatory arrangements.

1

Introduction: Corporate Norm-entrepreneurship and Global Governance

Effective and legitimate governance beyond the state faces considerable challenges. The traditional mode of interstate accords seems increasingly insufficient to provide reliable and sustainable solutions to collective problems at the global level. Against this background, emerging new forms of private self-regulation may be seen as possible solutions. To establish how far these expectations are justified and to what extent private contributions to global governance can be supplements or even substitutes for public regulation, the aims are as follows: to take stock, in empirical terms, of private contributions to transnational governance systematically as an expression of the new interplay among the state, the business sector, and civil society; to understand better the potential as well as the limits of private regulatory initiatives as components of the future global governance architecture; investigate under what conditions what kind of private contributions to governance beyond the state can be expected; and to evaluate, from a normative perspective, the implications of these contributions for the effectiveness, responsiveness, and reliability of public good provision as well as for power control and the self-determination of the addressees of private regulatory initiatives.

Governance beyond the state is characterized by remarkable individual and collective involvement of business corporations, notably in the socio-economic and environmental fields. There is obviously a shift going on in the division of labor between the public and the private sector in providing public goods. This shift toward transnational private governance goes along with the transformation of traditional roles of actors. The earlier distinction between governments as being public in form and public in purpose, while actors from civil society were regarded as private in form and public in purpose, and business corporations as being private in form and private in purpose, is no longer valid. As the Bremen TranState Research Centre rightly claims, this transition and role shift begins with the nation-state itself.

The golden age of statehood, ideally characterized by a complete overlap of its four basic dimensions – resources, law, legitimacy, and welfare – at the national level of the modern Organisation for Economic Co-operation and Development (OECD) state (see Leibfried and Zürn 2005), seems to be history in the age of globalization. With its decline since the late 1970s, various functions traditionally ascribed to the state have dispersed into the international realm (internationalization) and to new actors (privatization). The emerging 'postnational constellation' (Habermas 2001) is characterized by new regulatory arrangements in which the state shares responsibility with private actors. Governments change their role from providers to enablers of public goods.

The new phenomenon has been properly described as 'co-production of statehood' or 'co-performance of governance' (Schuppert 2008). If it is conceded that economic globalization creates challenges for political steering that exceed the capabilities of any single state, and even of intergovernmental governance systems, making use of the problem solving potential of nonstate actors in order to master these challenges more effectively seems to make perfect sense. These challenges call for 'arrangements in which public as well as private actors aim at solving societal problems or create opportunities, and aim at the care for the societal institutions within which these governing activities take place' (Kooiman 2000: 139).

Among the numerous strategies employed by national governments to increase their problem solving capability, the more direct involvement of private actors in the governance process is of particular interest. This step toward societal participation was not primarily motivated by democratic concerns but followed the rationale of increasing problem-solving effectiveness by utilizing the knowledge and other resources that only private actors could provide. Co-opting the former addressees of state regulation as partners in decision making could also increase the support and acceptance of political decisions. The expectation of a cooperative response by business actors to becoming partners in new governance arrangements relies on (1) market incentives for corporations to engage in norm setting and norm implementation, (2) corporations' strategic interests in avoiding reputational costs or legally binding public regulation, or (3) the exchange of information in learning processes designed to improve corporations' capacities to enact their supposedly intrinsically motivated willingness to 'do good'.

Within the traditional pluralist model of domestic policy-making and interest, intermediary societal lobbying groups were known as competitors for access to and influence on public policy decisions. At the domestic level, this model was first challenged when big nonstate interest groups had to be included in consensus-oriented, corporatist policy coordination and implementation. In their new roles, however, they were still dependent on recognition by the state (see Schmitter and Lehmbruch 1979). In the most recent phase of political modernization, even such corporatist patterns of interest intermediation have been left behind and a further dismantling of the hierarchical relations between public and private actors is taking place through policy-making and implementation in vertically differentiated political systems (Benz 2004: 127–30). Increasingly bypassing the traditional political institutions of the state, horizontal decision-making mechanisms have emerged, usually operating according to the modes of bargaining and arguing. On the one hand, this shift from government to governance reflects the state's response to 'societal actors claiming participation in the political process, while, on the other hand, cooperation with these actors offers the state the opportunity to obtain informational resources and can improve the acceptance of certain political decisions' (Mayntz 1993: 41, authors' translation). In the domestic context, the traditional notion of hierarchical state-society relations is giving way to the idea of the negotiating, enabling, or cooperative state. Sharing responsibility does not necessarily make the new state weaker than the older, interventionist golden age predecessor. The shadow of hierarchy is still present. But the post–golden age nation state is less keen on running things 'from above' than on regulating and monitoring self-regulation. It has begun to reduce its own governance contributions to functions that can exclusively, or most effectively, be provided by the public sector. Kooiman (2000: 139) thus speaks appropriately 'of *shifting* roles of government rather than of *shrinking* roles of government as part of such changing relationships'.

This pattern of originally domestic deregulation and sharing of authority with nonstate actors is 'increasingly [...] creeping into the international sphere' (Cutler et al. 1999b: 15). Today there seems to be a general belief that – very similar to that previously experienced in the national realm – intergovernmental regimes and organizations are inadequate political instruments for solving the collective action problems emanating from denationalized economic, social, and environmental processes. To regard 'states as the sole providers of public goods has become an increasingly inappropriate over-simplification' because technological and commercial forces, notably the market-driven diffusion of information technology, 'alter the relative capabilities of different types of actors to solve [...] collective action problems, in particular increasing the capacity of non-state actors relative to states' (Florini 2000: 15, 21). In fact, different types of actors can contribute specific resources: national governments have the monopoly on the legal authority to set collectively binding rules and to implement these rules with coercive power. Business corporations are equipped with economic and technological know-how and financial resources. Actors from civil society often claim moral and knowledge-based authority as their politically relevant resources.

Within this shift from an originally pluralist to a more network-like context of political decision making, not only states are affected by a fundamental role shift (see Gordenker and Weiss 1996; Florini 2000; Fuchs 2005;

Wolf 2008). Nongovernmental actors, such as those from civil society, are now facing the same challenge of having to redefine their roles. They, too, have to reflect upon their traditional role as watchdogs over the misbehavior of others, be it governments or corporations, when they enter into multistakeholder governance arrangements as partners of those whom they had formerly approached and to some extent still do observe with skeptical mistrust. The most significant role change concerns the much more direct involvement of transnational civic actors in core regulatory functions: originally they had focused either on the input phases of the political process, such as agenda setting, norm generation, and program development, or on the output side of the political process, taking on service functions in the implementation or evaluation of policies. Now their involvement is shifting from these peripheries to the actual centre of decision making within public-private or multistakeholder self-regulation. Rather than just acting as lobbyists who pressure governments or the private sector to protect political, economic, environmental, and human rights, nongovernmental organizations (NGOs) take on new responsibilities by establishing cooperative relationships with states and business as initiators or cooperative partners in joint governance initiatives (Doh 2008: 281–90). Within the new functional division of labor, NGOs are ascribed as having a real impact on how the world is governed (Van Rooy 2004) by contributing to a free, fair, and just global order (Taylor 2004). The 'global civil society' no longer merely addresses decision makers. NGOs participate directly as co-regulators in norm setting and norm implementing governance arrangements of a public-private or private-private nature.

Corporations may face the biggest task in re-inventing themselves as political actors in this changing governance environment. Their new role as actors with a public responsibility and as partners in the 'co-production of statehood' or 'co-performance of governance' (Schuppert 2008) rather than objects of state regulation and targets of NGO campaigning leaves Milton Friedman's doctrine behind for good: 'the social responsibility of business is to increase its profits' (Friedman 1970; see also Henderson 2001). Friedman's argument was based upon considerable preconditions that are highly questionable in the post–golden age nation-state: he regarded workers, suppliers, consumers, and, in general, the social community as protected by binding contracts and a competitive market system in which everybody can freely express their preferences. Companies were only responsible to their shareholders and have the duty of putting their needs first, to increase value for them. This view has become antiquated since economic globalization has been creating challenges for political steering that exceed the capabilities of any single state to solve problems of market externalities and incomplete contracts. With the growing need for the problem-solving potential of non-state actors to master these challenges more effectively, Friedman's doctrine became heavily contested. Scholars in Business Ethics discussed the potential of how to address ethical values in organizational management (Stakeholder Theory) and came up with a much more broad definition of corporate responsibility (Freeman 1984). Today the scope of corporate responsibility includes customers, suppliers, competitors, employees, the environment, local communities, and other stakeholders (Mullins 2005). Corporations have to cover social and political issues systematically (Donaldson 1989; De George 1993), such as how business ethics can be a central factor in managerial leadership in multinational and multicultural settings (Freeman 1991). Some authors operate with an instrumentalist understanding of corporate responsibility, debating whether corporate engagement in social and environmental issues pays in the long run (Berman et al. 1999), whereas others apply a social contract approach to ethically embed questions of societal responsibility (Donaldson and Dunfee 1999). Taking these debates as a starting point, privatization and internationalization imply that corporations engage in norm setting and norm implementing activities in the context of public-private or private-private governance arrangements.

1.1 Corporations as political actors: from problem causers to problem solvers?

With their involvement in transnational governance arrangements, the roles of governments, international organizations, civil society, and the private sector are shifting. The main goal of this research is reaching a more systematic understanding of the potential and limits of corporate contributions to governance beyond the state. This does not ignore the fact that corporations have and probably still do notoriously contribute to inequity, corruption, environmental degradation, human rights abuses, and violent conflicts in many parts of the world. 'Doing business is not a neutral activity, but an activity that might have negative and positive consequences for the societal environment' (Feil et al. 2008: 4). Apart from the numerous negative examples that portray the destructive societal influence of corporations, the international community increasingly appears to view corporations as powerful partners in global governance. In fact, global governance research has long identified transnational corporations (TNCs) as potent partners for solving collective action problems that call for the extension of public policy beyond the state (Reinicke 1998; Higgott et al. 2000; Reinicke and Deng 2000). Like the state and civil society, corporations are in the process of redefining their traditional roles, identities, and functions in the light of the growing regulatory demands to which they are exposed. This is a new phase in a long cycle during which business actors were addressees of public legal regulation ('norm-consumers') rather than as private regulators or partners in public-private governance arrangements. Even when business actors strayed beyond the economic realm into politics, they did so as lobbyists trying to influence public decision makers. When they contributed to the public good, they did so as charitable philanthropists, after work and not as part of their core business. The new self-commitments and public responsibilities expected from them as corporate citizens (Scherer and Palazzo 2008; Ruggie 2002; Matten and Crane 2005) go far beyond the traditional understanding of corporations as actors who are private in form *and* private, for example, commercial, in purpose. Recent research about corporations in conflict zones found companies engaging in the co-production of security (Feil et al. 2008: 26–7). However, these emerging patterns of 'business as partner' in governance also raise questions about the extent to which and under which conditions corporations take on responsibility to serve the public interest and provide public goods.

1.1.1   Corporate norm-entrepreneurship

A growing body of literature reflects the emergence of new governance patterns, including private standard-setting institutions in which corporations have taken on authoritative roles and regulatory functions (Cutler et al. 1999a; Hall and Biersteker 2002) previously ascribed to the state.

The transnational governance arrangements in which business actors are active as norm-entrepreneurs can be distinguished according to different actors' configurations. They may:

- still be initiated, sponsored, or even dominated by the public sector. In this case, the shadow of (public) hierarchy is still present, but the darkness of its shade may vary.
- consist of multistakeholder initiatives, where civic groups and business corporations meet on an equal footing.
- be pure instances of private self-regulation among business actors with no direct public sector or civil society participation.

Probably the best-known transnational governance arrangement sponsored by public actors is the UN Global Compact (Kell and Levin 2003; Schorlemer 2003; Rieth 2004). It provides a multistakeholder setting where corporations interact with public actors and civic groups to assist the UN implement universal values in the areas of human rights, labor, and the environment (also recently in the fight against corruption). The Global Reporting Initiative (GRI) is an example of a multistakeholder governance arrangement that includes corporations, accountancy agencies, human rights, environmental, labor, and governmental organizations. The initiative establishes a worldwide framework for voluntary sustainability reporting of public but mainly private organizations (Global Reporting Initiative 2003; Kolk 2004). The Wolfsberg Group serves as an illustration of a transnational regulatory initiative based purely on private self-regulation. In this initiative, 12 globally operating banks (Pieth and Aiolfi 2003a) develop and implement guidance documents for the prevention of money laundering. In addition to such collective initiatives, the debate on corporate social responsibility (CSR) has also increased corporate norm promotion at the level of individual companies. Company codes of conduct have spread into policy areas such as human rights, social standards, environmental protection, and the fight against corruption.

In all of these initiatives, companies act very similarly to the norm-entrepreneurship usually associated with actors from civil society. Taking the fight against corruption as an example, transnational corporations have played a major role in the reframing of corporate bribery activities that were formally seen as entirely legal and partially legitimate. These corporate activities have been called into question and it was agreed that new standards of behavior were required. TNCs engaged as 'meaning managers' by creating new 'cognitive frames' and establishing 'new ways of talking about and understanding issues' (Finnemore and Sikkink 1998: 897). Even though corporations may not have been the only or first actors to advocate a particular new norm, it does not diminish the quality of their norm-entrepreneurship but shows that corporate actors have to be included as part of a broader advocacy network which includes those actors working internationally on an issue.

In accordance with classical norm-entrepreneurship, corporate engagement for new standards of behavior often takes place against a preexisting normative space. In most cases, a new norm has to be established over a competing prior one (Finnemore and Sikkink 1998: 897). Corporate engagement in the new common standard of behavior in non-financial reporting (Dingwerth and Pattberg 2009; Kolk 2004) is an example. It did not take place in a normative vacuum but had to be established against the prior norm of fiduciary duty and financial reporting. In the early 1990s, non-financial reporting was first practiced and advocated by a small number of pioneering corporations, which published environmental reports. These non-financial reports thereafter became precedents and best practice for the creation of common guidelines that contributed to the delegitimization of nondisclosure. Corporations reframed the problem of nontransparency of non-financial issues in a new way and thereby reacted to increased public attention and growing demands for non-financial corporate information. For example, BASF AG Germany released its first environmental report in 1988 and Dow Chemical Canada Inc started individual non-financial disclosure in 1990. These two pioneering companies engaged as 'norm leaders', triggering the diffusion of the norm. Later on, companies such as the Aveda Corporation, General Motors, American Airlines, Coca-Cola, and McDonalds also acted as promoters of the norm by voluntarily testing common reporting guidelines (Brown et al. 2007: 4; Pattberg 2007: 162). Since 1997, non-financial reporting has moved from 'a fringe activity pioneered by socially conscious but non-mainstream companies into a credible and serious practice embraced by a number of major corporations' (Wheeler and

Elkington 2001: 4). It is an institutionalized standard of behavior in the GRI, making 'reporting on economic, social and environmental performance as routine and comparable as financial reporting' (Global Reporting Initiative 2003: 4).

Such examples of corporate norm promotion underline the most significant difference between classical norm-entrepreneurs and corporate norm-entrepreneurs because the latter target *themselves* with their reframing efforts. Corporate norm-entrepreneurship aims at self-regulation. Taking on the role of norm-entrepreneurs, corporations engage in establishing new normative standards for the business sector. This differs from the norm-entrepreneurship of NGOs and epistemic communities who usually want to commit other types of addressees, like states and business actors, to the norms they promote. Using the terminology of Nadelmann (1990) and Finnemore and Sikkink (1998), corporations act at two consecutive stages of norm emergence in two different roles simultaneously: as norm- (or moral-) entrepreneurs and as norm leaders or 'regime proponents'. As a consequence, the strategies and instruments of corporate norm-entrepreneurship also differ from those of other norm-entrepreneurs: NGOs, in seeking to change the practices of states, work mainly through discourse, shaming, and lobbying strategies. Corporations often start by changing their own behavior, thus offering best practice for imitation by other companies that may lead into collective self-commitments.

1.1.2   Three ways of understanding the norm-oriented engagement of business actors

But why should business actors accept and perform this new political role of norm entrepreneur? What will they make of it, and under what circumstances? The range of answers to these questions goes way beyond the predominantly skeptical views which have traditionally dominated the discourse about the 'privatization of world politics' (Brühl et al. 2001; Korten 1995).

The very notion of corporate, social, or environmental responsibility seems to contradict conventional wisdom that starts out from the actor-centered assumption that the prime function of business actors is, and has to be, profit maximization. Survival in the marketplace generally rules out norm-oriented behavior. No code of conduct would ultimately be capable of setting market demands by force. However, this assumption and the consequences derived from it are an inappropriate oversimplification. They neglect the fact that the marketplace is not the only environment that makes demands on business. Rational business actors have to take into account the challenges posed by globalized markets and those emanating from the state and from transnational civil society. The interaction of the three worlds of market, state, and civil society make up a normatively enriched environment, to the extent that 'market rationalism' may acquire a different meaning under these altering context conditions. In the face of public pressure or the threat of state regulation, 'doing good' may be the most rational strategy for business to evade the risks associated with adverse campaigning or public regulation (Conzelmann and Wolf 2007b).

This expectation rests on the assumption that private norm setting and norm implementation, which typically fall into the category of 'soft' and voluntary modes of governance, are driven by businesses' intention to avoid state intervention in the market. In order to achieve this goal, private self-regulation must succeed if it wants to prevent legally binding regulation being imposed. However, this embedding in pending public regulation could have yet another impact on private efforts trying to anticipate and prevent state intervention: even if public regulation follows at a later stage, its substance would be preshaped by the norms and rules of private self-regulation. These expectations of the potential impact of the fear of forced compliance go along with the suspicion that in the absence of this 'whip' the reliability of voluntary self-commitments would suffer. In order to meet certain demands on political regulation, private self-regulation would therefore always depend on the capability and the willingness of public actors to intervene.

Quite similar to the threat of state intervention, there is another environmental factor that could make corporate norm setting and norm implementation a rational strategy for business actors to pursue: the embedding of market actors in a societal environment in which civic groups are vigilant and strong enough to turn public attention to business conduct. In this case, the underlying assumption is that the reputational costs associated with public shaming will increase the likelihood of voluntary unilateral or multilateral normative self-commitments by companies and that their rules are actually implemented. Even if companies proclaim normative self-commitments only for strategic reasons without actually being convinced of their appropriateness, the importance of the societal environment lies in securing rule consistent behavior by helping the logic of rhetorical self-entrapment to unfold.

Such rationalist conceptualizations still rely on fear of coercion and self-interest as the only drivers for business contributions to global governance. In contrast to this, constructivists employ the logic of appropriateness and point to the emergence of a global epistemic community made up of likeminded corporate leaders, scientists, and public regulators who have defined certain standards of appropriate behavior for firms (Haufler 1999: 215). On the basis of these considerations and in trying to define their new role in relation to the public sector and transnational civil society, business actors have to choose from three ideal role models (see Wolf 2005): They can either follow a narrow market rationalism, a complex market rationalism, or an intrinsically norm-oriented behavior. While narrow market rationalism would consider societal and political forces as influential only insofar as they can be translated into short-term risks and opportunities in the marketplace, complex market rationality would anticipate reputational and political costs in the cost-benefit calculations of business actors. Finally, the existence of a normatively textured environment may also give rise to increased reflection on corporate responsibility and recognition of certain values as guiding principles for business conduct. The ultimate result of originally strategic norm-orientation may be an intrinsic motivation by business to observe and implement ethical principles even where there is no clear economic or political incentive to do so.

In the light of the choices described here, the notion that corporations still are and will remain private in form and primarily private in purpose when they engage in norm setting and norm implementation remains valid. In fact, the remarkable number of transnational private governance arrangements suggests that corporations have mutated into economic-political hybrids in the sense of being more or less private in form but definitely more than private in purpose and responsibility. This hybridism is also reflected by the multitude of rationales companies employ when they participate in transnational governance initiatives whose compliance mechanisms are based on highly varied assumptions about what will make business actors comply. Some rest on sanctioning through market mechanisms or rely on the threat of naming and shaming campaigns; others want to attract companies by appealing to their assumed interest in 'doing good' and by offering learning forums.

When we expect business corporations to redefine themselves as political actors and proactively contribute to the provision of public goods in the context of transnational governance initiatives, it is therefore not necessarily presupposed that they have abandoned their profit-oriented rationality and mutated into dedicated followers of a new logic of appropriateness. Corporations' engagement in norm setting and norm implementation still leaves enough room for very different assumptions about their motives. These motives can be, on the one hand, a more enlightened understanding of what the business case actually is under changing circumstances, to real ethical concerns, on the other. Here, neither the side of the rationalist nor that of the social-constructivist camp is taken in examining corporate norm-entrepreneurship. Instead, the general question of whether this is a phenomenon of strategic or intrinsic norm-orientation is left open. Different motivations leave space for corporate norm-entrepreneurship. Nevertheless, from the findings on the explanatory weight of the factors analyzed in Chapters 3 to 6 more can be learned about the validity of competing assumptions. After all, external incentives or pressures have to meet certain addressee dispositions to have effect, and the choice of particular governance arrangements can be interpreted as evidence of a predominant rationality.

1.1.3 What is new about corporate norm-entrepreneurship?

Is this role of corporations as norm-entrepreneurs really that new? Indeed, there is a long tradition of states outsourcing public functions to private entities, which is often overlooked in the narrow focus on the golden age of statehood. Granting royal charters to companies in the early modern period is an example (see Wolf 2010) of a reaction by governments that lacked the capacity or willingness to provide public goods effectively when faced with a growth of transborder economic and social transactions. The history of states sharing public responsibilities with private actors makes the golden age nation-state, in the shadow of whose self-assumed omnipotence companies could arrange themselves comfortably with Friedman's doctrine as their credo, look like an exception rather than the rule. At first glance, early modern states reacted very similarly to their postmodern counterparts of today, namely, by mobilizing private problem-solving resources and by sharing responsibilities with private actors. However, different from the early modern period when private actors acquired the political authority to perform state functions by formal delegation of state competencies, that is by the charters they were granted, private transnational governance contributions today mainly appear as voluntary self-commitments in reaction to public expectations. There are more or less soft invitations to private actors to take on responsibility for the provision of public goods. This change is again indicative of the role shifts of the actors involved.

Such invitations have frequently been put on the political agenda of international organizations, such as the United Nations or the World Bank, during the last decade. To mention only two examples: the former General Secretary of the United Nations, Kofi Annan, addressed the World Economic Forum on 31 January 1998 by saying: 'The United Nations once dealt only with governments. By now we know that peace and prosperity cannot be achieved without partnerships involving governments, international organizations, the business community and civil society. In today's world, we depend on each other' (Annan 1998). In a similar vein, the former president of the World Bank, James D. Wolfensohn, on 28 September 1999, advocated the need 'to build coalitions for change' (Wolfensohn 1999) with the private sector, civil society, and communities to assist governments in taking charge of their own development agendas with the participation of their citizens.

1.2 Corporate norm-entrepreneurship and the future global governance architecture

This study is firmly embedded in the governance paradigm as the appropriate conceptual framework to examine the future of governance beyond the state. In the broad notion of governance, it is best defined by distinguishing it from two traditional concepts used in describing political decision making: political steering and government. In contrast to political steering, governance has an institutional rather than actor centered focus (see Zürn 2005: 127; Mayntz 2008: 45–6). In contrast to the notion of government that highlights the traditional, legally binding, and hierarchical mode of setting and implementing collectively binding norms, governance comprises much more, namely, the 'totality of all forms of the intentional regulation of social affairs that coexist at a given territorial level' (Mayntz 2008: 55). Thus governance covers the whole range of concepts; voluntary private self-regulation, various forms of public-private co-regulation, and hierarchical government (Schuppert 2008: 26).

In fact, 'the blurring of boundaries and responsibilities for tackling social and economic issues' (Stoker 1998: 18) is one of the decisive features of governance in the postnational constellation. It challenges the traditional concept of government as public intervention by administrative law, backed by the coercive power of the state. This traditional hierarchical mode of public governance by government lost some of its significance in the course of the political modernization process that took place within most of the OECD countries. The 'limitations of traditional public command-and-control as a governing mechanism' (Kooiman 2000: 139) became obvious with the regulatory overstretch of the modern welfare state. The advent of globalization meant that when national governments promised to provide public goods or to prevent public 'bads' in fields such as macroeconomic planning or social safety, they were confronted with a new collective action problem: The causes and resources needed to combat them were beyond the command of any single government, and beyond the world of states as a whole.

For governance beyond the state, government has never been an appropriate model because of the lack of a *Leviathan* in an international system consisting of sovereign territorial states. Of course, coercion always has been and still is an omnipresent instrument for individual states or 'coalitions of the willing' to try to impose their will on others. However, this form of hierarchical political steering differs fundamentally from domestic public governing by government in that it is based on de facto instead of legitimate power and takes place under a shadow of anarchy rather than that of a *Leviathan*. More importantly, the standard mode of international public policy is based on treaty-based agreements rather than on the use of coercive measures. In the international sphere, even national governments perform their regulatory functions best not when the norms are imposed but when the norms and rules they try to implement are accepted as legitimate and serve the self-interest of those who are subject to those rules. In that sense, it becomes important to go beyond the fear of coercion as a compliance mechanism and to discuss alternatives conduits by which nonstate actors may contribute to the provision of public goods (see Conzelmann and Wolf 2007a).

However, an objection could be raised against the use of the governance paradigm for this study of the potential and limits of corporate contributions to norm setting and norm implementation: Thinking about politics in terms of governance is preoccupied almost exclusively with collective problem solving rather than with the much broader range of normative criteria against which the legitimacy of domestic political institutions and processes is usually measured. Indeed, the roots of the governance concept lie much more in policy analysis than in normative political theory. But even if there was this functional, problem-solving, and output bias of which the governance debate in general is often accused, and as a consequence of which the notion of the nature of politics seems to have shifted from exerting power to solving collective problems (see Mayntz 2008: 55–6), this does not preclude a critical perspective on the de facto power relationships between actors within governance institutions involved in collective problem solving. It is well acknowledged that extending the participation in collective decision-making arrangements to private actors does not just mean more inclusion and stakeholder involvement in the positive sense of better congruence between rule makers and rule takers, but that it can also create problems for governance in the public interest and therefore also for the legitimacy of governance. Participation and accountability can and do therefore play a crucial role in our understanding of the governance paradigm. Rather than neglecting demands on the input and throughput sides of legitimacy, reflexivity, interconnectedness, and a functional linkage between effectiveness and legitimacy demands is assumed, according to which an institution's right to rule is more likely to be accepted and its rules obeyed when they are regarded as legitimate. Purists of democratic theory may be disappointed by this functional view of input and throughput demands on political institutions and processes, but this is indeed the way to reconcile the tension between 'citizen participation and system effectiveness' (Dahl 1994) under the governance paradigm.

Another important implication has to be mentioned as it is part of the subscription to the governance paradigm as our analytical frame of reference. It concerns the role of the 'general interest' as a crucial normative measure for the evaluation of the involvement of private actors in transnational governance initiatives. According to the institutional- rather than the actor-centered focus of the governance paradigm, it has to be taken up not as a normative demand on the participating actors: 'Do behave in the general interest!' would overburden even the most role-shifted of profit-oriented private actors. It should instead be a demand on the institutional architecture and embedding of a given governance initiative that should be designed to facilitate the coordination of the individual interests of the interacting parties in such a way that, in the end, they can contribute to the general interest. Exactly because private governance cannot depend on actors who are geared toward the general interest – because they simply are not – the analytical and political challenge is to establish institutional frames that can channel the contributions of various self-interested actors 'to the millwheel of the general interest' (Schuppert 2008: 32). The general interest *enabling* transnational private governance institutions is therefore what is looked for.

1.3   Aim and structure of this book

The contributions of this book to the research on global governance can be summarized as follows:

First, there is conceptual groundwork. The new political role of corporations is still underconceptualized. Chapter 2 showcases a new analytical framework for a better understanding of business actors' contributions to norm setting and norm implementation within different patterns of private-private and public-private governance settings. Corporate contributions to transnational governance are conceptualized as a new type of norm-entrepreneurship.

Second, the main emphasis is put on the causal analysis of the conditions under which corporate norm-entrepreneurship is more or less likely to occur. Observing that corporations increasingly become proponents of normative standards for their own business activities, the causal reasons for this counterintuitive behavior are investigated. On the basis of a systematic application of existing or inductively generated hypotheses to the empirical data, numerous interviews were carried out at the level of individual companies and transnational private governance initiatives to examine the potential and the limits of governance contributions that can be expected from business actors. The explanatory value of nine factors from three different clusters of independent variables is analyzed (Chapters 3 to 5): The first cluster of variables (Chapter 3) comprises the social and political environment in which corporations are expected to act as norm entrepreneurs. In this cluster, the role of the transnational public, the home state, and the heterogeneity of the regulatory environment in which corporations operate is analyzed. The second cluster (Chapter 4) is at the company level and looks at the role of actors' characteristics. This chapter offers insight into the explanatory value of the vulnerability of a corporation, its ownership structure, and the significance of corporate culture for corporate norm-entrepreneurship. The third cluster of variables (Chapter 5) investigates the institutional characteristics of transnational governance initiatives in order to find out in what way they attract or hinder corporate norm-entrepreneurship. In this cluster, the factors steering mechanisms and actor configurations, institutional flexibility, and the legitimacy ascribed to a certain type of governance arrangement are investigated. In Chapter 6, general conclusions are drawn from a comparative assessment of the findings of the previous chapters, which explain corporate norm-entrepreneurship on the basis of certain combinations of necessary and facilitating conditions.

Third, the interest is not only in the conditions that make corporate norm-entrepreneurship more or less likely but also in a normative evaluation of the desirability of the new transnational governance arrangements in which private actors are involved and of the privatization of governance functions in general. In Chapter 7, the effectiveness of self-regulatory arrangements set and developed by corporations unilaterally or in cooperation with others is analyzed. First, a comprehensive model for assessing the effectiveness of corporations as norm-entrepreneurs is introduced. In order to get as broad a picture of potential effects as possible, effectiveness is examined at the actor level and at the structural level. Disaggregating effectiveness in its output, outcome and impact dimensions in the well-established tradition of policy research, the following criteria are applied to empirical case studies on unilateral and collective self-regulatory arrangements: norm commitment, change of behavior, identity shift at the actor level; goal attainment, contribution to normative order, and unintended consequences at the structural level. In Chapter 8, responsiveness, participation, accountability, and authority are introduced to examine the legitimacy of different types of unilateral and collective self-regulatory arrangements. Using the same empirical cases for the application of these theory-grounded legitimacy criteria to different types of individual and collective self-regulatory arrangements, fresh and systematically derived arguments are provided for the debate about the legitimacy of transnational private governance, which go beyond legitimacy perceptions that may be attributed to certain institutional arrangements by their participants.

Fourth, this study of corporations as political actors is not merely an academic enterprise but is a research based step toward advocating or rejecting certain options for the future institutional architecture of global governance. Linking the conclusions drawn from the causal analysis, effectiveness assessment, and normative evaluation, some policy-oriented recommendations are formulated in the final chapter (Chapter 9), in which the search for a new institutional architecture for transnational governance is returned to: Is there such a thing as an ideal functional division of labor between public and private governance contributions? What will and should be the role of the state and the 'shadow of hierarchy' in regulating private self-regulation? Rather than aiming at contributing to a 'new theory of the firm', these concluding considerations return to the big agenda of a new theory of statehood and public goods provision in the postnational constellation.

2
Basic Concepts and Assumptions

The aim of this book is to explore the conditions and the degree to which profit-oriented business corporations can be expected to make meaningful contributions to global governance by participating in setting and developing generally applicable norms – a phenomenon increasingly observable in transnational governance arrangements and considered under the label 'corporate norm-entrepreneurship' here. In what follows this concept is elaborated in more detail. A representative sample of systematic norm-entrepreneurs is selected as the basis of the empirical analysis in Chapters 3 to 5. Potential explanations for corporate norm-entrepreneurship are also presented and put to the test.

2.1 What is corporate norm-entrepreneurship?

The need to analyze the involvement of corporations in norm setting and norm development stems from both the empirical observation that TNCs engage extensively in norm-related behavior in this global governance age and that International Relations (IR) research, although researching extensively on the role of nonstate actors in norm emergence, has failed to consider corporations as norm-entrepreneurs. Therefore, before developing the concept of corporate norm-entrepreneurship, its place in IR theory is briefly reviewed.

In the early 1990s, Nadelmann contended that 'the dynamics by which norms emerge, evolve, and expand in international society have been the subject of strikingly little study' (Nadelmann 1990: 479). Since then, the constructivist turn in social sciences and the focus on rule- and norm-driven regime analysis in IR have contributed enormously to addressing this gap. One of the major findings was that agency is of crucial importance to the formation and diffusion of norms (Keck and Sikkink 1998; Risse et al. 1999; Brühl 2003). In Nadelmann's 'evolutionary pattern' (1990: 484) and in Finnemore and Sikkink's (1998) 'norm life cycle', norm or moral entrepreneurs are active in the first stages of the process, aiming to reframe a formerly unproblematic phenomenon or legitimate activity into a problematic or illegitimate activity. Norm-entrepreneurs have strong notions about appropriate behavior (Elgström 2000: 459) and 'attempt to convince a critical mass' (Finnemore and Sikkink 1998: 895) of 'principal protagonists' (Nadelmann 1990: 484) – almost exclusively state actors in the literature – to embrace newly established norms.

However, only a limited range of actors, such as activist networks (Keck and Sikkink 1998; Price 1998), 'epistemic communities' (Haas 1992), and, more recently, international organizations (Finnemore 1993; Schimmelfennig et al. 2003) and governments (Deitelhoff 2006) were regarded as agents with the potential for norm-entrepreneurship. Corporate social responsibility (CSR) has increased the awareness of corporate norm related behavior. Company codes of conduct and collective self-regulatory initiatives in policy areas such as human rights, social standards, environmental protection, and the fight against corruption are indicative of activities similar to those of classical norm-entrepreneurs. Actors qualify as a norm-entrepreneur when they engage in the early stages of a norm life cycle (Finnemore and Sikkink 1998; Nadelman 1990) to redefine 'an activity as a problem' (Nadelmann 1990: 482). Similar observations can be made about corporate behavior in the evolution of CSR norms. TNCs also engaged as 'meaning managers' by creating new 'cognitive frames' and establishing 'new ways of talking about and understanding issues' (Finnemore and Sikkink 1998: 897). A variety of corporate activities can serve this purpose. Two general behavioral patterns indicate corporate norm-entrepreneurship: norm setting and norm development. Corporations can support the setting or institutionalization of an entirely new norm by adopting a unilateral company code as best practice, by lobbying for it among its peers and by engaging in the creation of a collective self-regulatory initiative. Even after a norm has reached a certain level of acceptance and institutionalization a corporation can still be a norm-entrepreneur through norm development activities, for example, by engaging within governing bodies of initiatives or organizations supporting the norm or by participating in revision processes and thus further specifying a broader norm's exact content and implied requirements.

These two types of corporate behavior stand in contrast to the classic role of corporations who are subject to public norms with which they merely have to comply. In this role, corporations act as norm-consumers whose behavioral options are either norm acceptance or norm implementation. In contrast to norm consumers, norm-entrepreneurs are not only interested in accepting and implementing norms but in shaping these rules themselves.

As shown in Table 2.1, corporate norm-entrepreneurship can be unilateral (left-hand column) and collective (right-hand column): corporations engage in norm setting by regulating their own behavior (for example, in the form of a unilateral code of conduct) or that of their business partners (for instance, via supply chain management systems); or they can engage in

Table 2.1   Types of corporate norm-entrepreneurship

		Unilateral	Collective
Scope of norm obligation	Inward focus	Code of conduct	Self regulatory initiative
	Outward focus	Supply chain management	Best practice

collective processes of norm setting within self-regulatory initiatives where norm setting occurs in partnerships.

Firms not only set norms, they apply them, too. In norm-entrepreneurship with an internal focus, the entities engaging as norm-entrepreneurs are identical to the norm-consumers because the norm only addresses those who actively commit themselves. In externally focused norm-entrepreneurship, the roles of norm-entrepreneurs and norm-consumers fall apart because norm-entrepreneurs set norms with the aim of changing the behavior of other business actors who were not involved in the process of norm setting but who may be located in their wider sphere of influence. This differentiation is captured by the unilateral norm setting in the left hand column of Table 2.1: when a company acts as a norm-entrepreneur by developing an internal code of conduct the same company is also the consumer of the norm. However, a company code can also include a supply chain management system that reaches beyond the company to first and second tier suppliers. The suppliers take on the role of norm-consumers. This example also shows that Table 2.1 primarily stresses the analytical distinction between the directions in which the normative self-regulation of the business sector might take effect, even though the different directions may be addressed within one and the same empirical case.

2.1.1   Indicators of corporate norm-entrepreneurship[1]

Norm setting

Whenever corporations create a unilateral code or engage in the establishment of a self-regulatory initiative, they contribute to norm setting through voluntary agreement and therefore act and are classified as norm-entrepreneurs. In ideal terms, the concept of norm setting describes the deliberate creation of new collectively shared standards for appropriate behavior (Jepperson et al. 1996). Corporations, therefore, contribute to norm setting when they deliberately strive for new regulations of corporate behavior. However, the content of the norms to be set is usually not all that new or original. In fact, most of the norms agreed to by corporations within self-regulatory initiatives (or elsewhere) have previously existed in other bodies of law, usually public international law, just not with corporations as the addressees. Typically, norm setting by corporations does not entail the invention of an entirely new norm but rather the new commitment by corporations to a norm as a standard for *their* appropriate behavior. It is not the collective expectation that is fundamentally new but the application of that expectation to a new category of actors. Norm setting by corporations is a subphenomenon of the norm genesis model of 'genesis by voluntary planned agreement'. This is the most common model of norm setting in international affairs and is based on negotiations between a group of actors who agree by contract to norm a certain practice (Deitelhoff 2006: 45). The support a company lends to norm setting by planned agreement can take various forms and depends on the stage of emergence the norm has reached: where no code for corporate behavior or self-regulatory initiative is operative yet, a corporation establishes its own code of conduct in a policy area or fosters the creation of a new collective initiative. In the latter case, corporations voice the proposal for the norm in public or build alliances with other companies, civil society, international organizations, and even governments to initiate a process of norm institutionalization. Corporations thus get involved in an early stage of the norm cycle and engage in reframing a formerly legitimate activity as a problem (Nadelmann 1990; Finnemore and Sikkink 1998). Corporations have more than discursive mechanisms at their disposal to do this. They do not just advocate new norms but support the reframing process by changing their own practices and in so doing, set a positive example and become role models. Corporations may be among the founding members of an initiative promoting a newly proposed norm. By supporting a new norm before its widespread acceptance the corporation actively contributes to norm setting, even though it then plays the role of norm leader rather than norm-entrepreneur (Finnemore and Sikkink 1998: 895).

Norm development

While the concept of norm setting describes how previously nonexistent expectations of appropriate behavior emerge and how companies foster this process, norm development focuses on how the meaning of appropriateness within the norm undergoes incremental changes over time. Changes to a norm can affect its scope, content, and the procedures that serve as enforcement mechanisms. The process of norm development often involves more technical aspects than norm setting. Using the language of regime analysis as an analogy, norm setting would be closer – but not necessarily linked exclusively – to the principles and norms of an international regime, while norm development would relate more to its rules and procedures (Krasner 1983).

Often changes to the scope of a norm, its content or enforcement mechanisms within a self-regulatory initiative will take place as part of procedures explicitly designed for norm development, such as regular review processes. Therefore, corporate norm-entrepreneurs who contribute to norm development will usually not only be members of the initiative but will often be those representing its governing body. As with norm setting, corporate norm-entrepreneurship can be unilateral and collective, and inwardly or outwardly focused.

2.1.2   Indicators of corporate norm-consumership

In contrast to these two behavior patterns that signify norm-entrepreneurs, norm acceptance and implementation have always been required of corporations, as addressees of publicly set rules and norms. They are indications of corporate norm-consumership.

Norm implementation

Norm implementation refers to whether and how far corporations actually follow the norms that they have accepted as binding, either collectively, within the frameworks of self-regulatory initiatives, or in their own codes of conduct. However, while setting and developing norms may occur as collective and collaborative processes, norm implementation always requires individual effort from each corporation that has to comply and adjust its practices to the now required norm. Implementation can take many forms, depending on what the unilateral or collective initiative prescribes. The full implementation of any initiative will require an adaptation of the strategies, structures, and procedures of the company, in accordance with the respective norms prescribed by an initiative.

Whether norm implementation indicates a norm-entrepreneur or norm-consumer depends on the moment in 'world time' when the corporate activity takes place (Risse et al. 1999: 19–22).[2] Implementation as a form of norm-consumership would typically refer to norms that have already acquired prescriptive status. Before a norm has gained general acceptance implementation can be among the norm promoting activities of norm-entrepreneurs, as is often the case with best practice.

Norm acceptance

Norm acceptance, the second type of corporate norm related behavior that indicates a norm-consumer, implies a company's active acknowledgment that it is bound to a certain norm. It requires a commitment by the company to strive for compliance with the prescribed norm. The difference to similar best practice activities of norm-entrepreneurs is again found in 'world time': norm acceptance by norm consumers takes place *after* a norm has been institutionalized. It is practiced by, for example, acceding to an existing collective self-regulatory initiative. Most of these initiatives have established procedures for new companies to commit themselves to their norms and rules. Some only require a written statement expressing a company's commitment, whereas others have more formal accession criteria, which can even include the certification of norm conforming behavior.

2.2 How to identify corporate norm-entrepreneurs?

As laid out in the previous parts of this chapter, corporate norm-entrepreneurs engage in setting and developing norms and rules applicable to their own behavior rather than merely accepting and implementing those emanating from public bodies. Nevertheless, not all contemporary TNCs engage in norm-entrepreneurship. Vast variation exists: corporations not engaging at all in setting and developing new norms, corporations engaging sporadically, and corporations systematically profiting from any occasion they see for norm-entrepreneurship. Part II of this book attempts to identify the causes of this variation using a systematic comparison of corporate engagement. Since the interest is primarily in what motivates corporations to act as norm-entrepreneurs, positive examples of the dependent variable that serve the heuristic purpose of identifying potential causal paths leading to norm-entrepreneurship have been consciously selected (George and Bennett 2005: 23). Since the number of potential corporate norm-entrepreneurs is theoretically infinite, extreme cases (Gerring 2004) were selected; the corporations that engage in norm-entrepreneurship to a degree that is considered above average, quantitatively and qualitatively. To achieve this, a large number of corporations that demonstrated engagement in collective self-regulatory initiatives were sifted through. Although norm-entrepreneurship conceptually includes individual and collective norm setting activities, the primary focus here is on collective norm-entrepreneurs, for pragmatic and analytical reasons. In terms of research feasibility, norm-entrepreneurs in collective activities can be observed more easily and are highly likely to also be individual norm-entrepreneurs. In addition, norm-entrepreneurship in collective governance settings tends to be more persistent, institutionalized and more visible to competitors and the entire public. As a consequence, it is much harder for companies to revoke a former collective commitment without losing credibility. In contrast to this, individual norm-entrepreneurship mostly focuses on the supply chain of a company. Therefore, companies are more inclined to engage in an arbitrary way and commitments are of more temporary nature, changing whenever it suits the interests of the company.

The selection of highly active norm-entrepreneurs within collective self-regulatory initiatives was made in three steps: First, initiatives were identified that are representative of international self-regulatory arrangements – in terms of membership, issue areas covered and institutional design. Second, the general criteria signifying norm-entrepreneurship were translated into initiative specific indicators for corporate norm setting and norm development. Having used these indicators to isolate the corporations that were active as norm-entrepreneurs within each initiative, a quantitative overarching filter was applied to differentiate between corporations that are random, sporadic, or systematic norm-entrepreneurs.

2.2.1   Identifying representative collective self-regulatory initiatives

Case study selection started by identifying a sample of self-regulatory initiatives that represent different types of actors involved, steering instruments employed and issue areas covered. This sample was further narrowed down by focusing on those initiatives with the largest membership, including those that cover a broad range of topical areas, such as the UN Global Compact or the Global Reporting Initiative (GRI), and others that concentrate on more specific issue areas, such as the Wolfsberg Principles combating money laundering or Social Accountability (SA) 8000 on workplace standards. It has to be stressed that by definition, norm-entrepreneurship is not possible in every governance arrangement. As a result of particular institutional designs in some governance arrangements, such as the state led European Eco-Management and Audit Scheme (EMAS), norm-entrepreneurship is not possible. Since EMAS has no institutionalized role for corporate actors' participation, corporations can engage in lobbying efforts or accept and implement the rules and norms supplied by EMAS but cannot actively participate in their setting and development. EMAS, even though it works with innovative, soft steering mechanisms and incentives for voluntary compliance, is an example of top-down, state-led governance approaches that have no room for corporate norm setting or norm development activities. For these reasons, the selection of norm-entrepreneurs focused on the following six important governance settings: the Business Principles for Countering Bribery (Business Principles), the Business Social Compliance Initiative (BSCI), GRI, the UN Global Compact, SA 8000, and the Wolfsberg Principles. In all of these, norm setting and development by corporations are possible and observable phenomena.

Sample of self-regulatory initiatives

Social Accountability 8000[3]

The SA 8000 standard is a multistakeholder initiative that was initiated in 1996 by the US-based NGO, Social Accountability International (SAI), to establish a cross-industry standard for workplace conditions and a system of independent verification. It is one of the most recognized certification systems in producer countries around the world. By 2008, 1835 facilities in 68 countries had been certified. SA 8000 provides a framework for independent assessment by a third-party certification body. SA 8000 predominantly aims to increase the compliance record of corporations, focusing on the great number of suppliers and producers in developing countries. It spells out social accountability requirements for the International Labour Organization (ILO) core labor standards. Signatory corporations have to annually disclose the number of certified and non-certified suppliers. A centerpiece of the SA 8000 standard is requiring the establishment of management systems that set out the structures and procedures that companies must adopt in order to ensure that compliance with the standard is continuously reviewed.

The Business Principles for Countering Bribery[4]

The Business Principles for Countering Bribery (often simply called Business Principles) is a multistakeholder initiative instigated in 2002 by Transparency International (TI) and Social Accountability International (SAI) in cooperation with corporations, academics, trade unions, and civil society groups. The Business Principles are a tool to assist corporations in developing approaches to counter bribery and extortion in all business activities. It applies to bribery of public officials and private-to-private transactions. As a best practice tool, the Business Principles predominantly rely on learning and dialogue as steering mechanisms. A number of tools have been developed, such as a 'self-evaluation module' and an 'external independent verification tool' designed for companies wishing to obtain third-party verification. There are a dozen corporate members who actively provide advice on the development of the work program and supporting tools for the Business Principles for Countering Bribery.

The United Nations Global Compact[5]

The United Nations Global Compact was initiated in 1999 by former UN Secretary-General Kofi Annan at the World Economic Forum in Davos and launched in July 2000. The Global Compact is the largest (in terms of participating companies) and therefore probably most well known example of a multistakeholder, self-regulatory initiative worldwide. Corporations subscribing to the ten Global Compact Principles covering human rights, social standards, environmental protection, and anticorruption have to submit a clear statement of support on an annual basis and a Communication on Progress (COP) to document the progress they are making on internalizing the Principles within their operations. By 2009, the Global Compact had grown to more than 6000 participants, including over 5000 businesses in 120 countries around the world. Since its inception, the Global Compact has predominantly aimed to utilize the power of dialogue and transparency to identify, disseminate, and globalize corporate responsibility practices. Since 2005, the Global Compact has included formal procedures, such as 'integrity measures', including a delisting policy for noncomplying companies to ensure the integrity of the initiative.

The Wolfsberg Group[6]

The Wolfsberg Group is a collaboration of 12 of the world's largest banks and private financial institutions that convened with Transparency

International in 2000 to elaborate principles for combating money laundering in private banking operations. Since then, the group has produced standards and guidance documents on a number of related issues, such as the prevention of terrorist financing, money laundering in correspondent banking and trade finance, corruption, and so on. As their primary building block, the Wolfsberg Principles include common procedures for practicing customer due diligence and keeping watch over client relationships, especially with persons identified as being 'politically exposed'. Even though the group is a 'closed club' in the sense that no further financial institutions can become formal Wolfsberg members, it stimulates collective discussions within the financial sector as a whole at the annual Wolfsberg Forum.

The Global Reporting Initiative[7]

The Global Reporting Initiative (GRI), initiated in 1997 by the US-based NGO Coalition for Environmentally Responsible Economics (CERES) and the Tellus Institute, and joined by the United Nations Environmental Programme (UNEP) in 1999, is a multistakeholder process aiming to develop a common framework for voluntary reporting on the economic, environmental and societal impacts of corporate activities. The Global Reporting Initiative reporting guidelines undergo periodic revision cycles; the third generation was released in 2006. Since then, GRI based reports must self-declare an Application Level, expressing the degree of compliance with the guidelines. The accuracy of this self-declaration may be confirmed either by third parties or by the GRI. Since 2006, corporations are officially invited to refer to the GRI reporting framework in preparing their Communication on Progress for the Global Compact.

The Business Social Compliance Initiative[8]

The Business Social Compliance Initiative (BSCI) was founded in March 2003 as an initiative purely for the private sector to improve and monitor compliance with workers' rights in the global supply chain. The system is based on a code of conduct (SA 8000), enshrining principles from ILO's core conventions, and includes a comprehensive monitoring and qualification process that covers all products sourced from any country. The driving force behind the BSCI is the Brussels-based Foreign Trade Association (FTA). It is mainly intended as a sector solution for retail in Europe but is also open to any non-European company or business association. The BSCI offers a database exclusively to its members, containing supplier profiles and auditing information. It established roundtables in the major import markets of its members to strengthen stakeholder involvement and improve social standards in supplier countries.

2.2.2 Establishing initiative-specific indicators of norm-entrepreneurship

In each of these empirical governance settings, norm-entrepreneurship occurs in various forms that indicate general behavioral patterns observable in all of them. Therefore, to locate the most active norm-entrepreneurs within the six initiatives, general indicators of norm-entrepreneurship were developed and then translated into observable initiative-specific corporate activities. General behavior patterns that indicate norm-entrepreneurship are: participation in the foundation of an initiative that lends strong symbolic support to either newly emerging or not yet broadly accepted norms; participation in initiative working groups where existing norms are further specified and elaborated; membership in the initiative's governing bodies where norm development is given authoritative support; and commenting on draft guidelines or standards to be issued by the initiative to clarify its normative requirements. In Table 2.2, these general indicators are translated into specific ones for each of the six self-regulatory initiatives selected.

2.2.3 Differentiating random and sporadic from systematic norm-entrepreneurs

The classification of corporations as random, sporadic, or systematic norm-entrepreneurs is based on a comparison of their quantitative engagement within the collective self-regulatory initiatives identified (see Table 2.3). This engagement was identified by looking at relevant activities in the period from 2000 to 2006. Random norm-entrepreneurs are those that have been involved in norm-entrepreneurship only once in an initiative, by fulfilling one of the above-mentioned indicators for norm-entrepreneurship. This singular activity most likely resulted from coincidental effects rather than conscious corporate decisions to engage in norm-entrepreneurship. Therefore, random norm-entrepreneurs are not considered in the following chapters. Sporadic norm-entrepreneurs show a higher intensity of norm engagement in at least one or more self-regulatory initiatives by fulfilling at least two of the proposed criteria. These corporations are regarded as the standard type of norm-entrepreneurs. However, as the aim of this book is to find the potential and limits of corporate contributions to global governance, the interest primarily is in discovering the conditions that explain extreme cases of norm-entrepreneurship. Therefore, the main focus is on systematic norm-entrepreneurs and sporadic ones will only be looked at comparatively where reference to them provides further evidence of the conditions required for systematic norm-entrepreneurship. Systematic norm-entrepreneurs are defined by being active more often and in more diverse issue areas than their sporadic peers. For the purposes of this study, a corporation qualifies as a systematic norm-entrepreneur when it fulfills the indicators within at least three self-regulatory initiatives. These norm-entrepreneurs can be

Table 2.2   Initiative-specific indicators of corporate norm-entrepreneurship

Business Principles Countering Bribery (BPCB)
Steering Committee Member 2003
Steering Committee Member 2005
Comment on Business Principle Draft 2003

Business Social Compliance Initiative (BSCI)
Founding Member
Representative Committee Member 2005–06

UN Global Compact
Founding Member
Board of Directors 2002
Board of Directors 2003
Board of Directors 2006
Presenter at Learning Forum 2002
Presenter at Learning Forum 2004
Presenter at Learning Forum 2006

Global Reporting Initiative (GRI)
Founding Member
Steering Committee Member 2002
Participation in Revision or Measurement Working Group 2002
Participation in Sector Supplement Working Group 2000–06
Board of Directors/Stakeholder Council 2007

Social Accountability 8000
Founding Member
Signatory Member
Member of Advisory Board 1998
Member of Advisory Board 2005
Member of Advisory Board 2007

Wolfsberg Principles
Founding Member
Participant in drafting processes 2000–06

Table 2.3   Degrees of norm-entrepreneurship

Type of norm-entrepreneurship	Criteria
Systematic	Fulfilling indicators of norm-entrepreneurship in a minimum of three initiatives
Sporadic	Fulfilling more than one indicator of norm-entrepreneurship in a maximum of two initiatives
Random	Fulfilling no more than one indicator of norm-entrepreneurship in all six initiatives

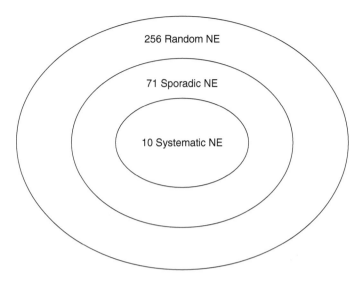

Figure 2.1 Corporate norm-entrepreneurs by type

considered – methodologically speaking – as extreme cases (Gerring 2004) in which norm-entrepreneurship exceeds the average degree.

The resulting numbers of norm-entrepreneurs in each category are displayed in Figure 2.1. The 10 systematic norm-entrepreneurs form the center of the qualitative analysis, on the basis of the assumption that this degree of norm-entrepreneurship (in at least three very different governance arrangements) cannot be accounted for by other, coincidental, factors but is the result of conscious decision making on the part of the respective corporations, which therefore seem to accept their new political role in the age of global governance.

The 10 systematic norm-entrepreneurs represent companies from various industries and home countries: BP, Credit Suisse, Deutsche Bank, France Telecom, Inditex, Rio Tinto, Sasol, Shell, Tata Group, and UBS. Each company was extensively investigated to confirm and explain the systematic degree of norm-entrepreneurship. Table 2.4 briefly summarizes key corporate data for the 10 norm-entrepreneurs, including the CSR-related initiatives in which they participate.

2.3   How to explain corporate norm-entrepreneurship?

After introducing the concept of corporate norm-entrepreneurship and identifying it as an empirical phenomenon in various governance settings, Chapters 3 to 5 engage in a causal analysis of the conditions under which corporate norm-entrepreneurship is more or less likely to occur. As a

Table 2.4 Key data about the systematic norm-entrepreneurs

Data Base	Industry	Business Segments	No. of Employees	Participating in
BP plc London, United Kingdom, www.bp.com	Extractive	Oil, gas, mineral oil products, gas stations, alternative energy products	92,000 (2008)	Global Compact, Global Reporting Initiative, Business Principles for Countering Bribery (these initiatives are covered in this study), Extractive Industries Transparency Initiative, Voluntary Principles on Security and Human Rights
Credit Suisse GRP AG ADR Zurich, Switzerland www.credit-suisse.com	Finance	Private banking, investment banking, asset management	47,800 (2008)	Global Compact, Global Reporting Initiative, Wolfsberg Group (these initiatives are covered in this study), United Nations Environmental Programme (UNEP), Finance Initiative, Equator Principles
Deutsche Bank AG NA O.N. Frankfurt/Main, Germany www.deutsche-bank.de	Finance	Global markets, global banking, asset management, private wealth management, private and business clients	80,456 (2008)	Global Compact, Global Reporting Initiative, Wolfsberg Group (these initiatives are covered in this study), UNEP Finance Initiative, World Business Council for Sustainable Development
France Telecom S.A. Paris, France www.francetelecom.com	Telecommunication	Fixed services, mobile services, internet services; distribution of content, health care, advertising on all platforms	186,049 (2008)	Global Compact, Global Reporting Initiative, Business Principles for Countering Bribery (these initiatives are covered in this study), Global e-Sustainability Initiative, Mobile Phone Partnership Initiative
Inditex S.A. La Coruna, Spain www.inditex.com	Retail	Textile design, manufacturing, distribution	89,112 (2008)	Global Compact, Global Reporting Initiative, Business Social Compliance Initiative (these initiatives are covered in this study)

Company	Sector	Products/Operations	Employees	Initiatives
Rio Tinto Limited & plc London, United Kingdom www.riotinto.com	Extractive	Iron ore, extraction of resources for energy consumption, industrial minerals (Talkum, Borax, and so on), aluminium, diamonds, copper, and gold	105,785 (2008)	Global Compact, Global Reporting Initiative, Business Principles for Countering Bribery (these initiatives are covered in this study), Extractive Industries Transparency Initiative (EITI), Voluntary Principles on Security and Human Rights
Royal Dutch Shell plc The Hague, Netherlands www.shell.com	Extractive	Oil, gas, petrochemicals, petrol stations	104,000 (2009)	Global Compact, Global Reporting Initiative, Business Principles for Countering Bribery (these initiatives are covered in this study), International Union for Conservation of Nature (IUCN), Extractive Industries Transparency Initiative (EITI), United Nations Partnership for Clean Fuels and Vehicles, Voluntary Principles on Security and Human Rights
TATA Group/ TATA STEEL Mumbai, India www.tatasteel.com	Steel	Crude steel production, manufacturing of steel products, steel building and construction applications	38,182 (2005–06)	Global Compact, Global Reporting Initiative, Business Principles for Countering Bribery, SA 8000 (these initiatives are covered in this study)
UBS AG Zurich, Switzerland www.ubs .com	Finance	Private and corporate banking, asset management, investment banking, private equity	79,166 (2008)	Global Compact, Global Reporting Initiative, Business Principles for Countering Bribery, Wolfsberg Group (these initiatives are covered in this study), UNEP Finance Initiative
SASOL Limited Johannesburg, South Africa www.sasol.com	Chemical	Commercial production and marketing of chemicals and liquid fuels, oil and gas exploration	32,000 (2008)	Global Compact, Global Reporting Initiative, SA 8000 (these initiatives are covered in this study), Responsible Care

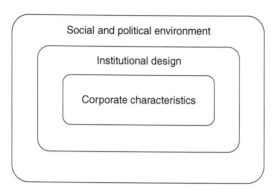

Figure 2.2   Variables encouraging corporate norm-entrepreneurship

starting point for this causal analysis, three clusters of variables have been developed that have an influence on norm-oriented corporate behavior (see Figure 2.2). Norm-entrepreneurship can be encouraged by: (a) the social and political environment; (b) specific corporate characteristics; and (c) the institutional design of self-regulatory initiatives.

2.3.1   The social and political environment

The social and political environment comprises a variety of factors that may affect the behavior of a company. Their relevance results from the assumption that no corporation is fully independent from the society in which it operates. Each company operates within one or more political systems, is subject to their laws, and depends on interaction with societal stakeholders, such as customers or investors who, in turn, might themselves be influenced by civil society activists. For the purpose of this study, three factors within the social and political environment were identified and are investigated for their explanatory power: transnational public pressure, relations between business and government in the home state and the heterogeneity of regulatory environments. Section 3.1 focuses on the influence of transnational civil society on corporate norm-related behavior. NGO pressure is the first factor that intuitively comes to mind when thinking about corporate concern for sustainability issues; it has already been suggested in several studies as an explanation for the origins of the CSR movement. To test the validity of this claim, initiatives of transnational NGOs are taken as indicative of societal pressure on corporations, and the level of pressure to which the 10 norm-entrepreneurs have been subjected is analyzed. In contrast to this, views voiced in interviews with initiative and corporate experts show that although societal pressure is indeed one of the primary factors leading to norm-entrepreneurship, its varying degrees cannot be seen as explanatory. Such pressure should instead be seen as a general background influence on TNCs in the global governance age.

To analyze home state characteristics as a causal factor in enhancing corporate norm-entrepreneurship, several theories are examined in Section 3.2, some from rationalist and others from constructivist thought. Surprisingly, both corporate law literature and the Varieties of Capitalism (VoC) approach are insufficient to explain cross-national variations in corporate norm-entrepreneurship. Therefore, the home state is reconceptualized along the lines of constructivist thought to make sense of the fact that different types of business-government relations may shape the identity of business actors and socialize them into following different procedural norms. It is argued that the extent to which a company engages in norm setting and norm development processes depends on the degree to which it has been socialized into the role of political actor by national business-government relations.

In Section 3.3, the heterogeneity of regulatory environments is proposed as an influence on a company's decision to engage in processes of norm setting and norm development. This argument comes from an empirical observation: Corporations increasingly have operations all over the globe and are confronted with extremely diverse regulatory standards in their day-to-day business operations in various host states. The underlying causal mechanism refers to heterogeneity constraining companies' strategic options and to increased costs of doing business on a global scale. Therefore, it is assumed that corporations exposed to heterogeneous regulatory environments are likely to engage in norm setting and norm development processes to reduce the costs of regulatory diversity.

2.3.2 Corporate characteristics

Factors of production, type of industry, legal form or size are features usually used to distinguish corporations. However, a brief analysis of these factors shows that their potential causal leverage for explaining corporate norm-entrepreneurship is limited. For example, among the 10 systematic norm-entrepreneurs are primary producers, manufacturers, retailers, and service businesses. Instead, the search for corporate variables has focused on characteristics that are related to the CSR debate, which stresses the importance of public perception, namely the vulnerability of a company. In addition, one classic 'hard' corporate characteristic, the ownership structure of a company, as well as a classic 'soft' one, corporate culture, have been chosen as potential causal factors that support norm-entrepreneurship.

In Section 4.1, intangible characteristics which may explain corporate engagement in norm-entrepreneurship are conceptualized as a company's vulnerability. As a causal factor, corporate vulnerability seeks to capture the fuzzy expectation that companies involved in misdeeds will either be sanctioned by society or self-reprimand. Due to their corporate property, some companies are more vulnerable to a loss of reputation or identity than others. Those who are more vulnerable attempt to compensate the ensuing risks by taking suitable pro-active and reactive steps to maintain and defend reputation and identity. To test the analytical value of the variable, corporate vulnerability is operationalized into two company properties: product type and brand. It is then investigated whether the risk of losing reputation is considerably higher for companies that produce consumer goods and whether companies associated with brands are more vulnerable to reputational losses and therefore more likely to engage in norm-entrepreneurship.

In Section 4.2, the ownership structure of a company, in terms of the level of ownership concentration, is examined. Following the principal agent logic, companies with dispersed shareholdings rarely have to be apprehensive of any external influence on a company's strategy. However, if shareholdings are concentrated, large investors might pursue more active strategies within a company. A genuine engagement in norm-entrepreneurship requires a high degree of commitment and an orientation that allows a longer time horizon, which might also lead to lower rates of return on equity investment in the short term. Owners have to be patient because a newly introduced CSR strategy may lead initially to performance deterioration. Moreover, this hypothesis has to be qualified according to the type of owner, whether government, institutional investor or individual. Some prefer short-term, others long-term, investment strategies. Looking first at the degree of ownership concentration, and, second, at the particular ownership mix, ownership structure is tested for whether it has any bearing on corporate norm-entrepreneurship.

Section 4.3 focuses on the corporate culture and investigates whether corporations can also undergo habitualization processes and whether norm-entrepreneurship, therefore, is not a wholly new phenomenon but, rather, a translation of what corporations have always been used to. For this purpose, a corporate culture is conceptualized as adaptable to norm-entrepreneurship when it can be understood as a culture of responsibility involving a corporate tradition or history of engagement in social or environmental not-for-profit activities. The deliberations of the experts interviewed establish the extent to which corporate representatives feel their companies are unconsciously used to the activities and therefore engage in norm-entrepreneurship out of routine rather than out of conscious decision making. Contrasting these deliberations with case studies on the historic engagement by the 10 systematic norm-entrepreneurs in not-for-profit activities, corporate culture is found to be highly significant in influencing corporate behavior.

2.3.3　Institutional design

The institutional environment of corporations consists of a great variety of collective self-regulatory arrangements, featuring designs that may attract or deter corporate engagement as norm-entrepreneurs. This argument differs from the previous ones in that institutional factors play a role as 'pull' rather that 'push' factors. For the purpose of this study, three institutional factors, namely, structural autonomy, flexibility of institutional rules and procedures, and the legitimacy corporations ascribe to a certain type of transnational governance arrangement were identified and investigated.

Section 5.1 analyzes the validity of the assumption that corporations prefer to engage in norm setting autonomously, without interference from other types of actors. Autonomy is said to be limited by two aspects of institutional design – the actor configuration and the steering instrument employed within an initiative. These two aspects are compared to the reasoning of interviewees on the importance of autonomy preservation. The variable is found to be highly significant – although in some aspects corporations seem more ready to accept or even support intrusions into their autonomy than might be expected.

In Section 5.2, flexibility of transnational governance arrangements is discussed as a means to attract companies to engage in norm setting and norm development, referring to research results on the nature of political institutions and processes of institutional change. Flexibility is conceptualized as a design pattern of self-regulatory initiatives capable of exerting influence on participating companies. Corporate norm-entrepreneurship is most likely to occur in moderately flexible institutions. This argument refers to a rationalist model of interaction: Corporations follow a cost-benefit ratio, weighing the foreseeable costs of corporate engagement against the benefits. The flexibility of self-regulatory initiatives is integrated as a factor in corporate cost-benefit analysis. Therefore, companies reduce regulatory complexity by participating in flexible institutions only to the extent that the costs of behavioral adjustment do not outweigh the benefits.

In Section 5.3, the focus shifts from objectively observable design features to the subjective perceptions of corporations: It is hypothesized that in deciding in which initiative to engage as norm-entrepreneurs, corporations are also driven by considerations of legitimacy. Legitimacy is also analyzed to establish whether it consists of the corporations own internalized ideas of legitimacy or whether they seek to fulfill the expectations of external actors. Corporate legitimacy criteria are identified from the interview data: they show that corporations are indeed driven by legitimacy considerations but that their concepts of legitimacy are rather flat or limited in comparison to demands voiced in the public sphere.

To test the nine hypotheses derived from the three clusters (Table 2.5), the 10 norm-entrepreneurs were empirically analyzed in detailed case studies based on secondary as well as primary sources. Apart from literature reviews and analyses of company, civil society and business associations' publications and websites, data were generated through semistructured expert interviews with representatives of the 10 companies and the 6 self-regulatory initiatives. It was agreed with the interviewees that personal and corporate anonymity would be preserved to avoid a social desirability bias

Table 2.5   Hypotheses to explain corporate norm-entrepreneurship

---

The social and political environment

H1 – Transnational Public
The more active the transnational public is in the environment of a corporation, the more the corporation is likely to engage in norm-entrepreneurship.

H2 – Home State Socialization
The more a company's home state provides enabling institutional structures, the more likely it will engage in corporate norm-entrepreneurship.

H3 – Heterogeneity of Regulatory Environments
The more a corporation is exposed to heterogeneous regulatory environments, the more likely it will engage in corporate norm-entrepreneurship.

Corporate Characteristics

H4 – Corporate Vulnerability
The more vulnerable a company is through its reputation or identity, the more it is likely to engage in corporate norm-entrepreneurship activities.

H5 – Ownership Structure
The more a company's shareholdings are concentrated with government, family investors, or pension funds as major shareholders, the more it is likely to engage in norm-entrepreneurship.

H6 – Corporate Culture
The more a corporation's culture is a 'culture of responsibility', the more it is likely to engage in norm-entrepreneurship.

Institutional Designs

H7 – Autonomy Preservation
The more a self-regulatory initiative preserves the autonomy of participating companies, the more appealing it will be for companies to engage in norm-entrepreneurship.

H8 – Flexibility
The more a self-regulatory initiative consists of moderately flexible institutions, the more corporations are likely to engage as norm-entrepreneurs.

H9 – Legitimacy
The more a self-regulatory initiative is perceived as legitimate, the more corporations are likely to act as norm-entrepreneurs.

---

in the answers. Therefore, all transcripts have been encoded as C1 to C11 for corporate representatives and I1 to I12 for representatives of self-regulatory initiatives. Interviews conducted in German have been translated but not indicated as such when referenced so that quotes cannot be associated with any particular interviewee. Additional insights have been derived from participatory observation in various expert meetings of self-regulatory initiatives between October 2005 and November 2008. For the causal analysis in Chapters 3 to 5, the interview data have been coded, in accordance with Chatham House rules.

Notes

1. A detailed introduction into the concept of norm-entrepreneurship (versus norm-consumership) is contained in the background paper by Flohr et al. (2008).

2. This implies that when norms have not yet reached taken-for-granted status (Finnemore and Sikkink 1998), acts of norm implementation can also be classified as norm-entrepreneurship. A similar distinction between early and late adopters is employed here, as is done in the classical norm-emergence models, by identifying the role of norm leaders or regime proponents as those active early in the norm life cycle.

3. See http://www.sa-intl.org/, date accessed 19 May 2009; Wick (2005), Leipziger (2001, 2003), Gilbert and Rasche (2007).

4. See http://www.transparency.org/global_priorities/private_sector/business_principles, date accessed 19 May 2009; Transparency International (2003, 2004, 2005, 2008a).

5. See http://www.unglobalcompact.org/, date accessed 19 May 2009; Kell and Levin (2003), Rieth (2004), Kell (2003).

6. See http://www.wolfsberg-principles.com/index.html, date accessed 19 May 2009; Hinterseer (2002); Pieth and Aiolfi (2003a, 2003b, 2004); Pieth (2006).

7. See http://www.globalreporting.org/Home, date accessed 19 May 2009; Gee and Slater (2005); KPMG (2002, 2005).

8. See http://www.bsci-eu.com/, date accessed 19 May 2009; Business Social Compliance Initiative (2005, 2006, 2007); Egels-Zandén and Wahlqvist (2007).

Part II

Causes of Corporate Norm-entrepreneurship

Part II of this volume examines the conditions under which corporate norm-entrepreneurship is more or less likely to occur. Three sets of explanatory factors are tested on the basis of empirical data from interviews with the representatives of companies and self-regulatory initiatives, and of secondary sources such as statistics, databases, and rankings.

Chapter 3 covers the social and political environment in which corporations operate. In the first section, the role of the pressure built up by transnational NGOs is analyzed. The emergence of corporate social responsibility (CSR) is commonly associated with NGO campaigns against single corporations or whole industries. We examine whether activist pressure also affects corporate norm-entrepreneurship. In the second section, we focus on the role of the home state of a company. In the age of globalization corporations are often considered to be 'stateless' actors. Yet, the home state may still matter by providing institutional incentives for corporate norm-related activities. To tackle this research question, different possible influences at the home state level are tested, including the level of regulation and the business-government relations. The last section investigates the heterogeneity of the regulatory environments that norm-entrepreneurs deal with. Transnational corporations are faced with the national laws of different states. Having to adapt to different regulatory environments may impose costs on corporations, which in turn may affect corporate norm-entrepreneurship.

Chapter 4 focuses on the characteristics at the company level that influence corporate norm-entrepreneurship. The first section explores the explanatory value of a corporation's vulnerability to reputational costs for its willingness to engage in norm-related activities. Companies do not want to lose their 'license to operate'. Reputation is understood here as an intangible characteristic of a corporation. An additional factor affecting corporate behavior is the type of ownership. The chapter analyzes in how far government or family ownership, or the dominance of institutional investors can explain corporate norm-entrepreneurship. The final section examines the role of organizational or corporate culture.

Chapter 5 investigates the institutional characteristics of transnational governance initiatives. Corporate norm-entrepreneurship can take place either unilaterally or in collective private-private, multistakeholder, or public-private governance arrangements. These different types of governance arrangements may encourage, limit, or prevent corporations' engagement as norm-entrepreneurs. However, there is still little knowledge about the extent to which existing or possible future institutional patterns can facilitate corporate norm-entrepreneurship. Section 1 investigates different types of actor configurations and steering instruments to find out how the structural autonomy of corporations in specific types of governance arrangements influences their behavior. The second section analyzes the flexibility of institutional rules and procedures. Section 3 focuses on the legitimacy that corporations ascribe to certain types of transnational governance arrangements and the influence of such legitimacy perceptions on corporate norm-entrepreneurship. The institutional factors investigated in chapter five differ from the preceding variables because they are likely to pull rather than push corporate norm-entrepreneurship. They do not explain why corporations change their behavior and become norm-entrepreneurs, but they determine what kind of governance arrangements corporations will look for once they have decided to become norm-entrepreneurs.

In Chapter 6, the findings of the causal analysis presented in the previous chapters are assessed in comparison. Two ideal-type pathways that are likely to lead to corporate norm-entrepreneurship are identified, based on different assumptions about the underlying rationalist or constructivist rationale of corporate actors, and on specific combinations of necessary and facilitating conditions.

3
The Social and Political Environment

3.1 Transnational public

The most intuitive answer to the question of what makes corporations engage in CSR activities and, more specifically, norm-entrepreneurship is public pressure. Because corporations are profit-maximizing enterprises, it is assumed that they do not develop any interest in beyond profit activities unless external factors exist. Corporations consider engaging in CSR only when civil society or consumers succeed in either reframing their moral demands into solid business cases or in awakening corporations' moral sensitivity (Gunningham and Rees 1997). How far this expectation holds true for corporate decisions to engage in norm-entrepreneurship is examined here. Given the dual character of the public as a structural variable and an actor endowed with intentionality (Habermas 1990; Gerhards 1994; Neidhardt 1994), it is assumed that structural conditions are necessary for a transnational public to function but that NGOs and other civil society actors form the basis of public pressure on corporations. Changes in the structure of international relations have enabled nonstate actors to become influential and the deliberate actions of transnational NGOs, for example, reinforce these changes.

3.1.1 Transnationalism as a prerequisite

This argument relies on the notion that macro-structural changes in international relations have allowed for the 'transnational public' to become a potential influencing factor in world politics: The international system has increasingly developed into a 'world society' characterized by growing institutionalization and the diffusion of actors and arenas of interaction (World Society Research Group 2000). As problem structures become globalized and problem solving capacities privatized, nonstate actors are no longer just the subject of state action but have become subjects of and active participants in transnational political processes (Weiss and Gordenker 1996). Even though pressure groups within nation states has been the traditional study focus (Arts 1998: 24), studies of transnational civil society exist, concluding that it exerts considerable influence on international politics, changing policy-making procedures at the international level and contributing to better or more desirable outcomes (Arts 1998; Willets 1996; Khagram et al. 2002; Keck and Sikkink 1998). Within this framework, often referred to as the 'new transnationalism' (Keohane and Nye 1972; Risse-Kappen 1995; Heins 2001; Dingwerth 2007), another shift has taken place recently: nonstate actors are increasingly refocusing their attention away from primarily targeting states to addressing other nonstate actors, such as corporations (Doh and Teegen 2003; Winston 2002). Probably one of the most visible aspects of this new phenomenon lies in the fact that a number of international NGOs who focus on human rights and environmental protection are wholly devoted to affecting corporate behavioral change (such as CorpWatch, Co-op America, Banktrack, Sweatshop Watch, and Corporate Europe Observatory). They are frustrated with the limited willingness of states to take legislative measures and instead channel their campaigns at corporations.

3.1.2   The origins of norm-entrepreneurship and public pressure

Transnational public pressure has previously been linked to corporate norm-entrepreneurship in publications referring to the early history of corporate social responsibility. The first instance of activist pressure for corporate behavior change was the anti-apartheid campaign, based in American student and church organizations pressuring corporations and investors to disinvest from South Africa (Klotz 1995: 97–100). The campaign ultimately resulted in the establishment of the Sullivan Principles, one of the first collective self-regulatory codes of conduct (Klein 2002: 346). Similar dynamics have proliferated since the mid-1990s when activist, media, and consumer campaigns targeted businesses such as Levi-Strauss, Matel and Disney, Nike, Wal-Mart, and Starbucks for exploitive practices in their supply chains. These campaigns spurred the creation of a variety of initiatives that involved the first instances of norm-entrepreneurship by corporations, such as the Levis Strauss Supplier Standards, Rugmark, and SA 8000 (Varley 1998: 12–13).

Who are those external actors exerting influence on corporate behavior: customers, investors, civil society actors, or the public? What is the behavioral logic behind corporate engagement in rule making when caused by public pressure? Which causal mechanisms link public pressure to corporate behavior change? When faced with new public expectations, raised particularly by transnational NGOs, it might either be the construction of a business case through mobilizing consumer or investor pressure, or corporations might be persuaded that their activities are morally wrong. Although activists will often resort to pressure strategies that involve other sectors of society, transnational NGOs are still assumed the decisive public force. The hypothesis is summarized as:

Hypothesis 1 (H1): The more active the transnational public is in the environment of a corporation, the more the corporation is likely to engage in norm-entrepreneurship.

3.1.3 The construction of a business case by transnational public pressure

Macro-structural changes in the international system have increased the weight of nonstate and civil society actors in particular, as the main elements of the transnational public. The assumption that public pressure can force corporate behavior change relies to a certain extent on a classical understanding of corporations who follow a purely profit-driven rationale and engage in seemingly nonprofit activities only when they can be transformed into a business case, either through generating additional profit or preventing additional costs (Take 2002: 73). Several alternative pathways are possible to achieve this end but, as the historical examples above show, all of them usually rely on the activities of specialized groups within society, namely activists, deliberately aiming to create a business case for corporations. These actors will usually try to involve other subsets of society to reinforce their goals. For example, consumers, through their consumption decisions, can influence the profits of a firm directly and use this power to achieve behavior change. The public can also exert pressure on a corporation from the supply rather than the demand side: investors can withhold finances from a corporation if it does not act in accordance with their expectations (Kong et al. 2002). Activists might also harm the reputation of businesses, which can indirectly translate into pecuniary loss or benefit. However, this last method presupposes the corporation's market rationality to be of the complex kind – where the calculation of costs and profits includes intangible assets, such as the corporation's reputation (Haufler 2001: 26–7; see also Section 4.1 on vulnerability). This logic thus moves away from rationalist concepts of material incentives as being the only relevant ones and assumes corporations also to be sensitive to purely social pressure (Schimmelfennig 2003: 410–11).

In his study of NGO influence in world politics, Take differentiates between three levels of influence; national, international, and societal, asserting that the societal is often overlooked in studies of NGO strategies (Take 2002: 68). NGO activities targeting corporations belong to this category. It can be differentiated further into campaigns that seek to incur economic costs on corporations through consumer boycotts, institutionalized monitoring by NGOs, and eco-sponsoring that seeks to reward corporations for good behavior with a positive public image. Take also compares the indirect targeting of corporations by raising the awareness of their customers to NGO strategies of educating voters to exert their political influence on election candidates.[1] These distinctions emphasize that NGOs are only one of several public actors who can potentially influence corporations, although they are probably the one who strives the most deliberately to put pressure on corporations. Strategies differ even when aiming at the same goals, depending on the assumptions made about corporate constitution and sensitivity.

Civil society can raise awareness of putative corporate wrongdoings and put them on the public agenda. Corporations have to react to avoid negative, tangible, and intangible effects. These types of business cases are distinguished by the different subsets of the public they involve (consumers, investors, civil society) or by the type of costs through which they seek to incur influence (revenues, reputation, finances). From this rationalist perspective, advocated in International Political Economy (IPE) (Stopford et al. 1991; Fuchs 2005) and by theories of corporatism (Ottaway 2001), businesses' reactions to this pressure are primarily regarded as a means of taming rather than empowering civil society actors ('global corporatism'), whose impact on corporations would therefore only trigger the development of new strategies of profit-maximization.

3.1.4   The moral case made by the transnational public

The second mechanism that could explain corporate behavior change triggered by public pressure supposes that corporations may not always be driven by profits alone and may be affected by normative change at the international level (Rieth and Zimmer 2004), civil society lobbying and new cognitive frames by which companies judge activities formerly considered legitimate (Finnemore and Sikkink 1998; Nadelmann 1990). This process may start as pure lip service, that is, as a strategic behavior employed by actors who are unwilling to change their normative frames but who strive for international recognition. As research of states under normative pressure has shown, it can lead to self-entrapment and result in internalization and moral conviction (Risse et al. 1999). Just as states can be socialized into wholly new identities and behavioral constraints, corporations might also be able to undergo identity changes when cognitively challenged from the outside. Even though research on this is still scarce, the same framing and social construction techniques that persuade states of new normative standards (Deitelhoff 2006) could also have an affect on corporations and set off similar processes of strategic self-entrapment.

For this kind of 'corporate identity change' through the spread of global norms, the modes of interaction employed by civil society are of crucial importance. As demonstrated by Rieth and Zimmer (2004), companies are more likely to accept new standards of appropriate behavior when NGOs transform their strategies away from confrontation and toward collaboration in multistakeholder settings (see also Mark-Ungericht 2001; Heins 2005).[2] Shaming campaigns prevent companies from being persuaded by normative arguments. For persuasion to have effect, interactions must be discursive and aimed at learning, rather than confrontational and aimed at coercion. By employing coercive strategies on corporations who specifically violate norms with strong normative force, NGOs run the risk of reducing the weight that their argument could have in discourse. Hence, NGOs have started to become more flexible. Having traditionally taken on the role of confronters, convinced that corporations will act only when their financial interests are threatened (business case), NGOs increasingly now play the role of engagers, trying to draw corporations into dialogue and persuade them to change their behavior by means of ethical and prudential arguments (moral case) (Winston 2002; Rieth and Göbel 2005). For corporations, it seems to be increasingly difficult to escape the normatively textured environment they see themselves confronted with and where they seek to appease via new modes of institutionalized dialogue (Mark-Ungericht 2001: 57–8), this opens pathways for moral persuasion that can be promoted by an active transnational public.

3.1.5 Identifying the role of public pressure

Following Hypothesis 1, it is assumed that transnational NGOs have the capacity to influence the public agenda, deliberately mobilize larger parts of the public and generate pressure by targeting corporations. The website of the Business and Human Rights Resource Centre[3] is 'tracking the positive and negative impacts of over 4000 companies worldwide' and although it focuses on corporate activities and misdeeds primarily in the field of human rights, it can serve as a useful indicator of transnational public attention levels. The number of posts on the site indicates the level of public pressure on a corporation. However, the principal indicator is not the number of hits targeting one specific company but, rather, those targeting a specific industry sector because only a few exceptional civil society campaigns have focused on single companies. In the majority of cases, an entire industry sector was targeted. Targeting one company from a sector often puts the spotlight on its peers, as seen in the campaigns against Nike and Starbucks that resulted in closer scrutiny of the whole apparel and coffee industries. Therefore, the number of posts targeting an industry sector serves as an approximation of the level of transnational civil society activity. To substantiate further the claim that there is a causal relationship between the pressure created by NGOs and corporate norm-entrepreneurship, qualitative data from expert interviews are consulted as well. The interview data are also helpful for identifying what exact causal mechanisms are at work as interviewees referred to civil society pressure as a cause for engagement and, more specifically, to either the costs or moral convictions underlying their companies' decisions.

Applying Hypothesis 1 to the available empirical data, the prime expectation is that the corporations most actively involved in norm-entrepreneurship were targeted by civil society campaigns to above average degrees, resulting in above average numbers of hits on the website. Vice versa, corporations and sectors that have not attracted much civil society attention and therefore have fewer hits on the website are not expected to significantly engage in norm-entrepreneurship.

Quantitative analysis

The number of posts on the Business and Human Rights website indicates the variance in intensity with which the public follows the activities of different industry sectors. Table 3.1 shows the 10 norm-entrepreneurs identified in Chapter 2 and the numbers of hits their industry sectors have received. Since the website lists posts in cumulative categories such as 'natural resources', comprising 'mining' and 'oil, gas and coal' as subcategories and gives separate numbers for each of these, the following table lists the number of hits for the relevant subcategories as well as their aggregated sums. The findings rely only on the numbers of hits received in the subcategories in which a company is active. They are highlighted in bolt print and their aggregate can be found under the title 'Total hits of relevance' at the end of each row.

Looking at the total hits within sectors first, the extractive industry ('natural resources') has received more than twice the attention of the financial sector and a third more than the apparel industry. The technology and chemicals sectors are even further behind. This considerable variance in public pressure stands in contrast with the high level of norm-entrepreneurship of all of the ten selected outstanding norm-entrepreneurs. However, it would be premature to draw conclusions from these findings without contrasting them to the levels of attention received by other corporations less active as norm-entrepreneurs. Indeed, this further test yields more interesting results: When the hits of the subsectors of the selected norm-entrepreneurs are compared with those of other subsectors, few have been exposed to equally high levels of attention as even those least targeted among the sample. Leaving aside the diversified companies such as Sasol and Tata – where it is difficult to disentangle the targeting of which of their many product lines influences them most – the lowest results are found for the subsectors 'technology, telecom and electronics' (1035 hits) and 'finance and banking' (1119 hits). In fact, out of the 188 listed subsectors, only three – 'agriculture and livestock' (1228), 'food and beverages' (1042), and 'pharmaceuticals' (1381) – surpass one or both of these two least targeted of the norm-entrepreneurs and even then it is only to a small degree.

A minimum level of public attention seems to be a necessary condition for outstanding norm-entrepreneurship. All of the systematic norm-entrepreneurs belong to industry sectors that have been targeted above a certain minimum degree. However, in all of the highly targeted sectors there are also large numbers of corporations not engaged in norm-entrepreneurship, at least not systematically. Transnational public pressure alone cannot function as a sufficient condition to foster norm-entrepreneurship.

Table 3.1 Industry sector hits on the business and human rights website

Company	Hits on business and human rights website	
BP	**Natural resources (total hits)**	**6,153**
Shell	Cork	2
	Diamond	431
	Logging & lumber	709
	Mining	1,728
	Oil, gas, & coal	**3,036**
	Paper & cardboard	192
	Petrol stations	**13**
	Sand	2
	Stone quarries	40
	Total hits of relevance	**3,049**
Credit Suisse	**Finance (total hits)**	**1,385**
Deutsche Bank	**Finance & banking**	**1,119**
UBS	Insurance	232
	Stock exchanges	34
	Total hits of relevance	**1,119**
France Telecom	**Technology (total hits)**	**1,162**
	Internet companies	127
	Technology, telecom, and electronics	**1,035**
	Total hits of relevance	**1,035**
Inditex	**Apparel & textile (total hits)**	**1,971**
	Clothing & textile	**1,406**
	Footwear	**530**
	Leather & tanneries	**35**
	Total hits of relevance	**1,971**
Rio Tinto	**Natural Resources (total hits)**	**6,153**
	Cork	2
	Diamond	431
	Logging & lumber	709
	Mining	**1,728**
	Oil, gas, & coal	3,036
	Paper & cardboard	192
	Petrol stations	13
	Sand	2
	Stone quarries	40
	Total hits of relevance	**1,728**
Sasol	**Chemical (total hits)**	**1,260**
	Adhesives & glue	8
	Chemical: General	**747**
	Cleaning products	12
	Dye	5
	Ethanol	**6**
	Fertilizer	39

Continued

Table 3.1   Continued

Company	Hits on business and human rights website	
	Industrial gases	12
	Ink	2
	Paint	33
	Pesticide	371
	Refrigerant	25
	Total hits of relevance:	**786**
	Natural Resources (total hits)	**6,153**
	Cork	2
	Diamond	431
	Logging & lumber	709
	Mining	1,728
	Oil, gas, & coal	**3,036**
	Paper & cardboard	192
	Petrol stations	13
	Sand	2
	Stone quarries	40
	Total hits of relevance:	**3,036**
Tata Group/Tata Motors/Tata Steel	**Metals/plastics/basic materials (total hits)**	**579**
	Fiberglass	4
	Foam	1
	Glass	54
	Metals & steel	**422**
	Plastics	68
	Rubber	29
	Soda ash	1
	Transport (total hits)	**1,108**
	Transport: General	47
	Aircraft/airline	247
	Airports	17
	Auto parts	35
	Auto rental	4
	Auto wrecking & salvage	1
	Automobile & other motor vehicles	**627**
	Bicycle	4
	Bus	14
	Ferry	5
	Railroad	67
	Snowmobile	1
	Taxi	4
	Tire	35
	Conglomerates	**218**
	Diversified/Conglomerates	**218**
	Total hits of relevance	**1,267**

Source: http://www.business-humanrights.org/Home, accessed 1 January 2006.

Qualitative analysis

Further insight into whether and how much corporations were motivated by being heavily targeted – or whether the correlation is merely coincidental – is achieved by analyzing the qualitative data from interviews with corporate experts. Potential clues are expected to explain why transnational public pressure seems to motivate some corporations but not others. The significant influence of NGO pressure on corporate behavior and specifically in inducing norm-entrepreneurship was confirmed in most interviews with representatives of individual companies and self-regulatory initiatives – as is exemplified by the following statement: 'We could easily become the target of an NGO campaign because we are highly exposed. [...] For that reason, it is of course very important that we do much more than the minimum for the sake of prevention. For we know it is always about reputation and about avoiding negative perception. Therefore, we do considerably more as a means of anticipation, so to say' (C11, 24 May 2006). This statement explains why norm-entrepreneurship is a chosen reaction to civil society pressure: Engagement in norm setting shows responsibility beyond the minimum degree required in a somewhat proactive and anticipatory way – in the hope of preventing further negative pressure in the future. It is interesting that public influence on corporations strongly depends on whether NGOs succeed in mobilizing a broader base among other segments of society that can exert influence upon corporations: 'Civil society is the voice that is heard [...] but only those topics are successful that find support in the broader public' (C2, 11 September 2007). It seems more appropriate to speak of the influence of the societal environment rather than narrowing it down to civil society. As one company representative stated, 'We surely follow the civil society debate, if you want to reduce it to NGOs. However, there are so many stakeholder groups that we have to take into account that we rather try to have a general picture of the overall societal environment' (C2, 11 September 2007). While many statements explicitly referred to transnational NGOs, others also stressed the strong influence of home state-specific societal pressure: 'In each country the stakeholder community is a little different, especially in terms of trade unions and critical NGOs which address these topics to corporations. As a result, the companies from countries with particularly aggressive campaigns, above all Germany, Sweden and the Netherlands, have an important incentive to say, "Yes, we actually want to do more"' (I13, 28 July 2006).

Another notion that figured very prominently, especially in statements from initiative representatives, was that the differing degrees to which specific companies have been or are targeted by campaigns do not make significant differences to corporate behavior anymore once the corporations realize that they are generally under scrutiny. Therefore, they no longer react to single instances of pressure but take public scrutiny as something they constantly have to be aware of: 'Company X might not have been targeted to the same extent as company Y has. But they know that the whole sector is in the spotlight. They are all under heavy fire, at all times' (I5, 28 April 2006). The following statement also supports this pending tendency of public pressure: 'Without a doubt, when globalization really took off in the 1990s, it was of course the [...] oil corporations that first became subject to activists' attacks as well as to critical media coverage. [...] Meanwhile, there is no corporation, no single sector that is not affected by those [attacks], [...] whether it is services or industry or consumer products' (I2, 27 March 2006). Once general public awareness and attention to corporate misdeeds has passed a certain threshold, the temporarily heightened or lowered regard for specific industries or companies becomes less relevant. Hence, the level of public pressure should not be conceived of as a variable but represents a constant factor, functioning as a sort of 'background noise' experienced by and having an impact on all contemporary corporations in all sectors.

This relevance of 'world time' (Risse et al. 1999: 19–22) as a factor also seems to be of high importance if norm-entrepreneurship is understood as a specific subcategory of CSR behavior that is not necessarily the automatic reaction to NGO pressure but might develop over time and only if additional conditions are fulfilled. Representatives from various corporations outlined the difficulty that arises when NGO pressure stimulates them to engage in norm-entrepreneurship but the same NGOs then do not enter into constructive dialogue. Pressure alone, therefore, seems to lead to only short-lived norm-entrepreneurship when NGOs are not ready to switch their strategy from confrontational to cooperative later in the process. This view is confirmed: 'This is another issue where corporations have difficulties: the stakeholder dialogue. There is dialogue, there is a lot of criticism, but we find it difficult to establish constructive collaboration with some of the stakeholders. That is always a pity because we see that they also have experience in this domain and they know where the problems are. They approach the corporations, but if one invites them to sit down together and to try to find a way to solve the problem for good, then the willingness of many of them is very limited' (I13, 28 July 2006).

As this last statement highlights, learning within and among corporations and civil society actors also plays an important role as a causal mechanism for corporate norm-entrepreneurship. It suggests that corporations may be engaging in rule setting because of persuasion and with a real interest in improving their behavior. A representative of a company not among the most highly targeted of our sample even went as far as saying that it is an interest in learning more than a fear of being targeted that makes companies get involved with civil society 'because we think we can progress with them and improve our environmental behavior. [...] We think we can learn something from them and the partnership could be constructive. We have no special reason to be concerned about the NGOs and do not fear to be a target' (C8, 10 January 2008). One initiative representative even stressed a sequential logic in the causal mechanisms that works in the opposite direction to those usually identified in International Relations (IR) research, where actors start to adapt their behavior strategically before changing their cognitive frames. 'Originally, it was all a question of morality; the NGOs, the press, media, students and partly also the consumers, they all 'made the moral case'. That's how it actually began. But nowadays, it is more and more turning into a business case' (I2, 27 March 2006). However, some experts argued much more skeptically about the corporate potential for persuasion and learning. They stressed that NGO pressure can, at maximum, lead to the redefinition of a business case without affecting the rationalist logic of profit maximization: 'We all saw that scandals are extremely difficult to manage. [...] These all [have] enormous 'complexity' costs. [...] The corporation wanted to better handle the reputational risk that impacted the capital markets, the external communication and media relations. I do not believe that it wanted to improve society. It is more trivial than that' (I7, 15 May 2006).

3.1.6 Conclusions

These findings underline the significance of the transnational public, which is exemplified by the pressure of transnational NGOs, but in a slightly modified way. While this factor is without doubt influential – as confirmed by experts from corporations and self-regulatory initiatives alike – the data suggest some specifications: The levels of attention that the systematic norm-entrepreneurs receive from the transnational public vary significantly. However, the levels are still generally higher than in the sectors in which they do not operate. Taken together with the repeatedly stated expert views that corporations are generally aware of the scrutiny they are under and that the differing degrees of this scrutiny between single corporations or sectors are of less relevance, it can be concluded that the pressure built up by the transnational public functions as 'background noise' that all corporations are sensitive to. This background noise was created over the past decade and has been kept up to a generally high level by NGOs. It seems to be a prerequisite for corporations to engage in norm-entrepreneurship but cannot fully explain why some do and some do not. There is reason to assume that the background noise, having a minimum level of general public attention to corporate misdeeds and capacity to exert pressure upon corporations, is a necessary condition for any norm-entrepreneurship to occur. Unfortunately, this cannot ultimately be proven within this study for methodological reasons since both conditions, the existence of a certain amount of societal pressure upon corporations and the existence of corporate norm-entrepreneurship, have coincided since the early 1990s. Because of this, a straightforward research design that allows for a systematic comparison cannot be constructed here to prove the causal connection.

Nevertheless, there is good reason to believe that a significantly high level of pressure from transnational NGOs is a sufficient condition for corporate norm-entrepreneurship: No corporation has been identified to date that in being heavily targeted by at least one civil society campaign has not responded by engaging as a norm-entrepreneur, either individually or in collective self-regulatory initiatives. Examples not examined here include Coca-Cola, Nike, WestLB, and Union Carbide. When severely pressured, all reacted by engaging in norm setting, either individually, such as the Coca-Cola Code of Business Conduct or the Nike Code of Conduct, or collectively, such as WestLB's involvement in the Equator Principles or Union Carbide as an active member of the Responsible Care Initiative.

3.2   The home state

The home state – the state where a company is legally incorporated (Muchlinski 2007; Zerk 2006) – is a controversial factor in the debate on corporate behavior change. There are two contradictory views: In the globalization debate, companies are usually portrayed as de-nationalized or stateless entities that are purely guided by 'their own bottom lines – without regard to any national or local interest' (Korten 1995: 127). In this view, the state is seriously challenged by the internationalization of production and TNCs' disregard for the boundaries of territorial politics. Some scholars suggest that the home state, a variable formerly considered important in corporate behavior, is suffering a significant loss of influence and have concluded that the emergence of new forms of private authority is synonymous with a general weakening or retreat of the state (Ohmae 1995; Strange 1996). Comparative law, politics and IPE approaches claim that the home state still matters as a factor in explaining corporate behavior (Doremus et al. 1999; Nölke and Taylor 2007). Linking these contributions to the study of corporate norm-entrepreneurship, this section investigates whether institutional structures at the domestic level enhance or inhibit corporate engagement in norm setting and norm development processes by testing the validity of two causal mechanisms.

Hypothesis 2 (H2):   The more a company's home state provides enabling institutional structures, the more likely it will engage in corporate norm-entrepreneurship.

Corporate law literature, comparative political economy, and comparative politics literature are examined in search of possible causal mechanisms and appropriate indicators to measure home state influence on corporate behavioral change. Assuming a rationalist rationale, the empirical analysis first looks for the explanatory value in the level of regulation approach, analyzing the home states of the ten systematic norm-entrepreneurs. An alternative explanation is then tested, based on the business-government relations approach, which follows constructivist thinking (Wolf et al. 2010).

In seven country case studies, the dominant type of business-government relations in the home states of the 10 systematic norm-entrepreneurs is analyzed as a factor either enhancing or inhibiting corporate behavioral change. Finally, the empirical analysis is expanded, looking for cross-national variations in corporate norm-entrepreneurship in two collective self-regulatory initiatives and two additional countries that have interesting numbers of corporate norm-entrepreneurs.

3.2.1 The business case – the national level of regulation

One way of conceptualizing the home state's influence on corporate norm-entrepreneurship is to follow the assumption that the home state's level of regulation determines company behavior. As Braithwaite and Drahos argue, the national level of regulation defines the scope and boundaries of corporate activities (Braithwaite and Drahos 2000) and drives corporate behavior change even outside the home state. Companies always attempt to create a level playing field to reduce competitive disadvantage internationally and to make the same level of regulation applicable to their competitors. In order to achieve this leveling, they seek to make voluntary standards of behavior (equal to those they are subject to in their home states) applicable to all competing corporations. The underlying rationalist causal mechanism assumes that corporations calculate the cost of regulatory diversity: Companies compare the level of regulation they are used to complying with in their home states with the regulatory obligations their competitors face. Scholars also put forward this argument in comparative political economy, particularly in the Varieties of Capitalism (VoC) approach (Crouch and Streeck 1997; Hall and Soskice 2001; Nölke and Taylor 2007; Streeck and Yamamura 2001).[4]

This logic corresponds with statements in expert interviews, in which national regulation by the home state was portrayed as creating incentives for corporate action: 'Sometimes the state says: "if you do not regulate yourself, it will be regulated by law". From my point of view, the state should do this more often; it creates incentives' (I7, 15 May 2006). One company representative explained that his company does business all over the globe, complying with the standards prevailing in the home state: 'And if you go to a country with a weak legislative system or a country like Qatar where the environmental legislation is basically absent: What do you do when you enter that market? [...] Even though the country does not have legislation in a specific field, we will still do it the way we do it in (our home state), to comply with minimum standards. In other words, we try to engage with the country to lift the standards while setting the example by not doing something recklessly or to obviously contravene good or best practices in the rest of the world. So the political area is important for us' (C5, 8 November 2007). These statements provide initial empirical clues of the national level of regulation working on corporate behavior change. According to another interviewee, 'for us, the distinction between home state and host state almost no longer exists. We have two home markets [...] The same might go for other internationally operating companies. However, if we participate in projects or business far away from our home states or home markets this engagement might have impacts in the home state. I think we are expected to comply with the same norms and values that apply to our headquarters, to our home state, [and] as far as possible, also in our operations worldwide' (C11, 24 May 2006). Such statements support the expectation that the ten systematic norm-entrepreneurs should originate from highly regulated home states.

3.2.2   The constructivist case – national socialization

Following a constructivist path, a causal mechanism can be derived by combining corporatist research in comparative politics with socialization literature. In comparative politics literature, policy styles, decision-making procedures, and mechanisms for societal involvement within a country are regarded as conditions that determine how far companies are likely to take on public roles. Characteristics of national economies influence the varying degrees to which corporations are accustomed to interacting with government in a cooperative manner. Corporatist research differentiates national political systems along two interrelated dimensions: The degree to which interest intermediation is organized and centralized within a national economy, and the degree to which these organized interests are regularly consulted in legislative processes (Lijphart 1999: 171; Schmitter 1982: 262–3). The latter is referred to as 'concertation' and is in contrast to the opposite mode of policy making, 'pressure', where interest groups seek to influence the policy process from outside (Schmitter 1982: 263). Corporatist systems are different to liberal systems where interaction between business and government is not institutionalized but is the outcome of political competition and bargaining. Finally, in interventionist systems the state dominates business-government relations significantly by unilaterally enforcing strict policies (Crouch 1993; Katzenstein 1985).

This general analysis can be further differentiated into specific national styles of business regulation. 'Adversarial legalism'[5] characterizes a type of business-government relationship that is exemplified by the United States, while in nonadversarial relationships, such as the UK, corporations act in partnership with government entities (Vogel 1986; Kagan and Axelrad 1997).[6] Such business-government relations at the national level are institutions of socialization that can alter the identities and preferences of companies. The underlying causal mechanism is a constructivist one, which is quite similar to the understanding of international socialization in IR, in which actors are socialized into a new community by being 'taught' the norms constitutive of and applied in that community (Finnemore 1996; Schimmelfennig 2003: 406). Departing from the assumption that corporations will usually be opposed to or not interested in taking on public functions by providing regulation as a public good, constructivism assumes that such preferences, and thereby certain aspects of the social identity of corporations, can be altered. In this argument, companies are nationally socialized into specific norms of procedural character, prescribing how norm-setting processes should be organized and how public goods should be provided – in either cooperation or confrontation with public and private actors.

Accordingly, companies that are exposed to cooperative business-government relations at the national level are more likely to take on a pro-active role at the transnational level as well. Companies that are used to adversarial relations or those dominated by heavy government intervention are unlikely to engage as norm-entrepreneurs. The reaction of corporations faced with the challenge of substantial new norms from the outside world, such as emerging CSR norms, depends on the procedural norms they have been socialized into nationally. The 10 companies that took on political functions 'away from home', engaging in systematic corporate norm-entrepreneurship, are assumed to originate from home states with cooperative business-government relations that invite companies to take on public functions, participating in political processes 'at home'.

3.2.3 Measuring the level of regulation

To find out more about the home state potential to enhance corporate behavioral change toward norm-entrepreneurship along either of the described causal mechanisms, the home states of the 10 systematic norm-entrepreneurs were examined. To test the rationalist argument, the level of regulation was measured using the Environmental Regulatory Regime Index (ERRI), which summarizes country environmental regulatory systems (Esty and Porter 2002, 2005).[7] To test the constructivist argument, evidence of cooperative or confrontational business-government relations that might enhance or inhibit corporate norm-entrepreneurship activities was sought.

As illustrated in Table 3.2, the 10 companies originate from 7 different home states. Two countries, Switzerland and the United Kingdom, seem to particularly foster norm-entrepreneurship.

According to the level of regulation approach, corporate norm-entrepreneurs originate from home states with an extensive environmental regulation. The seven home states should feature similarly high levels of environmental regulation. However, there are significant cross-national differences in the level of environmental regulation (Table 3.3).

The seven corporate home states spread across the statistical distribution; countries such as Switzerland had a high level of environmental regulation (1.631), countries such as the United Kingdom had a medium level (1.185), and countries such as India had low levels (–0.759). Even though countries with high levels of regulation, such as Switzerland and Germany, apparently foster norm-entrepreneurship, some systematic norm-entrepreneurs originate from countries with significantly lower levels of regulation, such

Table 3.2   Home state distribution per systematic norm-entrepreneur

Systematic norm-entrepreneur	Home state
Credit Suisse	Switzerland
UBS	Switzerland
Deutsche Bank	Germany
Inditex	Spain
France Telecom	France
BP Plc	UK
Rio Tinto	UK
Royal Dutch/Shell	UK
Tata Group	India
Sasol	South Africa

Table 3.3   Corporate home states and their ERRI ranking 2002

Corporate home states	ERRI
Switzerland	1.631
Germany	1.522
France	1.464
Great Britain	1.185
Spain	0.437
South Africa	−0.029
India	−0.759

as South Africa or India. Most interestingly, Great Britain, the country with the highest number of systematic norm-entrepreneurs, scores only inter-mediately for its level of regulation.

Similar results were found when additional indices were used to indicate the strength of public policies that might encourage responsible business practices (Bertelsmann Stiftung 2007; Zadek and MacGillivray 2007). These group home states such as France, Germany, the United Kingdom and the United States together as 'innovators' or 'second level maturity countries', as these countries are most advanced in embedding responsible business practices into national policy. However, with no company from the United States among the 10 systematic norm-entrepreneurs, this approach to meas-uring national regulation cannot explain the influence of the home state on corporate norm-entrepreneurship either.

3.2.4   Measuring national business-government relations

To measure the business-government relations[8] in a company's home state, comparative politics literature differentiates between two types of relations, based on the prevailing cooperative or confrontational policy styles: Adversarial economies with clear-cut, hierarchical, top-down approaches to regulation are contrasted to corporatist types of business-government relations. In what follows, each of the seven home states is classified as having confrontational or collaborative business-government relations. Cooperative interaction between business and government supposedly predisposes companies to engage in norm setting and norm development processes. Therefore, each systematic norm-entrepreneur is assumed to originate from a home state with cooperative business government interactions.[9]

France

French business-government relations operate from a historical background of a close relationship between government and industry, accepting that the state has an almost 'mercantilist' concern with French economic interests (Cawson et al. 1987: 10). Because of the accepted monopoly of the state and the strong belief in its responsibility for the common welfare, there is a deep mistrust of intermediary organizations. According to the traditional understanding of how to divide private and public responsibilities, public authority enjoys a much higher degree of legitimacy than the market.[10] In France, the executive is strong, the legislature weak and the bureaucracy predominant. Interest group politics and lobbying are often seen as illegitimate (Schmidt 1996: 179) and social welfare is predominantly the state's responsibility (Blasco and Zolner 2008: 25). Corporatist research finds France to be only weakly corporatist in nature because, despite strongly organized interest groups, concertation does not lead to consensus and sector ideologies remain adversarial (Lehmbruch 1982: 22). France has a socially corporatist system, where labor organizations play a much more important role than capital ones (Katzenstein 1985: 104–5). The role of the French state in business-government relations is described as predominantly 'interventionist' or 'dirigiste' (Schmidt 1996: 46–8). The French government continues to intervene in business, albeit through laws and incentives intended to make the economy more competitive and to 'moralize' business and labor relations (Schmidt 2003: 547). Because French companies have no history of collaborating with government, they are expected to be less proactive in CSR norm setting and norm development processes.

Germany

In terms of the participation of business in policy making and the institutions enabling it, Germany is a typical example of corporatism. It has a high degree of interest group centralization and, above all, concertation mechanisms that make trilateral consultation on policy making the rule rather than the exception – although there might not be statutory entitlements granting rights to such consultations (Lehmbruch 1982: 20). Even though the German policy style might be classed as partly adversarial, as it relies on complex legalistic rules, the rules are usually made in consultation with or even by industry itself via institutions that facilitate government-industry cooperation (Kollmann and Prakash 2001: 418–20). German corporations are highly used to participating in setting prescriptive rules for their own behavior within the German national context – due to corporatist decision-making processes and institutions that make it likely that such functions have been internalized over time and accepted as part of the identity of corporations. Although corporate CSR behavior has not reached its full potential, German business-government relations seem to provide a solid foundation for norm-entrepreneurship and CSR engagement in general (Habisch et al. 2005).

India

Since its independence, India has shifted its policies on business over time (Evans 1995). It turned toward a policy of 'Indianization', with more self-reliance socially, economically and politically. The Indian government adopted an interventionist policy approach to development that 'was not only blessed by business elites, but was largely authorized by them' (Reed 2002: 252). In Indian business-government relations, the 'active and dominant participation by the government in economic activities resulted in the creation of a protected, highly regulated, public sector-dominated economic environment' (Lal and Clement 2005: 85).[11] Up until the early 1990s, India's economy consisted of a licensing system requiring government permission for establishing and expanding capacity, excessively high rates of corporate and personal taxation, severe restrictions on imports of goods and technology, and tight controls on foreign investment and foreign exchange transactions (Nayar 1998: 2453). Consequently, the political role of business was limited: 'Economic and political elites developed models of governance that have primarily served their own interest rather than those of society as a whole' (Reed 2002: 249). However, in the second half of the 1990s, India moved away from the interventionist policy style of 'high regulation internally and high protection externally to a situation of moderate regulation and moderate protection' (Nayar 1998: 2453). Like other developing countries, where economic actors have come to play a more prominent role and given a greater say by governments (Whitley 2001), India undertook a program of liberal economic reforms, giving business an increasing intermediation role, taking over public functions. Therefore, India is a country in transition from rather interventionist to collaborative business-government relations.

South Africa

South African corporations are also exposed to a national institutional environment that is in transition. South African business-government relations have changed profoundly since the end of apartheid. Under the apartheid regime, business had to follow the rules of the government. There were tough controls on ownership and activities permitted under the apartheid regime (Chabane et al. 2006). This phase of confrontational business-government relations was accelerated by the withdrawal of foreign capital and implementation of economic sanctions against South Africa, which adversely affected South African business (Harshe 1993). South Africa's shift toward democracy after the Government of National Unity took over in April 1994 meant that more cooperative business-government relations developed (Taylor 2007). The government introduced fundamental changes, including liberalization and black economic empowerment (BEE) policies, and the integration of previously excluded racial and ethnic groups. Black-owned economic groups gradually emerged (Ponte et al. 2007). Solving the ethical problems of the disadvantaged players in the economy had top priority in South African businesses (Rossouw 1997: 1546). In 1994, the government launched an initiative to promote business culture in South Africa. The King Report[12] on corporate governance included the creation of a code of ethical practice for enterprises. Currently, South Africa's governing and corporate elites are proponents of best practice in corporate governance and financial regulation, and the reports of the King Committee in 1994 and 2002 – referred to as King I and King II – provide the framework for debate on corporate governance in South Africa (Andreasson 2007: 2). They show the tendency to increasingly rely on voluntary business measures instead of government intervention. Although South African companies only have a short tradition of responsibility,[13] business-government relations have profoundly changed; companies are increasingly engaged politically.

Spain
Spain is commonly portrayed as a 'mixed economy' (Rhodes and Molina 2007) that conforms largely with the 'state capitalism' model (see Schmidt 2002: 141) where dynamic networks of small and medium-sized enterprises constitute the backbone of the national economy. There are no monopolistic and encompassing unions (membership rates are estimated at between 10 and 19 percent and are among the lowest in the OECD) but there is weakly coordinated bargaining at central, sectoral, and firm levels. State actors continue to play a direct role in shaping business-labor relations (Royo 2007: 49). The state, authoritarian and officially Catholic (represented by General Franco's regime), originally imposed a politicized version of the common good, which came to dominate social, economic and cultural life (Argandona 1999: 156). Even after Franco's death, state actors still played an important role in the Spanish economy (Royo 2004: 7). Although European market integration and international competition create pressures to promote social bargaining and offer incentives to Spanish social actors to address new challenges through social pacts, Spain lacks encompassing labor market institutions. However, it has developed some coordination capacity over time (Royo 2004, 2008): Tripartite bargaining collapsed after 1986, reemerging

in the mid-1990s, with 25 agreements between 1994 and 2005 (Royo 2007: 49–50). Over the past decade, there have been few notable cases of cooperation among firms, unions, and regional governments.[14] In the absence of structured and institutionalized top-level bargaining (Hamann 1998: 433), Spanish companies interact with a government that is a major institutional actor who often intervenes in the resolution of coordination problems.

Switzerland

Switzerland is a home state with a general blurring of the state-society distinction. It is commonly referred to as a small coordinated market economy with a long tradition in cooperative policy styles. This is symbolized by the practice of the government receiving formal, written opinions of the main interest groups before a law proposal is submitted to the parliament. The legal basis of this practice is the Swiss constitution of 1947 that states that interested economic associations have to be consulted during the development of laws and may be called on to cooperate in their implementation (Siaroff 1999: 187). Swiss companies have a long tradition of acting politically in cooperative business-government relations and within highly corporatist decision making procedures (Siaroff 1999: 186). According to corporatist research, cooperation between business and core labor in Switzerland occurs in a much more decentralized way than in purely corporatist nations with national tripartism (Armingeon 1997: 171–2).

The United Kingdom

The institutional representation of business interests in the United Kingdom is comparatively weak and underdeveloped (Grant 1993: 104–5). Business organizations and labor unions are fragmented in size, sector and territory, and lack public law status as well as personal, financial, and political resources.[15] Despite this, there is a surprisingly strong partnership between government and individual corporations, leading to the term British 'company state' (Grant 2004: 411), as opposed to corporatist state. British business-government relations are generally characterized as nonadversarial. The United Kingdom system of regulation is based on mutual trust between business and government. Legislation in the United Kingdom encourages business self-regulation. For example, environmental regulation is not done through precise emission limits or generally stringent binding laws but through non-binding guidelines that can be flexibly adapted to local conditions by individual administrative or regulatory agencies (Kollmann and Prakash 2001: 420). U.K. business associations insist on preserving this national regulatory style against European Union attempts to harmonize (Vogel 1986: 21). In the current debate on British corporate social responsibility (CSR) policy, unions are considered more as part of the problem than the solution. They are criticized for their lowest common denominator dynamic, lacking the proactive behavior that some leading companies are ready to show. The

British government prefers direct consultation with individual corporations (Coen and Grant 2006: 23) and so always offers business the chance to directly influence U.K. policies in short-term, issue-specific arrangements. U.K. business has a substantial interest in the British government setting binding regulations – coherent with business interests – as a threshold to the emerging markets. Up until now, the government has been trapped in traditional reluctance to intervene in the market: 'UK plc. is ill-served by lowest-common-denominator lobbying' (Ward and Smith 2006: 36). In summary, U.K. business is very much acquainted with a cooperative approach to policy making, with the government as a partner.

Empirical Results

As summarized in Table 3.4, cooperative business-government relations exist in five out of the seven home states of the sample of systematic norm-entrepreneurs.

France and Spain have confrontational relations that do not explain the proactive behavior of France Telecom and Inditex. In these two cases, company characteristics may play a role as causal factors that potentially enhance corporate norm-entrepreneurship (see Chapter 4.3). France Telecom, as a formerly state-owned company, has a long tradition in its corporate culture of acting politically and may therefore be a likely candidate for taking on a political role in norm setting and norm development processes. As far as the family-owned company Inditex is concerned, this argument cannot be upheld. In this case, there must be additional factors involved that can account for its decision to engage in corporate norm-entrepreneurship.

Despite these two outliers, the home state analysis provided some clues about the validity of the business-government approach as an explanation

Table 3.4 Different types of business-government relations

Systematic norm-entrepreneur	Home state	Cooperative business-government relations	Confrontational business-government relations
Credit Suisse	Switzerland	X	
UBS	Switzerland	X	
Deutsche Bank	Germany	X	
Inditex	Spain		X
France Telecom	France		X
BP Plc	UK	X	
Rio Tinto	UK	X	
Royal Dutch/Shell	UK	X	
Tata Group	India	X	
Sasol	South Africa	X	

for the proactive engagement of at least eight of the ten systematic norm-entrepreneurs. However, the sample of systematic norm-entrepreneurs may not allow for more generalized inferences because there are only a few home states involved. Quantitative analysis of corporate norm-entrepreneurship in two self-regulatory initiatives expanded the sample of companies surveyed to 71 sporadic norm-entrepreneurs. The larger sample size was used to gain more evidence of the assumed causal link between cooperative business-government relations and corporate norm-entrepreneurship.

Quantitative analysis

To investigate the explanatory power of the business-government argument further, the Global Compact and the Global Reporting Initiative (GRI) were selected[16] to analyze the ratios of corporate norm-consumers versus sporadic norm-entrepreneurs from different home states. Following the business-government relations approach, the two self-regulatory initiatives were assumed to show high levels of norm-entrepreneurship among corporations from countries with cooperative business-government relations and low levels from countries with confrontational relations. Starting with the Global Compact (Figure 3.1), a significant difference was observed in the ratio between corporate norm-consumers and norm-entrepreneurs (see also Wolf et al. 2010).

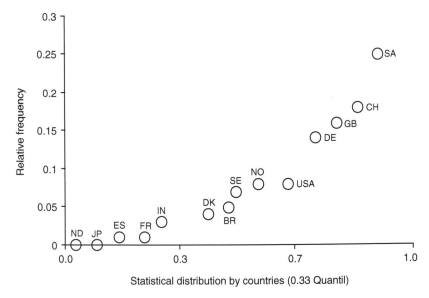

Figure 3.1   Ratio of sporadic norm-entrepreneurs vs. norm-consumers within the Global Compact

Similar to the results of the qualitative analysis, some countries, such as Spain, France, the Netherlands, and Japan, produce hardly any norm-entre-preneurs, while others, such as Germany, the United Kingdom, Switzerland, and South Africa, host a comparatively high number of norm-entrepreneurs. As an illustrative example, 49 German companies had signed up to the Global Compact by 2006, which qualifies all of them as norm-consumers. Seven of these companies also contributed to norm setting or norm development, for example, as founding members of the Global Compact or by participating in learning forum events, which qualifies them as norm-entrepreneurs. Based on these numbers, Germany has a ratio of norm-entrepreneurs to norm-consumers of 0.14.[17] France, Spain, Japan, and the United States all have a rather low turnout of norm-entrepreneurs compared to their OECD peers, with the United States only having half the ratio of the United Kingdom, for example.

The examination of the ratio of norm-entrepreneurs versus norm-consumers within the GRI underscores most of the findings from the Global Compact analysis (Figure 3.2).

To take Germany as an illustration again, 46 German companies prepared their sustainability reports using the GRI reporting guidelines, thus showing norm-consumership. Six of them engaged in structured feedback processes and other norm development activities, qualifying them as corporate norm-entrepreneurs. This results in a ratio of 0.13 for German corporations. It is remarkable that Germany and the United Kingdom are again among

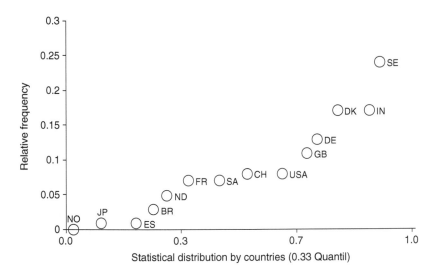

Figure 3.2 Ratio of sporadic norm-entrepreneurs and norm-consumers within the GRI

the companies with high ratios. A poorer turnout of norm-entrepreneurs in France and the United States and even lower ratios in Spain and Japan are again noticeable, which also confirms the findings of the Global Compact analysis.

These results together demonstrate that there are significant cross-national variations that support the findings from the previous qualitative analysis of the seven home states of the systematic norm-entrepreneurs: Some countries with cooperative business-government relations and a significantly high degree of corporate norm-entrepreneurship were detected, such as Germany and the United Kingdom. Among the countries with an average ratio of norm-entrepreneurs to norm-consumers are Switzerland, India, South Africa, France, and the United States. Countries that had disproportionately low ratios of norm-entrepreneurs in both self-regulatory initiatives are Japan and Spain.

Whereas most empirical results correspond with the previous findings, the United States and Japan (for different reasons) are anomalous cases whose business-government relations deserve a closer look. The average turnout of American corporate norm-entrepreneurs is surprising because no systematic norm-entrepreneur in the original sample originated from the United States. Japan's low ratio in corporate norm-entrepreneurship leads to the assumption of confrontational or, at least, uncooperative relations.

The United States
Interest intermediation in the United States is usually highly liberal with a variety of small interest groups, competing rather than cooperating in their public policy goals. Due to Americans' historical distrust of corporate power and suspicion of business-government cooperation, government officials have understandably been reluctant to justify particular policies on the grounds of their benefits to a particular – civilian – industry (Vogel 1987: 94). Tripartite concertation is unheard of in the United States, probably due to the most distinct feature of American business-government relations: Not by coincidence, the term 'adversarial legalism' was originally coined with reference to the United States (Kagan 1991). American regulation is not based on partnership nor does it show any flexibility or discretion in its administration. It consists of classic command and control mechanisms, entailing many more legal formalities: public notice and comment, open hearings, restrictions on informal contracts, legalistically specified evidentiary and scientific standards, mandatory official findings, and responses to interest group arguments (Kagan and Axelrad 1997: 153). Probably most importantly, any new regulation is usually challenged in court by the industries addressed by it, showing the stark contrast between confrontation in the United States and collaboration in the United Kingdom and Germany (Vogel 1986).[18] This underlines the noncollaborative interaction mode of business-government relations which – according to the hypothesis – should

lead to the conclusion that U.S. companies have no history of co-performing public functions with the government or setting CSR rules for their own behavior. The case of the U.S. shows, however, that the business-government approach might be useful to explain the non-existence of *systematic* norm-entrepreneurs among U.S. companies but it is not sufficient to explain the average number for sporadic norm-entrepreneurship.

Japan

There are no Japanese companies among the 10 systematic norm-entrepreneurs and only a low number of sporadic norm-entrepreneurs was found in the GRI and Global Compact analysis. This finding is surprising when taking a closer look at the cooperative business-government relations. In Japan, this relationship rests upon a special cultural setting that builds on a cohesive policy style that takes unilateral company engagement for granted. This approach differs from formal institutionalized Western approaches because of particularities in the Japanese economy and society. In the model of community, both individuals and companies alike are traditionally regarded as members of Japanese society and hence responsible for it. Therefore, business-government relations follow a comparatively 'society friendly' approach that is reflected by the close relationship between business and national government, which is described as 'reciprocal consent' (Samuels 1987: 336). According to Sako, Japanese welfare capitalism was reinforced by the government (instead of competing with it), enterprise unions (who were part of the team), corporate governance and a value system emphasizing reciprocal obligations and trust (Sako 1992). Nevertheless, Japanese capitalism differs in many ways from the welfare capitalism of Germany or the stock market capitalism of the United Kingdom and the United States. The role of Japanese business in society is more harmonious. Dore contrasts the Japanese business employee community view with an Anglo-American property view (Dore 1993). Although Japanese companies act on a global scale, they still comprise national, or at least regional, characteristics. Predominantly, business engagement for public purposes is much more focused on unilateral company behavior. This is typically manifested in a long-standing commitment of the individual company to workforce welfare and employment for life.[19] Japanese companies have become aware of CSR topics, although somewhat later than the United States and Europe (Tanimoto and Suzuki 2005: 3). In the 1990s, business roundtables and major business associations such as Keidanren, Doyukai, and Mecenat played an important role in leading individual corporations to act in the common interest (Taka 1997: 1502). In 2003, the Japan Association of Corporate Executives, Keizai Doyukai, published an influential report, defining and spreading CSR among Japanese companies (Keizai Doyukai 2003: 173–4). Japanese corporations are aware of CSR but tend to avoid legally binding obligations and formal administrative processes: 'Japanese firms predominantly use cultural mechanisms, such as philosophy and guiding principles, to address such issues. The planning and management of the most important issues is conducted through teams or committees, and little formal monitoring is conducted' (Lewin et al. 1995: 95). The comparatively low rate of norm-entrepreneurship in Japan can therefore be explained by the internal orientation of corporations combined with a supportive but rather inactive government. Accordingly, Japanese corporations are not used to participating in the setting of prescriptive rules for their own behavior within the Japanese national context due to the dominant approach that focuses on inward rather than outward reaching company behavior. The Japanese case also shows that cooperative business-government relations do not necessarily lead to corporate norm-entrepreneurship.

3.2.5   Conclusion

The analytical steps taken in this section can be summarized as follows: whether companies take on the role of norm-entrepreneurs at the international level depends on the type of interaction between business and government at the national level. Corporate attitudes to regulation seem to be constructed by the social institutions and procedures they are 'used to' at the national level. The seven country case studies have shown that almost all of the systematic norm-entrepreneurs from our sample originate from home states with cooperative business-government relations, such as Germany, India, South Africa, Switzerland, and the United Kingdom. Although the proactive engagement by France Telecom and Inditex, from France and Spain, respectively, could not be explained, interesting links to potential other factors were detected in both cases.

The quantitative analysis of the ratio of corporate norm-consumers to sporadic norm-entrepreneurs in one country, as represented in the Global Compact and the GRI, has shown results confirming the correspondence of cooperative business-government relations with a significantly high degree of corporate norm-entrepreneurship. As the analysis of the United States showed, confrontational business-government relations could explain the lack of American corporate norm-entrepreneurship. However, the findings on Japan make it clear that cooperative relations between business and government do not necessarily enhance corporate norm-entrepreneurship. Still, being socialized into such relations in the home state context seems to be a highly significant factor when it comes to corporate engagement in norm setting and norm development processes.

3.3   The heterogeneity of regulatory environments

In IR research on regionalism and economic integration, the heterogeneity of regulatory environments is widely acknowledged to characterize the diversity of various regulatory systems in different regions in the world

(Coleman and Underhill 1998; Söderbaum and Shaw 2003). Heterogeneity is a contextual factor influencing actors' behavior options. In a rationalist model of interaction, the costs of dealing with heterogeneous regulatory environments are included in an actor's cost-benefit calculations. In this mode, heterogeneity predominantly restricts an actor's behavior options. However, heterogeneity can also potentially stimulate actors' decisions to harmonize regulatory standards and create political institutions to regain behavioral freedom or to lower the cost of regulatory diversity. Stretching this assumption even further, companies are interested in establishing common rules of behavior to reduce regulatory diversity and hence lower transaction costs. To analyze the causal influence of heterogeneous environments on corporate norm-entrepreneurship the following initial hypothesis was tested:

Hypothesis 3 (H3): The more a corporation is exposed to heterogeneous regulatory environments, the more likely it will engage in corporate norm-entrepreneurship.

First, the possible underlying causal mechanisms and indicators used to measure the level of cross-national heterogeneity are introduced. Then the host states of the 10 systematic norm-entrepreneurs are mapped to establish the heterogeneity of regulatory environments these companies are exposed to in quantitative terms. In the next step, the level of regulation in select corporate host and home states is investigated. To measure the value of cross-national regulatory heterogeneity, the Global Competitiveness Index (GCI) ranking 2008–09 is used as an indicator. Finally, the labor market regulations of select states within the European Economic Area (EEA) are analyzed to examine whether companies still experience cross-national, regulatory heterogeneity if their three most important host states are located in one integrated regional trade area.

3.3.1 The business case – creating the level playing field

Research on economic integration processes argues that regulatory heterogeneity has an influence on behavior change. As an analytical concept, heterogeneity differentiates geographic regions and represents a distinctive feature that indicates the degree of cross-regional regulatory diversity (Chen and Mattoo 2008: 839). Focusing on processes of international trade and economic integration, heterogeneity is a factor that influences public actors' decisions to establish a global free trade framework. In research on 'economic regionalism', heterogeneity is both a barrier to economic cooperation and a stimulatory force for processes of convergence. Looking at political harmonization and integration processes commonly defined as the replacement of differing standards with common regulation, a causal mechanism is at work that might be transferred to corporations engaging in corporate norm-entrepreneurship. Public actors react to regulatory diversity by integrating separate national economies into larger blocs or communities. This lowers the costs of barriers to international free trade and builds an atmosphere for enduring private investments, trade activities (Schuler and Brown 1999: 468) and increased welfare gains (Sampson 2003: 10).[20] This process is commonly described as 'economic regionalism'[21] (Robson 1998: 1). The causal link between regulatory heterogeneity and economic regionalism refers to a rationalist model of interaction that assumes public actors as calculating the costs of regulatory diversity against the benefits of economic harmonization efforts. Accordingly, public actors are interested in 'leveling the playing field'. In the calculation, regulatory heterogeneity functions as a nontariff barrier because it raises the fixed and sunk costs of market entry for companies in export markets (Kox and Lejour 2005: 19). Companies have to cope with regulatory heterogeneity and to abide by different standards in their home and host states (Ganslandt and Markusen 2001: 6). This causes high additional transaction costs. A similar argument is put forward about the motives of business actors in the debate on CSR. Thus, a level playing field as a common baseline for operating practice would constitute an important improvement because it provides information about what type of behavior is socially expected and calls on all corporations to adhere to the same standards (Waddock 2004: 315). As Hopkins argues, corporations are interested in long-term profits and stability and therefore seek to create a level playing field which provides a minimum set of rules for socially responsible behavior (Hopkins 2003: xii). Common standards reduce the risk of competitive disadvantages that result from socially responsible engagement (Hopkins 2003: 40).[22] Following these arguments, companies, similar to public actors in economic regionalism, are likely to create institutions that have a level playing field. As a factor potentially enhancing corporate norm-entrepreneurship, the heterogeneity of regulatory environments is a relational concept that starts from the level of regulation in a corporation's home state. Companies are used to a certain level of regulation in their home state. The cross-national regulatory heterogeneity to which a company is exposed is composed of different regulatory standards in home and host states.

3.3.2   The moral case

Although most literature refers to the business case when analyzing the influence of heterogeneity on behavior change, some Business Ethics scholars put forward a moral argument. Referring to a constructivist rationale, Palazzo and Scherer argue that common standards of corporate behavior are in the interest of corporations because 'the idea of conformity to some more or less implicit rules of some more or less contained social communities on the global level is currently difficult to achieve' (Palazzo and Scherer 2007: 26). Following this argument, corporations are likely to promote a level playing field to satisfy larger societal demands to justify their legitimacy (Palazzo and Scherer 2007: 33).

However, the analysis here primarily relies on the business case argument: Homogeneous regulatory environments reduce operating costs in foreign environments (De Groot et al. 2004: 111). To prevent different standards of behavior and competitive disadvantage, companies are assumed to create a level playing field. Hence, it is expected that all 10 systematic norm-entrepreneurs are exposed to heterogeneous regulatory environments in their global operations.

3.3.3 Measuring the heterogeneity of regulatory environments

Despite the apparent economic integration and harmonization in several regions of the world, corporations still operate, produce, and trade in very diverse regulatory environments. This is substantiated by mapping the group of systematic norm-entrepreneurs' host states. Home and selected host states are then examined more closely to measure the degree of regulatory heterogeneity according to the Global Competitiveness Index (GCI) ranking 2008–09 (Porter and Schwab 2008), provided by the Global Competitiveness Report (GCR) of the World Economic Forum.[23] First launched in 2004, the Global Competitiveness Index ranking includes macroeconomic and microeconomic factors of competitiveness. The revised version of 2008 also includes indicators of more general conditions that create opportunities for higher productivity across the economy, such as the quality of public institutions or the average skill level of the labor force (Porter and Schwab 2008: 44). The difference between the ranks of the home state and selected host states of a company provides an additional measurement of the degree of cross-national regulatory heterogeneity. According to the heterogeneity hypothesis, the home and host states of all systematic norm-entrepreneurs should spread along the Global Competitiveness Index ranking.

3.3.4 Empirical analysis of the role of the heterogeneity of regulatory environments

The following empirical analysis builds on primary and secondary data: First, quantitative data from company publications are used to identify the global span of corporate activities in their most important host states. These host state data are then aggregated to the level of the most important regional trade areas (RTA) (which are harmonized internally but differ from each other in their economic and political regulatory environments) to control for the misleading impression of a large number of host states in the same, homogeneous trade area. The following trade areas were selected according to their size, global political influence, and geographic orientation (Gavin and Langenhove 2003: 280): the North American Free-Trade Agreement (NAFTA),[24] the European Economic Area (EEA),[25] the Association of Southeast Asian Nations (ASEAN),[26] the Mercado Común del Sur or Common Market of the South (MERCOSUR),[27] and the Economic Community of West African States (ECOWAS).[28] The Global Competitiveness Index was then applied and primary data from expert interviews with representatives of self-regulatory initiatives and corporations were used to complete the picture.

Quantitative analysis

As shown in Table 3.5, the mapping of the total number of corporate host states per systematic norm-entrepreneur reveals a global distribution of host states for each of the systematic norm-entrepreneurs, spreading from developing to industrialized states,[29] and ranging from 17 for the Tata Group to 127 for Shell.

These findings provide initial support for the link between heterogeneous regulatory environments and corporate norm-entrepreneurship. The geographical distribution of corporate host states over the selected regional trade areas, as illustrated in Table 3.6, also shows that all systematic norm-entrepreneur are operating in at least four areas.

Table 3.5 Total number of corporate host states

Systematic norm-entrepreneur	Total number of host states
Credit Suisse	51
UBS	52
Deutsche Bank	61
Inditex	67
France Telecom (including Orange)	31
BP Plc	26
Rio Tinto	18
Royal Dutch/Shell	127
Tata Group	17
Sasol	23

Table 3.6 Corporate host states of systematic norm-entrepreneurs located in selected RTA

Systematic norm-entrepreneur	NAFTA	EEA	ASEAN	MERCO-SUR	ECOWAS	Additional host states
Credit Suisse	X	X	X	X	/	19
UBS	X	X	X	X	/	19
Deutsche Bank	X	X	X	X	X	26
Inditex	X	X	X	X	/	24
France Telecom	X	X	X	/	X	14
BP Plc	X	X	X	X	X	10
Rio Tinto	X	X	X	X	X	8
Royal/Dutch Shell	X	X	X	X	X	67
Tata Group	X	X	X	/	X	9
Sasol	X	X	X	/	X	11

These findings provide additional support for the assumed link between the heterogeneity of regulatory environments and corporate norm-entrepreneurship. However, such heterogeneity does not provide a sufficient explanation for norm-entrepreneurship: There are other corporations operating in diverse regulatory environments without engaging in norm setting and norm development processes. Coca Cola and Siemens, for example, are active in similar host states and in all five trade areas, as are norm-entrepreneurs Deutsche Bank, BP, Rio Tinto, and Royal Dutch/Shell.

The relevance of the heterogeneity hypothesis is further supported by the significant cross-national regulatory Global Competitiveness Index score differences that were identified for all ten norm-entrepreneurs. In the Global Competitiveness Index ranking of 2008–09, results from 134 states range from the highest rank, the United States, with a 5.74 score, to the lowest, Chad, with a 2.85 score (see Porter and Schwab 2008: 43). Table 3.7 shows the three most important host states of each systematic norm-entrepreneur, selected according to corporate investments, in terms of production intensity and local concentration of facilities.

Royal Dutch/Shell's most important host states range from a 3.81 score (Nigeria), over Mexico (4.23) to Canada (5.37). Such large differences were not found in any other company. The three most important host states of Rio Tinto, for example, all have comparatively high GCI rankings (the United States 5.74, Australia 5.20, Canada 5.37).

Taking the spread between the home state and the lowest ranking host state in the GCI ranking as a further measure (see Table 3.8), significant cross-national regulatory heterogeneity was detected in all cases. The Global Competitiveness Index score difference between the home state and the lowest ranking host state ranges from 2.42 for Rio Tinto and Shell to 0.96 for Tata.

Even the comparatively low cross-national regulatory values of Inditex (1.16), Sasol (1.53), and Tata (0.96) can be explained by these three norm-entrepreneurs coming from home states with only medium scores in the GCI ranking (Spain 4.72, South Africa 4.41, India 4.33). The findings from the score difference analysis further support the assumption that heterogeneous regulatory environments enhance corporate norm-entrepreneurship. All systematic norm-entrepreneurs showed significant cross-national regulatory GCI score differences, span their activities all over the globe, and operate in at least four of the five selected regional trade areas.

Although regulatory heterogeneity was found in the home state/host state analysis, the lowest ranking corporate host state might not be important enough to exert influence on corporate behavior change. As in the case of France Telecom, the three most important corporate host states are all located in one politically harmonized and economically integrated trade area. In this situation a systematic norm-entrepreneur would not be exposed to cross-national regulatory heterogeneity. The national labor market regulation[30]

Table 3.7 Corporate home and host states in the Global Competitiveness Index (GCI) ranking 2008–09

Systematic norm-entrepreneur			GCI rank	GCI score
BP	Home state	UK	12	5.30
	Most important	Angola	n/a	n/a
	host states	Azerbaijan	69	4.10
		Russia	51	4.31
	Lowest ranking host state	Venezuela	105	3.56
Credit Suisse	Home state	Switzerland	2	5.61
	Most important	Italy	49	4.53
	host states	USA	1	5.74
		Germany	7	5.46
	Lowest ranking host state	Venezuela	105	3.56
Deutsche Bank	Home state	Germany	7	5.46
	Most important	Italy	49	4.35
	host states	Spain	29	4.72
		USA	1	5.74
	Lowest ranking host state	Pakistan	101	3.65
France Telecom	Home state	France	16	5.22
	Most important	UK	12	5.30
	host states	Spain	29	4.72
		Poland	53	4.28
	Lowest ranking host state	Uganda	128	3.35
Inditex	Home state	Spain	29	4.72
	Most important	Portugal	43	4.47
	host states	Mexico	60	4.23
		France	16	5.22
	Lowest ranking host state	Venezuela	105	3.56
Rio Tinto	Home state	UK	12	5.30
	Most important	USA	1	5.74
	host states	Australia	18	5.20
		Canada	10	5.37
	Lowest ranking state	Zimbabwe	133	2.88
Royal Dutch/Shell	Home state	UK	12	5.30
	Most important	Canada	10	5.37
	host states	Mexico	60	4.23
		Nigeria	94	3.81
	Lowest ranking host state	Zimbabwe	133	2.88

Continued

Table 3.7 Continued

Systematic norm-entrepreneur			GCI rank	GCI score
Sasol	Home state	South Africa	45	4.41
	Most important host states	USA	1	5.74
		Germany	7	5.46
		Italy	49	4.35
	Lowest ranking host state	Zimbabwe	133	2.88
Tata Group	Home state	India	50	4.33
	Most important host states	China	30	4.70
		UK	12	5.30
		South Africa	45	4.41
	Lowest ranking host state	Nepal	126	3.37
UBS	Home state	Switzerland	2	5.61
	Most important host states	USA	1	5.74
		Italy	49	4.35
		UK	12	5.30
	Lowest ranking host state	Argentina	88	3.87

Source: Own research.

of the host states within the EEA was examined. Certainly European economic integration aims at reducing traditional trade barriers by liberalizing and harmonizing efforts (Sampson 2003: 3–4). However, European labor market regulation harmonization is still limited because of member states protecting their comparative advantages and preserving their national regulatory diversity (Dehejia and Yiagadeesen 2006: 6). Here, the member states still operate on the 'lowest common denominator of standards' (Gitterman 2003: 8) and policy decisions are governed by domestic issues (Dehejia and Yiagadeesen 2006: 2; Boeri et al. 1999: 40). Applied to Hypothesis H3, systematic norm-entrepreneurs with host states located in the EEA still have to cope with highly inflexible labor markets, such as in France and the Czech Republic, and with countries that have much more freedom for employers and companies, such as the United Kingdom and Bulgaria (Javorcik and Spatareanu 2005: 377). For instance, Shell and Deutsche Bank operate in France, the United Kingdom, and Bulgaria. Royal Dutch/Shell and Inditex do business in Belgium, Denmark, France, and Germany, and all 10 companies operate in the United Kingdom.

Heterogeneity within the EEA is increased by the diversity of labor market policies in the Central and Eastern European States (CEE), which are less

Table 3.8   The home state and host state variance in the Global Competitiveness Index (GCI) ranking 2008–09

Systematic norm-entrepreneur	Home state	Lowest ranking host state	GCI score difference
BP	UK	Venezuela	1.74
Credit Suisse	Switzerland	Venezuela	2.05
Deutsche Bank	Germany	Pakistan	1.81
France Telecom	France	Uganda	1.87
Inditex	Spain	Venezuela	1.16
Rio Tinto	UK	Zimbabwe	2.42
Shell	UK	Zimbabwe	2.42
Sasol Ltd.	South Africa	Zimbabwe	1.53
Tata Group	India	Nepal	0.96
UBS	Switzerland	Argentina	1.74

flexible than in the United Kingdom but more flexible than in southern European member states (Svenjar 2004: 103; Riboud et al. 2002: 8). In addition, there are differences among CEE states. For instance, Poland and the Czech Republic are at different ends of the flexibility scale for employment restrictions, with Poland being more flexible than its Czech counterpart (Riboud et al. 2002). Taking Credit Suisse, Inditex, Shell, and UBS as illustrative examples, these systematic norm-entrepreneurs simultaneously operate in Poland and in the Czech Republic and are therefore exposed to cross-national regulatory diversity within a particular region. As the empirical findings from the analysis of the European labor market regulation show, even if the three most important corporate host states are located in one single trade area, companies are still exposed to cross-national regulatory heterogeneity.

Qualitative analysis

These empirical findings also correspond with the qualitative data gained from expert interviews. Most company representatives believe they are exposed to high regulatory diversity. As one interviewee pointed out: 'Laws are going to be really, really different in the Middle East than they are in the Asia-Pacific, than they are in the US, than they are in certain southern European countries, for example, or than they are in northern European countries' (C10, 23 May 2006). Operating in heterogeneous regulatory environments is also perceived as a huge challenge for doing business on a global scale. As one company representative stressed, the large number of host states in which a company operates poses problems due to diverse national laws: 'When you are involved in that many, there are of course national laws and regulations that are fine in some countries and that are not fine in others. In some, homosexuality is illegal or simply does not exist, as we have been told, or that trade union meetings are not allowed. How do you accommodate these things? That is very difficult! If you look at our business principles, [...] we apply them to certain national regulations, [which is] very tough. How do you balance those things? Do you mention trade unions or labor conditions at work or labor practices or do you say human rights or is there something else you can say?' (C4, 10 October 2007).

Another company representative, referring to the influence of heterogeneous regulatory environments, stated that the challenge begins with operating outside the home state: 'The challenge comes to us when we move outside the boundaries of the country. For example, if we go and invest in Nigeria or when we build a plant in Qatar in the Middle East we operate under different conditions where our constitution does not cover our activities. And this applies when you need to unpack the specific principles in that context for that country and see whether you can still comply with that specific principle. That does not say that we operate with a different set of norms when we operate outside of Africa but you still have to comply with the laws of that specific country' (C5, 8 November 2007).

Similarly, one representative of a self-regulatory initiative explained: 'There are different situations to face, such as high standard countries, low standard countries, failing states, inefficient states, corrupt states, regulated societies and very regulated societies. A company that operates globally has this huge challenge of facing dozens of different situations. On the one hand, companies operating in Stuttgart face the world's highest social standards and on the other hand, the same company operating in Beijing has to deal with basic questions of human rights. This is a huge challenge' (I1, 27 March 2006). Another company representative referred to the example of cross-national variations in environmental regulation, pointing out the differences between high and low levels of regulation: 'When you go into Qatar there are no environmental laws. But we will use the World Bank standards as the minimum requirements against which we will build our plants and operate. In the US, for example, the waste legislation is much stricter than the World Bank standards and then we will comply with the stricter conditions. The same applies for emissions, for example, in Germany or in the EU. The regulation is much more advanced than in other countries at this point in time and we just adapt to the local requirements' (C5, 8 November 2007).

Stressing the regulatory heterogeneity for specific industries, such as the banking sector, another interviewee explained: 'So the US banks have to apply OFAC [Office for Foreign Assets Control in the US Treasury Department Office] sanctions, no matter where they operate, for terrorist financing. That puts our US members in a slightly problematic situation, for example, in Germany where it is illegal, by law, not by guidance, by law, to apply a third nation's sanctions program. That gives you one example of some of the difficulties that we face in multiple jurisdictions on a daily basis' (C10, 23 May 2006). Also referring to heterogeneous regulatory environments, one company representative stressed, as a main reason to engage in processes of norm setting and norm development, that 'Sometimes we face the situation that in our home state something is regulated whereas this regulation is absent in our host state, or that in both states there is no regulation at all. But banks need common standards because otherwise their behavior would have negative consequences. That is why we start setting norms for ourselves' (C2, 11 September 2007).

3.3.5 Conclusions

The findings from the empirical analysis of the corporate home and host states and qualitative interviews support the assumption that heterogeneous regulatory environments enhance corporate norm-entrepreneurship. All systematic norm-entrepreneurs are exposed to high cross-national regulatory diversity. Each of them operates in host states that spread all over the globe and are located in different regional trade areas. Applying the results from the Global Competitiveness Index ranking 2008–09, significant score differences were detected among corporate home and host states. As exemplified by the European labor market regulation, even if systematic norm-entrepreneurs only operate in one trade area, such as the EEA, they are still exposed to regulatory heterogeneity.

As a relational concept, the heterogeneity of regulatory environments stimulates corporations to strive for a level playing field and avoid the competitive disadvantages that arise from different standards in home and host states. Whereas the level of regulation in the home state was not influential on its own (Section 3.2 analysis), under the condition of cross-national heterogeneity the national level of regulation seems to constitute a necessary condition for corporate norm-entrepreneurship. Companies lower the costs of different regulatory standards by creating institutions that guarantee a level playing field. However, as illustrated by the example of Coca Cola and Siemens, heterogeneity of regulatory environments is not sufficient alone but is a necessary condition for corporate norm-entrepreneurship.

Notes

1. A similar distinction is drawn by Arts, who differentiates between pressure and protest groups (Arts 1998: 51). Other studies suggest that depending on the extent to which a corporation resists cooperating with NGOs, cooperative or more confrontational tactics are applied (Rieth and Göbel 2005: 259).
2. In trying to explain under what circumstances NGOs use which kind of strategies on corporations, Heins found that they are more likely to be confrontational the

more the corporations' business impacts on 'habeas corpus issues', meaning the most fundamental human rights to life and physical integrity. He therefore identifies businesses in the areas of health, nutrition and reproduction as most likely to be targeted by NGO-shaming campaigns (Heins 2005: 181).

3. See http://www.business-humanrights.org/Home, date accessed 19 May 2009. The site's main purpose is to provide easy, one-stop access to information for companies, nongovernmental organizations (NGOs), and others. It receives over 1.5 million hits per month. Although the site is a collection of information from a multitude of sources, the great majority of posts on the site and therefore of information publicly available stems from, relates to, or references civil society activities.

4. The VoC approach analyses diverse macroeconomic and institutional characteristics of capitalist systems influencing corporate behavior change. It differentiates between two ideal types of capitalist systems by using a broad range of variables, such as the financial system, corporate governance, and industrial relations (Hall and Soskice 2001: 17–18; Jackson and Deeg 2006: 11–12). However, suffering from a rather deterministic perspective on corporate behavior change, the VoC approach does not clearly answer the question of what underlying causal mechanisms are assumed to influence corporate behavior change, nor does it precisely declare whether a rationalist or constructivist logic of action is presumed (see Wolf et al. 2010).

5. First, adversarial legalism differs from informal methods of resolving disputes or making policy decisions, such as mediation, expert professional judgment, or bargaining among political authorities. Second, in adversarial legalism, litigants and their lawyers play active roles in the policy implementation and decision-making process; hence the style differs from governance that is legally formal but more hierarchical or bureaucratic (Kagan and Axelrad 1997: 152).

6. This typology has also been employed by Kollmann and Prakash to explain the cross-national variation in business acceptance rates of the voluntary eco-management schemes EMAS and ISO 14000 (Kollmann and Prakash 2001: 418–20). They suggest that voluntary schemes are more likely to be implemented in non-adversarial regulatory systems because adversarial ones will not allow for the incentives necessary to make them attractive.

7. To measure the level of regulation prevailing in a company's home state, the levels of environmental regulation can be employed as proxies because it can be assumed that environmental regulation will only be of high quality in countries with generally comprehensive regulatory systems.

8. The focus is exclusively on certain types of business-government interactions within the national institutional environment of companies. Nevertheless, it should be noted that state-business relations can emerge in various forms and involve various actors, not only business and government (Cawson et al. 1987; Streeck and Schmitter 1985).

9. It has to be noted that these institutions, especially within countries in transformation, such as India and South Africa, are constantly developing. Therefore, the following classification of cooperative versus confrontational types of business government relations is understood as an analytical approximation.

10. With regard to post-1789 France, scholars turn to different factors to explain this. First, French republicanism with its discourse on the 'general interest' – *la morale de l'intérêt general* – stating that the state, standing beyond civil society and the market, can and should define rationally what is best for the nation and

serve its interests. On the contrary, civil society and the market are considered to act in favor of their own particular interests rather than for the common good. Thus, private actors have enjoyed little legitimacy in comparison to the state (Blasco and Zolner 2008: 24).

11. Within this setting, 'the private sector was required to contribute to India's economic growth in ways envisaged by the government planners. Not only did the government determine where businesses could invest in terms of location, but it also identified what businesses could produce, what they could sell, and what prices they could charge' (Lal and Clement 2005: 84).

12. The King Report (see Institute of Directors 1994) was formed under the auspices of the Institute of Directors (IoD) with the support from the South African Chamber of Business (SACOB), the Chartered Institute of Secretaries and Administrators (CIS), the South African Institute of Chartered Accountants (SAICA), the Johannesburg Stock Exchange (JSE), and the South African Institute of Business Ethics (SAIBE).

13. The political engagement of South African business has always been backed by political support from foreign political and/or business actors or an international consensus toward liberal economy and market (Handley 2005).

14. As pointed out by Royo, 'in the Basque country, the cooperation of the regional government, firms, employers association and unions has led to the development of industrial clusters in sectors such as machine tools. There are similar examples in Catalonia and Madrid' (Royo 2007: 59).

15. For instance, the leading business organization Confederation of British Industry (CBI) has been constrained by broad membership, an internal structure of special committees and most important a policy of the lowest common denominator, generally more reactive than active in driving their interests (Grant 1993: 105, 111). The CBI has the strong advantage of a cooperative relationship with New Labor despite a tighter net of regulation, because of UK's blocking position to EU regulation which might impact on business competition (Grant 2004: 417).

16. The case selection of the Global Compact and the GRI was designed to control for potential alternative explanatory variables, such as specific industries, particular issue area or specific incentive structures. Last but not least, the selected case studies should include a significant number of companies so that a distortion by a small-n partiality could be controlled.

17. By making use of descriptive statistics a quantile function was applied which mathematically corresponds to the inverse of the cumulative of the distribution function. Values were calculated for the following three quantiles (0–0.33; 0.33–0.66; 0.66–1) and generated margins for the norm-entrepreneurship distribution in the Global Compact and the GRI across countries (see Wolf et al. 2010).

18. In accord with this assessment, one interviewee argued: 'The US does a lot on paper because otherwise if companies do not have a code of conduct, they are usually brought to court' (I5, 28 April 2006).

19. Nevertheless, there is evidence of profound changes in society concerning lifetime employment and an increase in the number of unemployed people in Japan. Dore argues that job-hopping by regular workers still remains a rarity in Japan and has shown little or no growth between 1985 and 2002 (Dore 2004).

20. As Kneller indicates, politically harmonized areas with aligned trading conditions and low barriers for market entry go hand in hand with benefits for companies engaging in certain economic regions (Kneller et al. 2008: 664).

21. Since the end of the 1990s, national economies increasingly lowered traditional barriers to trade, like tariffs and/or quotas, and actively participated in multilateral, regional, and bilateral trade and investment agreements (Schuler and Brown 1999: 454). However, the impact of economic regionalism on lowering regulatory heterogeneity is controversial. As Sampson argues, it can also lead to disfunctionalities in the case of increased competition between fortress-like regional trade agreements (Sampson 2003: 5).

22. However, it should be noted that although companies express their will to level the playing field and therefore engage in norm setting and norm development, they do not necessarily have to implement and/or comply with certain standards.

23. The Global Competitiveness Report is recognized as a global ranking of country competitiveness as well as a tool for benchmarking strengths and weaknesses (Porter and Schwab 2008: 43). Currently, the Global Competitiveness Index ranking incorporates 12 pillars of competitiveness to provide a comprehensive picture of the competitiveness of countries around the world. These pillars include institutions, infrastructure, macroeconomic stability, health and primary education, higher education and training, goods market efficiency, labor market efficiency, financial market sophistication, technological readiness, market size, business sophistication, and innovation. For more details about the 12 pillars of competitiveness of the Global Competitiveness Index ranking, see http://www.weforum.org/en/media/Latest%20Press%20Releases/PR_GCR082/, date accessed 25 October 2008.

24. NAFTA finalized the emerging economic integration in North America with a free trade area between Canada, the United States, and Mexico, where 'tariff and non-tariff barriers to trade in goods and services among the NAFTA countries have fallen, and cross-border flow of capital and investment have been facilitated' (Abbott 2000: 193). Corporations operating in the NAFTA area can build upon an independent and long-term framework for investment, however, the NAFTA trade rules currently have the tendency to create a protected market within the free trade area (Scherer 2004: 8–9).

25. As today's role model for regional integration processes, the European Economic Area (EEA) constitutes a common European market with free movement for people, goods, and services. The Integration of the European Economic Community was the first step to political integration and gained further momentum with the final declaration of the Single European market, finalized in 1992, and plans for a common currency. During the final steps, non-tariff trade barriers, which were used as protectionist means by some member states, should especially be removed (Kohler-Koch et al. 2003: 69). With the Treaty of Maastricht in 1993, the former European Community deepened into a political and economic union. Companies engaging in the EEA face a highly integrated and harmonized economic environment.

26. ASEAN was founded in August 1967 by Indonesia, Malaysia, the Philippines, Singapore, and Thailand; since then, Brunei, Cambodia, Laos, Vietnam, and Myanmar have joined. It constitutes a security arrangement between postcolonial states and intends to accelerate economic growth, social progress, and cultural development in the region through joint endeavors in the spirit of equality and partnership to strengthen the foundation for a prosperous and peaceful community of Southeast Asian Nations. It relies on a strong norm of non-interference as the basis for regional cooperation and stability. Companies currently

operating in the ASEAN region face an economic environment that is still characterized by non-tariff barriers to trade and a fragmented market structure.

27. Argentina, Brazil, Paraguay, and Uruguay established MERCOSUR in 1991 by signing the Treaty of Asunción. It is an instrument to accelerate economic integration in the formerly strictly protected South American markets. Today, further associate members comprise Chile, Bolivia, Peru, Columbia, and Ecuador, which have equal access to the free trade area. MERCOSUR serves as a universal, nontariff, free trade zone with a degree of harmonization in 'trading with third parties' policies adopted (Vaillant 2005: 54–5). Although MERCOSUR established a free market area and adopted a common external tariff (Paiva 2003: 132), nontariff barriers continue to influence intra-regional trade (Vaillant 2005: 60).

28. ECOWAS was established by the Treaty of Lagos signed in 1975 by 15 African states with the objective of promoting trade, cooperation, and self-reliance in West Africa. In 1993, a revised ECOWAS treaty was signed to accelerate economic integration and to increase political cooperation. ECOWAS has comparatively low levels of political harmonization and regulation.

29. Notably, every systematic norm-entrepreneur operates in at least one of the BRIC states (Goldman Sachs 2003) which contributed roughly 28 percent of global growth in U.S. dollar terms between 2000 and 2005 (Goldman Sachs 2005: 4); Sasol and France Telecom operating in China; Rio Tinto in India and Brazil; Tata in Russia and Brazil; BP in China, Russia, and Brazil; Inditex in China, Russia, and Brazil; and Credit Suisse, UBS, Deutsche Bank, and Royal Dutch/Shell with maximum activity in all four BRIC states. According to Goldman Sachs, China and India will become the world's dominant suppliers of manufactured goods and services, and Brazil and Russia will become comparably dominant suppliers of raw materials. Although Goldman Sachs points out the potential of the BRICs to form a powerful economic bloc, it does not refer to the BRICs as a unique political alliance such as the European Union or a formal trading association (Goldman Sachs 2005).

30. Whereas economic regulation can be broadly defined as the use of coercive power of the government to restrict the decisions of economic agents, employment legislation refers to rules and regulations that govern unfair dismissal, restrictions on lay-offs for economic reasons, compulsory severance payment, minimum notice periods, and administrative authorization (Boeri et al. 1999: 2).

4
Actor Characteristics

4.1 Corporate vulnerability

Every company possesses tangible and intangible characteristics. Tangible ones, such as ownership structure, are fundamental to any company. Intangible ones emerge over time, either through intentional effort or as unintended side effects. Intangible assets are gaining more attention in management science and practice as they are sources of value creation and are therefore driving forces in corporate behavior.

In the following, the intangible characteristics of a corporation, which may explain corporate engagement in norm-entrepreneurship, are conceptualized as a company's vulnerability. This concept has two aspects: On the one hand, vulnerability is relational. This is known as 'corporate reputation' and is generally defined as stakeholders' collective judgments of a corporation. Barnett et al. (2006: 34) stress that such judgments accumulate and vary over time. Consequently, reputation capital may ebb and flow. The second component of vulnerability refers to self-perception and is best described as the corporation's 'identity'. As a causal factor, corporate vulnerability seeks to capture the fuzzy expectation that companies involved in misdeeds will either self-reprimand or be sanctioned by society. The risk of sanctions is higher or lower depending on certain qualities. Therefore, vulnerability is interlinked with societal pressure, a factor described in Section 3.1 but located within the corporation itself. Popular examples, such as the criticism of Shell for improper disposal of the oil storage buoy, Brent Spar, and the company's alleged involvement in killings and human rights abuses in Nigeria, and Nike, who was accused of using child labor, indicate that some companies are more vulnerable to public scrutiny than others and have suffered more severely from changes to their reputation and/or identity. It is assumed that if a company is not vulnerable, societal pressure will not be influential upon it or will not even emerge.

Vulnerability can, in principle, result from one of two sources, through one of two mechanisms: In a rationalist logic of consequences, the loss of a corporation's reputation capital[1] may result in objective costs. Or, following the logic of appropriateness, a corporation has developed a specific, socially defined identity so that action contradicting it will result in cognitive dissonance, that is, an identity crisis. It is assumed that the more a company is vulnerable to external or internal pressure (a loss in its reputation capital or a cognitive identity crisis), the more likely it will undertake extra corporate social responsibility measures and, more specifically, engage in corporate norm-entrepreneurship as either a means to create and maintain reputation capital or to realign identity with practice. In International Relations (IR), the concept of vulnerability was put on the agenda by Keohane and Nye (1977) as 'vulnerability interdependence', focusing on the relationship of two actors (usually states) and the degree to which they are able to cope with the costs of changes in this relationship. While the concept of reputation takes up this relational aspect, for example, between a company and its stakeholders (Haufler 2001; Rieth and Zimmer 2004),[2] identity, in contrast, is basically self-referential as it reflects a company's own sense of appropriateness, which is also likely to be influenced by normative expectations in its environment.

On the basis of these conceptual considerations, it is argued that, due to their corporate properties, some companies are more vulnerable to a loss of reputation or identity than others. Those who are more vulnerable attempt to compensate the ensuing risks by taking suitable proactive and reactive steps to maintain and defend reputation and identity, possibly by engaging in norm-related behavior individually or as a member of collective self-regulatory initiatives. It is hypothesized that the more a company is vulnerable to a loss in corporate reputation capital, the more likely it will engage in corporate norm-entrepreneurship activities.

Hypothesis 4 (H4):   The more vulnerable a company is through its reputation or identity, the more it is likely to engage in corporate norm-entrepreneurship activities.

4.1.1   Causal mechanisms

'An organization can have many reputations' (Wood et al. 2006: 207), or, put differently, it has many sources of vulnerability. Due to its many possible sources, corporate vulnerability can set off causal mechanisms that emphasize either the business case or the moral case.

The business case

Although reputation is an intangible asset, it still can have very tangible consequences for a company's long-term success or failure, by generating benefits or producing costs. As nonphysical sources of value generated by innovation, organization design, or human resources practices (Lev 2001: 7, 21), intangible assets have acquired a prominent place in modern markets.

Increasing competition and the advent of information technology, among other factors, led to an increase in their significance in the 1980s and 1990s.[3] Even if such estimates did not accurately reflect reality, significant costs can arise from inadequately dealing with negative stakeholder perception (Epstein 2008: 180; Donaldson and Preston 1995). Reputation is regarded by some as the most valuable asset to manage and maximize. A good reputation can attract and keep away customers, investors, and employees (Alsop 2004).

A company's interest in developing its intangible assets is therefore totally rational. The management of the functional and social components of reputation (Schranz 2007: 79–81) follows a pure logic of consequences. Functional reputation includes all that is necessary to achieve the most important goals of a company and to generate profits (Carroll 1979). It overwhelmingly focuses on financial performance; all aspects that have a direct effect on corporate sales and profits are considered relevant (Holliday et al. 2002: 28–30). In contrast, social reputation focuses on norm compliance and on whether a company behaves in accordance with ethical standards. Although norms and values are also involved in social reputation, the cost-benefit aspect and the instrumental function of reputation prevails. Therefore, because of both functional and social reputations, companies aim to satisfy the expectations of external actors. With the diversity of factors that can potentially affect reputation, it is necessary for a company to have considered actions and procedures in place because, even if it produces the best products and services, when faced with a bad reputation it still runs the risk of losing its financial basis. The handling of reputation capital affects revenues, stock prices, operational efficiency, creation of new markets, and treatment by government regulators. It can have huge effects on the financial bottom line of a company. Thus, reputation capital management becomes a primary tool for managing risks that emanate from perceived socially irresponsible behavior (Visser et al. 2007: 391, 403). This is a complex issue, since reputational risks and opportunities are difficult to measure.

Against this background, a company that has a brand and produces consumer goods may regard itself as being particularly vulnerable to losing its reputation capital. For such a company, misbehavior and subsequent civil society campaigns are more likely to have negative effects on its financial situation (Klein 2000). Companies with no branded products and business-to-business sales run a lower risk of losing reputation capital because they hold less of it in the first place. Being aware of their risks, vulnerable companies take preventive measures against negative media attention. By engaging in norm setting exercises, companies invest in their corporate reputation capital as insurance and a risk reduction strategy (Fieseler 2008: 144). Norm-oriented behavior can therefore serve a company's goal of increasing shareholder value (SustainAbility and UNEP 2001). The more convincingly a company can demonstrate the future financial benefits from norm-oriented behavior, the more likely the markets will recognize and reward it (Holliday et al. 2002: 29). Companies also have to be aware that it may take years to build up reputation capital because it has to be earned by repeated proof (Hague 2008) and can be destroyed overnight.

The moral case

As outlined earlier, the vulnerability of a company can stem from the reputation capital it has to lose and can be connected to its self-perception and identity. In contrast to the business case, the moral case for CSR and norm oriented behavior implies action based on fundamental values concerning companies' responsibilities toward society rather than on a market rationale or legal obligations set and enforced by the state (Visser et al. 2007: 329–32). The relevance of a moral case to corporate behavior presupposes that in a normatively structured environment companies act in accordance with societal norms and values because they have internalized certain norms and societal expectations as being natural, rightful, expected, and legitimate. According to this supposition, the identities of companies are influenced by the fact that they regard themselves as (corporate) citizens, and as such, follow the practices and expectations of the surrounding institutions. As part of a social collective, they act in a way that they regard as appropriate (March and Olsen 1998) because even business companies cannot have a nonconforming identity.

In contrast to reputation risk management approaches that can be controlled by managers, a company's identity or image cannot. A company may try to control its image via communication strategies (Wood et al. 2006: 207–8) but the short-term influence of management is limited to the essential set of values that define and differentiate it from others. The values are expressed through the company's vision and mission and the way it envisages and conducts its business. A company is expected to act consistently with its identity and the image it portrays to others.

If a company acts in accordance with socially accepted norms, it creates an image through which it can gain stakeholders' trust, confidence, and support (Dowling 2001). However, it can undergo identity change to the degree that its actions are not in accordance with internalized standards of appropriateness, which can cause identity crises. Thus, a company becomes vulnerable when its identity and public image begin to separate. In such a situation norm-entrepreneurship can reconcile societal expectations with the company's own value propositions. Where companies have brand products in their portfolio, this constructivist causal mechanism may well occur subsequent to action prompted by following the business case. As the business model of such companies relies on conveying a positive public image of their products, the internal pressure for identity alignment also increases.

Referring to the spiral model of norm socialization, such companies may go through different phases (Risse et al. 1999; Rieth and Zimmer 2004) of dialogue with civil society and in the end find themselves self-entrapped. This self-entrapment can eventually lead to identity change when a company has finally accepted, internalized, or at least habitualized a certain norm. The company may then also promote this norm internally and externally. Once it has built up a certain value-based identity, it is likely to engage in setting up and developing new norms that reflect its value proposition and will inspire others to act in the same way. Crane and Matten (2007: 53) expect companies that have gone through such a socialization process to not only implement norm oriented corporate social responsibility (CSR) behavior, such as designing stakeholder dialogues and initiating community development, but to go beyond what is legally or economically required and anticipate future expectations (see also Carroll 1979).

4.1.2 Operationalization of corporate vulnerability

Of the two components of corporate vulnerability, identity is much more difficult to operationalize than reputational capital. However, even reputation has no consensus in definition across academic disciplines or among academics and practitioners (Bennett and Kottasz 2000; Fombrun and Riel 1997; Barnett et al. 2006). Consultants regard corporate reputation as a comprehensive concept that includes aspects such as excellent leadership, emotional appeal, and high financial performance. Traditionally, research focused mostly on financial variables, taking the difference between market value and the value of a company's assets to constitute the reputational capital of a company.[4] More recent studies measure reputation based on assessments or perceptions of company stakeholders, such as the 'reputation quotient', 'reputational audit', and the 'corporate personality scale' approaches (Epstein 2008: 181), or on the internal assessment of nonquantitative factors. In this vein, formal reputation audits were conducted, often complemented by external information (Cravens et al. 2003: 205).[5]

For the empirical test in this study, product type and brand were chosen as indicators of corporate reputation, which, according to Lev (2001), are related to the innovation and organization intangibles.

Product type is an intangible property of a company that refers to the channel of distribution. In general, intermediate and final goods can be determined. Intermediate goods go into the production of final goods, either by becoming part of the final product or by changing it beyond recognition, as in the case of raw materials or synthetic materials. A final good is ultimately consumed and does not require any further processing. Consumer goods are a common type of final good specifically intended for the mass market. The distinction between intermediate and final goods can also be made by simply referring to the business-to-business (B2B) and business-to-consumer (B2C) types of transactions.

For companies that produce consumer goods, the risk of reputation loss is considerably higher as large numbers of stakeholders are involved. In contrast, companies engaged in B2B transactions depend less on public opinion. It can also be assumed that within the business world, normative expectations are less significant than in civil society or among consumers. Therefore, it is hypothesized that B2B type corporations are less likely to engage in norm-entrepreneurship for reputation preservation. When they do so nevertheless, it could be an indicator of the logic of appropriateness, operating on the basis of corporate identity. However, this would need to be supported by views expressed in interviews.

A *brand* is a name, phrase, symbol, or other identifying characteristic of a product or service to create recognition by the consumer.[6] This usually occurs over a period of time with multiple exposures and positive experiences. Negative experiences with the product can also create brand awareness, although not the kind a company usually wants to achieve. Assets like brands are referred to as 'knowledge assets' or 'intellectual capital' and do not possess physical or financial embodiments. They could therefore also be defined as nonphysical claims to future assets. Brands can be legally protected (for example, as a trademark) and be classified as 'intellectual property' (Lev 2001: 5). Very often brands are employed to create an image that identifies a product and differentiates it from its competitors. Over time and in a best case scenario, an image becomes associated with a level of credibility, quality, and satisfaction in the consumer's mind. In a crowded and complex market, brands assist consumers by standing for certain benefits and values.

4.1.3   Empirical results

Hypothesis H4 was tested with quantitative and qualitative data. Product type and brand were used to identify the level of vulnerability. First, 10 systematic norm-entrepreneurs were examined. In the quantitative test, the hypothesis would have been supported if all 10 shared the same properties. Second, 71 sporadic norm-entrepreneurs were examined to learn more about the analytical status of the variable (Table 4.4). Given that a company brand is based on subjective stakeholder perceptions, whereas product type can be assessed more objectively, further evidence was sought from interview data to learn how far corporate identity or reputation accounts for the influence of vulnerability on norm-entrepreneurship.

Quantitative analysis

A strong correlation could be observed in product type between producing an end product and being active as a norm-entrepreneur. Nine out of ten systematic norm-entrepreneurs produce end products (Table 4.1). Since 1 of the 10 systematic norm-entrepreneurs, Rio Tinto, is a mining company producing intermediate products, product type cannot be classified as a necessary condition: There have to be other influences or factors that can also make a company a norm-entrepreneur. Nevertheless, a supplementary test of the larger

Table 4.1 Norm-entrepreneurship (NE) and product type

	End product	Intermediate product
Systematic NE (10)	9	1
Sporadic NE (71)	59	12

Source: Authors' research.

Table 4.2 Norm-entrepreneurship (NE) and brand status (global level)

	Brand	No Brand
Systematic NE (9)	4	5
Sporadic NE (48)	12	36

Source: Authors' research.

group of sporadic norm-entrepreneurs supported the first finding: 80 percent of the companies who engaged at least to a certain degree in norm setting activities were also producers of end products. Companies that produce end products seem to be very likely candidates for norm setting activities.

To determine how much a brand matters for a company's norm-entrepreneurship is more difficult because the operationalization of 'brand' generates a number of problems: a brand may only be of significance temporarily or it may be geographically limited. In general, it is contestable whether the brand value of a transnational company should be determined at the global or national level as some companies have brand status at the national but not the global level. The indicator must be tested at both levels. As most surveys measuring the brand value of companies exclude purely B2B, all companies that solely produce intermediate products also had to be excluded from the brand analysis. For this reason, Rio Tinto was not included in the sample of systematic norm-entrepreneurs in the brand status analysis.

The Top 100 Best Global Brands Ranking by Interbrand, one of the biggest brand consultancies worldwide, was used to correlate the indicator brand with the 10 systematic and the 71 sporadic norm-entrepreneurs.[7]

Based on this global brand ranking, only four of the remaining nine systematic norm-entrepreneurs are classified as having a brand (Table 4.2). Of the sporadic norm-entrepreneurs, only some 25 percent have a brand. These findings underline the lack of importance of this indicator at the global level.

At the national level, seven home states of norm-entrepreneurs were examined. While the data for Brazil, France, South Africa, and Switzerland are also based on the Interbrand ranking, those for Germany[8], the United

Table 4.3 Norm-entrepreneurship (NE) and brand status (national level)

	Brand	No Brand
Brazil (4 NE)	2	2
Switzerland (6 NE)	4	2
Germany (10 NE)	9	1
France (4 NE)	3	1
South Africa (4 NE)	1	3
UK (11 NE)	7	4
US (16 NE)	7	9

Source: Aggregated data from ranking organizations.

Kingdom,[9] and the United States[10] come from different rating organizations. The data indicate that brand matters more at the national level (Table 4.3). In most countries, the majority of sporadic norm-entrepreneurs are listed in national brand rankings, with the exception of South Africa and the United States.[11] In these countries, the importance of the home state on companies' behavior becomes relevant again (see Section 3.2).

Qualitative analysis

The quantitative data support the assumption that companies with a vulnerability that is based on their reputation as producers of end products and on their brand status (at the national level) are indeed more inclined to take on the role of norm-entrepreneurs. However, to get more clarity about the extent to which this influence of vulnerability on norm-entrepreneurship is related to identity and prompts a company to operate according to the logic of appropriateness rather than a rationalist logic, additional qualitative data from interviews were examined. From these, a slight tendency to strategic reasoning outplaying moral concerns was derived, although value- and norm-related arguments were also presented by the interviewees.

As the following examples show, companies and initiative representatives share the view that companies producing consumer-oriented products are more vulnerable than others to losing reputation: 'It would be sort of naive to deny that companies that are closer to consumers [...] are more pro-active, just because they have to do it. This is the business case' (I4, 27 April 2006). 'Customers sometimes react immediately if they are unsatisfied with a company. We as a retail company are more affected by changing public sentiments than others' (C2, 11 September 2007). The fear that consumers might vote with their feet increases when a company carries a brand. According to another company representative, big companies with brand products run a considerably higher risk of being publicly targeted by civil society groups and eventually losing their reputation (C2, 11 September 2007).

All expected arguments, as laid out earlier, were presented; from stressing the identity of a company and its effect on norm-related engagement, to justifications that highlighted the importance of defensive risk management strategies to a company. Although the qualitative data overwhelmingly indicate that the business case dominates the moral case, when moral arguments were proposed it often remained unclear whether reference to norms served the instrumental purpose of selling cost-benefit-oriented behavior as ethical. Some company representatives were quite irresolute on this and found it difficult to come up with stringent explanations for why they think norm oriented activities are important for their company: 'It brings a certain reputational advantage, but ultimately the thing that people hold on to share-wise is not because we are green but because we make money and (...) that we don't kill people while we are doing that. So, I would not say that our CSR engagement is necessarily done or has brought a huge reputational advantage' (C6, 20 November 2007). Company representatives who emphasized the identity and value proposition also underlined that a brand is not 'very strongly associated with products. For us, the brand is far more about the whole process of who we are. And who [...] is more important then what [the company] is doing!' (C1, 22 July 2007). Some companies engage in norm oriented behavior because this was the will of their founders (C8, 10 January 2008). Obviously, company identity relates to the identity of influential individuals who imprint their personal value judgments on corporate behavior.

Still, the majority of interviewees emphasized the importance of risk management when asked why reputation related arguments drive norm oriented activities: 'Historically, it all developed from the risk management approach. CSR in general and its different elements were a lot about risk and risk prevention. Of course, people prefer using the term 'reputational risk' but it is other risks that are at stake. It's business risks. That is definitely one component' (C3, 21 September 2007); 'These Initiatives strengthen our reputation globally, they reduce risk and enhance customer loyalty' (C9, 5 February 2008). Others underlined the long-term and indirect effects of inadequate reputation management. Short-term, purely profit motivated action might undermine long-term profits: 'The damage one entails in the long run, definitely in terms of reputation but possibly also in hard facts, in numbers in the annual report, is ultimately bigger than the one business opportunity that one might have to forego. [...] I do believe that some will get engaged because it concerns their returns when the corporation has bad reputation or does not have an adequate risk management. That will have financial consequences' (C3, 12 September 2007).

Last but not least, the defensive nature of corporate vulnerability management was stressed: 'If it doesn't happen, it can bring negative reputational value publicly. [...] But actually doing it is not bringing you any reputational value. It is a reputation defense strategy as opposed to a promotion strategy. [...] I would not say that we are part of Global Compact because that makes us sell more [products]. It doesn't! We would wish it did, because then we would get senior management really eager about it. But no, it is difficult to show that link. I think that the fact that if you don't do it or if it goes wrong, the reputational impact comes – it is always a reactive kind of thing, but once you are in a good place and nothing has happened recently, people kind of forget of it' (C6, 20 November 2007).

4.1.4   Conclusions

A company's vulnerability, via its brand and end products, has an influence that needs to be qualified. Value derived from reputation (Fombrun and van Riel 1997) does not necessarily lead to pro-active norm setting behavior. On the one hand, companies that produce end products are much more likely to engage in corporate norm-entrepreneurship; on the other hand, reputation capital in the form of a positive brand value is less significant than expected. While most of the systematic and sporadic norm-entrepreneurs produce final goods, carrying a brand does not correlate with norm-entrepreneurship. Brand companies who are also active norm-entrepreneurs come from certain home countries; this suggests possible linkages with the home state variable, as discussed in Section 3.2.

Since consumer products are a highly significant factor, questions remain concerning Rio Tinto, the only systematic norm-entrepreneur in our sample with a B2B channel of distribution. A Rio Tinto ex-CEO's statement points to a possible answer for this seeming inconsistency: 'To say that criticisms are ill-founded, to remind critics that they depend on mineral products, and to engage in education, advertising and public relations campaigns have all been to little or no avail. Mining's reputation continues to deteriorate' (Briskey et al. 2001). Companies that have reputation to lose are not the only ones influenced by this vulnerability; those with a particularly negative reputation may seek to overcompensate. The former CEO states that conventional corporate reactions to criticism could not reverse the bad image of the mining industry. Because of this, the industry engaged in stakeholder dialogue, especially with nongovernmental organizations, and supported a new global mining philosophy, including social and environmental and economic concerns. Interviewees at Rio Tinto underlined the specific challenges the company faces as a member of a sector with a particularly low reputation. The anomoly of Rio Tinto therefore stresses rather than raises doubts about the finding that a brand name and reputation are important drivers: They matter to corporations with pure B2B transactions once they have been highly affected in a negative way.

Despite the assumed underlying logic of action, a careful examination of the vulnerability of corporations showed that the majority of companies

Table 4.4 Systematic/sporadic Norm-entrepreneurs, brand value, and product type

No.	Corporation	HS[a]	Branch/sector	Brand/no brand	Product type[b]
1	Aracruz Cellulose S.A.	BR	Natural resources		Final
2	Natura Cosmeticos S/A	BR	Cosmetics/chemicals		Final
3	Petrobras	BR	Natural resources		Intermediate
4	Samarco Mineracao S.A.	BR	Natural resources		Intermediate
5	Charles Vögele	CH	Textiles/clothes		Final
6	Credit Suisse	CH	Banking		Final
7	Migros	CH	Retail		Final
8	Novartis Int.	CH	Chemicals/pharmaceuticals	Brand	Final
9	Société Générale Surveillance	CH	Inspection/certificates		Intermediate
10	UBS	CH	Banking	Brand	Final
11	BASF	DE	Chemicals		Final
12	Bayer	DE	Chemicals		Final
13	Daimler Chrysler	DE	Automobiles	Brand	Final
14	Deutsche Bank	DE	Banking		Final
15	Deutsche Telekom	DE	Telecommunications		Final
16	Henkel	DE	Chemicals		Final
17	OTTO	DE	Retail and service		Final
18	SAP	DE	Software development	Brand	Intermediate
19	Siemens	DE	Software/technologies	Brand	Final
20	VW	DE	Automobiles	Brand	Final
21	Novo Nordisk	DK	Chemicals/pharmaceuticals		Final
22	Banco Santander	ES	Banking		Final
23	Inditex	ES	Textiles/clothes	Brand	Final
24	France Telecom	FR	Telecommunications		Final
25	Groupe Renault	FR	Automobiles		Final
26	Suez	FR	Energy supply		Final
27	Total	FR	Natural resources		Final

Continued

Table 4.4 Continued

No.	Corporation	HS[a]	Branch/sector	Brand/no brand	Product type[b]
28	BHP Billiton	GB	Natural resources		Final
29	BP Plc	GB	Natural resources	Brand	Final
30	British Airways	GB	Tourism		Final
31	British Telecom	GB	Telecommunications		Final
32	HSBC	GB	Banking/insurance	Brand	Final
33	Pearson plc	GB	Media		Final
34	Rio Tinto	GB	Natural resources		Intermediate
35	Royal Dutch Shell plc	GB	Natural resources	Brand	Final
36	Standard Chartered Bank	GB	Finance		Final
37	TXU Europe	GB	Energy supply		Final
38	Unilever	GB	Food & beverage		Final
39	Esquel Group	HK	Textiles/clothes		Final
40	Infosys Technologies Ltd.	IN	Software		Final
41	Tata Group	IN	Various activities		Final
42	Panasonic	JP	Engineering/electronics	Brand	Final
43	ABN Amro	NL	Banking/insurance		Final
44	TNT Express	NL	Transport		Final
45	Norsk Hydro	NO	Natural resources/ aluminum		Intermediate
46	Ericsson	SE	Telecommunications		Final
47	ESAB	SE	Engineering		Intermediate
48	H&M	SE	Textiles/clothes		Final
49	ITT Flygt	SE	Engineering (pumps)		Final

50	Tex Line	SG	Equipment (pipes)		Intermediate
51	Avon	US	Cosmetics/ chemicals	Brand	Final
52	Baxter Int.	US	Health products		Final
53	Calvert Group	US	Inspection/certificates		Intermediate
54	Dole Food	US	Food & beverage		Final
55	Eileen Fisher	US	Textiles/clothes		Final
56	FedEx	US	Logistics		Final
57	Ford Eu./Ford	US	Automobiles	Brand	Final
58	GAP	US	Textiles/clothes	Brand	Final
59	General Electric	US	Engineering/electronics	Brand	Final
60	General Motors	US	Automobiles		Final
61	Goldman Sachs Group	US	Investments	Brand	Intermediate
62	Nike	US	Textiles/clothes/shoes	Brand	Final
63	Pfizer	US	Chemicals/pharmaceuticals	Brand	Final
64	Procter & Gamble	US	Chemicals		Final
65	Reebok	US	Textiles/clothes/shoes		Final
66	Toys 'R' Us	US	Toys		Final
67	AngloGold	ZA	Natural resources/mining		Intermediate
68	Eskom	ZA	Energy supply		Final
69	Kumba Resources	ZA	Natural resources		Intermediate
70	Sasol	ZA	Natural resources		Final
71	Kaingu Mines	ZM	Natural resources		Intermediate

[a] Home state or country of origin.
[b] In case a company produces intermediate and end products, the classification 'end product' is applied.

engaging in norm-entrepreneurship are driven by a logic of consequences. Producers of end products who are more exposed to reputation risks are most likely to engage in norm-entrepreneurship. Brand companies who might be expected to develop norm oriented identities, turned out to engage less regularly in this type of behavior. Although some interviewees presented identity related and normatively structured arguments, cost-benefit considerations were still dominant. However, there are signs that in the long run companies start internalizing norms and values previously advocated for strategic reasons and that, over time, these norms might even be institutionalized (Gunningham and Rees 1997: 376–82). This pattern can particularly be observed among some of the systematic norm-entrepreneurs.

The variable of corporate vulnerability, especially in its intermediate versus consumer product variant, can be classified as highly significant even though it does not constitute a necessary condition for norm oriented behavior. On the one hand, companies that have a certain degree of reputation capital in the form of consumer products, especially when branded, make substantial efforts to maintain it and prevent potential campaigns against them. On the other hand, as the Rio Tinto case shows, companies with no end consumer business but who operate in a sector with a highly negative reputation might also engage in norm-entrepreneurship.

4.2   Ownership structure

When discussing the characteristics that companies possess and their resulting influence on corporate behavior, the issue of ownership is often the first to arise. The owner has special legal rights, for example, to rent or sell the company, and presumably an influence on strategic direction, particularly regarding norm-related behavior.

Company ownership structures can differ widely. Individuals and financial institutions are the usual shareholders of publicly listed companies. Individuals, families, and groups of individual shareholders usually own nonlisted companies. States are often major shareholders in companies of national interest, such as those in the energy industry, and cooperatives are wholly owned by their employees. Most of the modern transnational companies are private companies with diffuse ownership (Jensen and Meckling 1976: 6). In privately owned companies, ownership and control is usually separated.[12] This raises the issue of corporate governance, which delineates the rules and practices by which companies are directed. In general, corporate governance includes all mechanisms within corporations that affect decision making (Schmidt 2004). At the management level, these mechanisms are rules and practices by which businesses are operated and controlled. Corporate governance also regulates a corporation's relationship with its stakeholders, including financiers, customers, employees, management representatives, government, and the community.

The relationship between financiers who are also owners of the company and management is particularly critical in corporate strategy development. The relationship very often causes friction between the two parties and is one of the main challenges of corporate governance. Recurrent sources of conflict include divergent interests of owners and managers and whether firms can be run for the benefit of both management and owners (Mayer 2003: 84).[13] The relationship between owners and management is best characterized by the principal-agent concept. The central dilemma is how to get the managers (agents) to act in the best interests of the owners (principals), knowing that the managers have an informational advantage (Richter and Furubotn 1999). The most important problem that arises for the owner is how to manage and reduce agency costs, a type of transaction cost incurred when owners attempt to ensure that managers act in their principals' interest.[14] How much management decisions to engage in norm-related activities can be influenced by the owners of a company is a valid research question. The management informational advantage may be an incentive to cheat and maximize personal gain at the owner's expense (Alchian and Demsetz 1972; Pollack 1997; Jensen and Meckling 1976). It is also expected that management is more likely to pursue short-term interests and invest in concrete, not fuzzy, projects, being less interested in norm-related activities. Which conditions enable owners to minimize agency costs and have an influence on management decision making?

The principal-agent concept is employed to analyze whether company owners exert influence on managers to engage in corporate norm-entrepreneurship, particularly whether concentrated or dispersed shareholdings have any bearing on management decisions to engage in norm setting and development activities. If owners in general do have an impact on their company's norm setting activities there have to be clear indications that they have some influence on management decisions regarding norm-related behavior.

Ownership can be differentiated into a number of different types, two of which are relevant to this research: ownership concentration and ownership mix (Xiaonian and Yan 1997: 2–3; Köke 1999: 3).

Only in companies where a significant portion of the shares has concentrated ownership owners are able to exert considerable pressure on corporate managers. The potential management (agency) costs are contingent on the level of ownership concentration. When shareholdings are disperse and assuming that owners rarely have strategic interest in the company they are investing in, owners primarily want to maximize returns on their investment and are not interested in direct control of the company (Rappaport 1986). In contrast, if the shareholdings are concentrated, large investors tend to pursue strategies more actively within the company. In this case, agency costs are smaller because owners also have insider knowledge and, because of long-term commitments and intense internal company relations, can pressure management to follow their strategic priorities. Dispersed groups of investors do not have the same options at their disposal (Börsch 2007: 17–20). Accordingly, ownership structure might play a prominent role in influencing the possible corporate norm-entrepreneurship activities of a company.

Concentrated shareholdings encourage long-term strategies and are expected to make corporate norm-entrepreneurship more likely. Dispersed shareholdings give managers more leeway in decision making, putting an emphasis on short-term successes, thus hindering engagement in norm setting and development processes. For norm-entrepreneurship, a high degree of ownership commitment is required. This orientation allows for a long-term strategy that might have to take lower rates of return into account in the short term. Concentrated shareholdings imply that long-term oriented owners are more patient if a newly introduced CSR strategy might initially weaken economic performance. In contrast, companies with dispersed shareholdings might adopt general CSR strategies and behave as norm-consumers but would rarely engage in norm-entrepreneurship activities. They prefer to remain flexible to adapt to change and free to exercise the exit option and stop norm-related activities if they are in direct conflict with the goals of a self-regulatory initiative. In companies with dispersed shareholdings, it is expected that short-term oriented shareholder values prevail (Börsch 2007: 18). It is hypothesized that the more concentrated shareholdings are in a company and the more owners have the power to decide whether to engage as norm-entrepreneurs, the more likely that corporate norm-entrepreneurship will occur.

Because of this hypothesis, *ownership mix* becomes of interest. Some owners could be more interested in the norm-related activities of their company than others. In addition, different types of owners might use different strategies to influence management.

To examine whether different types of owners prefer to get actively involved in corporate strategies equally, three types of owners are examined: governments, institutional investors and individuals (Köke 1999). The third category of owners, individuals, is further differentiated into family-owned companies (or family investors) and thus expands the research framework to include nonlisted companies. Generally, it is assumed that governments and individuals are primarily concerned with preserving their original investment, a steady income, and capital appreciation. Firms governed by state bureaucrats mostly lack the incentive to maximize shareholder value (Shapiro and Willig 1990). Family investors have a desire to protect family assets (Dyer and Whetten 2008), and apply employee and community friendly policies, stressing mid- and long-term considerations in the process (Stavrou et al. 2007). The potential roles of creditors, insurance companies, universal banks and pension funds, which form the group 'corporate shareholders', are diverse. The merits and influence of institutional investors have been highly debated (Köke 1999: 6). Creditors as shareholders might force a company to forego investment opportunities with a long-term horizon for smaller short-term gains. In contrast, pension funds, as a particular version of institutional investor, have a reputation of acting as good monitors, pursuing long-term strategies. Pension funds these days emphasize the pursuit of sustainable economic returns through increased shareholder engagement, negative screening, and divestment (Bengtsson 2007: 977).

A two-factor hypothesis is set up, focusing on the concentration of shareholdings and shareholder type. A company with concentrated shareholdings, involving government, family investors and pension funds, is more likely to engage in corporate norm-entrepreneurship than a company with dispersed shareholdings. In addition, a company with concentrated shareholders who are mainly creditors or mainstream investors as major shareholders is less likely to engage in corporate norm-entrepreneurship.

Hypothesis 5 (H5): The more a company's shareholdings are concentrated with government, family investors, or pension funds as major shareholders, the more it is likely to engage in norm-entrepreneurship.

In existing research on the explanatory power of ownership structure, most scholars were primarily interested in the correlation between ownership and financial performance (Xiaonian and Yan 1997; Mathiesen 2002) or efficiency (Köke 1999). Some researchers have applied the principal-agent concept to look at the causal link between ownership and corporate social performance as it relates to norm-consumership.

For example, Barnea and Rubin investigated 3000 U.S. companies for the effects of agency costs on corporate social performance. They showed that in times of profit, it is not at odds with a firm's revenue-maximization strategy to increase CSR activities and that conflicts between managers and owners are less likely to occur. However, managers tend to 'over-invest' in CSR policies because of personal reputation concerns (Barnea and Rubin 2006). As a result, conflicts take place when the costs of CSR investment are more than the revenue expected and received from it. In these circumstances, shareholders feel burdened with CSR expenditure, as they are primarily interested in maximizing profits (Barnea and Rubin 2006: 1).[15] A similar study by Consolandi and colleagues focused on the relationship between ownership structure, corporate financial performance (CFP) and corporate social performance (CSP). The authors found a positive correlation between the first two: Concentrated shareholdings lead to better CFP, while the relationship between CFP and CSP lacks any parallels (Consolandi et al. 2006: 11–12). These results hint at some sort of causal effect between ownership structure and norm-entrepreneurship. However, it has to be stressed that ordinary CSR measures, as described in the literature to date, refer to norm-consumership and not to norm-entrepreneurship.

Goergen and Renneboog analyzed the effects of ownership structure, defined as shareholder management and social issue participation, on CSR in 500 U.S. firms (2002). They argued that major shareholders are more visible to the wider public. They will engage in CSR measures because they are interested in trying to keep the firm's image clean. In addition, it was suggested that the application of higher CSR standards might result in better financial performance; low levels of CSR having negative effects on the firm's value. Consequently, major shareholders are expected to be concerned about improving a company's CSR profile (Goergen and Renneboog 2002: 5). Goergen and Renneboog could not find any significant correlation between ownership structure and CSR activities.

4.2.1   Business case – the short- and long-term perspective

To analyze the causal value of ownership, two theoretical assumptions about the motivations of owners are applied: narrow market rationalism and complex market rationalism (Conzelmann and Wolf 2007b). While both point to the 'business case', the former refers to a rational choice reflection that is limited to the short-term, material, cost-benefit calculations of a *Homo economicus*, whereas the latter extends the rationalist notion of the logic of consequences to the long-term implications of the reputation costs resulting from corporate activities. A causal mechanism is introduced which differentiates between short- and long-term perspectives to analyze whether ownership has any effect on norm-entrepreneurship (Consolandi et al. 2006: 11).

In the *short-term perspective*, it can be argued that companies with a short time line for calculating costs and benefits usually have owners (and shareholders) with only a temporary stake in the company.[16] Their primary goal presumably is the maximization of shareholder value and they do not want managers to allocate funds to long-term investments. Norm setting activities would be considered conspicuous social programs with no or negative effect on the financial bottom line.

Owners following a short-term approach claim that any type of additional CSR engagement primarily adds costs, which in turn lowers the short-term profitability at the expense of return on owner capital. This attitude is described as 'shareholder primacy'. It stresses a cost and risk reduction approach that does not seriously recognize the possibility of a CSR business case (Kurucz et al. 2008: 101). As a result, managers focus on classical economic accounting indicators, such as earning-per-share growth, return on equity or those stemming from the contemporary shareholder value approach that focuses primarily on the cash flow and shareholder return.

Owners of this type do not have any altering influence on managers, because managers are considered short-term oriented and naturally refrain from any risky norm-entrepreneurship activities. Independent of the origin of an investor, the owner, whether a government, an individual or a creditor, would follow a narrow market rationalism, focus on short-term profitability and hence grant extensive autonomy to the management.

In a *long-term perspective*, companies with concentrated shareholdings have owners that are directly interested in the long-term strategy of a company.[17] These owners with often long-term holdings are more open-minded to the possibility of adopting elaborate CSR strategies, including norm-setting activities. They may be interested in norm-entrepreneurship because they see a potential additional – economic and possibly social – value in engaging in norm-related activities. It is assumed that owners with long-term investment views are also more inclined to pursue more comprehensive management approaches that focus not only on short-term profits and do not solely emphasize economic indicators. Underlying this approach are notions of complex market rationalism. Owners realize that corporations have at least some sort of social obligation beyond complying with economic and legal responsibilities, looking at social responsiveness and social responsibility, ethical and philanthropic aspects (Carroll 1979, 2004). These types of owners try to integrate economic and noneconomic views into their deliberations, applying a 'triple bottom line' approach of financial, social and environmental elements (Elkington 1998). They are regarded as interrelated and therefore have to be aligned with the overall corporate goal of sustaining growth and providing value to shareholders (Roselle 2005: 115). Based on this approach, economic profits are achieved in the mid- and long term, particularly if socially responsible aspects are adhered to in the short term. Environmental and social points of view are considered not only as a risk but also as an opportunity (Schaltegger and Figge 1997). The inclusion of environmental protection and compliance with social standards are met with less resistance from owners because they might lead to higher long-term earnings. Successful management of sustainability performance is achieved only if the management of environmental and social issues is in line with increased competitiveness and economic performance (Schaltegger and Wagner 2006: 4).

Thus, companies with concentrated shareholdings might follow an enlightened version of the logic of consequences and be proactive in self-regulatory initiatives because certain owners want to see their company well positioned for future challenges and to be economically successful in the mid- and long term. As a result, owners with a large stake in the company would also aim to install like-minded managers and support management approaches that keep agency costs down.

Different types of owners underscore and reinforce the mechanisms inherent in a long-term perspective. When governments finance commercial enterprises, they are still committed to the common good and public welfare. The same might hold true for individual and family-owned companies because they are under less pressure to generate short-term returns for shareholders. The extent that a governmental investor will try to influence management decisions to engage in CSR is also contingent on national developments, particularly whether a public CSR policy has been developed that is enforced and actively pursued by governmental actors. Possible examples are countries such as the United Kingdom, where the government acts as a driver of CSR by mandating reporting, increasing transparency through soft forms of regulation, and providing incentives and awareness raising activities (Bertelsmann Stiftung 2007: 32–3). Typical incentive schemes might involve the inclusion of CSR criteria in public procurement tenders. However, companies from OECD countries need to be differentiated from emerging market TNCs. National governments of developing countries frequently regard foreign investment as an opportunity to increase their influence in the global arena, especially in key national industries. They exert influence over the activities of 'their partly-owned' companies with the goal to enhance national (political) objectives and increase the performance of their economy (Dunning et al. 2007: 13–14). It is expected that state owned – or state controlled – companies from 'challenger' countries will put less emphasis on norm-related activities than ones from OECD countries.

Individual and family ownership can have an impact on management CSR activities as family owners invest in socially responsible behavior if it serves to protect the family's assets. Some studies stress that this can be positively associated with strategic flexibility and an ability to pursue new opportunities and respond to threats in the competitive environment, depending on a family firm's culture of commitment to business (Zahra et al. 2008). Family owners very often apply employee and community friendly policies (Stavrou et al. 2007). This indicates that family companies might be able to sense new trends, such as CSR, and to consider engaging in norm-entrepreneurship activities as relevant economic value drivers.

The role of creditors and pension funds in particular in corporate norm-related activities has only recently gained attention. Pension funds are the largest investment blocks in most countries and dominate the stock market where they invest. So far, these types of mainstream investors have taken a rather indifferent view of CSR-related activities. Their primary objectives were to preserve the original investment, a steady income, and capital appreciation because the business case for CSR activities has been far from clear to date. Until the late 1990s, public and private pension funds did not significantly push CSR activities. They generally took on the role of monitors because they have no business relationship with their investment. In recent years, socially responsible investment (SRI), which is an investment practice that includes the evaluation of social, environmental, and ethical issues, has gained momentum (Sparkes and Cowton 2004; Visser et al. 2007: 424). Socially responsible investors have integrated CSR and sustainability policies (as indicators for risk management) in the search for successful long-term investments. SRI is the attempt to consider the social, environmental and ethical consequences of investment within the context of rigorous financial analysis (Vivo and Franch 2009). Only lately have pension funds received more public attention due to shareholder activism. Activists apply various tactics. For example, they voice their opinion at shareholder meetings by filing shareholder resolutions that challenge companies about allegedly unethical practices (Crane and Matten 2007: 250). Because asset managers have a fiduciary duty to vote on these resolutions and, in some countries, such as the United States, to disclose their voting policies, shareholders can raise public awareness of CSR issues. Through the application of these measures, public pension funds are starting to become a potentially powerful catalyst for corporate social and environmentally responsible activities (Hess 2007; Sjöström 2008). A prominent example is the transfer of the Norwegian Petroleum Fund, which administers and invests the state's revenues from the oil industry, into a public fund with an ethical investment policy.

It is expected that owners with a short-term outlook would rarely try to influence management decision making processes. Owners who are part of an anonymous mass of dispersed shareholders are solely interested in short-term profitability. They expect managers to do everything that is necessary to serve their interests, which implies that they will not engage in any costly forms of norm-entrepreneurship activities. On the contrary, owners with a long-term outlook consider environmental and social issues as an opportunity that can also be economically attractive. If they control a critical number of shares, they could directly influence management to consider norm-related activities as a salient corporate strategy.

Looking in more detail at these types of owners, governments, and families can be expected to have a long-term view, whereas creditors have a short-term view. Governments are prone to support norm-related activities if they have already introduced CSR aspects into their national legislation, such as in public procurement tenders. Family owners are expected to do the same, especially if they feature a corporate culture that focuses on employee and community friendly policies (Section 4.3). Creditors focus mostly on preserving investments. Pension funds, due to their long-term orientation and in line with their recent reorientation toward ethically oriented investment strategies, may be more open to norm-related corporate activities.

4.2.2 Measuring ownership

Links between owners, management, and norm-entrepreneurship activities are sought in two steps. First, the degree of ownership concentration is examined. This is a precondition for testing whether there are significant correlations between ownership structure and norm-entrepreneurship. The ownership of a company is 'concentrated' if major owners hold 5 percent or more of the voting shares.[18] Each owner whose share package exceeds 5 percent is considered capable of exerting influence on management. In the second step, the hypothesis is analyzed to see if governmental, family, or pension fund ownership is more prevalent (Xiaonian and Yan 1997: 2–3; Köke 1999: 3). To account for the different types of ownership, two empirical samples are used, covering 71 corporate norm-entrepreneurs altogether. In addition to the 10 systematic norm-entrepreneurs, the 61 companies that were identified as sporadic norm-entrepreneurs are also included in the empirical analysis. Finally, to find out whether the previously detected correlation in relationships also indicates causal links, interviews with representatives of companies and self-regulatory initiatives were conducted to gather additional empirical evidence.

Quantitative analysis of ownership structure relevance

An analysis of the ownership structure of the two samples shows that six out of the ten systematic norm-entrepreneurs have concentrated shareholdings (Table 4.5). This does not convincingly demonstrate the significance of concentrated shareholdings compared to dispersed shareholdings. The percentage of concentrated shareholdings is only slightly higher among sporadic norm-entrepreneurs. Approximately two-thirds of the sporadic norm-entrepreneurs have owners that hold more than 5 percent of the shares. These preliminary results suggest only a limited potential relevance of the relationship between owners and managers that is typical of concentrated shareholdings.

A more detailed look at owner type reduces the significance of this preliminary result: Although all types of investors – public, private, individual, and family owners – are represented in this sample, there are a striking number of institutional investors, in the form of asset managers and the like. In the sample of systematic norm-entrepreneurs, nine have investors from this sector but only five pass the 5 percent threshold. Among the 61 sporadic norm-entrepreneurs, also half of the owners are of institutional origin. Since pension funds – as the type of long-term institutional owner presumed to increase CSR engagement, including norm-entrepreneurship – are exceptions among the institutional investors, these findings further weaken the hypothesis: asset managers and the like are typical examples of investors not interested in exerting control over the companies in which they hold shares but exclusively looking to maximize their returns. It is highly unlikely that sporadic or systematic norm-entrepreneurship can be explained by concentrated ownership by institutional investors.

Looking more closely at the actual influence of those types of owners that were hypothesized to generally show greater interest in fostering ethical corporate policies, only three among the 10 systematic norm-entrepreneurs (Table 4.5) have major shareholdings by governments (France Telekom and Sasol) or individual and family investors (Inditex). These relations are similar to those among the 61 sporadic norm-entrepreneurs (Figure 4.1). All that can be concluded here is that, while there are individual instances of norm-entrepreneurship that might be explained by ownership structure (such as the cases of France Telekom or Inditex), the mix of owners and especially the presence of governments or individuals cannot explain all instances of norm-entrepreneurship and thus does not constitute a necessary factor.

Qualitative analysis of ownership influence

Based on the empirical results of the quantitative analysis, the variable 'owner-ship structure' currently has no significant impact on norm-entrepreneurship. It neither supports nor prevents corporations from becoming norm-entrepre-neurs. Qualitative analysis supports these results. Most of the interviewees stressed that norm-related activities had not been a priority for the owners of a company. However, there were some hints that concentrated shareholdings, in particular governmental and family ones, might start playing a larger role in the future.

When asked about whether the ownership structure of a company and the different types of shareholders play a role in norm-related activities, a company representative answered straightforwardly: 'When you go to a shareholders' meeting, so far there have not been many questions on CSR' (C3, 12 September 2007). Another one stated that 'we have never, in terms of CSR, received any negative feedback or criticism from our shareholders' (C5, 8 November 2007). An interviewee alluded to the fact that single own-ers and shareholders rarely have any say on particular corporate policies

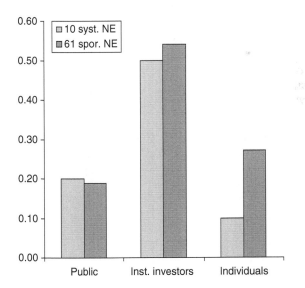

Figure 4.1 Shareholder structure of sporadic and systematic norm-entrepreneurs (percentage of public, institutional investors, and individual owners)

Source: Authors' research.

Table 4.5 Ownership structure of systematic norm-entrepreneurs

NE	As of	Free float		Type of shareholder	
			Public	Institutional investors	Individuals
Credit Suisse (CH)	31.12.07	87.46%		Chase Nominees Ltd. (GB) 9.74% AXA SA (FR) 6.98%	
UBS (CH)	31.12.06	90.40%		The Depository Trust Company (USA) 13.21% Chase Nominees Ltd (GB) 8.81%	
Deutsche Bank (DE)	31.12.06	100%		Barclays PLC (GB) 3.6% UBS (CH) 3.1%	
Inditex (ES)	31.12.06	75.35%		Institutional Investor in total 36.52%: ROSP Corunna Participaciones Empresariales, S.L. 6.9% Chase Nominees LTD. (GB) 5.974%	Gartler, S.L (ES) 50.01% Partler, S.L (ES) 9.28% Other individuals 4.18% Employees 3.64%
France Telecom	31.03.06	67.55%	French State 18.18% ERAP 14,27%		
British Petroleum	31.12.05	89.60%		Kuwait Investment Office 3.32%* Barclays PLC 3.47% Legal/General Investment Management 3.57%	

Rio Tinto (GB)	25.04.07	88.95%		Barclays Plc 4.02% The Capital Group Companies Inc 3.9% Legal & General Group Plc (UK) 3,13%
Royal Dutch Shell (GB)	27.02.07	100.00%		The Capital Group Companies Inc. 7.24% Barclays Bank plc 6.45% Legal & General Group plc 3.9%
TATA Steel (IN)	30.09.08	66.05%	Government 0.02%	Bank Financial Institutions/ Insurance Companies 18.05% Foreign Institutional Investors 19.82 % Mutual Funds 4.95%
Sasol (SA)	30.06.06	k.A.	Public Investment Corporation Ltd. 13.8% Industrial Development Corporation of South Africa Ltd. 7.8%	Sasol Investment Company Ltd. 8.8% PIC Equities (SA) 10.8 % Old Mutual Asset Managers (SA) 8.1 % Stanlib Ltd (SA) 4.4 % Capital Int'l Inc (US) 4.3 %

Legend: NE: norm-entrepreneur
Grey: *companies with concentrated shareholdings*
White: companies with dispersed shareholdings

in incorporated companies: 'Because our company is a publicly listed company, the owners do not have any direct influence on operational business' (C9, 8 February 2008). One interviewee was quite surprised about questions regarding the relevance of ownership: 'To be honest, I have never thought about CSR from this perspective. I do not think that the ownership mix has an influence. Maybe a big shareholder might have the opportunity to have an effect on management decision, but at our company this has not happened so far' (C3, 12 September 2007). The argument was even turned around; one interviewee stated that 'because our company is an incorporated company, owners have only a limited direct influence on the operational business' (C9, 5 February 2008). Another company representative stressed that 'in French, an incorporated company is translated as "societé anonym", which provides a good account of reality. We have millions of shareholders, big and small ones, even hedge funds, but they do not have a say in our daily business' (C2, 11 September 2007).

Some respondents pointed to the fact that publicly listed companies were more under scrutiny than others but that this does not mean that they are more active than nonlisted companies. In no interviews was any significant owner influence mentioned. Some shareholders became more interested in management decisions on CSR activities, but no credible pressure has been exerted on management so far. In addition, some company representatives considered investing in their company as a long-term investment: 'From a shareholder perspective we are very safe and you invest in us for the long term. [...] We know our shareholders are expecting a return in 20 years time. So it does give us some leeway, the way that we operate our business. [...] Within our team, I do not feel the pressure of our shareholders or the owners' (C7, 21 November 2007).

The interviews did not support the expectation that a company is more inclined toward norm-related activities if it has a certain type of owner. A representative of a company with strong governmental shareholdings stressed that 'the way of doing business is the way of a private company. [...] The influence of the public shareholders is that they vote and that they may choose the CEO' (C8, 10 January 2008), like any other shareholder. The same results hold true for companies that have family owners. Although there was only one family-owned company in the sample, the majority of the respondents provided numerous good and bad examples of family ownership and norm-related activities. One company representative suggested that 'owner-operated businesses have a better chance from the beginning to act ethically and more responsible. In contrast, incorporated companies have to "learn" what that means and need external pressure' (C2, 11 September 2007). Another interviewee put the emphasis on 'personal leadership' and that 'good behavior depends on having a determined, charismatic leader' (I3, 27 March 2006). Again, no general causal pattern could be established.

Interviewees stressed that, while investors in the past rarely pushed companies toward norm-related activities, this has started to change with the current trend of socially responsible investment (SRI): 'There are these sustainability oriented shareholders, yet they only form a small group of shareholders which are interested in our engagement in CSR activities. But remember, they are negligibly small in comparison to the bulk of other shareholders' (C2, 11 September 2007). However, as another company representative pointed out: 'In the longer term there might be a proliferation of socially responsible investors. [...] Their influence is growing. [...] They are small but they are influential' (C4, 10 October 2007). Some companies have already reacted to this increasing attention from activist shareholders but the overall effect is still rather small, as one company representative reports: 'Yes, there is pressure from the investors. We try to go out and tell our investors about our sustainable development programs and about the value added to our reputation. FTSE4 Good and the Dow Jones Sustainability Index help that. But actually the vast majority of the investor world is not particularly interested in that stake, though it is changing' (C7, 21 November 2007).

Interestingly, two company representatives emphasized that the origin of shareholders might play an important role (the home state variable is analyzed in Section 3.2.): 'Like other companies, we do not have massive numbers of foreign owners. [...] But most of the shareholders are very much here [in the home country of the company]. That, of course, influences us' (C7, 21 November 2006). The interviewee associated this sort of home state influence with a certain kind of ownership influence on corporate behavior: Owners who are considered risk averse or have a conservative reputation might affect a corporation's strategy.

In summary, only a few company representatives attributed relevance to ownership structure in norm-related activities. Some believed that it might become an issue in the future, particularly in family owned companies, pension funds, and SRI. This would indeed support recent research on the influence of pension funds and family owned companies. However, clear evidence of any significant causal effect of ownership type could not be detected. Overall, the analysis surprisingly showed that the variable 'ownership structure' has no decisive effect on the norm-related behavior of companies. However, reinforced by the financial crises in 2008 and the ensuing decline in confidence in short-term investments, the increasing amount of money invested in SRI funds could be taken as a sign that long-term owner and investor views might play a much larger role in the future than in the past.

4.2.3 Conclusion

Neither concentrated shareholdings nor any particular owner type can explain the sporadic or systematic activities of corporate norm-entrepreneurs.

There are slight indications that some types of owners are present more often than others but their causal effect could not be traced. Public pension funds and socially responsible investors might direct companies into more norm-related behavior in the near future but their small percentage of company ownership and overall investment is currently still too insignificant. It might be interesting to further examine the role of government and family owners to determine whether individual instances of norm-entrepreneurship can be sufficiently explained by their influence, particularly when considered with the results of Section 3.2: The home state variable explained 8 out of the 10 cases of systematic norm-entrepreneurship. It seems striking that the remaining two – from the fairly interventionist home states Spain and France – have a government and a private individual in control of the company.

Other shareholder criteria could be of interest in other correlations, such as the origin (home state) of the owner or the industry sector. However, the influence of ownership on norm-entrepreneurship seems to be negligible. The fact that owners seem to generally exert little influence on norm-entrepreneurship points to the potential importance of corporate leadership by managers, which deserves more attention in future research.

4.3　Corporate culture

Corporate or organizational culture figures prominently in sociology and management sciences as a causal factor in explaining an organization's structure or strategy and as a phenomenon defined, for example, by the larger societal culture or the nature of the problems an organization has to cope with (Pfahler 2006: 36–40). In this study it is assumed that corporate culture can make corporations more or less likely to engage in norm-entrepreneurship. Without prior experience in related matters a company cannot easily take on corporate norm-entrepreneurship because the behavior requires particular cognitive predispositions and factual resources. It is therefore assumed that an existing 'culture of responsibility' is more adaptable to norm-entrepreneurship than other variants of corporate culture. Companies habitualized to engaging in activities beyond their core business and contributing to public good provision prior to the rise of societal expectations of corporate engagement in norm setting and opportunities for norm-entrepreneurship will follow the same scripted behavioral paths in these new challenges.[19]

Hypothesis 6 (H6):　The more a corporation's culture is a 'culture of responsibility', the more it is likely to engage in norm-entrepreneurship.

4.3.1　Learning as a causal mechanism

Institutional learning is a key concept for drawing a possible causal connection between a traditional culture of responsibility and engagement in norm-entrepreneurship. In departing from the zero hypothesis of narrow market rationalism (corporations follow profit-maximizing strategies only), the motivation for acting as norm-entrepreneurs might be hard to establish. Sociological versions of neo-institutionalist organizational theories recognize that corporations need to be cognitively 'ready' to engage in any activity (Hall and Taylor 1996: 16). Just like individuals confronted with new and highly complex problem structures in their environment, they tend to rely on scripted role behavior to reduce complexity (Gioia and Poole 1984; Hall and Taylor 1996; Preisendörfer 2005: 145–52). Accordingly, it is likely that corporations who already have a tradition of and mechanisms available for processing demands that go beyond pure profit-maximizing strategies will react in the same way to demands or opportunities to engage in norm-entrepreneurship.

This reasoning implies that norm-entrepreneurship – as a form of script processing – is not necessarily a consciously chosen behavioral strategy but results from habitualized routines (Gioia and Poole 1984: 449). Therefore, assuming there is explanatory value in corporate culture does not mean that corporate norm-entrepreneurs are normatively convinced of doing the right thing. They are not necessarily undergoing a cycle of double-loop learning resulting in a modification of their underlying values, interests and goals (Argyris and Schön 1978, 1996). However, script acquisition – the point in time when a corporation first starts to develop its culture of responsibility – requires a certain amount of active cognition. This process can be enhanced by interaction, rewards and reinforcement processes. While interaction, communication, and dialogue have the potential to foster persuasion (Checkel 2001; Schimmelfennig 2003), social or material rewards and punishments for enacting a company culture of responsibility can also make a corporation follow the script in adopting strategies of norm-entrepreneurship.[20]

4.3.2 Identifying an adaptable culture of responsibility

The operationalization of 'corporate culture' thus needs to capture two very different dimensions of the concept: First, what is the actual and observable content of the 'culture of responsibility' that is assumed to be particularly adaptable to norm-entrepreneurship? Second, what indicators signal that norm-entrepreneurs have already been habitualized into acting in accordance with a culture of responsibility to a degree where they, by reflex, react with similar strategies when they are confronted with new demands and opportunities, such as engaging in norm-entrepreneurship?

The content of a culture of responsibility

Schein's distinction of three levels of organizational culture, ranging from subconscious basic assumptions about the nature of the world, to values and behaviors as its more observable manifestations (Schein 1989: 13–21) holds relevance but the focus of this study is on the visible manifestations of corporate culture. These can be verbal references to corporate culture, or, as an attempt to objectify what an adaptable culture consists of, forms of corporate engagement in beyond-profit activities. These two manifestations are understood as expressions of the underlying values and basic assumptions of a corporation that form an overall corporate culture of responsibility. The visible artifacts, whether verbal or behavioral, are thus taken as indicators of the overall corporate culture. By identifying the responsible activities of a corporation, it is assumed that a culture of responsibility exists and is the source from which these activities are derived.

A corporate culture of responsibility comprises activities that are not part of a corporation's business activities. Business could still function, the product produced, and service provided even if the responsible activity was not practiced. A characteristic of activities that flow from a culture of responsibility is that they are dispensable to a corporation with a purely business culture. However, for responsibility to qualify as a part of organizational culture, a corporation would have to view itself and its role as defined by responsible behavior rather than regarding it as an add-on to business activities. This implies that philanthropic activities with no effect on business activities are not proxies for a corporate culture of responsibility. Philanthropy and norm-entrepreneurship differ too much from one another in their degree of infiltration into the core business practice of the corporation.

Another set of activities has to be excluded from the definition of a culture of responsibility, namely corporate lobbying activities. Even though lobbying – as an inherently political activity – comes close to the political character of norm-entrepreneurship and could be regarded as highly connected, there is again a fundamental difference between the two. Political lobbying approaches the political decision making process from the outside and only through deliberate choice. Norm-entrepreneurship implies a degree of involvement in public affairs and therefore a role-shift that goes beyond what would be necessary to ensure business benefit. A culture of responsibility – for public affairs though not necessarily for the public good – therefore has to be distinguished from a culture of political involvement in terms of adaptability to norm-entrepreneurship.

Indicators of a culture of responsibility are found in the internal and external activities of a company. Internal activities can aim to improve the situation of employees beyond a legally required degree, such as special vocational programs, gender-equality measures, or extraordinary participatory mechanisms. Externally oriented aspects of a responsible culture are found in environmental protection or in being sensitive to political issues. Responsible activities could consist, for example, in establishing beyond compliance waste-management systems, or in distancing the company from repressive regimes, a classic example being the withdrawal of firms from South Africa in the times of apartheid, which demonstrated a degree of responsiveness to demands for beyond-profit activities. A culture of responsibility can also have more sector-specific characteristics. For example, environmental policies are considered almost indispensable to a culture of responsibility in the extractive industry. Issues connected to transparent information policies have greater relevance to the banking sector.

Habitualization of a culture of responsibility

For an activity to be classified as a habitualized script of behavior it must reach a certain level of intensity. Established long-term processes resulting in repetitive patterns of behavior are more indicative than single or isolated instances of 'doing good'. Ideally, a certain degree of institutionalization that ensures reliable adoption of such behavior in any situation will also be discernable. Hence, the focus is on identifying existing structures and policies within corporations that back behavioral routines engrained in the corporate DNA. Relevant actions should have a certain degree of regularity, even if behavior may still sometimes contradict structure and policy. The intensity of behavior required for adaptability will be most clearly established where special branches or departments exercise responsibility and are not mere add-ons without links to core business departments. Gunningham and Rees quote Selznick: 'a corporate conscience consists of specific arrangements for making accountability an integral part of corporate decision making. The main strategy is institutionalization' and 'the great task of institutional design is to build moral competence into the structure of the enterprise' (Gunningham and Rees 1997: 381–2).[21]

There is also a difference between a culture of responsibility – as a rather apolitical practice of 'doing good' – and the more recent public expectations of corporations taking on an explicitly political role as co-providers of governance functions. These expectations are embedded in the paradigm shift toward a relationship between the public and private sector as partners in the provision of public goods which is not based on hierarchy. The former apolitical practice of doing good is rooted in the time when the roles of the two were still distinct and even the highest expectations of corporate responsibility did not go beyond issues within the businesses' realm of influence. Hence, a distinction between the dependent variable (corporate norm-entrepreneurship) and the independent variable (corporate culture) can be drawn with a timeline: Activities that represent a culture of responsibility must be searched for and intensively practiced before this paradigm shift occurred and expectations of a corporate role-shift were made. The United Nations Conference on Environment and Development in Rio de Janeiro in 1992 serves as the empirical watershed for distinguishing corporate political activities that occurred in the 'new age' of global governance that followed the golden age of the nation state. To draw a clear differentiating line in corporate norm-entrepreneurship (the dependent variable), only those activities indicative of a culture of responsibility (the independent variable) that can be identified as part of a company's tradition prior to this date are taken into account.

Data and method

Organizational culture is obviously a complex construct and difficult to measure in quantitative terms or according to precise indicators. To determine the character of the ten selected norm-entrepreneurs' corporate culture a qualitative approach was used, primarily based on how corporations describe themselves rather than on objective data portraying a factually observable corporate culture. Accordingly, data from expert interviews were first used to identify the cognitive influence of culture upon the corporation, the expectation being that corporate representatives regularly refer to their corporate culture, that is, responsible practices and activities with a long tradition, as the background for their current engagement as norm-entrepreneurs. Habitualization, in particular, was assumed if the adequacy and appropriateness of such activities are taken for granted. In terms of figures of speech that could underpin the hypothesis, people involved in norm-entrepreneurship are expected to be aware of the connection between previous beyond-profit activities and current norm-entrepreneurship and to naturally draw argumentative links between them.

The visible 'third' level of organizational culture was identified in short case studies on the selected corporations, based on primary and secondary accounts of the internally and externally oriented activities assumed to flow from a culture of responsibility. Although corporate publications and self-descriptions may not be sufficiently reliable sources in general, in this context they contain the desired evidence. Cognitive processes, such as habitualization and scripted role behavior, become operational in subjective accounts of history. Even if a corporation does not live up to its perceived culture, self-perception is important to decision making on norm-entrepreneurship.

If, as assumed here, corporate norm-entrepreneurship rests on a preexisting corporate culture of responsibility, it is expected that the ten identified norm-entrepreneurs would show a high level of adaptability in their pre-norm-entrepreneurship activities. Presumably, they will have exercised the internally and externally directed activities that were identified as indicative of a culture of responsibility, not as ad-hoc responses to external stimuli but with a certain regularity and based on established and institutionalized processes. As this degree of institutionalization also depends on material and personal resources allocated by the corporation to these activities, the companies will typically have specific departments and staff. It is also expected that evidence of written or oral testimony of specific policies and processes will be found and that staff in general will be aware of these.

4.3.3 Evidence from primary data

It is highly striking that several representatives of initiatives named a culture of responsibility as one of the most influential factors in the corporate decision to engage in norm-entrepreneurship. The following statement is indicative: 'If a corporation has a certain tradition in the area of social responsibility or maybe environmental protection, it is much more likely that it will participate in this initiative than if that corporation was more aligned [with] other topics' (I14, 5 September 2006). One business representative explicitly related his corporation's current frontrunner position as a norm-entrepreneur in several contemporary self-regulatory initiatives to its long history of going beyond legal compliance in welfare and public goods provision, arguing exactly along the lines of an earlier statement. 'When it comes to norm formation, which means innovative entrepreneurship and the appliance of norms which formerly were nonexisting and nonaccepted standards, it really means that these entrepreneurs played a part in pioneering and innovating something. [...] For instance, we started a number of best practices for labor. When it was unheard of [...] we [...] thought of having workers compensation, worker committees, a nursery for mothers with children who come to work. Now these things are all setting up certain norms, which became law [...] fifty years ago. [...]This is something that characterizes norm-formative behavior' (C1, 22 July 2007).

Another expert linked the behavior of corporations to the internal allocation of resources, underlining that a certain amount of institutionalization is necessary for a culture of responsibility to enable norm-entrepreneurship: 'Obviously, the maturity of corporations differs. [...] There are all those which only just started to approach the topic and have to discover it for themselves. They have to establish their own internal processes and are busy with that task. They are, in a sense, trying to catch up and they do not have the capacity to participate immediately. Where the internal organizational structure is often a one man show, where there is no infrastructure, where data first have to be generated and their quality is questionable, the people responsible are [too] overstrained to participate in advanced processes on top of that (I7, 15 May 2006). Several interviewees drew this link between the availability of resources and the possibility of engagement in norm-entrepreneurship: 'Very often it is a single person who has to do this job on top [of their normal work load]. [...] Of course, then it is difficult for a corporation to be even more pro-active in a project than is required. Possibly they are willing, but they are lacking the capacity' (I13, 28 July 2006). As assumed, the necessary resources for norm-entrepreneurship are more likely to be provided in corporations who are accustomed to allocating resources for beyond-profit activities.

Other statements emphasized the importance of institutional venues for norm-entrepreneurship to flourish: 'It has to be part of the corporate culture otherwise it will not be lived. The intention has to be incorporated into the business processes and operations. The most important thing is to have space for discourse within the corporation: A designated space where the dilemmas and conflicts can be discussed' (I7, 15 May 2006). Where a culture of responsibility is not habitualized and practices flowing from it are not internalized but questioned, 'people in middle management and lower levels of the hierarchy are bending over backwards for this but have to struggle internally with the board of management to achieve something. Therefore, it is necessary to have awareness of this topic internally, to have sensitivity and to acknowledge the necessity of making it transparent' (I13, 28 July 2006).

There was one initiative representative who saw cultural factors as irrelevant, highlighting that engaging in new collective mechanisms can be equally attractive to corporations who have had 'a long-running tradition in social monitoring and CSR generally' (I13, 28 July 2006) as it is to those without such a tradition. Within the collective initiative that the spokesperson represents, traditions in the area of responsibility vary largely among the norm-entrepreneurs. 'From the beginning, quite a lot of corporations were interested in this idea [of collectivizing a monitoring system], especially [...] those corporations [that] did not have a system of their own [...] and were searching for a new one. On the other hand, it was also attractive [to] those corporations [that] already had an [...] internal monitoring system because they, too, recognized that a collective approach might [...] have more authority and efficiency' (I13, 28 July 2006).

Initiative and corporate representatives almost unanimously underlined the importance of a culture of responsibility: a tradition of engaging in beyond-profit activities. The substantive and procedural aspects of such a tradition were also acknowledged as important. Corporate representatives referred to their history of beyond-the-law engagement, for example, in workers' rights protection, as a driver of their current norm-setting activities. The necessity of a minimum of institutionalization and CSR resource provision was underlined because without them corporations are not able to notice new engagement possibilities. Evidence was also found to confirm the expectation that engagement in norm-entrepreneurship is difficult for a company that is only at the early stages of institutionalizing responsibility internally. Although this was doubted by one expert, there was ample support for the assumption that habitualization to CSR-related behavior increases the likelihood of engaging in norm-entrepreneurship

4.3.4   Analysis of secondary data

To further substantiate the hypothesis, the behavior of the ten norm-entrepreneurs was analyzed for beyond-profit activities directed toward internal and external stakeholders traditionally practiced by the company, according to its own and third party accounts.

British Petroleum

BP is active primarily in the extractive industry and repeatedly faces the problems endemic to this sector. Although criticized on many occasions, BP stands out as a company that accepted its responsibilities to external actors and within certain issue areas considerably earlier than many of its peers. In the early 1980s, after an at the time rather uncommon process of stakeholder consultation, BP institutionalized a special group within the Public Affairs and Information department at headquarter level that was responsible for the four areas of donations, sponsorships, education and community affairs, with the latter being of particular importance. BP explicitly described the activities as being part of its own 'enlightened self-interest' (BP 1982: 2–3) and stated that 'the aims of BP's community and educational affairs policy are therefore an integral part of the overall commercial objectives of the company' (BP 1982: 6). BP's efforts to benefit communities were especially prominent in South Africa where it sought to foster desegregation in the 1980s (Browne 1997: 8–9). Even though BP was widely criticized for not disinvesting from South Africa and being involved in human rights violations via a subsidiary in Indonesia (ICEM 1997: 24), the company strove early on to engage with and to assume responsibilities to external stakeholders in an institutionalized manner.

Similar observations hold true for BP's awareness of its environmental responsibilities. BP drew massive criticism from NGOs, such as Multinational Monitor and Citizen Action, for a number of accidents that led to massive habitat degradation: But it also developed a sense of responsibility for the detrimental environmental effects of its operations and accepted its role model position: 'as the largest company in the United Kingdom, BP has a special responsibility for setting a lead in good energy management' (BP 1979: 4). In the 1970s, the company engaged extensively in renewable energy research, set up an Energy Conservation Committee and consulted its customers on these issues (BP 1977, 1979). By not filing for patents for its energy-efficient technologies, BP shared its expertise with competitors (Lamb 1970: 2). According to the company, 'throughout the 1970s and 1980s, environmental concerns were increasingly core to BP's culture' (BP 2008).

BP's inward-directed activities, in addition to an institutionalized Employees' Relations Department dedicated to the classic function of attracting and retaining suitable staff (Rock 1968), are demonstrated for example by deliberate attempts to increase the number of shares held by staff. For example, 20,000 people, equaling more than 60 percent of staff employed in the United Kingdom, owned shares in the early 1980s (Walters 1984: 4). In sum, BP institutionalized avenues for the enactment of a culture of responsibility long before the concept of CSR was invented, although largely based on a rational understanding of enlightened self-interest. Their focus was outward-oriented but policies on employees followed a similar pattern.

Credit Suisse

As seems to be the case with banks in general, the beyond-profit activities of Credit Suisse originally focused on sports and cultural sponsoring and philanthropy. In this sense, its culture was a traditional banking culture until the end of the 1970s. However, because of the Chiasso scandal in 1977, the bank – in collaboration with several peers – developed an early approach to responsibility: Issue management became a sort of early warning system. The bank started to have regular and more specific contact with the media and political actors (Jung 2000: 379), changing its approach to public communication from 'information to communication or from monologue to the exchange of thoughts of the bank with its customers, employees and the public' (Jung 2000: 382). For example, the bank, within a larger consortium of banking institutions, had regular exchanges with a number of NGOs on apartheid issues in South Africa (Rogge 1997: 348). A far reaching consequence of the Chiasso scandal was the development of new forms of self-regulation by several Swiss banks, referred to as a milestone for the establishment of business ethics in banking (Jung 2000: 245, 290).

Credit Suisse showed their environmental awareness as early as the 1970s, establishing a 10-year energy conversation program in 1977 (Credit Suisse Group 1998b: 14–15) and creating and continuously advancing an environmental management system since the early 1990s (Credit Suisse Group 1998a: 2–3). Concrete measures consisted of, for example, reduction in energy usage, educational measures, creating a position concerned with environmental issues in 1989 and a working group on the issue in 1991 (Credit Suisse Group 1998b: 14–15). Also in 1990, protection of the environment was incorporated into the official corporate philosophy and Credit Suisse was the first Swiss bank to introduce an environmental technology fund. Even before that, in 1986, an ethical-ecological fund was set up in the United Kingdom (Credit Suisse Group 1998b: 21–8). In 1992, on the edge of the new age of global governance, Credit Suisse signed the United Nations Environment Programme Financial Initiative for Banks, which, according to the bank, proves its commitment to sustainability and put Credit Suisse at the forefront of enacting a culture of responsibility.

Deutsche Bank

Deutsche Bank is the rare case in the ten systematic norm-entrepreneurs where the prevailing corporate culture can only be construed as a culture of responsibility with difficulty. The prevalent management style was long described as an 'among us culture' ('Unter-uns-Kultur') and communication with external actors as obdurate, defiant, arrogant and ignorant (Schwarz 2003: 29, 40). The bank's information policy never extended beyond what was legally required (Büschgen 1995: 656). Until 1970, it was an 'established principle in Deutsche Bank to avoid public attention by any means' (Schwarz 2003: 44). Management on all levels was organized as collectivities so that no individual was ever held responsible (Schwarz 2003: 29). Even when the more open and progressive Herrhausen became CEO, there was little and slow change in communication policies, he replaced the prior 'concealment tactics' with open acknowledgement of the bank's power (Schwarz 2003: 48–9; Büschgen 1995: 648).

However, with regard to its internally oriented responsibility, such as employment policies, Deutsche Bank earned praise for several socially oriented measures in the 1980s: The extension of apprenticeship positions beyond the necessary amount resulted from 'social and socio-political deliberations' and the bank's desire to 'take its socio-political responsibility seriously' (Büschgen 1995: 627). Gender equality policies also figured prominently. For example, a campaign on 'women in leadership positions' was launched in 1973 and the number of female executives rose from 3 in 1975 to 39 in 1992 and in 1988 a woman was appointed to the executive board for the first time. In the extremely conservative German banking business, this was without precedent (Büschgen 1995: 628).

The bank's environmental efforts seem to not extend before the late 1980s but it claims to have been the first bank to engage in Debt for Nature Swaps, writing off outstanding debts or handing them over to, for example, the World Wildlife Fund for Nature (Jeucken 2001: 77; Büschgen 1995: 672). In 1992, the bank joined the United Nations Environment Programme Financial Initiative, further evidence of its changing attitude toward beyond-profit activities (Deutsche Bank 2002, 2008).

France Telecom

France Telecom represents a special case in the sample, as it was originally a state-run business and was only privatized in 1988. The Direction Générale des Télécommunications was an integral part of the state's administration, which, by its very nature, pursues beyond-profit interests. Providing telecommunication connections was in itself seen as a public good. Hence, France Telecom was and still is influenced by the history and self-perception of providing a public service, a notion that also figured prominently in interviews with France Telecom representatives. Even though France Telecom's culture of responsibility cannot be measured by specific activities exercised, the culture is still entrenched by the company's very nature of having been a public service provider.

Inditex

For Inditex, hardly any documentation of its past activities exists, presumably due to it being the youngest company of the systematic norm-entrepreneurs. Founded in 1975 and set up in its current structure in 1985, its history only briefly predates the watershed after which new and quite different demands on corporate involvement in beyond-profit activities arose. Inditex is also the only truly 'family-run' corporation in the sample.

Amancio Ortega Gaona almost single-handedly founded the corporation and remains the majority shareholder. Since he is known for keeping a very low public-profile (Kersting 2001; Manager Magazin 2001), it is not surprising that little to no corporate history data is available. It is not possible to establish whether it is lack of available information that gives the impression of a limited traditional engagement in beyond-profit activities or whether there is an actual lack of a culture of responsibility. However, assuming that any type of corporate culture, responsible or not, needs a sufficient period to develop and mature before it can be assumed to determine corporate behavioral patterns, it can be theorized that Inditex has not yet completed any habitualization processes.

Rio Tinto

Rio Tinto has always drawn serious criticism, for example for neglect of trade union rights, abuse of indigenous peoples and environmental degradation, to mention a few (ICEM 1997; Jones et al. 2007). Even if the company was one of the 'bad guys' in environmental or human rights issues, it also developed a growing awareness and acceptance of these responsibilities early on. Concerning outward directed beyond-profit activities, Rio Tinto engaged heavily in community support and established social infrastructure wherever it operated, for example already at the beginning of the twentieth century in Spain (McIntosh and Thomas 2001 xviii). The company always claimed to place high importance on empowering local populations through employment of locals, selling stocks to locals and encouraging locals to be on the company board (Rio Tinto 1973: Foreword). One self-portrayal that stems from a time prior to the global governance debate (with its demands for a new role of business as co-provider of governance functions) is especially telling in terms of Rio Tinto's perception of its community engagement at the advent of the 'new age'. It understood its responsibility toward communities as the support of local industries, agriculture, and enterprises (Rio Tinto 1992: 11) and stated that 'the overriding principles which run through all the activities are partnership with the local community and the promotion of self sufficiency' (Rio Tinto 1992: 11; Duncan 1967: 24).

Rio Tinto's awareness of political responsibility is demonstrated by its subsidiary operating in Apartheid South Africa, stating already in a publication of 1987 that Rio Tinto 'is utterly opposed to Apartheid' and making all its payments under the European Economic Committee Code of Conduct. All salaries were above the general standards (Rio Tinto 1987: 1–2). The company won the Top Safety Award of the National Occupational Safety Association in 1986 in South Africa (Rio Tinto 1987). The following quotation is especially indicative of Rio Tinto's awareness of having to respond to changing external demands: 'the philosophy of a rapidly expanding company presumably must be constantly evolving to meet the changing world scene and, particularly in our case, the changing political conditions and attitudes of governments' (Wright 1968).

Shell

Shell got the attention of a critical transnational public in the 1990s, mainly for its involvement in tragedies, such as the hanging of Ken Saro-Wiwa in Nigeria, and scandals, like Brent Spar. While acknowledging that severe company misdeeds were causal in these events, the company must also be considered as one of the early examples of corporations accepting responsibility beyond profit interests. As one of the most visible early artifacts of this, in 1976, following a bribery scandal in Italy and accusations of selling oil to then Rhodesia (Zimbabwe) despite official embargos, the company drew up a set of principles describing its responsibilities in a variety of issue areas such as corruption, health, safety, and environment issues. Shell named four groups to whom it was responsible: shareholders, employees, customers, and society – with responsibilities to society at the center of the principles. Each Country Chairman was personally responsible to ensure respect for the principles and had to report about their implementation on an annual basis at headquarters. Managers faced 'serious consequences' for violation and persons violating the core principle, the prohibition of corruption, were fired – which made the company 'revolutionary' at the time (Stadler 2004: 134, see also 147–54).

Sasol

Sasol is a very delicate case of exhibiting a culture of responsibility. South Africa not only is the company's home state but Sasol was a state-owned company already during apartheid and is therefore easily associated with the policy of apartheid itself. In fact, activists seeking to put pressure on the government often targeted Sasol (FundingUniverse 2008). Remarkably, even before the end of the apartheid regime, there were statements like the following from Sasol: 'Sasol's ethical responsibility extends beyond its shareholders and the technological milieu in which it operates. It also has a social responsibility toward its own people, the communities in which it operates and the country as a whole' (Wessels 1990: 142).

Sasol has a record of extensively engaging in larger community affairs. For example, it built two complete towns, Sasolburg and Secunda, as extensions of its operational facilities. The company's activities in the administration of these towns went far beyond donations to schools or hospitals. For instance, at Secunda it established a health committee that represented the first local authority in a town which did not officially exist. Elected representatives later replaced this authority, thus the management of Sasol established democratic structures (Wessels 1990: 38–62). Sasol staff were authorized to execute governance tasks such as provision of order and security, medical services, and education (Wessels 1990: 64).

Sasol's behavior in racial politics is ambiguous. On the one hand, Sasol built separate towns for white, black, and colored people at Secunda. On the other hand, 'blacks were trained on a scale never before equaled in South Africa' (Wessels 1990: 38, 64).

In the 1970s, Sasol launched an informal environmental management system, which was the precursor of modern standards like ISO 14001 (Sasol 1996: 24). Later in the 1980s, the company's executive board deliberately lowered extraction rates to enhance mine safety and decrease negative impacts above ground (Sasol 1996: 29–30). The corporation also engaged in voluntary environmental impact assessment with local authorities before building some of its facilities (Sasol 1996: 35). In 1991, Sasol signed its first official environmental policy and revised it in 1995 (Sasol 1996: 5).

Sasol was a strong promoter of education that was considered crucial for social and economic development. In 1977, the corporation established its own primary school and installed comprehensive training programs for unskilled workers, the scope of which extended much further than the projects themselves and made an important contribution to the country's overall skilled labor market (Wessels 1990).

Tata

Tata has always portrayed itself as more than just a commercial enterprise. There is strong evidence of a culture of responsibility in many issue areas. In inward oriented policies, relations with employees are characterized by a 'human attitude' where 'man is the core of Tata Steel' (Pandey 1989: 13). Social services and labor welfare were incorporated in Tata's activities in the 1930s. JRD Tata, who led the company from 1938 to 1988, was a forerunner but already said of Tata's founder Jamshedji Nasarwanji Tata 'the way he thought about workers nobody in India or abroad thought at that time' (quoted in Lala 1992: 197). Tata introduced the 8-hour working day in 1911 when other steel companies still had ten or twelve hour working days (Lala 1992: 238). Tata is reported to have had 'a tradition of providing excellent welfare measures for employees' and medical services as well as education in the corporation's 26 schools were free for employees until class X' (Pandey 1989: 264). In 1947, the company created an employees department, the first of its kind in India (Tata Steel 2007). Its functions extended to social services and supervision of compliance with the provisions of the Factories Act and the Mines Act, public relations work, [...] maintenance of contacts and relations with the workers' union, supervision of conditions of work and payment of wages of contractors' labor (Pandey 1989: 17–18).

Tata's high regard for social issues beyond its profit activities is best summarized by the following quotation: 'Probably no other family has ever contributed as much in the way of wise guidance, economic development and advancing philanthropy, to any country as the Tatas have to India, both before and since Independence' (John Canning, quoted in Lala 1992: 307).

UBS

UBS has a remarkable record of beyond-profit activities that leaves little doubt of the existence of a culture of responsibility in this company. In terms of internally oriented policies, gender equality has been high on the agenda since the 1980s. From 1983 to 1996, the percentage of women in the company rose from 5.1 percent 12.9 percent, and in 1991 UBS, together with other banks, worked out a concept to ensure equal opportunities, enhancing the compatibility of family and work life. In the same year, UBS opened the first day nursery for its employees (Rogge 1997: 310–11).

The bank was regarded as a pioneer in retirement issues as early as 1920. Its service always went beyond what the law required. The bank offered an early retirement option, implemented its own casualty insurance before it was required by law, and has offered voluntary health insurance since 1987 (Rogge 1997: 322–30). The UBS communication policy, originally following Swiss banks' general preference for secrecy, began to change during the 1960s to a permanent seeking of 'understanding and sympathy' for the bank's cause (Rogge 1997: 327, 346). This change was brought about partly by negative headlines on money laundering, insider trading, bank confidentiality, Apartheid South Africa, trafficking and Mafia connections (Rogge 1997: 347–8.). A set of due diligence procedures for banking was introduced in 1977, the bank becoming a role model for self-regulation (Rogge 1997: 348). In Apartheid South Africa, the bank made meetings with diverse interest groups, religious parties and charitable organizations routine. Concerning environmental responsibility, in 1990 a company concept was developed that comprised ecology in the corporation, product ecology, personal and education, and communication as the areas of action. Like Deutsche Bank, the other norm-entrepreneur from the banking sector, UBS joined the UNEP Finance Initiative in 1992.

4.3.5 Summary

Most of the sample of ten norm-entrepreneurs had a strong tradition of engaging in beyond-profit activities before they became norm-entrepreneurs. Significant contributions to society were measured in all three indicative areas of internal and external engagement: workers' rights, environmental protection, and political engagement. Especially concerning the latter, the extent to which the ten norm-entrepreneurs sought to take on the issue of apartheid in South Africa is striking. Nevertheless, few of the 10 were comprehensively active in all of these areas equally, with Shell and BP being true exceptions. Instead, as might have been expected, an industry sector bias was observed: the financial businesses seem to orient engagement toward their workforce whereas extractive businesses, such as Rio Tinto or Sasol, primarily foster community affairs. Equally, few of the companies had set up comprehensive departments dealing with all the aspects of corporate responsibility. However, most of the norm-entrepreneurs institutionalized their policies at least to some degree.

4.3.6   Conclusion

The evidence to support the explanatory power of a culture of responsibility is highly significant. Virtually all of the expert interviewees emphasized the importance of culture and tradition in influencing corporate norm-entrepreneurship. A number of them even explicitly reasoned along the lines of this research in stating that norm-entrepreneurship represents a continuation of what their companies had been accustomed to for decades. Additionally, case studies on the corporate histories revealed that at least a significant majority has always been engaged to a notable degree in relevant beyond-profit activities for the benefit of internal and/or external stakeholders. There were no conclusive data on Inditex and skepticism about the few beyond-profit activities of Deutsche Bank. This leaves 8 out of 10 norm-entrepreneurs that had a significant culture of responsibility prior to engaging in norm-entrepreneurship activities.

It needs to be emphasized again that the conceptualization of a culture of responsibility by no means supposes that norm-entrepreneurs have always been do-gooders. It can still be claimed that those who have always attempted to contribute to the provision of public goods, albeit only to a limited degree compared to the potentially negative impact of their overall operations, have developed a cognitive predisposition that made them more likely to follow similarly scripted role behavior when confronted with pathways to norm-entrepreneurship. There might be reason to believe that a minimum level of a traditional culture of responsibility is a necessary condition for norm-entrepreneurship. There are, however, considerable difficulties in defining a threshold for such a minimum, and at least one of the cases in our sample, Inditex, seems to be lacking any discernable and operational corporate culture. Due to its significantly younger age, Inditex could hardly have established a reliable culture of responsibility prior to the timeline watershed in 1992 anyway. The factor also does not amount to being a sufficient condition on its own. Without having included them here, it can be safely assumed that corporations exist that do not qualify as norm-entrepreneurs, at least not as systematic ones but possess a culture of responsibility.

Notes

1. Also often defined as the company's value beyond its financial and physical assets (Epstein 2008: 181).
2. In IR the concept of reputation was first introduced by Jonathan Mercer's challenge of classic deterrence theory (Mercer 1996).
3. In 1978, 5 percent of all assets were intangible; in 1998, 72 percent of all assets were intangible. Currently 75–85 percent of all assets are said to be intangible (Chareonsuk and Chansa-Ngavej 2008).
4. For example, most of the management literature about corporate reputation is interested in reputation capital in terms of market value. An excellent overview of the value of intangible assets is given by Cravens et al. (2003).

5. The comprehensive 'reputation index' approach introduced by Cravens et al. offers important insights into the various components of corporate reputation capital but refers primarily to organizational culture, which is treated as a separate explanatory factor in this study (see Section 4.3). It is mingled with the dependent variable used here by including corporate, social, and environmental policies, for example, by examining whether the implementation of CSR activities leads to gains in a company's reputation and legitimacy (Kurucz et al. 2008: 90–1).

6. A legal name for a brand is a trademark; when it identifies or represents a firm, it is called a brand name (Business Dictionary Online 2008, http://www.business-dictionary.com/definition/brand.html, date accessed 13 March 2009).

7. According to this ranking, 'brands' are subject to five basic conditions: (1) substantial public available financial information, (2) internationality scope – at least one-third of revenues from outside the home state, (3) market facing brands (consumer, not corporate, brands), (4) positive Economic Value Added (EVA), (5) not purely B2B audience (http://www.interbrand.com/best_global_brands_methodology.aspx?langid=1000, date accessed 25 November 2008).

8. Semion Brand-Broker GmbH, a German branding enterprise, rates German companies. However, the criteria of their list differ somewhat from those of Interbrand. They are divided into four main categories: financial value, brand protection, brand strength, and brand image (http://www.branding-kaeuffer.com/value/value2007.html, date accessed 15 January 2009).

9. The data for the United Kingdom stem from Superbrand, an organization that determines brand through the following three criteria: quality (representation of quality products and services); reliability (trust in consistent performance and maintenance of product and service standards at all customer touch points); and distinction (popularity in the brand's sector, suitable differentiation from its competitors, and unique personality and values within market place). (http://www.superbrands.uk.com/, date accessed 15 January 2009).

10. The Delahaye Index used for the United States represents a quarterly assessment of how news media coverage affects the corporate reputation of the hundred largest U.S. companies. The index is calculated in two steps. First, America's most prominent national news sources are reviewed for news coverage of the Top 100 U.S. companies. Then, the result for each one represents a ratio between positive and negative 'reputation-driving attributes' in news stories. Like the aforementioned brand measuring methods, the Delahaye Index also uses five indicators: stakeholder relations, financial management, products and services, organizational integrity, and organizational strength (http://www.finanznachrichten.de/nachrichten-2005-05/4807747-microsoft-tops-delahaye-s-index-of-best-u-s-corporate-reputations-wal-mart-disney-and-verizon-move-higher-as-aig-takes-fall-004.htm, date accessed 25 November 2008).

11. To further substantiate this conclusion an analysis of additional countries (by applying the same methods to a larger sample of random norm-entrepreneurs) could perhaps provide additional insights.

12. A separation between the ownership and control of companies became a widely discussed issue during the twentieth century, especially in the United States and the United Kingdom, where shareholders have tended to be more passive. Managers were viewed as having come to occupy controlling positions as the scale of industry grew. This position has changed to some extent since the 1980s, as privatization, management buy-outs, restructuring and share incentive plans

led to greater shares ownership by managers and produced less passive share-holders.

13. The corporate governance structure is more complex than it initially appears. Most private and publicly listed companies have a board of directors that is responsible for governing the company. The shareholders' role is to appoint the directors and the auditors. The responsibilities of the board include setting the company's strategic goals, providing leadership to put them into effect, supervising the management of the business and reporting to the shareholders on their stewardship. The board's actions are subject to laws, regulations, and the wishes of the shareholders (owners) in the general meeting.

14. Agency costs include the costs of investigating and selecting appropriate agents, gaining information to set performance standards, monitoring agents, bonding payments by the agents and residual losses.

15. According to Barnea and Rubin, insider ownership can have two potential outcomes: on the one hand, the augmentation of the number of insiders should lead to bigger CSR engagement; on the other hand, the bigger the insider share is, the more likely they are to bear the costs of a potential reduction in the firm's value through CSR policies (Barnea and Rubin 2006: 2).

16. This short-term perspective applies an argument similar to the 'managerial opportunism hypothesis' of Consolandi et al. (2006: 2).

17. In contrast to the short-term perspective, a long-term perspective applies an argument similar to the 'social impact hypothesis' (see Consolandi et al. 2006: 11–12).

18. There are different approaches to determining ownership concentration. While some authors, like (Shleifer and Vishny 1986), consider only the largest block of shares, Köke (1999) evaluates the three biggest owners of a company regardless of how much their shares add up to. However, it is widely accepted that 5 percent of a company's shares, which constitutes one of the central legal notification threshold in most share corporation acts around the world, is a feasible indicator.

19. The relevance of corporate culture is supported by the contingency theory in sociology, which claims that a specific situational setting predetermines and confines the choices of organizations (Preisendörfer 2005: 78–94). This argument strengthens the case that the specific corporate strategy of norm-entrepreneurship may not evolve easily from any type of corporate culture but relies on specific preexisting settings.

20. Despite this emphasis on the potential of material rewards for reinforcing habitualization, it is assumed that there is a constructivist mechanism underlying the causal logic of this hypothesis. Nevertheless, the role of corporate culture in fostering norm-entrepreneurship could be constructed according to purely rational logics. Sociology's transaction cost theory, as one of many theories understanding organizations as rational actors, supports this interpretation: Organizational structure is always a function of the transaction problems *(Transaktionsschwierigkeit)* faced by the organization (Preisendörfer 2005: 44). If norm-entrepreneurship is understood as one of a corporation's possible reactions to a problem that imposes especially high transaction costs, it can be expected that this behavioral path can and will only be followed by those actors whose organizational structures already supply the necessary resources, as a result of prior attempts to reduce transaction costs in similar areas. Where no such resources can be relied upon to implement norm-entrepreneurship, transaction

costs might prove prohibitively high for corporations with no such prior experience. Therefore, differently equipped corporations may follow different behavioral paths when faced with similar problems.

21. Gunningham and Rees contend that companies develop a 'moral capacity' and support the importance of socialization processes – reinforced through institutionalization – as a prerequisite for companies becoming responsible. For them, the decisive question revolves around how 'normative principles and practices are built into the operative structure' and they contend 'it is a question of institutionalization' (Gunningham and Rees 1997: 380–1).

5
Institutional Arrangements

5.1 Structural autonomy

International Relations (IR) research on transnational governance arrangements has always accorded an important role to institutional design (Schäferhoff et al. 2007: 16). It is usually differentiated along two dimensions: the number and types of actors participating in the arrangement (actor configuration), and the types of interactions prevalent between the actors within the arrangement (steering instruments) (Börzel and Risse 2005; Scharpf 2000a). Both factors are assumed to have equal influence on the decision by actors to participate and on the performance of the arrangements.

In this Section, these characteristics of governance arrangements are tested for their appeal to corporations that decide to act as norm-entrepreneurs. It is assumed that both aspects, the actor configuration and the steering instrument, are influential in corporate decisions. However, when building on a rationalist model of interaction, where companies anticipate the costs and benefits of their decisions in terms of self-interest preservation, the dimensions of institutional design turn out to be two sides of the same coin: both describe the degree to which institutions guarantee corporate behavioral freedom. Departing from assumptions about actor preferences in actor-centered institutionalism (any actor's self-interest can be defined objectively as the strive for self-preservation, autonomy, and growth (Scharpf 2000a: 117; see also Wolf 2000)), it is assumed that corporations will have a preference for institutions that give them the highest degree of autonomy. This interest in autonomy preservation involves a substantive and a procedural goal: in terms of substance, corporate self-preservation, autonomy and growth are all tied to the institution of the market, meaning corporations view their self-interest as served best through market-enabling and market-preserving measures and rules. In procedural terms, corporate interest in preserving autonomy suggests that they prefer to engage in governance processes that will not constrain their choices more than necessary.

The substantive and procedural aspects of corporate self-interest are closely related. Whenever governance arrangements do not restrain corporate autonomy procedurally, the rules made within these arrangements will most likely serve to establish and maintain markets. Nevertheless, the procedural interest of corporations in autonomy preservation is of special importance when analyzing the appeal of institutional design because both of its dimensions, actor configuration and steering instruments, have the potential to restrict corporate autonomy.

Actor configurations involving other types of actors, such as public or civil-society, limit the autonomy of corporations. Presumably, norm setting by corporations follows different preferences and differs significantly in its logic, mechanisms, and regulatory approaches from norm setting when performed by other actors. To enact their preferences, corporations wish to play a prominent or influential role within the institutional setting of an initiative. Therefore, when the primary impetus within an initiative comes from states or civil society, corporations will have little incentive to participate, remaining in their classic role of norm addressees because they anticipate that their interests and methods of norm design are unlikely to find support. They prefer to engage unilaterally or in purely corporate initiatives. Although a strong state role within an initiative might be useful for enhancing compliance, exactly this fear of coercion may prevent corporations from taking part in the first place.

A similar logic can be assumed in the appeal of the steering instrument to corporations: Steering mechanisms traditionally understood as 'strong' or most effective in constraining behavior, such as sanctions, significantly reduce the autonomy of corporations within a self-regulatory arrangement. Norm-entrepreneurship becomes more likely within 'softer' and more autonomy protecting steering mechanisms. Again, a shadow of hierarchy involving the threat of coercion or 'informal' coercion by monitoring and shaming mechanisms might be effective in ensuring compliance but might not attract norm-entrepreneurship. These considerations led to the following hypothesis:

Hypothesis 7 (H7):   The more a self-regulatory initiative preserves the autonomy of participating companies, the more appealing it will be for companies to engage in norm-entrepreneurship.

The test of this hypothesis proceeds as follows: first, structural autonomy is operationalized as a causal factor by distinguishing between its components, actor configuration, and steering instruments. The literature on each is then reviewed to identify possible causal mechanisms. Finally, corporate engagement in self-regulatory arrangements that have varying degrees of corporate autonomy is analyzed empirically to find evidence of the significance of the two indicators.

5.1.1   Measuring structural autonomy

The configuration of actors

The configuration of actors within a governance arrangement can describe the relative importance of the roles played by actors within self-regulatory initiatives. It is a two-dimensional concept that includes the 'scope' and 'quality' (Dingwerth 2007) of participation. As Koenig-Archibugi notes, research on global governance arrangements has focused on two questions: why international institutions differ in the degree of their inclusiveness and in the relative power accorded to their members in agenda setting, decision making and factual influence (Koenig-Archibugi 2006: 11). The conceptualization firstly captures which types of actors participate within the given framework and differentiates between internationally embedded initiatives which include, as a minimum, business and state actors but that might also involve civil society, private-private initiatives in which business and civil society collaborate without state participation, and purely private initiatives consisting exclusively of business actors. The mere enumeration of participants alone does not provide much information about the relative weight of each type of actor: it is necessary to identify the respective lead actor in each initiative. The lead actor is an actor whose approval is required for all decisions and who therefore possesses a kind of veto power. Accordingly, three types of veto players generate three types of initiatives: state-led, NGO-led, and business-led.

The analysis of actor configurations in governance arrangements and policy networks is a well covered topic in transnational governance research. However, the focus is usually on their influence on policy outcomes (Börzel and Risse 2005) or on the normative evaluation of patterns of participation (Benner et al. 2004), not on their influence on actors' decisions to participate. This question has only been addressed in research on public-private partnerships (PPPs), as one specific type of arrangement.[1] Access to public tender, reputational gains, and knowledge are positioned as the most important incentives for corporations to engage in PPPs. Autonomy preservation is added in this analysis, as another incentive especially important in norm-entrepreneurship initiatives. It is assumed that corporations will only collaborate in norm-entrepreneurship with other types of actors when they are not able to establish or preserve markets on their own – which signifies the substantive dimension of their self-interest in autonomy preservation.[2] Corporations engage in self-regulation – instead of seeking public regulation – whenever effective self-regulation is possible without the state's enforcement power – whether because of an oligopolistic market structure that makes free-riding difficult and monitoring easy or strongly organized business associations that are able to solve collective action problems (Hönke et al. 2008: 17–8; Ronit and Schneider 1999: 245–6). To further support the expectation that corporations generally prefer to act independently at the international level, it could be argued that states cannot make use of their domestic enforcement powers to enforce international rules on foreign corporations.

The steering instrument

Steering instruments vary in the degree and type of obligation, whether legal, cost/benefit or persuasive (Conzelmann and Wolf 2007a, 2007b; Risse 2004). To achieve norm compliance, they may rely on sanctions and hierarchical relationships between the participating actors (Brunsson and Jacobsson 2000; Jacobsson and Sahlin-Andersson 2006) or on vertical relationships and monitoring and evaluating instruments (Power 1997). Even though, in practice, they are often combined and occur in hybrid forms, the following three ideal types are used in the empirical analysis:

1. *Coercion* influences corporate behavior predominantly through pseudo-legal sanctions to ensure compliance. Self-regulatory initiatives employing coercive steering measures typically comprise public actors that have coercive power at their disposal. Coercive steering corresponds to the potential of legal regulation and the 'shadow of hierarchy' exercised by state actors. According to the main assumption, companies that seek to maintain their behavioral autonomy do not engage in initiatives that rely on coercive steering in any extensive way, that is, on the shadow of legal regulation. Corporate norm-entrepreneurship in self-regulatory initiatives that have coercive steering instruments should not be observed, except in times of economic crises when corporations might sacrifice their procedural interest for their substantive one to preserve their autonomy.
2. As a comparatively soft mode, interest based *cost-benefit steering* relies on market mechanisms and assures compliance through monitoring and performance reviews. Costs can either be material (financial losses) or reputational (public naming and shaming). The benefits are competitive advantages deriving from high ratings and rankings and a good reputation. Companies may benefit from the certification or reporting practices of cost-benefit steering by attracting new investors or by gaining a better position in the market for socially responsible investment (SRI). Companies that prefer initiatives that preserve their behavioral autonomy are also more likely to engage as norm-entrepreneurs in initiatives based on cost-benefit steering than on coercive measures.
3. The steering instrument of *information* is based on the mechanism of learning and predominantly corresponds to information asymmetries and knowledge gaps in the company environment. Even more than the instrument of cost-benefit, it represents a soft mode of steering, influencing company behavior without imposing hard sanctions for non-compliance. The idea that steering by information influences corporate behavioral change rests upon the rationale that companies are interested

in information about their environments to reduce uncertainties they face in their daily business activities. Self-regulatory initiatives that focus on steering by information typically include institutional settings such as learning forums or policy dialogues where companies can cooperate and mutually share their expertise and best practice. Another argument, which refers to constructivist thought, is that companies may persuade one another of the appropriateness of certain norms and policies in open discursive dialogues. Because learning activities imply a lack of interference and behavioral autonomy, companies see no additional costs in participating in initiatives that focus on steering by information. Instead, they anticipate benefits such as building capacities and reputation.

5.1.2   Analyzing the role of structural autonomy

Operating under the assumption that there is a general strategic interest in maintaining and increasing behavioral autonomy, corporate norm-entrepreneurship is expected primarily in institutional arrangements that do not constrain this autonomy, that is, within purely private initiatives that focus on cost-benefit or information-based modes of governance. To test this hypothesis, evidence was sought of the two indicators in the self-regulatory initiatives in which the selected norm-entrepreneurs are engaged. If the hypothesis is correct, the norm-entrepreneurs should be found predominately in initiatives that preserve the autonomy of corporations because of their institutional designs. It is a common methodological difficulty that the subjective nature of actor preferences cannot be equated with 'revealed preferences' (Scharpf 2000a). To make sure that their observed participation actually reflects the actors' preferred choices, interview data will be used. Secondly, statements by corporate and initiative representatives are examined to find out whether autonomy preservation is as important to corporate institutional preferences as assumed.

The role of actor configurations

Although purely business-led initiatives, such as the Wolfsberg Principles or the Business Social Compliance Initiative (BSCI), are found in the sample used to identify systematic norm-entrepreneurs, we also find norm-entrepreneurs in initiatives with a mixed actor configuration. In these, norm-entrepreneurs are neither the only nor the lead type. Is autonomy preservation of considerably less importance to corporations than expected?

The mere fact that nonbusiness-led initiatives in which corporations engage as norm-entrepreneurs exist does not prove that corporations have no preference for business-led initiatives. The reasons why such initiatives exist are likely to be multicausal and influenced by more than just corporate preferences. Even among corporations there may be conflicting preferences: They might prefer business-led initiatives for reasons of autonomy preservation and multistakeholder initiatives might appeal to them for reasons of legitimacy perception (Section 5.3). Nevertheless, there is evidence in the secondary data that supports the theoretical argument to a degree. Initiatives conceptualized by business actors alone, or at least led by them from the beginning, rarely evolve into multistakeholder undertakings – whereas initiatives not led by business often become more inclusive over time. A case in point is the Wolfsberg Group: even though its initial steps were undertaken in close collaboration with academic and civil society actors, business took the lead and the initiative, over time, stepped back from the multistakeholder approach and evolved its purely private character (Pieth 2006: 10).

Corporations are active within initiatives that have actor configurations they would not have chosen if they had other options. Interviews with company and initiative representatives suggest that there is a strong preference for institutions that give them independence from the influence of other actors. For example, one representative from a purely private initiative stressed that corporations, as the addressees of the initiative's norms, should be free to decide within the initiative, without interference from politics: 'We have intentionally tried to keep politics out of this process. To put it differently: in the end it is the corporations that have to implement these norms in their supply chains and they should decide how it should be done' (I13, 28 July 2006). Several business representatives pointed out that involvement of other actors might limit opportunities for corporate norm-entrepreneurship and considered their involvement in initiatives such as Global Reporting Initiative (GRI) or the Business Principles for Countering Bribery (BPCB), which are clearly led by civil society actors, as having minor importance. The following corporate statement is a case in point: 'As concerns the GRI, we, just like other corporations, have only given some feedback. [...] The same goes for the BPCB. [...] There was nothing that could be qualified as regular dialogue. That can hardly be compared to our engagement with the GC, not to mention the Wolfsberg Group, where we developed the whole thing by ourselves' (C3, 12 September 2007).

Another argument frequently put forward by interviewees was that cooperation among corporate peers who used to perceive each other exclusively as competitors is a value in itself: '[These standards] were developed by peers. This is very important that the competitors participated in the creation of the principles. [...] This actor configuration was optimal' (I2, 27 March 2006). Another interviewee appreciated 'that corporations the size of ours took the initiative to cross what we would normally see as competitive boundaries and consult with each other and try to come up with standards or what we would refer to as norms' (I9, 23 May 2006). Such statements prove that initiatives with exclusive cooperation between corporations are seen as fulfilling important functions that are less likely to be achieved in the presence of other actors. Corporate representatives also emphasized their uniqueness as experts on relevant subjects and their ability to develop adequate and realistic standards superior to the usually imprecise ones set by the public sector: 'Very often what we need is to convey these topics to non-experts. [...] And when I approach them with the OECD guidelines or the UN Charter, they just run off' (C3, 12 September 2007). The following statement demonstrates the fundamental doubt whether intergovernmental processes can achieve genuine collaboration: 'There was very little interaction with the private sector about what they desire the private institutions to do. [...] So it was desire for information rather than a common collaboration which perhaps may have yielded different results' (I9, 23 May 2006).

Apart from all these statements supporting the autonomy assumption, it was also suggested that multistakeholder processes are essential in a corporation's decision to get involved in norm-setting activities: 'The coalition approach, the multistakeholder approach, bringing in NGOs and trade unions and businesses all the time, at every point makes it possible to produce a more mature program, more sensible approaches, and is more likely to be successful' (I3, 27 March 2006). The importance of creating a common understanding of a problem through involving all relevant actors was underlined: 'There is a bias towards multiparty structures, particularly since in our industry not everybody has a common understanding on these issues. So if we were to do it on an industry level, we probably would have not got very far' (C6, 20 November 2007).

It is difficult to draw clear conclusions about the relevance of autonomy preservation to corporate norm-entrepreneurship decisions from such a diversity of statements on the preferred configurations of actors. Nevertheless, the fact that initiatives exclusively or at least significantly led by corporations rarely become more inclusive over time – as is the case with other types of initiatives – suggests a preference for governance arrangements that allow for autonomous rule making.

The role of the steering instrument

None of the six selected self-regulatory initiatives in which the 10 systematic norm-entrepreneurs participated constrains the behavioral autonomy of the participating corporations by coercive measures. As shown in Table 5.1, they all predominantly rely on soft modes of governance based either on information or cost-benefit as steering instruments. Three out of six focus on steering by information: the Wolfsberg Group, the Global Compact and BPCB, the other three focus on cost-benefit steering: the GRI, SA 8000, and the BSCI.

Some interviewees stressed the importance of ongoing policy dialogues in the Global Compact, 'because you can come back and tell your colleagues what other groups are doing and report their views' (C7, 21 November 2007).[3] However, the 'softness' of the Global Compact's governance mode was questioned: 'If you say the Global Compact (GC) has neither formal monitoring [...] nor sanction mechanisms in the case of non-compliance,

Table 5.1 Steering instruments and norm-entrepreneurship

Steering instrument	Self-regulatory initiative	Distribution of systematic norm-entrepreneurs
Cost-benefit	GRI	10
	SA 8000	2
	BSCI	1
Information	Wolfsberg Group	3
	Global Compact	10
	BPCP	6

there are still [...] informal sanction mechanisms: If we are committed to the GC, and effectively non-compliance behavior [is demonstrated], this is a contradiction. If this becomes public, our reputation is affected, thus we are sanctioned by the public. For us, this poses a great risk. For smaller and less known corporations this, certainly, implies less of a risk' (C2, 11 September 2007). These informal or public sanctions are still far less tough steering instruments than coercion.

All banks in the sample – Credit Suisse, Deutsche Bank, and UBS – engage in the Wolfsberg group, an example of a self-regulatory initiative solely relying on steering by information and having the main intention of providing guidance and best practice on how to design banking operations. The initiative does not strive to monitor or enforce the standards nor are there any other formal mechanisms to ensure compliance and implementation. Each of the guidance documents issued or revised by the group has undergone an extensive process of consultation. One company representative described the autonomy preserving 'beauty of this approach, [...] that it's still down to the individual company to decide how they handle this' (I9, 23 May 2006).

Somewhat surprisingly, cost-benefit is not less popular as a steering instrument than the even softer information. All systematic norm-entrepreneurs participate in the GRI, an illustrative example of an initiative focusing on cost-benefit steering. This finding may be indicative of a more general trend toward reporting (C7, 21 November 2007) but – more importantly here – it also stresses corporate preference for market affiliated cost-benefit steering: 'In the end, the market is the driving force. The GRI is a very market driven institution. Finally, in everything we do we want the markets [to] react and to establish it as mainstream. And of course, we listen to what the markets say. We listen very little to politics' (I11, 30 May 2006).

None of the initiatives where the systematic norm-entrepreneurs are active rely on coercive elements to any extensive degree. This is in accordance with the findings from the qualitative interviews on cost-benefit and information steering, which are generally preferred by companies, and supports the preliminary assumption that corporate norm-entrepreneurs are more likely to engage in initiatives that preserve their behavioral autonomy by using softer modes of steering. However, the question remains of whether initiatives that include coercive steering instruments generally inhibit corporate norm-entrepreneurship. The qualitative data gained from the interviews give a mixed picture about the compatibility of coercive steering and corporate norm-entrepreneurship.

To find out whether coercive elements in self-regulatory initiatives are incompatible with norm-entrepreneurship, it is interesting to look for an initiative that expanded or changed its mode of steering over time by introducing coercive elements. In such a case, companies could resign from the initiative, accept the changes without actively protesting against them, or actively lobby for and support the introduction of coercive elements. According to the hypothesis, companies would be expected to resign from an initiative after these institutional changes were introduced and there would be an overall decline in levels of corporate norm-entrepreneurship within the initiative, perhaps accepting changes but not supporting the introduction of coercive elements.

The UN Global Compact is probably the most well known example of self-regulatory initiatives (Kell and Levin 2003; Schorlemer 2003; Rieth 2004). It has gradually introduced coercive steering elements. As an originally 'non-coercive approach toward corporate responsibility' (Thérien and Pouliot 2006), the Global Compact was intended to be neither a regulatory instrument nor a code of conduct, but a value-based platform designed to promote institutional learning. Companies were welcome to participate in a number of available engagement mechanisms, but not required to (Kell 2003). The Global Compact was not originally designed, mandated ,or equipped to monitor or measure participant performance or norm compliance.

In 2005, the former UN Secretary-General, Kofi Annan, on the recommendation of the Global Compact Advisory Council, introduced formal procedures (Integrity Measures) that marked a move toward more coercive steering elements. Companies were required to communicate annually to their stakeholders on progress made in implementing the ten principles. Companies failing to issue this Communication on Progress (CoP) are listed as 'noncommunicating' upon missing the first annual deadline, then as 'inactive' when they miss the second consecutive annual deadline, then delisted. The delisting policy was first implemented in January 2008, when 394 companies were removed from the list of participants.[4]

Despite the comprehensive review of the governance system of the Global Compact and the large number of companies that were removed from the participant list, the overall number of participants continues to rise. During the first half of 2008, 701 new companies joined the Global Compact, increasing the total number of business participants to 4619, and the total number of all participants – companies plus nonbusiness stakeholders – to 5982.[5] Of the 71 sporadic norm-entrepreneurs examined here, 39 are active as norm-entrepreneurs within the Global Compact. Despite coercive steering elements being introduced, none of these companies left the initiative after 2005.[6] One sporadic norm-entrepreneur, Banco Santander, one of the world's leading banks, even signed up to the Global Compact after the establishment of the Integrity Measures. An even stronger indicator of the least expected scenario is that companies actively participated in establishing the Integrity Measures. This includes the 10 systematic norm-entrepreneurs, which all continued their engagement, if not actively supporting the change after 2005. While companies are more likely to engage in initiatives that focus on noncoercive steering measures, the case of the Global Compact illustrates that coercive elements do not necessarily inhibit corporate norm-entrepreneurship.

5.1.3 Conclusions

The empirical findings on both aspects of structural autonomy indicate that corporate norm-entrepreneurship is more likely to occur in self-regulatory initiatives that preserve corporate autonomy. Autonomy is not severely restricted in any of the initiatives in the sample. Corporate and initiative representatives generally acknowledged the importance of room for autonomous corporate engagement in initiatives. These general observations still hold true when disaggregating the findings for each of the indicators – although with some necessary qualifications. While none of the initiatives in the sample employ fully coercive steering instruments (strongly supporting the hypothesis), corporate norm-entrepreneurship goes hand in hand with a variety of actor configurations – a finding that seems to reduce the significance of this variable. However, the interviews showed that corporate representatives view their activities within purely private sector initiatives as a higher quality of norm-entrepreneurship than their activities within the two private-private and NGO-led initiatives of the sample. This again supports the assumption that norm-entrepreneurship needs a certain amount of room for autonomous corporate behavior – implying that governance arrangements that provide this room are more appealing to potential norm-entrepreneurs. Corporations also seem to view their autonomy as being more restricted by the involvement of civil society than by public sector actors.

Actor centered institutionalism might provide a clue as to why corporations still engage in initiatives involving public actors despite their preference for autonomy preservation. Conflicting preferences can arise when actor preferences have multiple components, such as self-interest, normative expectations, and identity (Scharpf 2000a: 117–18). While they may prefer purely private self-regulation for reasons of self-interest in autonomy, they might seek public-private forms of co-regulation because of normative expectations (Section 5.3).

Autonomy preservation and the corresponding institutional design provide neither a necessary nor a sufficient explanation: in fact, none of the causal factors of self-regulatory initiatives can. All 10 systematic norm-entrepreneurs also engage in initiatives whose characteristics run contrary to assumptions. Within each of the initiatives that fulfill the criteria of autonomy preservation, there are corporations who are only norm-consumers. In addition, the case study on the Global Compact shows that corporations actually tolerate higher levels of coercive mechanisms than the hypothesis suggests. Some systematic norm-entrepreneurs even contributed to their introduction.

5.2   Flexibility

Institutional flexibility is a descriptive term that characterizes the features of international organizations and regimes that enable them to cope with new challenges more effectively. In particular, it is a key dynamic in European integration (Warleigh 2002). Other examples of flexible or 'dynamic' (Gehring 1994) institutions are the World Trade Organization's (WTO) Special and Different Treatment (SDT) and the Clean Development Mechanisms and Joint Implementation within the Kyoto Protocol. In this study, flexibility characterizes a design pattern in collective transnational governance arrangements: the existence or absence of institutional structures and procedures that allow for change. Flexible design patterns are continually reshaped in the repeated interplay between participating actors. The assumption here is that collective norm-entrepreneurship may be more attractive to corporations if the envisaged or already existing institutional design of a collective self-regulatory arrangement fulfills certain requirements for flexibility.

To conceptualize the flexibility of self-regulatory initiatives as a 'pull factor' for engagement, a concept from sociology and IR research is employed. This concept of flexibility distinguishes the extent to which institutions have static or flexible structures and procedures. Rather than examining the impact of such differences on the effectiveness of institutions, the interest lies in the attractiveness of the differences to potential corporate norm-entrepreneurs. As a design pattern of self-regulatory initiatives, flexibility is assumed to exert an influence on actors' decisions to participate. The underlying causal mechanism refers to a rationalist model of interaction: the flexibility of self-regulatory initiatives is a factor in the cost-benefit analysis that influences the decision to engage as a norm-entrepreneur. However, the effects attributed to flexibility are controversial. On the one hand, flexibility can decrease the costs of external complexity by creating common rules of behavior for all participating actors. On the other hand, highly flexible institutions can increase the costs of cooperation by requiring permanent behavior change. The middle ground position assumes that companies engage in institutions that have moderate flexibility, seeking to reduce regulatory complexity by participating in flexible institutions only when the costs of behavioral adjustment do not outweigh the benefits.

Hypothesis 8 (H8): The more a self-regulatory initiative consists of moderately flexible institutions, the more corporations are likely to engage as norm-entrepreneurs.

In the following, the causal mechanisms underlying Hypothesis 8 are described. Three self-regulatory initiative types are used as indicators to measure degrees of flexibility: technical, procedural, and meta flexible. In the empirical test on the causal link between corporate norm-entrepreneurship and the flexibility of transnational governance arrangements, engagement by the 10 systematic norm-entrepreneurs is related to the degree of flexibility in the six self-regulatory initiatives, introduced in Chapter 2.

5.2.1 Underlying causal mechanisms

Looking for reasons why and how the flexibility of institutional arrangements influences corporate norm-entrepreneurship, useful links can be drawn to research in which, as an equivalent to institutional structures enabling behavioral change, flexibility constitutes part of the design pattern of political institutions. The latter are commonly understood as 'systems of rule in which goals are pursued through the exercise of control' (Rosenau 1997: 145). These institutions indirectly affect the incentives for action and ideally help to solve collective action problems. In rational choice theory, institutions therefore serve as settings of 'strategic interactions among individuals who calculate the costs and benefits of an action and then make the choice that maximizes their goals' (Levi 1987: 685; Hall and Taylor 1996: 10–13). According to Levi, participating actors create and maintain institutions through their choices (Levi 1987: 687). Thus, the flexibility of political institutions is a contextual factor, framing strategic interactions and affecting actors' behavior, primarily providing greater or lesser degrees of certainty about the present and future behavior of others.

There are two contradictory views about which kind of institutions are more attractive for actors; flexible or static. In the literature on the performance of economic institutions, North refers to the persistence of stable institutions as an incentive structure that encourages individual effort and investment in physical and human capital and in new technology (North 1990). Similarly, the stability of institutions has emerged as a dominant factor in various conceptual approaches that explicitly assume political institutions to impact on actors' behavior (Pierson 2004; Thelen 2004). As sociological institutionalism stresses, static institutions provide institutional stability and are more attractive to actors in their efforts to overcome external uncertainty and constraint. This leads to the creation of homogeneous institutional structures, also referred to as 'institutional isomorphism'[7] (DiMaggio and Powell 1983). The idea of actors preferring static institutions relates back to a rational choice model of interaction suggesting that actors strive for the benefits from preventing the uncertainty that surrounds political institutions. Stability represents a viable part of the operational capability of a given institution and guarantees reciprocal credibility on the part of participating actors. In this understanding, flexible structures and procedures raise security concerns of actors and may threaten an institution's credibility[8] (Labitzke 2008: 38–9). Applying these considerations to this study, companies hesitate to change institutional rules because, although reform might allow them to realize an immediate gain in the issue – at hand, there is great uncertainty about the potential impact of new rules and decisions not yet foreseen (Shepsle 1986).

However, a different body of literature regards static institutions as inadequate because they generally restrict an actor's behavioral autonomy. Relating this approach to institutional incentives for corporations to act as norm-entrepreneurs, Mark-Ungericht and Weiskopf argue that static institutions constrain corporate actors to a clear definition of where their responsibility begins and ends (Mark-Ungericht and Weiskopf 2007: 293). Companies might therefore be interested in flexible institutions that offer an enabling setting for corporate adjustments to complex external circumstances. A flexible institution can provide relevant information about the actions that others are likely to take in response to or simultaneously with the actor's own action.[9] Moreover, they affect individual action by altering an actor's expectations, offering institutional structures and procedures that enhance an actor's ability to adapt to new situations (Koremenos et al. 2001: 773). Relating these considerations to corporate norm-entrepreneurship, the voluntary and innovative nature of some self-regulatory initiatives may facilitate corporate engagement (International Organization of Employees 2003: 5–6). Therefore, corporations may favor flexible over static institutions as the flexible institution can provide opportunities to develop and freely select more compatible and appropriate measures.

In summary, there are two contradictory views in the literature. The middle ground is taken in this study: it is assumed that moderately flexible initiatives are most attractive to corporations performing cost-benefit analyses to determine engagement. Moderately flexible institutions allow companies to pursue their own interests directly whilst engaging in collective processes of norm setting and norm development (Warleigh 2002: 33) and without bearing the costs of permanent behavior change. Accordingly, we expect that corporate norm-entrepreneurs tend to avoid inflexible and highly flexible institutions: inflexible institutions inhibit adjustment to external demands and highly flexible institutions impose costs because they demand permanent behavior change.

5.2.2 Measuring flexibility

Self-regulatory initiatives can be highly flexible, moderately flexible, and inflexible. Flexibility matters at the meta, procedural, and technical levels of a self-regulatory initiative. The levels are used here to measure flexibility.[10]

Technical flexibility facilitates the alteration (creation, development, abandonment) of technical standards. Its material output follows practical requirements associated with problem solving. It is the most common type of flexibility.

Procedural flexibility reflects the structural aspects of governance and concerns institutional output, such as the creation of rights and obligations that help to calculate the behavior of other actors. In this study, procedural flexibility indicates changes in the institutional practices and procedures that occur while the institutional framework of a self-regulatory initiative evolves over time.

Meta flexibility refers to changes in the universal principles and norms that govern the governors. They are usually moral in nature and aim to respond to an existing normative gap through normative output. In this analysis, meta flexibility indicates changes in the fundamental aims and principles of a self-regulatory initiative. These changes typically comprise the creation, development, and alteration of constitutional norms, for example, the addition of the tenth principle to the Global Compact. There are not a large number of self-regulatory initiatives featuring meta flexibility, due to their focus on problem fields, such frameworks usually remain robust. Self-regulatory initiatives are classified according to their flexibility as follows: Initiatives with only technical flexibility (if they have any at all) have a 'low flexibility'; initiatives that include technical and procedural flexibility are regarded as 'moderately flexible'; and initiatives with technical, procedural, and meta flexibility qualify as 'highly flexible'.

One example of an initiative with low flexibility is the European Eco-Management and Audit Scheme (EMAS). EMAS does not have institutional structures or formal procedures that allow for direct corporate engagement in norm-related processes, even though EMAS includes complex, institutionalized rules and procedures to ensure the norm compliance of participating corporations.[11] As an extremely static initiative, EMAS does not provide much opportunity for companies to be involved in norm setting and development processes. In contrast, the Global Reporting Initiative (GRI) is an example of a highly flexible initiative with technical, procedural, and meta flexibility. Established in 1999 to create a globally accepted framework for corporate sustainability reporting (Kolk 2003; 2004), it includes highly flexible structures. All GRI norms involve an ongoing, formal, and highly institutionalized review procedure (Global Reporting Initiative 2002). The development of the GRI reporting guidelines takes place in a three-phase review cycle during which GRI participants can submit their input if desired (Gee and Slater 2005). During a 90-day Public Comment Period (phase 1), companies comment on a draft document of the reporting guidelines. Comments received in this period are reviewed by the GRI Technical Advisory Committee and find their way into a new pilot version of the reporting guidelines (phase 2). Companies are able to use and test the pilot version of the reporting guidelines as the basis for their sustainability reporting practices for one year. After the pilot version is available, the GRI establishes a Structured Feedback Process (SFP) (phase 3). In this phase, companies contribute reports on their individual experience with the pilot. Based on the results from the SFP, the Technical Advisory Committee, the Board of Directors, and the Stakeholder Council release a new version of the reporting guidelines that then enters into a new institutional review cycle. Moreover, the GRI offers several institutional settings, such as working groups or sector supplements, to develop indicators for industry sectors in permanent norm development processes. All these manifold structures and procedures qualify this initiative as highly flexible. However, the GRI is not attractive to all companies wanting to engage in norm setting and norm development processes because of the high costs of permanent behavior change.

According to the hypothesis here, moderately flexible initiatives, where the benefits of behavioral adjustment outweigh the costs, are the most attractive ones to companies who want to engage in norm setting and norm development processes. An example of an initiative with technical and procedural flexibility is the Extractive Industries Transparency Initiative (EITI)[12], established in 2002, which aims to improve transparency and accountability in the extractive sector. The EITI Business Guide outlines how companies can support the implementation of the initiative at the national level by, for instance, taking part in a multistakeholder process. With the establishment of the EITI Board in 2006, the initiative responded to growing needs for strategic direction, credibility, outreach, and advocacy.

5.2.3   Empirical analysis of the role of flexibility

In measuring the role of institutional flexibility as a 'pull factor' attracting collective corporate norm-entrepreneurship, quantitative data from company publications, secondary sources on self-regulatory initiatives, and qualitative data from expert interviews were used to relate the engagement of the 10 systematic norm-entrepreneurs in the six initiatives introduced in Chapter 2 with the degree of flexibility within these governance arrangements. For Hypothesis 8 to hold true, all of the initiatives in which the systematic norm-entrepreneurs engage have to qualify as moderately flexible. Table 5.2 applies the flexibility indicators to the six initiatives.

This overview indicates that all initiatives include at least technical and procedural flexibility. Comparative analysis of the six self-regulatory initiatives shows that no initiative offers only technical flexibility, supporting the assumption that static initiatives do not facilitate engagement in corporate norm-entrepreneurship. This conclusion is further confirmed by expert statements, such as one interviewee's praise of a self-regulatory initiative whose 'principles are not carved in stone forever' (I7, 15 May 2006). Similarly, one representative explained his company's support for a certain collective norm-entrepreneurship framework 'because it is not a static process. It is an evolutionary process and it evolves as is required by the evolution of the industry and the evolution of the regulatory environment' (C10, 23 May 2006). 'The risk of an initiative being too inflexible and therefore to lose relevance over time' was also measured against the opposite problem 'that certain initiatives develop too fast for certain companies' (C2, 11 September 2007).

Such statements confirm the middle ground assumption that moderate flexibility is the most attractive initiative architecture to companies wanting to engage in corporate norm-entrepreneurship. Three initiatives – the Global Reporting Initiative, the Global Compact and the Wolfsberg Group – have technical, procedural, and meta flexibility and therefore qualify as highly flexible. Nevertheless, they have attracted corporate norm-entrepreneurship. Does this contradict the assumption that highly flexible institutions constrain corporate norm-entrepreneurship? A company representative highlighted while discussing the Global Reporting Initiative that highly flexible institutions do not necessarily constrain corporate norm-entrepreneurship: 'We see the changes in the guidelines themselves as a positive approach and one that we embrace. It is definitely not a burden on us. We are actively involved in the whole process of reviewing the guidelines and I would not say negotiating but interacting with the Global Reporting Initiative in terms of how we see how the next generation should be' (C5, 8 November 2007).

The sample was then broadened beyond the six initiatives referred to so far to find where the 10 systematic norm-entrepreneurs engage in other collective processes of norm setting and norm development. If institutional arrangements with low flexibility do not attract companies, the systematic norm-entrepreneurs should not be engaging in such initiatives. As shown in Table 5.3, the 10 companies additionally engage in the Voluntary Principles on Security and Human Rights,[13] the Equator Principles,[14] the Partnering Against Corruption Initiative,[15] Extractive Industries Transparency Initiative, and the European Telecommunications Network Operators' Association.[16]

5.2.4   Conclusions

All of these additional initiatives that corporations have engaged in as norm-entrepreneurs (Credit Suisse in the Equator Principles; France Telecom in the European Telecommunications Network Operators Association; BP and Shell in Extractive Industries Transparency Initiative; Shell, BP and Rio Tinto in the Voluntary Principles on Security and Human Rights; and Rio Tinto and Shell in the Partnering Against Corruption Initiative) are moderately flexible. To find the systematic norm-entrepreneurs in these initiatives further confirms the importance of existing flexibility. Despite the great diversity of institutional architectures in transnational governance arrangements, systematic norm-entrepreneurs are predominantly engaged in initiatives that comprise at least technical and procedural flexibility and therefore

Table 5.2 The flexibility of the six selected initiatives

Initiative	Meta flexibility	Procedural flexibility	Technical flexibility
Global Compact	10th Principle	Integrity Measures (2005); new governance framework (August 2005), annual updates of governing framework, creation of working groups to advance the core issues	'How To' guides; additional measures at the point of commitment (corporate board approval required along with CEO commitment)
Global Reporting Initiative	Change from G2 to G3; Increase of sustainability minimum	Working groups; sector supplements	Guidelines updated incrementally from the previous revision cycles; G3 Guidelines draft plan for new revision priorities, (2009–10)
Wolfsberg Principles	Statement on the Financing of Terrorism (January 2002)	Revision of the Wolfsberg Anti-Money Laundering Principles for Private Banking (May 2002)	Introduction of payment message standards in November 2008; update of the definition of Politically Exposed Persons (PEP); release of the Wolfsberg Anti-Money Laundering Principles for Correspondent Banking, (November 2002); statement endorsing measures to enhance the transparency of international wire transfers to promote the effectiveness of global anti-money laundering and anti-terrorist financing programs (with The Clearing House Association LLC)
SA 8000		Social Accountability Accreditation Services (SAAS) started as a department within Social Accountability International (SAI)	Periodical revision – 3rd draft

	in 1997 and formally established as a not-for-profit organization in 2007; Social Accountability in Sustainable Agriculture (SASA) joint the International Social and Environmental Accreditation and Labelling Alliance (ISEAL) research project with the Fairtrade Labelling Organization International (FLO), the Sustainable Agriculture Network (SAN), and the International Federation of Organic Agriculture Movements (IFOAM) launched in January 2002. SASA Final Report on Social Standards and Social Auditing Methodologies (August 2004)	
Business Principles	SME (Small and Medium Enterprises) Edition of the principles, (30 January 2008); creation of external independent verification tool; creation of self-evaluation module	The SME edition includes a practical guidance document on how to develop an anti-bribery program tailored to the size and resources of individual businesses and provides sample codes of conduct and sample rules on gifts and entertainment, an area often problematic for small enterprises. Launched the FTSE 4Good criteria for Countering Bribery in 2006 Launching the UK ACCA Sustainability Reporting Awards
Business Social Compliance Initiative	Working groups (for example permanent working group on system development)	Business Social Compliance Initiative Code of Conduct (March 2004, revised November 2006); Business Social Compliance Initiative Management Manual and Audit Guidelines

Table 5.3 Flexibility assessment of additional initiatives

Initiative	Meta flexibility	Procedural flexibility	Technical flexibility
Voluntary Principles on Security and Human Rights		Steering Committee with rotating membership of governments, NGOs and companies established January 2003 Secretariat established January 2004	Voluntary Principles website launched November 2004 Voluntary Principles Plenary opened participation to more extractive companies, NGOs, and host governments (April 2006) Formal participation criteria introduced May 2006
Equator Principles	New requirement, Principle 10, requiring Equator Principles Financial Institutions to report publicly on their Equator Principles implementation experience	Subsequent updating process in 2006 led to newly revised set of Equator Principles	New Performance Standards introduced February 2006 (much stronger and clearer requirements)
Partnering Against Corruption Initiative		July 2006 First Partnering Against Corruption Initiative Country Signatory Network launched in Romania in collaboration with the American Chamber of Commerce	Partnering Against Corruption Initiative Principles for Countering Bribery

| Extractive Industries Transparency Initiative | International Secretariat opened in Oslo with a 'Transparency Week'. 15 countries welcomed as Extractive Industries Transparency Initiative Candidate Countries in 2007 Extractive Industries Transparency Initiative Board established in September 2006 | Validation methodology agreed by board at meeting in Accra in February 2008 |
| European Telecommunications Network Operators Association | Annual conferences Position papers present member companies' views on a wide range of technical, regulatory and trade issues to EU decision-makers, national governments and the public. They are developed internally by European Telecommunications Network Operators Association (ETNO) working groups or, occasionally, in co-operation with third parties, such as other industry associations. | ETNO's Environmental Charter January 2004 ETNO's environmental reports issued every two years to reflect the trend of Signatories' environmental performance Environmental and sustainability charters |

qualify as moderately flexible. Such an institutional design is most likely to attract corporate norm-entrepreneurship. The empirical test also confirms that initiatives with little or no flexibility do not attract corporate norm setting and norm development. However, cases of corporate norm-entrepreneurship were unexpected found in highly flexible initiatives, such as the Global Reporting Initiative, the Global Compact, the Wolfsberg Group, and the Equator Principles. Corporate norm-entrepreneurship is also possible under conditions of high flexibility. Moderately flexibility in initiatives is a necessary condition in the institutional architecture of a self-regulatory transnational governance arrangement for individual norm-entrepreneurs to engage in collective norm-entrepreneurship. Moderately or highly flexible institutional arrangements do attract corporate norm-entrepreneurship but, as the participation of companies who remain norm-consumers within such initiatives shows, they do not automatically result in norm-entrepreneurship.

5.3   Legitimacy perceptions

The changing character of international relations and the roles of the actors involved have led to an increased interest in the normative foundations of a 'new transnationalism' (Dingwerth 2007). A growing number of studies investigate the legitimacy of transnational governance arrangements; understood as either their 'acceptability', based on normative theory, or 'acceptance' as a sociological phenomenon. Legitimacy is either an end in itself (Wolf 2002, 2006; Held 2005) or instrumental for compliance with certain governance structures (Franck 1990; Hurd 1999). It is assumed that corporations base their decisions on whether to engage as norm-entrepreneurs in a collective initiative on their estimation of the general acceptance of the initiative. This assumption is based on the sociological approach to legitimacy as a social construct or, as Suchman put it, 'legitimacy is possessed objectively, yet created subjectively' and 'represents a reaction of observers to an organization as they see it' (Suchman 1995: 574). This ascription can be 'pragmatic, based on audience self-interest; moral, based on normative approval; and cognitive, based on comprehensibility and taken-for-grantedness' (Suchman 1995: 571). Which of these actually influences a corporation's decision to act as a norm-entrepreneur depends on the causal mechanism that underpins hypothesis 9:

Hypothesis 9 (H9):   The more a self-regulatory initiative is perceived as legitimate, the more corporations are likely to act as norm-entrepreneurs.

5.3.1   Legitimacy for whom and for what?

There is a growing number of studies that either analyze empirically the extent to which transnational governance arrangements can be seen as legitimate (Dingwerth 2007; Pattberg 2005) or devise normative frameworks for such an analysis (Buchanan and Keohane 2006; Flohr et al. 2008; Wolf 2002, 2006). There is less research about how far the legitimacy of these institutions functions as a causal factor. A notable exception – although dealing with a different question – are Beisheim and Dingwerth who analyze the influence of procedural legitimacy characteristics of private transnational governance arrangements on behavior change among norm addressees. They conclude that procedural aspects of legitimacy, such as inclusiveness, deliberativeness, accountability, and transparency, are linked to compliance through three social mechanisms: ownership, social learning or persuasion and social control (Beisheim and Dingwerth 2008). Despite this notable advance in tying legitimacy to outcomes, the findings are not applicable to this study because the factors enabling or inhibiting norm compliance differ from those encouraging corporations to engage in norm-entrepreneurship. Nevertheless, they generally support the view that legitimacy affects corporations' decisions.

In Suchman's typology of legitimacy as something granted by external audiences, pragmatic, moral, and cognitive legitimacy each follow their own logic of self interest, moral persuasion or taken-for-grantedness (Suchman 1995; Cashore 2002). In corporations' decisions for or against norm-entrepreneurship, the causal logic depends on the audience from who corporations seek acceptance: legitimacy can either be understood as acceptance by the general public, including government authorities, by the members of a self-regulatory initiative or by the corporate norm-entrepreneurs themselves.

Acceptance in the eyes of the public

In a classical understanding of corporations as merely strategic profit seekers, their preference for seemingly legitimate initiatives is motivated by rational self-interest, in terms of positive pay-offs or cost-avoidance. In this logic, 'the quest for public acceptance is a central driver' in designing institutions according to legitimacy expectations (Dingwerth 2007: 187) – but it is for purely strategic reasons that corporate actors seek to justify self-regulation as legitimate in the eyes of public authorities and their constituencies who might otherwise call for public regulatory intervention. Consequently, corporate norm-entrepreneurs are likely to cooperate in initiatives that they assume are perceived as legitimate by critical audiences – including public actors – because this offers them the best normative defense for their private rule setting activities (Gunningham and Rees 1997: 366, 370, 391).

Acceptance in the eyes of co-regulators

When acting as norm-entrepreneurs, corporations face the same problems of finding acceptance and ensuring compliance with their rules[17] as other, usually public, actors.[18] A second possible mechanism behind legitimacy as an explanation for norm-entrepreneurs' preference for certain types of collective initiatives could therefore be their interest in enhancing compliance with the norms they want to set. Such a shared perception of legitimacy concerning a given initiative among rule addressees may be an equal or even more potent driver of compliance than coercion, for example (Beisheim and Dingwerth 2008; Franck 1990; Hurd 1999; Porter and Ronit 2005: 51). Where a self-regulatory initiative constitutes a multistakeholder process, corporations might also depend on the acceptance of other types of co-regulators, such as NGOs or public sector participants, to ensure the initiative's success – whether in terms of prevention of regulation or public good provision.

This explanation still implies a merely strategic application of legitimacy, as opposed to a reference to legitimacy that follows the logic of appropriateness. However, it still supposes corporate norm-entrepreneurs to be aware of the role change they undergo when engaging in rule making for actors other than themselves and of the accountability relationships and enhanced normative requirements that they construct and put upon themselves (Koenig-Archibugi 2004). The preference for a certain type of initiative is less a function of the corporate norm-entrepreneur's idea of legitimacy but of its strategic perception of other actors' legitimacy expectations – since the norm-entrepreneurs aim to satisfy these to either enhance norm followership or ensure that the initiative succeeds in whatever the corporations aim to achieve.

Acceptance in the norm-entrepreneurs' own eyes

While the two previously described mechanisms rely on straight forward rationalist understandings of legitimacy used instrumentally by norm-entrepreneurs to achieve their goals, the causal mechanism underlying Hypothesis 9 (the explanatory value of legitimacy perceptions) could also be described by following a constructivist argument. In this case, the legitimacy perceptions of other actors are irrelevant. Corporations' choice to engage in initiatives that fulfill their own legitimacy expectations could either be conscious and – in Suchman's (1995) terminology – based on moral persuasion, or it could flow from habitualization – Suchman's cognitive legitimacy – where a certain type of appropriate conduct has been internalized.

It has to be noted, however, that the legitimacy criteria of norm-entrepreneurs need not necessarily meet the demands of the 'right thing to do' in a moral sense. Following Suchman's logic of pragmatic legitimacy, a rational application of legitimacy criteria might lead corporations to accept those initiatives as legitimate that promise the best material pay-offs. This widely shared assumption is exemplified by the Forest Stewardship Council's interest in increasing its legitimacy (and therefore also its attractiveness) among corporate stakeholders by providing and stressing material incentives to corporations in the form of increased market access (Cashore 2002: 517).

5.3.2 Identifying legitimacy perceptions

As employed here, the sociological construction of legitimacy as acceptance is ascribed to self-regulatory initiatives by corporations. Conceptualizing legitimacy as an independent variable, therefore, clearly requires application of inductive research methods to identify its influence. Accordingly, the prime indicators used here for the variable legitimacy perception are derived from the corporations' own deliberations, most significantly from pronounced reference to it in corporate statements. Since the legitimacy ascribed by corporations can be based on either their own value judgments or their perceptions of the expectations of other actors, the operationalization of the variable has three steps. First, legitimacy criteria are identified that are discussed in the public sphere and could therefore form the basis of corporate perceptions of the public's expectations. Second, the data gathered in interviews with initiative representatives are analyzed as a proxy to explicating the legitimacy criteria employed by co-regulators. Finally, the data gathered from interviews with company representatives are used to reconstruct the corporations' own notions of legitimate governance arrangements.[19] If, as suggested in Hypothesis 9, legitimacy perceptions have an influence upon corporate decisions to engage as norm-entrepreneurs in certain types of collective initiatives, these perceptions should be reflected in corporations' actual behavior – that is, in the institutional design of the initiatives in which they act as norm-entrepreneurs. The last step contrasts data that portray this behavior with corporate deliberations.

Legitimacy criteria in the public sphere

The assumption here is that corporations will prefer to engage as norm-entrepreneurs in those initiatives that actors with a potential influence upon them[20] perceive to be legitimate. In order for corporations to develop an understanding of what other actors might require from a legitimate governance arrangement, such criteria have to be communicated in the public domain.[21] The following three documents were chosen as representative because they explicitly address global governance institutions in which private sector actors are involved. Additionally, it can be assumed that corporations, in seeking to identify other actors' legitimacy demands they might wish to meet, will have distilled their notions about such demands from similar documents:

(1) AccountAbility, a British-based NGO, is dedicated to 'promoting accountability for sustainable development'.[22] In its report, 'Governing Collaboration', 12 global cross-sector partnerships were evaluated on legitimacy, strategy and performance (AccountAbility 2008: 26–7). Legitimacy is reflected in 'structures and policies that clarify authority in decision making, inclusiveness of stakeholders, processes to engage stakeholders, adequate representation of stakeholder interests, establishing mechanisms

to enable all concerns to be voiced, dispute resolution mechanisms, making decisions and performance outcomes transparent, and securing trust among participants' (AccountAbility 2008: 37; see also 28). Despite this rather ambitious list, there is an evident emphasis on input-oriented criteria and process requirements of legitimacy. Aspects relating to effectiveness and output legitimacy are subsumed under strategy and performance (AccountAbility 2008: 39–44).

(2) In 2003, representatives of four major NGOs sent an open letter to the Deputy Secretary General of the United Nations, expressing their concerns about the Global Compact's performance over the previous three years (Amnesty International et al. 2003).[23] Even if not explicitly referring to legitimacy as a concept, but speaking of a need for 'mechanisms' or 'methods of accountability' as being their main concern, expectations of legitimacy in global governance institutions can still be identified in this letter. While placing high importance on output-related criteria in the first three of the letter's four bullet points, the NGOs also stressed the importance of participation by asking that stakeholder involvement be improved, in particular, by having a more balanced and fair selection of stakeholders.

(3) In 2007, the Independent Evaluation Group (IEG),[24] an independent unit within the World Bank Group, published the 'Sourcebook for Evaluating Global and Regional Partnership Programs (GRPP)'. Legitimacy of partnership programs was designed as a criterion to assess the governance and management of GRPPs. It is defined as 'the extent to which the governance and management structures permit and facilitate the effective participation and voice of the different categories of stakeholders in the major governance and management decisions, taking into account their respective roles and relative importance' (Independent Evaluation Group 2007: 76). Further criteria include accountability (which has to be ensured along the chain of command), responsibility, fairness, transparency, efficiency, and personal probity (meaning that members of the governing entities should exercise personal and professional integrity and avoid possible conflict of interests) (Independent Evaluation Group 2007: 75–8). Again, there is an emphasis on criteria for effective participation and accountable procedures. Output-related criteria, such as efficiency and responsibility, are also incorporated (Independent Evaluation Group 2007: 77–8).

Table 5.4 summarizes the criteria found in the three documents and categorizes them along the typologies of Suchman (1995) and Dingwerth (2007):

In summary, while popular demands that legitimacy requirements fulfilled by global governance arrangements cover a wide range of aspects, including the majority of those also addressed in academic treatments of the

Table 5.4 Legitimacy criteria in the public sphere

	Consequential	Procedural			Structural	Personal
		Inclusiveness	Deliberative quality	Democratic control		
Accountability standards	Separate strategy; performance criteria	Inclusiveness; processes to engage stakeholders adequate representation of their interests	Securing trust; space for all concerns to be voiced	Incentives, transparency, and enforcement mechanisms to hold the powerful to account	Dispute resolution mechanism	
Open NGO letter to Global Compact	Evidence of progress; leadership on human rights principles	Stakeholder engagement: balanced selection process of corporations and NGOs		Accountability mechanisms; monitoring of reporting; clear criteria for dealing with noncompliance	Complaint mechanism; ombudsman	
World Bank Sourcebook	Responsibility; efficiency	Effective participation	Fairness	Accountability along the chain of command; transparency		Probity; Professional and personal integrity

subject, the prime concern of external stakeholders such as NGOs or evaluative bodies such as the IEG rests with procedural determinants of legitimacy. Among them, requirements for inclusive processes and accountability mechanisms stand out. The primary points of reference for evaluating the degree to which such public demands have an influence on corporate decisions are the inclusiveness of self-regulatory initiatives and the provision of accountability mechanisms. To assess inclusiveness, relevant indicators are the types of actors who participate (corporate, civil society, public) and whether participants can be considered as representative, for example in terms of geographic proportion. To operationalize the more complex criterion of accountability, it has to be acknowledged that to provide appropriate accountability mechanisms, at least a minimum degree of institutionalization is required. Relevant indicators for meeting this requirement can be a statute or other kind of constitutional foundation of an initiative that clearly outlines governance structures and allocates responsibilities as well as accountabilities along all its levels.

Legitimacy perceptions of initiative representatives

As explained earlier, corporations might seek acceptance of their norm setting activities from several audiences, bringing the legitimacy expectations of different kinds of actors into play. Among these, the legitimacy perceptions of co-regulators can be of special importance. Without their acceptance, a self-regulatory initiative will not come into existence, not allow corporations to participate or not survive periods of pressure or crisis. To assess what the perceptions of co-regulators are and how far they exert an influence on corporations' decisions to engage as norm-entrepreneurs in collective initiatives, the statements of initiative representatives are assumed to be indicative.

The initiative experts' statements provide ample evidence for the importance of legitimacy in general and specific legitimacy criteria. Many of them strongly supported the aspect of inclusiveness and congruency between rule makers and addressees. They explicitly pointed to the need to develop inclusive institutional designs in order to achieve legitimacy: 'I think that the two sides of the effort to maintain our integrity are the multistakeholder nature, that the standard is legitimate and the process is legitimate, that it includes the people who should be included' (I3, 27 March 2006).

However, inclusiveness is not always understood in the classic sense of improving input legitimacy via self-determination but may rather serve as a means to improve results or level the playing fields for corporations. One expert, in line with many others, emphasized the necessity of including the expertise of professional peers in rule setting processes: 'As a corporation I should refer to these principles, because in my opinion they are rather well in line with actual practice and have a certain credibility. They were not developed by a worker's council, an auditing firm or by an NGO. But they were developed by peers. [...] They do not only have the seal of one NGO, but instead, the seal of those affected' (I7, 15 May 2006). This reference to practical relevance points to the underlying, output oriented understanding of legitimacy. The importance of professional expertise as a prerequisite for acceptance by corporations was repeatedly highlighted.

Several initiative representatives also stressed that an initiative is more likely to gain acceptance from its various audiences when it is based on generally accepted norms and rules: 'The legitimization of the principles brings us much "soft power" and support [...], support we would have never earned if the principles were not based on international framework agreements' (I2, 27 March 2006). Initiative representatives repeatedly put forward this argument. Binding norms of international law were recognized to be of special importance here: 'Of course, on the ideational level these principles have the broadest possible global foundation because they are based on conventions and declarations which were signed, ratified and implemented by the vast majority of states' (I1, 27 March 2006).

In addition to the legitimizing force of norms, the importance of collaboration with legally legitimized actors – such as international organizations or governments – was underlined frequently. As one initiative representative put it: 'If one knows that an initiative has intergovernmental blessing and is actively supported by the social partners, one has a completely different foundation for one's own corporate policies in the respective area' (I4, 27 April 2006). The participation of international organizations was also advocated as relevant for another source of procedural legitimacy, namely deliberation: 'I believe legitimacy is a decisive aspect for this initiative. [...] The international organization provides a platform where they [the corporations] can openly and honestly exchange views about the varying challenges' (I1, 27 March 2006). Under the cover of an international organization, a new form of dialogue is deemed possible between the participants – in some cases even leading to role and identity transformation: 'The roof of the international organization offers the chance to get involved with actors who would not have talked to one another only a few years ago, such as corporations and NGOs. In this sense, the initiative's achievement is its pragmatic success in bringing people together in a very constructive dialog. And this is to a large degree due to the international organization and its general acceptance as a public actor who offers a 'non-threatening-environment' (I1, 27 March 2006).

In summary, all expert statements from the initiatives analyzed underscore the critical role that legitimacy of self-regulatory initiatives plays in the corporations' decisions to engage. While their conceptualization of legitimacy places high importance on the criteria of inclusiveness as an aspect prominent in public sphere understandings of legitimacy as well, accountability structures figured less prominently. However, other aspects of legitimacy were not expected to be so prominent and were seen as highly important, in particular the role of substantive criteria for input legitimacy, such as a foundation in international law, and process-oriented criteria, such as room for deliberation.

Although these inputs from the initiative side can only give indirect clues as to how corporations construct legitimacy and how much they are influenced by these constructions, the reasoning for specific legitimacy criteria is of relevance to the hypothesis. From the postulate that legitimacy is a social construct based on collectively shared beliefs and values, it can be assumed that corporate legitimacy perceptions are also based on the views of co-regulators, partly because of the interaction between the participants in self-regulatory initiatives and the resulting possibility of mutually shared understandings. Therefore, the legitimacy perceptions within initiatives are likely to have an influence on corporate constructions of legitimacy.

Corporate legitimacy perceptions[25]

As has been shown, whether it is the corporation's own legitimacy expectations or its perception of others that influences its behavioral decisions depends on the causal mechanism that is operational. Corporations might strategically seek to satisfy external actors' demands for legitimacy or act in accordance with their own understandings of legitimacy, perhaps motivated by material pay-offs, moral convictions, or cognitive habitualization. Which of these logics and therefore conceptions of legitimacy motivates corporate behavior can only be derived from reconstruction of corporate perceptions. Even the legitimacy perceptions of other actors go through this filter and can only exert influence to the degree they find recognition in the corporate horizons.

Explicit reference to the term legitimacy is not the only evidence of corporations looking for public acceptance of their norm setting activities. Whenever corporations attempt to objectivize the sources on which they base their authority, pointing to supposedly objective criteria to justify their activities and invoke external approval, their belief in the importance of legitimacy becomes operational. Justification can be sought in all domains of legitimacy: Corporations might refer to material pay-offs for those affected by their rules, to consequential, procedural, or structural aspects of 'doing the right thing' or to taken-for-grantedness. By demonstrating their perceived need for justification, no matter on what basis, corporations show the relevance of the socially constructed variable, legitimacy perception. Against this background, corporate norm-entrepreneurs could be expected to be active in initiatives fulfilling the criteria identified as most prominent in the public sphere. These are, on the one hand, initiatives that are conceived as multistakeholder forums or that at least allow for multiple actors to participate and affect decision making. Furthermore, one should expect corporate norm-entrepreneurs in initiatives that provide for institutionalized accountability structures and mechanisms to ensure responsiveness to stakeholder concerns.

Looking at the corporate interview data, there are generally less references to legitimacy as a concept and less attempts to justify corporate engagement in norm-entrepreneurship by resorting to possible legitimacy criteria than in the interviews with initiative representatives. This could mean that legitimacy perceptions play less of an important role for corporations in determining decisions about norm-entrepreneurship after all. However, the secondary data on the institutional contexts of norm-entrepreneurship behavior still lend some support to the hypothesis, especially in the criteria of inclusiveness and accountability: Several of the initiatives in the sample exhibit strong multistakeholder characteristics – such as the Global Compact or the Global Reporting Initiative. Both are designed to bring together a large variety of stakeholders, including corporations, business associations, trade unions, NGOs, international organizations, and academia, and offer meaningful roles for these actors at all relevant governance levels. Furthermore, the Global Compact met demands for the improvement of its accountability structure by introducing the 'integrity measures', providing better monitoring and sanction mechanisms. The fact that corporate norm-entrepreneurship takes place in these initiatives suggests that corporations either take external demands for inclusiveness and accountability seriously, or are themselves convinced of the benefit in such institutional designs, notably their multistakeholder character. In fact, the primary interview data reveal that corporate representatives support the importance of multistakeholder processes for their decision to participate based on output oriented reasoning: 'If it is multistakeholder, normally you have companies, NGOs, other levels of civil society and sometimes government. It can be quite frustrating when you are sitting around the table and not all of these groups are equally represented. Because then the initiative starts to fail!' (C7, 21 November 2007).

On the other hand, one can also find several examples of initiatives that clearly contradict the hypothesis: the Wolfsberg Principles and the Business Social Compliance Initiative are exclusively private sector initiatives with no discernible institutionalized role for other types of actors. Looking beyond the sample of initiatives analyzed here, one can easily identify similarly exclusive arrangements that were set up and run by corporate norm-entrepreneurs alone, such as Responsible Care or the Equator Principles. These observations lead to the conclusion that even if corporations seem to value the legitimacy of multistakeholder processes to a certain degree, lack of this variable clearly does not prevent them from cooperating in initiatives not exhibiting it. Initiatives for which the impetus came primarily from within the private sector rarely develop into larger multistakeholder processes but remain pure business initiatives.

Interestingly enough, however, even in the initiatives that are barely multistakeholder arrangements, there are corporate representatives trying to point to the involvement of other actors, however small, to justify the initiative's design: 'The process of developing the guidelines is, of course, maybe led by the members but it is not exclusively up to them to decide. Within the group, there are initiatives that aim to involve other types of actors – such as the transnational ones. The group holds good relationships with individual government agencies and international organizations' (C11, 24 May 2006). Corporations, even if not always acting accordingly, are influenced by perceptions of what is legitimate for global governance arrangements, at least to the degree where they feel a need to discursively acknowledge the validity of certain legitimacy criteria. This justification, referring to the participation of other types of actors, was prominent among the corporate interviewees. To give only one example: 'I believe a success factor for such initiatives is a third party actor who is accepted, credible and disposes of know-how. It becomes obvious when I name the relevant examples: the Wolfsberg Principles with Transparency International, the Equator Principles with the IFC-Guidelines, the Global Compact with the UN as a whole, with ILO or UNEP. [...] It is rather this neutral third party actor who provides communality but also contributes know-how and legitimacy' (C2, 11 September 2007). In many statements, the credibility of third party participants was linked with their expertise and knowledge, their 'broad support in society', and with having 'no reservations against the private sector' (C2, 11 September 2007).

For the second criteria prominent in public demands for legitimacy in global governance arrangements, accountability, it is remarkable that the same initiatives that are dominated rather strongly by business also show comparably low degrees of institutionalization, making it difficult to identify clear lines of accountability. For example, the Wolfsberg Group operates on a totally informal basis. Neither accession criteria nor governance structures have ever been spelled out explicitly. In contrast, none of the initiatives that come close to genuine multistakeholder processes are institutionalized. This leads to the assumption that actors other than corporations generally prefer and push institutionalization and the establishment of accountability structures. Additional evidence of this is that NGOs regularly call for improved accountability of self-regulatory initiatives, whether in initiatives in which they have some sort of voice, such as the Global Compact, or no role at all, such as the Equator Principles (BankTrack 2005).

Institutionalization of accountability structures seems to exert little influence as a pull factor for corporations to engage in collective norm-entrepreneurship – a point further underlined by the fact that there was little discursive reference to these factors. This impression has to be specified, however. Lack of accountability is seen as unproblematic because corporations do not see themselves as acting as a 'half-state authority', supervising and controlling their peers, within private sector initiatives. This distinction reflects the awareness that purely private initiatives lack the legitimacy to regulate third parties. They cannot impose strong accountability features and therefore have to rely on voluntary commitment. Thus, in the corporations' beliefs, accountability demands can only be raised in the context of highly institutionalized forms of regulation, that is, those that are avoided by them if they can choose. This is implied in statements of the following kind: 'Here, one has to differentiate clearly that it is not the aim of the initiative to establish a supervisory authority which verifies that individual corporations, maybe even nonmembers, abide by the best practice. It is a voluntary effort. [...] We do not exist to control who implements the principles, like a governmental agency would' (C11, 24 May 2006).

5.3.3 Conclusions

Legitimacy perceptions are a pull factor in corporate decisions to engage in collective norm-entrepreneurship. However, while there was considerable general support for the relevance of legitimacy, corporate experts seemed to resort to the concept considerably less often than the representatives of self-regulatory initiatives. Additionally, corporate behavior seems to lend only limited support to the hypothesis: Corporations regularly engage as norm-entrepreneurs within initiatives that fulfill few of the most prominent criteria for legitimacy – such as inclusiveness and accountability. Nevertheless, corporate representatives regularly resort to justifications based on legitimacy criteria for their involvement in rule making. In linking these diverging observations of corporations, on the one hand, engaging in initiatives that do not fulfill legitimacy criteria of participation and accountability but, on the other hand, seeking to justify their engagement by referring to these criteria – one could conclude that corporations do accept and engage in legitimacy discourses. This attempt to justify obviously noninclusive initiatives by referring to whatever little room for participation they enable, suggests that corporations are more externally pressured to legitimize their actions than they themselves believe in the value of participatory legitimacy beyond the inclusion of (their) professional expertise. Furthermore, the fact that substantive sources of input legitimacy, such as a base in applicable international law, were prominently applied by co-regulators but did not appear in corporate deliberations, shows the limits of this external influence on corporate legitimacy perceptions.

Corporations are indeed influenced by certain perceptions or discourses of legitimacy but their own conception of legitimacy is rather limited in scope when compared to the expectations of the public or their co-regulators. Even though they rhetorically acknowledge the importance of inclusiveness, a low level of it apparently fulfills their expectations, at least for the input side of legitimacy. Accountability, as a criterion prominent in the public sphere, matters little to corporations or co-regulators. However, corporations seem to be ready to ascribe legitimacy to true multistakeholder processes when they also improve outputs. Even then, they may find it difficult to heed the call of such legitimized initiatives: As shown in Section 5.1, the more inclusive an initiative is, the less room it leaves for corporate autonomy – another value enshrined in corporate preferences. Knowing that 'all selves are self-divided', as pointed out by Walzer, because they simultaneously enact roles, possess identities and hold ideas (Gunningham and Rees 1997: 372), one has to acknowledge that corporations seem to be torn between aims based on moral convictions and those based on self-interest (Scharpf 2000a: 117–18).

Notes

1. Two approaches can be identified (Andonova 2006; Schäferhoff et al. 2007: 10–13). Some authors explain PPPs by referring to a functional logic according to which the transnationalization of problem structures creates a demand for public-private collaboration as the only means of closing the ensuing governance gaps (Reinicke and Deng 2000). In criticism of this it has been asserted that, rather than flowing automatically from whatever governance gap may be identified, PPPs are the product of action by voluntarist political agents whose incentive structures are served best through the creation of a PPP (Andonova 2006).

2. This argument is broadly in line with the findings of Hönke and colleagues who provide an analysis of conditions that influence corporate choices to engage in one of three types of regulation to improve environmental standards – public, public-private co-regulation, or private self-regulation, but within the national context (Hönke et al. 2008: 35–6). In contrast, this research seeks to understand which of the available forums at the transnational level are most attractive to corporations that want to engage in norm-entrepreneurship.

3. However, others were more critical of the intended learning effects: 'I do not know if we learn a lot – specifically from the Global Compact. We learnt a lot from, for example, the network and other UN agencies, etc. Do we go and learn a lot from that? I am not a hundred percent sure' (C4, 10 October 2007).

4. Since then, an additional 236 companies have been delisted – bringing the total number of companies delisted since the policy was implemented to 630. In addition, 317 companies are currently listed as 'inactive' on the website, of which 184 were at risk of being delisted in 2008; http://www.unglobalcompact.org/AboutTheGC/integrity.html, date accessed 6 September 2008.

5. Global Compact 2008; see http://www.unglobalcompact.org/newsandevents/news_archives/2008_06_25.html, date accessed 5 September 2008.

6. Regarding the implementation of the CoP policy, only 1 of the 39 sporadic norm-entrepreneurs failed to provide a link to a CoP on the Global Compact website: in the Global Compact participant list, Esquel Group is marked by a yellow exclamation point that indicates that a Global Compact participant either failed to develop a CoP by the relevant deadline or has not yet provided a link to a CoP. See http://www.unglobalcompact.org/, date accessed 6 September 2008.

7. The concept of institutional isomorphism comprises three distinct mechanisms of institutional change: 'coercive isomorphism' that is stimulated by pressures from other organizations, 'mimetic processes' that result from uncertainty encouraging imitation, and 'normative pressures' that derive from professions entering organizations and thus lead to inter-organizational socialization processes (see DiMaggio and Powell 1983).

8. According to Labitzke, there are five types of institutional change – adaptation (detail changes), reform (reformulation of rules based on common principles), new order (new organization of rules due to a breach of common principles), transformation (phase-like change of the institutional system), and revolution (abrupt change of the institutional system). In this context, it is probable that the more intensive the institutional change the more undesirable it is for companies (Labitzke 2008: 44)

9. Organizations also induce processes of institutional change. These 'transformational organizations' possess the capacity to transform their institutional environment with discontinuous changes in normative patterns or institutional rules (Hage and Mote 2008).

10. This distinction follows Kooiman's three orders of governing: first, second, and meta (Kooiman 2000).

11. Companies that want to receive an EMAS registration have to carry out four clearly defined norm compliance steps: Firstly, they have to conduct an environmental review, considering all environmental aspects of the organization's activities, products and services, methods to assess these, the legal and regulatory framework and existing environmental management practices and procedures. Secondly, companies have to establish environmental management systems aimed at achieving the organization's environmental policy defined by top management. Thirdly, companies have to carry out an environmental audit assessing, in particular, the management system in place and in conformity with the organization's policy and program as well as the company's compliance with relevant environmental regulatory requirements. Fourthly, companies have to provide a statement of their environmental performance that also lays down the future steps to be undertaken to continuously improve environmental performance. An accredited EMAS verifier must approve the environmental review, the audit procedure and the environmental statement, and the validated statement needs to be registered and publicly available before an organization can use the EMAS logo.

12. http://eitransparency.org/, date accessed 21 November 2008. The EITI members are governments, companies and civil society actors working to establish a global standard for managing revenues from natural resources. EITI has been implemented in some countries, is supported by others, and has various stakeholder groups.

13. http://www.voluntaryprinciples.org/, date accessed 23 April 2009. The Voluntary Principles guides companies in maintaining the safety and security of their operations within an operating framework that ensures respect for human rights and fundamental freedoms.

14. http://www.equator-principles.com/index.shtml/, date accessed 23 April 2009. The Equator Principles is a financial industry benchmark for determining, assessing, and managing social and environmental risk in project financing.

15. http://www.weforum.org/en/initiatives/paci/index.htm/, date accessed 23 April 2009. The Partnering Against Corruption Initiative of the World Economic Forum is a business driven effort to combat global corruption.

16. http://www.etno.be/, date accessed 23 April 2009. The European Telecommunications Network Operators Association develops regulatory and trading policies for the European telecommunications marketplace.

17. Although it is questionable whether corporations really are interested in achieving compliance with their self-regulatory rules, such underlying motivation is captured by the previous paragraph about legitimacy as a defense strategy.

18. In Cashore's terms, corporations could be seen here as 'tier I audiences', that is, as 'organizations that have a direct interest in the policies and procedures of the organizations they legitimate'. In his example of forest certification, this is the forest companies, industry associations, forest landowners, environmental groups, and consuming businesses. In contrast, 'Tier II are those audiences within civil society that have a less direct but equally important role in granting legitimacy' and that are distinguished by 'the values and attitudes of civil society' (Cashore 2002: 511).

19. For practical reasons related to the nature of the data, it is not possible to separate the operationalization of sociological legitimacy perceptions – meaning the reconstruction of legitimacy criteria that initiative and corporate experts employed – from the analysis of the influence accorded to them by the same interviewees.

20. See also the chapters on transnational public and ownership structure.

21. Although the criteria will mostly be similar to those identified in academic research on legitimacy (Chapter 8) it is important that the indicators be derived from political or campaigning documents rather than from academic research.

22. http://www.accountability21.net/, date accessed 20 April 2009.

23. http://www.globalpolicy.org/ngos/ngo-un/access/2003/0606compact.htm, date accessed 20 April 2009.

24. http://www.worldbank.org/oed/, date accessed 20 April 2009.

25. As was to be expected, most interviewees accepted and supported the importance of a general notion of legitimacy as it figured in the semi-structured questionnaires. Since legitimacy is a concept generally accompanied by positive connotations, it is no surprise that interviewees did not deny its value. Therefore, instances of mere mentioning of legitimacy are of little validity when not accompanied by further references, proving the interviewee's awareness of its importance prior to the interview situation.

6
Comparisons for Conclusions: Different Paths to Corporate Norm-entrepreneurship

As the causal analysis in the previous chapters has shown, a number of factors influence corporations' decisions to engage in norm-entrepreneurship. Therefore, any attempt at explaining the conditions under which corporations are likely to act as norm-entrepreneurs is necessarily a complex undertaking. Causal factors can result from characteristics of the corporations themselves (Chapter 3) or their environment (Chapter 4) and act as *push* factors for individual norm-entrepreneurship. Other factors emanate from institutional designs of self-regulatory initiatives (Chapter 5) which may be attractive to corporations. The latter can be regarded as *pull* factors, in the sense that they direct corporate norm-entrepreneurship toward engaging in certain collective initiatives, rather than others, or from individual toward collective norm-entrepreneurship. These factors do not explain norm-entrepreneurship itself but the unilateral or collective shape it is likely to assume.

Although it is true for all of the factors that they – at best – increase the probability of corporate norm-entrepreneurship and therefore do not 'cause' it in a strong deterministic or law-like sense, the degree to which they affect companies' choice to act as norm-entrepreneurs still differs. While several factors were found to play a role in all instances of systematic norm-entrepreneurship by the ten companies in this study, none of them provides a sufficient explanation alone. Although they correlate with systematic norm-entrepreneurship, they can also correlate with sporadic norm-entrepreneurship or even only norm-consumership. Against this background and bearing these caveats in mind, it makes sense to focus the analysis by looking more closely at how certain combinations of the factors put to test in the previous chapters can increase the likelihood of individual and collective corporate norm-entrepreneurship. The findings of Chapters 3 to 5 make a distinction between necessary factors or 'conditional variables' (see van Evera 1997: 10) and additional or significant factors, which in certain combinations can pave the way to individual and collective forms of norm-entrepreneurship. These findings are presented as two different narratives, helpful to demonstrate that 'different roads lead to Rome'. They also show that, although they have to be looked at separately in analytical terms, causal mechanisms that follow a more rationalist understanding of corporate behavior and others based on a more constructivist understanding can mutually reinforce each other and provide an integrated account of systematic corporate norm-entrepreneurship. Within both narratives (which are based on the same necessary factors), additional factors are significant in explaining systematic norm-entrepreneurship.

6.1   Necessary pre-conditions

Three of the nine factors analyzed in Chapters 3 to 5 are *necessary* conditions for systematic norm-entrepreneurship: the pressure of the transnational public, the heterogeneity of regulatory environments, and the flexibility of the institutional design of a collective initiative. Since the latter becomes a necessary *pull* factor only at the second stage (when individual norm-entrepreneurs have to decide whether they want to engage in collective norm-entrepreneurship), this factor is treated separately from the two necessary *push* factors. After all, institutional flexibility is not thought necessary to facilitate norm-entrepreneurship but is a necessary bridge between unilateral and collective corporate norm-entrepreneurship.

The two other necessary conditions, heterogeneity of regulatory environments and transnational public pressure, both stem from the cluster of variables describing the corporations' social and political environments. This leads to a significant conclusion: Corporations are more strongly influenced by external forces than is often suggested in critical globalization literature where they are portrayed as powerful actors, immune to state or other actors' interference, and more likely to control than be controlled by them. The importance of this finding is revisited in the final chapter, which examines the bridge between forms of corporate norm-entrepreneurship likely to occur when necessary conditions and significant factors are present, and forms regarded as meaningful and desirable components of global governance architecture that meet demands of effectiveness and legitimacy.

That corporate engagement in norm-entrepreneurship might firstly be the result of external factors does not mean that normative beliefs (for example, of managers) do not matter in corporate decision making. Rather, the conclusion about what generally drives corporations to engage in activities beyond their commercial interests is that intrinsic corporate willingness to 'do good' is less important than 'doing well by doing good' (Conzelmann and Wolf 2007b): creating win-win situations that suit moral and profit motives (Graafland 2002; Pies and Sardison 2006). Corporations achieve this by taking on norm-related activities for strategic reasons, such as reputational risk management or reducing the costs resulting from a heterogeneous regulatory environment. Indeed, the causal mechanisms connecting either heterogeneous environments or transnational public pressure to norm-entrepreneurship all show that their force results primarily from rational calculations: Corporations exposed to heterogeneous regulatory environments engage as norm-entrepreneurs to level the playing field and thus reduce the costs of adjustment that they would otherwise face. According to the evidence from expert interviews, corporations under transnational societal pressure engage as norm-entrepreneurs because there is a business case to do so. They then may – or may not – internalize normative expectations of them to keep 'the license to operate' but they do not become norm-entrepreneurs because of prior internalization. Corporations have to be exposed to a heterogeneous regulatory environment or to transnational public pressure before they engage as norm-entrepreneurs.

Therefore, before demonstrating that both a rationalist and a constructivist narrative can trace the process that leads a corporation to norm-entrepreneurship, it has to be conceded that the business case – and therefore a rationalist logic – underlies both cases. At least in one way, the two factors may also be mutually reinforcing: When corporations are active in several countries, they are potential targets for transnational civil society because they create more 'room for attack'. However, the combined force of heterogeneous regulatory conditions and a certain amount of transnational public pressure does not automatically result in corporate norm-entrepreneurship nor provide a sufficient explanation but does increase its likelihood. For example, numerous corporations in the extractive and apparel industries, such as Exxon, Chevron, or Nike, although all heavily targeted by transnational NGOs they do not engage in individual or collective norm setting activities to a degree comparable to Shell, BP, or Inditex. There are also many corporations active in a large number of countries and exposed to extreme heterogeneity, such as Siemens, Toyota, and General Electrics, that have not yet figured as systematic norm-entrepreneurs – at least not within the sample of self-regulatory initiatives studied here.

Based on the findings of Chapters 3 to 5, the paths that are most likely to lead to individual and collective norm-entrepreneurship are illustrated in Figure 6.1. They represent two parallel narratives that both start from heterogeneous regulatory environments and a certain amount of transnational civil society pressure as necessary conditions for individual corporate norm-entrepreneurship, and that both lead to collective norm-entrepreneurship under the necessary condition of institutional flexibility within the initiatives in which it is most likely to occur. The two narratives encompass additional conditions, telling either a rationalist or constructivist story and providing distinct causal mechanisms. One narrative focuses on corporate vulnerability and autonomy preservation as further important explanations of individual and collective norm-entrepreneurship (the rationalist path),

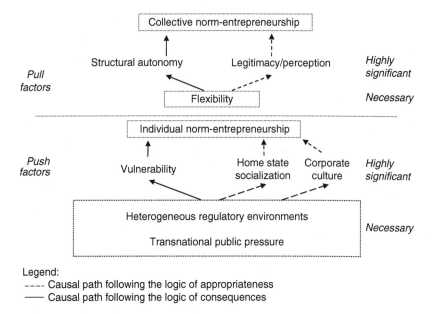

Figure 6.1   Paths to corporate norm-entrepreneurship

and the other stresses the importance of home state socialization, a corporate culture of responsibility and the legitimacy ascribed to collective self-regulatory arrangements (the constructivist path). Under the assumption that corporate decisions are influenced by their anticipated consequences and normative appropriateness, the two paths may run parallel and be taken simultaneously.

6.2   The rationalist narrative – from vulnerability to norm-entrepreneurship

As rational actors, corporations are expected to seize any opportunity to make profits while trying to avoid costs. By creating costs or hindering profits, heterogeneous regulatory environments and transnational NGO pressure are the most important drivers of corporate norm-entrepreneurship. Both factors create a strong business case for systematically seeking norm-entrepreneurship opportunities. For example, companies who operate in many different regulatory environments face higher transaction costs in adapting their compliance policy to many national regulations, in comparison with companies that operate in small and homogeneous countries and regions. Similarly, the vulnerability to loss of reputation capital increases when companies are directly exposed to end consumers because they produce final goods. The impact of this driver of norm-entrepreneurship is further strengthened when the products are branded, providing NGOs with widely visible targets and enough appeal for a public campaign, as in the cases of Tata and Inditex. The driver is weak when a company only produces for industrial customers even though it may be active around the globe, such as SAP, or under societal pressure, such as Union Carbide/Dow Chemical. Similarly, exposure to consumers in multiple and heterogeneous jurisdictions can increase the risk of not satisfying multiple – legally encouraged – expectations.

While, individually, the two necessary and the additional factor with high significance might only push a corporation toward norm-consumership, heterogeneous environments, transnational pressure and corporate vulnerability working in conjunction strongly reinforce the interest in proactively avoiding costs and are likely to channel a company toward norm-entrepreneurship.

6.3 The constructivist narrative – norm-entrepreneurship via home state socialization

Starting from the assumption that norm-related policies and activities of corporations are not solely and continuously profit driven but may also be based on and triggered by beliefs, values, and ideas, an alternative explanation of norm-entrepreneurship is possible. Again, the necessary conditions of heterogeneity and transnational public pressure serve as starting points: All systematic norm-entrepreneurship observed emerged from these conditions. However, the alternative path leads not via corporate vulnerability but via home state socialization and/or a habitualized culture of responsibility. As shown, both of these factors exert significant influence on a corporation's likelihood to engage in norm-entrepreneurship. On the one hand, the prevailing type of business-government relations in the home state of a corporation can socialize corporations into certain expectations of how norms applicable to their behavior should be set. Having been habituated to procedural norms in their home state, corporations faced with heterogeneous environments and transnational public pressure will not calculate the costs and benefits of engaging in norm setting activities but apply the role they have learned as the 'natural' way of reacting to any required or desirable norm setting demands. They will therefore engage in norm setting processes independently of their vulnerability to profit or reputation capital losses. The norm-entrepreneurship of Rio Tinto is a case in point here. Companies such as BASF and BHP Billiton serve as further examples: both stem from countries featuring collaborative business-government relations and both strongly engage in norm-entrepreneurship activities (although outside the sample of self-regulatory initiatives examined here).

On the other hand, as shown in Chapter 4.3, the cognitive predisposition that makes corporations engage in norm setting activities out of mere taken-for-grantedness, cannot only result from socialization by external forces but can be an internal process: Traditional enactment of a culture of responsibility over many years and already in times of the golden age nation state might lead corporations to resort to proactive engagement habitually also in the modern age of global governance and with regards to demands for norm setting activities.

Again, the causal factors subsumed in the constructivist narrative fulfill the function of transforming the corporate preference resulting from the necessary factors: heterogeneity of regulatory environments and transnational NGOs create a certain pressure to abide by international norms that might just as well be dealt with via mere norm-consumership. But a particular home state socialization or corporate culture can turn this rational preference into a taken-for-granted resort to engagement in the creation of these norms. The habitualization either to collaborative norm setting processes or to generally responsible behavior resulting respectively from external or internal socialization processes encourages and promotes proactive norm-entrepreneurship.

6.4   The *pull* factors

Based on the test of nine hypotheses in Chapters 3 to 5, the rationalist and constructivist narratives offer two independent and complementary but not mutually exclusive explanations of corporations acting as norm-entrepreneurs. They show that different configurations of factors can lead to the same result: norm-entrepreneurship. Even after they develop the intention, corporate norm-entrepreneurs still face various options to enact it. The most fundamental choice for corporations contributing to transnational governance is the one between individual or collective norm-entrepreneurship, with the latter appearing generally more interesting because of its higher degree of long-term reliability. However, even the most favorable configuration of causal factors discussed so far only pushes corporations toward individual norm-entrepreneurship. In search of additional factors in the hypotheses tested in Chapter 5 that could attract corporations to collective self-regulatory initiatives, the flexibility of the institutional design proved to be a necessary *pull* factor for corporate norm-entrepreneurs to 'go collective': none of the 10 systematic norm-entrepreneurs engage in a fully inflexible collective self-regulatory initiative. By inversion, this means that even when all of the discussed conditions are in place, according to the constructivist and the rationalist narrative, norm-entrepreneurs will prefer unilateral action unless there exist sufficiently flexible collective initiatives in the issue area of interest to them. However, the numerous collective self-regulatory initiatives that already exist indicate that this hurdle between individual and collective norm-entrepreneurship can be overcome.

While flexibility constitutes a necessary condition in institutional designs to attract collective corporate norm-entrepreneurship, two other characteristics of collective governance arrangements were also identified as relevant factors for corporate norm-entrepreneurs to engage in collective initiatives. One of them, the degree to which an institution preserves or restricts the autonomy of its participants, increases the likelihood of collective norm-entrepreneurship along the rationalist path. Under the assumption that corporate norm-entrepreneurs are interested in autonomy preservation, they would prefer to engage in purely private initiatives. As outlined in Chapter 5, the more inclusive an initiative is (and this is, above all, the case in multi-stakeholder arrangements) the less room it leaves for corporate autonomy and the less attractive it will be. On the other hand, in the constructivist narrative empirical findings strongly support the view that corporations also want to believe that the initiatives in which they cooperate are legitimate. However, legitimacy perceptions put forward by representatives in interviews ('it includes the people that should be included') do not necessarily point to encompassing broad stakeholder participation either. After all, even the members of the Wolfsberg Group regard it as a 'legitimate' initiative, in terms of including expertise and knowledge as well as building on generally agreed principles. Thus, corporations' interest in legitimacy allows for very specific notions of legitimacy and reflects participatory demands that may even be compatible with their interest in preserving autonomy. To make collective norm-entrepreneurship more likely, the institutional design of the governance arrangements in which corporate norm-entrepreneurs collaborate must take into account their specific legitimacy perceptions and their interest in preserving autonomy. In Chapter 9, the question is addressed of how the pull factors that make certain types of collective norm-entrepreneurship more likely than others can be manipulated in a way that also make 'meaningful' forms of collective norm-entrepreneurship possible. In Part III of this volume, criteria to qualify collective transnational private governance arrangements as meaningful contributions to global governance are developed and applied to existing initiatives.

Part III

Evaluating Corporate Norm-entrepreneurship

In the previous part of this volume, general explanatory patterns for corporate norm-entrepreneurship were sought. On the basis of a systematic application of existing and inductively generated hypotheses on the empirical data, conclusions were formed about the relevance of a broad range of factors for explaining corporate norm setting and norm implementation.

Part III adds a normative perspective to the political role of corporations as norm-entrepreneurs by addressing the desirability of involving corporations in emerging postnational governance in terms of their effectiveness as well as legitimacy. Normative reflections on governance have been heavily influenced by Fritz Scharpf's basic distinction between output and input legitimacy (Scharpf 1999). Chapters 7 and 8 reflect this distinction, which is similar to the one between governance *for* the people and governance *by* the people. However, over both chapters, these categories are further disaggregated into more specific output, input and throughput related evaluation criteria that are derived from the different disciplinary discourses in policy analysis and normative political theory, to allow a differentiating assessment of the strengths and weaknesses of corporate norm-entrepreneurship in transnational self-regulatory arrangements.

In policy research, *effectiveness* is the most important yardstick for the evaluation of private contributions to governance. The evaluation of corporate norm-entrepreneurship in Chapter 7 follows this tradition and focuses on the effectiveness of different types of individual and collective (self-)regulatory governance arrangements. The empirical cases to which an elaborate set of effectiveness criteria is applied cover an individual company code as well as collective corporate norm-entrepreneurship in private-private, multi-stakeholder and public-private governance arrangements. The conceptual framework employed for their evaluation starts out from the assumption that corporations are subjects and objects of corporate norm-entrepreneurship. Effectiveness is thus analyzed at the actor level as well as at the structural level. To provide a comprehensive picture of the effectiveness of corporate norm-entrepreneurship, at the actor level 'output' is disaggregated into effects in terms of norm commitment (output in a narrow sense), change of behavior (outcome) and identity shift (impact). At the structural level, further impacts are evaluated with regard to goal attainment, contributions to normative order and unintended consequences. Thus the extended framework for analyzing the effectiveness of corporate norm-entrepreneurship not only covers material and visible effects of corporate norm-entrepreneurship but also includes effects on the beliefs of actors and on the development of rules and norms in the transnational sphere.

From the perspective of normative political theory even the sophisticated set of output oriented criteria applied in Chapter 7 would not suffice for a comprehensive evaluation of the new political role of corporations. Chapter 8 therefore addresses *legitimacy* criteria that are widely recognized in political theory: responsiveness, self-determination, accountability, and authority. These normative standards entail theory-grounded criteria of acceptability that go beyond the empirical legitimacy perceptions investigated in Chapter 5 as a potential explanation for the preference of participation in certain institutional arrangements. They focus on the 'government by the people' aspects of legitimacy but at the same time blur the boundaries between input and output notions of legitimacy, taking into account the interrelatedness of the two. Their application follows the assumption that the legitimacy of corporate norm-entrepreneurship is closely linked to the legitimacy of the transnational private governance arrangements in which this norm-entrepreneurship takes place. Thus it can only be fully assessed by bringing together legitimacy-providing sources of authority attributed to the actors' level with the legitimacy demands of certain governance arrangements at the structural and procedural level which determine the value of the former as legitimacy providers. For reasons of coherence, the same empirical cases are used as in Chapter 7, representing corporate norm-entrepreneurship in individual company codes and collective private-private, multistakeholder, and public-private governance arrangements. In addition to comparing the legitimacy potential of corporate norm-entrepreneurship within different actors' configurations, special attention is also paid to whether the focus of corporate norm-entrepreneurship is inward or outward.

Obviously, the challenges of governance beyond the state are too complex not to involve business actors in addressing them but also are too sensitive and 'public' in nature to rely on the self-regulation of actors alone who are primarily motivated by the 'business case'. Starting out from the shortcomings identified in the previous chapters, Chapter 9 makes some policy recommendations to exhaust the full potential of corporate norm-entrepreneurship as a meaningful private contribution to global governance by providing a regulatory framework for 'embedded private norm-entrepreneurship' that could reconcile the 'public case' with the 'business case'. Thus the concluding considerations return to the 'big' agenda of a new theory of statehood and public goods provision in the postnational constellation. They advocate rules for the constitutionalization of transnational private self-regulation that are based on a Neo-Westphalian rather than supranational or heterarchical approach to the political order of an emerging world society.

7
The Effectiveness of Transnational Private Governance

Global governance research only recently discovered the output dimension of transnational self-regulatory arrangements (Börzel and Risse 2002, 2005; Rieth and Zimmer 2004: 28; Conzelmann and Wolf 2007a, 2007b). Adequate yardsticks are still sought to evaluate the effectiveness of norm and rule setting by corporate actors, alone or in cooperation with states and NGOs, and in individual or collective self-regulatory arrangements. To fill this gap, a comprehensive conceptual framework is developed to assess the effectiveness of corporate contributions to global governance. A consolidated model for assessing corporate norm-entrepreneurship is introduced and applied to select individual and collective self-regulatory arrangements.

7.1 Developing a conceptual frame for analyzing the effectiveness of institutions

Lasswell's query – *who gets what, when, and how* – remains one of the crucial questions when analyzing the actual effects of regulatory efforts. Questions regarding effectiveness that are common in policy analysis in the domestic context only recently gained center stage in IR. Transnational challenges in environmental politics (Cusimano 2000) first triggered systematic research on the effectiveness of international regimes. Young and Levy introduced types of effectiveness: problem solving, legal, economic, normative, and political (Young and Levy 1999); and Oran Young distinguished between simple and complex performance (Young 2002). Simple performance means that an institution's own criteria for success are met; complex performance 'involves longer causal chains, and encompasses negative as well as positive effects' (Young 2002: 15; see also Breitmeier and Wolf 1993; Bomann-Larsen and Wiggen 2004).[1]

Another approach to analyzing the effectiveness of institutions is based on David Easton's distinction among output, outcome, and impact (Easton 1965).[2] The output of an institution is defined as commitments that actors have agreed on. Outputs can include 'regulations, programs, and organizational arrangements' (Young 1999: III; see also Huckel et al. 2007: 59). The outcome of an institution is defined as the change in behavior of participating actors in accordance with outputs (Young 1999: III). Impact refers to an institution's contributions to problem solving, which are considered effective if problems that led to the creation of an institution are solved or at least alleviated (Underdal 2002). Huckel and colleagues used this framework to analyze self-regulatory arrangements, including business actors (Huckel et al. 2007), and address the methodological challenges, particularly the complex nature of the impact dimension. Apart from the problem of attributing causality, seemingly simple questions, such as 'impact on what' or 'goal attainment by whose standards', have to be dealt with before carrying out an analysis (Wolf 2007; see also Dingwerth 2004). After all, 'effective' corporate norm-entrepreneurship does not necessarily contribute to good governance. Do corporations act as norm-entrepreneurs in the public interest and, if so, to what extent?

In Business Ethics, the effectiveness of business codes has been widely examined yielding varying results: 'largely counterproductive, ineffective, insufficient, not enough, not very effective, uncertain, doubtful, little impact, less effective than their proponents think, needed, necessary, valuable, vital, invaluable, effective and successful' (Kaptein and Schwartz 2008: 113). Such studies often do not differentiate between types of business codes, such as explicit or implicit, distinct or formal, or limited or extended prescriptions, and are not very precise when it comes to terminology (Collier and Esteban 2007; Bhattacharya et al. 2009; Stevens 2008). As a result, the dimensions of effectiveness measured remain elusive. Assessing the effectiveness of self-regulatory arrangements is a challenging task, especially when it comes to the analysis of corporate norm-entrepreneurship. A conceptual framework for assessing the effectiveness of corporate norm-entrepreneurship is used here that is applicable to different types of self-regulatory arrangements and distinguishes between effects at actor and structural levels, that is, on the corporations participating in self-regulatory arrangements, and on their overall environment (Table 7.1).

Table 7.1   Different dimensions of the effectiveness of self-regulatory arrangements

	A	B	C	D	E	F
Level	Output	Outcome			Impact	
Actor	Norm commitment	Change of behavior	Identity shift			
Structural				Contribution to goal attainment	Contribution to normative order	Unintended consequences

7.1.1 The actor level

Individual and collective self-regulatory arrangements can have various effects on the participating actors, such as commitment to a norm, change in corporate behavior, and change in the identity of an actor.

(A) Norm commitment can be signaled by the introduction of an individual or collective code of conduct that guides the day-to-day business routines and underlines sustainable corporate visions and strategies. Further indicators of such a commitment are the establishment of new operational workflows and procedures, including revisions of the company's organizational structure, for example, the installation of a CSR department or a sustainability board. These procedural or institutional outputs are the first steps toward implementation of the often vaguely formulated code of conduct.

(B) A corporation can change its behavior in accordance with a self-regulatory arrangement by actively applying and implementing these new procedures. For example, 'whistleblower' hotlines can be installed at external law offices or trustable internal units for reporting violations of new corporate guidelines, which can be investigated and penalized if necessary. The basic difference between dimensions A and B is the code conversion and implementation. For example, if suppliers do not comply with a new code of conduct, they will be warned or advised to engage in training programs and, if the situation does not improve, a contract may be terminated.

(C) A shift in the identity of an actor implies a change in the 'principled beliefs' (Goldstein and Keohane 1993: 9) that define interests, goals, and preferences (Abdelal et al. 2006: 701). A typical example is the extension of the financial bottom line to include social and ecological aspects. As a result, new corporate strategies and major investments are screened for profit maximization and their social and ecological consequences.

7.1.2 The structural level

Effects on the structural level are commonly subsumed under the impact label. In contrast to changes on the actor level that are limited to those explicitly accepting a particular governance arrangement, changes on the structural level go beyond this to include effects on third parties and the overall political environment. They comprise contributions to a new or redefined normative order or to the solution of the problem at hand but they might also lead to unintended, and possibly negative, consequences.

(D) Goal attainment is a measure of the extent to which a regulatory arrangement's self-stated goals are attained over time (Young 1994: 143). It considers specific and often measurable goals, targets, or benchmarks. If it were the envisaged goal of a political regulation to reduce the percentage of forced labor or guarantee freedom of association in a given country, a significant improvement would have to be shown by presenting data for specified time-periods. However, attempts to establish degrees of goal attainment are faced with the difficulties of retrieving sound empirical data and the methodological challenge of attributing causality. Apart from the self-regulatory arrangement, a number of other factors might be influencing the degree of goal attainment.

(E)   An individual or collective self-regulatory arrangement can contribute to a system of norms and shared expectations (Parsons 1951) that go beyond the policy field in which it was established. The more effective a new type of sectoral regulation is, the more likely that it has an influence on *collective expectations* of proper corporate behavior in general (Jepperson et al. 1996: 54) and therefore on the broader normative environment. It can set a precedent for what public and private actors are supposed to deliver. Role components, such as best practices developed by individual corporations or a group of companies, might become the principal normative patterns defining what desirable corporate behavior is in general. This has wider implications on expectations of business actors beyond a particular industry or geographical region.

(F)   Finally, individual or collective self-regulatory arrangements can have both positive and negative unintended consequences. Such externalities can have harmful effects on third parties or other policy areas, or in the shift in power relationships between public and private actors. State actors who assign regulatory competences to private actors may become dependent on them.

7.2   Empirical application

To identify the potential and limitations of what individual and collective self-regulation can achieve, examples of arrangements with particularly far-reaching regulatory scope were chosen. While these empirical cases portray 'as much corporate norm-entrepreneurship as possible', their selection does not prejudice the quality of their governance contributions. As an example of an individual, entirely private, governance arrangement, the Shell General Business Principles were chosen. Different types of collective governance arrangements are represented by the Wolfsberg Principles, as a private self-regulatory initiative, the UN Global Compact, as a public-private arrangement, and the Global Reporting Initiative, as a multistakeholder arrangement.

All these examples are striking for their high-profile membership – Shell being one of the most important corporations of its sector, and the three collective initiatives generally comprising almost all of the biggest transnational corporations and representing the large majority of actors in their relevant markets. Most importantly, all four initiatives take a comprehensive approach to regulating the issue or policy area in which they are engaged. The regulations they produce are extensive in their aspired scope and therefore likely to have far-reaching effects. While Shell and the Global Compact take an extensive but somewhat less precise approach to regulating all aspects of business responsibility, the GRI and the Wolfsberg Principles focus more on clearly delineated issue areas and regulate these with very precise prescriptions.

Shell's General Principles were established to guide the full range of Shell's operations and business activities. In combination with the company code of conduct, it provides guidance on behavior and complying with internationally accepted rules and norms in various issue areas. Similarly, the Global Compact's norms seek to establish overarching normative principles applicable to all corporations in all sectors and all of their activities. In comparison, the Wolfsberg Principles may seem much more limited in its regulatory scope – the fight against money laundering. This limited goal, however, is approached comprehensively by the Wolfsberg members and is translated into more and more banking business areas with each additional guidance document issued. In a similar way, the GRI's goal of establishing standards for sustainability reporting is furthered from a variety of angles simultaneously, through constantly developing and improving the reporting standards.

7.2.1 Shell

Despite constant clashes between Shell and its stakeholders, particularly over the company's misconduct in Nigeria, various instances of environmental degradation and bad treatment of local employees, Shell has long been regarded as a frontrunner in CSR-related matters. Shell's General Business Principles represents one of the most far-reaching codes of conduct adopted by a transnational corporation and has been selected as an individual self-regulatory arrangement.

In 1976, a formal set of principles was set up by Shell and has been updated on a regular basis. The principles only gained prominence in 1997 with the publication of Shell's first Health, Safety and Environment Report (Shell 1997). According to Shell, its General Business Principles commit the company 'to contribute to sustainable development, balancing short and

Table 7.2 Case selection of comprehensive individual and collective self-regulatory arrangements

	Individual governance arrangements	Collective governance arrangements		
Actor configuration	Entirely private	Private-private	Public-private	Multistakeholder
Empirical examples	Shell	Wolfsberg Principles	Global Compact	Global Reporting Initiative

long-term interests and integrating economic, environmental and social considerations into our decision making'. The Code of Conduct, introduced in 2006, 'guides employees on how to apply the Shell General Business Principles in line with its core values of "honesty, integrity and respect". It is designed to provide practical advice on how to comply with laws and regulations and how to relate to customers, communities and colleagues' (Shell 2006a). The General Business Principles testify to Shell's commitment to business ethics and sustainable development. The code of conduct is an 80-page document with detailed guidance on how to practically implement the Shell General Business Principles.

Norm commitment

Since the introduction of its General Principles and first sustainability report, Shell has constantly reaffirmed its commitment by gradually establishing new organizational procedures 'to help us better manage our social and ethical responsibilities' (Shell 1998: 5). The Social Responsibility Committee meets regularly with local staff and stakeholders and reports to the board (Shell 2006b). Shell has acknowledged its responsibility in areas such as human rights and climate change and has issued guideline documents for management and training purposes. Even critics regard the company as a significant player in renewable energy (Frynas 2005). Shell has established internal accountability structures (Social Responsibility Committee and the Shell Internal Audit for Fraud, Shell 2008: 35) and a helpline for staff and business partners to report bribery and corruption concerns (Shell 2008: 32). Mandatory internal training programs were established to give its Business Principles more effect in practice.

However, the effects of most of these policies are not known to external stakeholders. Some of the programs cannot be assessed due to a lack of data access. For example, the independence of analyses of the helpline is not guaranteed and relevant information about job security for 'whistleblowers' is not provided (OneWorldTrust 2008).

Externally, suppliers and partners in joint ventures are also encouraged to adopt the Business Principles. Learning mechanisms are installed to ensure contractor compliance (Stadler 2004: 154). To emphasize its commitment to applying its business principles to supply chains, Shell has conducted mandatory training courses for 2000 people in 60 countries since 2004, when voluntary workshops did not reach target numbers. The Code of Conduct attests to a high degree Shell's overall commitment to its social responsibilities.

Change of behavior

In the late 1990s, Shell spent large sums of money on communication campaigns. The focus of its activities has shifted over time. Various internally and externally oriented changes in behavior can now be observed. They range from requiring each country representative to complete an 'annual internal questionnaire' on compliance with the General Principles (Shell 2008: 32) to the implementation of community projects to improve the local standard of living – although the latter were criticized for being drawn up in a nonparticipatory, top-down way (Frynas 2001: 43). Shell is consistently listed high in CSR and sustainability rankings and in relevant sustainability indices, setting new standards that constitute new benchmarks for its partners and competitors.

It is difficult to come up with a firm assessment of actual changes in anti-bribery and anti-corruption (Shell 2006a: 24–37). In the notorious case of Nigeria, Shell is ranked far above average for implementing its anticorruption policy, showing that companies can change a deeply rooted culture of corruption. A number of cases of bribery and fraud have been reported to the Audit Committee of the board and the total number of violations is provided in the sustainability report along with the total number of staff dismissed and contracts terminated (Shell 2008: 32). This makes Shell's efforts extraordinarily transparent but does not answer the question of whether Shell employees are now less involved in issues of bribery.

Shell has also started implementing its Business Principles within its supply chain. It regularly reviews its business relationships. Terminations of contracts are possible when the suppliers fail to meet agreed criteria (Shell 2008: 32). Shell has a monitoring system in place. There are internal reports listing the number of countries where Shell's Business Principles is included in contracts, the number of countries where contractors, subcontractors, and suppliers have been screened for compliance, and the number of contracts Shell cancelled and joint ventures it divested from because of incompatibility with the Principles. However, the data are not made available to the public (Stratos 2007), leaving doubt about the validity of the claimed effectiveness in day-to-day business operations. The latest OECD Watch shows implementation problems in joint venture parts of the company (OECD 2009). Shell has changed its behavior, but doubts remain over the extent that the company implements its code of conduct in sensitive areas systematically, such as supplier management and anticorruption.

Identity shift

Shell has had an identity shift since the 1990s, reflected in its statement 'that the basic interests of business and society are entirely compatible – that there does not have to be a choice between profits and principles' (Shell 1998: 6). Years of civil society campaigning have taken their toll. Shell has come a long way and acknowledged its bad record in all CSR issues. According to Rieth and Zimmer (2004: 28–30), Shell's gradual acceptance of the CSR norm and continuous extension of its CSR policy at local, national and global levels, and its change in line of argument are the result of a process of self-entrapment. Targeted by persistent NGO pressure, shamed by the violation of human rights in Nigeria and accused of environmental degradation, Shell started to reflect on its corporate strategy. The company seemed to realize that its bad record was a result of focusing only on the financial bottom line, and increasingly attempted to give the principle of sustainability equal consideration (Shell 2009). The Chief Executive Officer's (CEO) public statements support this identity shift; he reflected on Shell's position in society in times of globalization and took responsibility for future commitments to social investment and anticorruption measures (van der Veer 2005).[3] This does not mean that Shell achieved the full understanding of all stakeholders. At times, the basic concerns of local communities are still ignored and the adoption of social and ecological programs still have to be internally justified as an answer to bad publicity that might harm the firm's reputation (Frynas 2001: 44; 2005: 585–8). This indicates that every employee has not yet internalized the new corporate policies. The credibility of its identity change is backed up by external sources. 'Shell meets all good practice principles for environmental and social impact evaluation, including engaging external stakeholders in the evaluation of activities which have impacted them, being open and transparent about evaluation results, using those results to inform future decision making, and evaluation of both evaluation goals and evaluation policies' (OneWorldTrust 2008). There is significant evidence that Shell actually 'walks the talk'.

Contributions to goal attainment

Whether the unilateral governance contributions of a single corporate norm-entrepreneur such as Shell can have major effects on goal attainment is questionable. Realistically, it can hardly be expected that the overall situation in social welfare or environmental conditions in Shell's host states (such as Mexico, Nigeria, and Russia) has changed for the better due to Shell's engagement. Yet, Shell's efforts have had effects at least at the procedural level. Again using the fight against corruption as an example, Shell's commitment to its code of conduct led to greater inclusion of civil society organizations in problem-solving efforts. Overall, Shell's degree of transparency also stands out in comparison to its key competitors and other major transnational corporations, although its impact beyond the corporate sphere remains limited. According to Transparency International's data about the likelihood of companies bribing public officials, the oil and gas sector remains the top offenders. There is some improvement, notably in Nigeria.[4] To what degree this improvement can be attributed to Shell's anti-corruption efforts in this country is hard to assess. Some reports claim that the effectiveness of Shell's community projects was limited, small-scale (Frynas 2001: 42), and did not address the core needs of the people. According to Frynas, less than one-third of Shell's development projects were successful (Frynas 2005: 587–8). Overall, Shell's track record shows positive signs of improvement, for a transnational company working in challenging environments, but has significant problems in meeting its own high demands.

Contributions to normative order

Shell's efforts have contributed to the new public image of the extractive industry as a whole. Its comprehensive anticorruption program and its revenue transparency policy should be considered as best practice. They have demonstrated that it is possible to fight corruption even in countries with disastrous transparency records where a company runs the risk of losing business to free riders (Transparency International 2008b). Shell's activities have been a building block for a new system of norms and rules supported by the Extractive Industries Transparency Initiative (EITI) that aims to improve transparency and accountability in the extractive sector.

Shell is considered as a role model for not just the extractive industry but for companies in general as they apply modern techniques, such as materiality analysis, and stress the importance of an external verification of sustainability reports. Shell has cooperated with the Danish Institute for Human Rights (DIHR) to develop corporate human rights policies (DIHR 2006) and has provided environmental best practice for the whole industry for the protection of the Grey Whale habitat in the Shakalin region. Given the limited degree that any single company can contribute to normative orders, Shell has been at the forefront of the CSR movement since its early days and has significantly contributed to the larger normative shift toward responsibility as a value for measuring business success. The company is still regarded as a CSR trendsetter, constantly participating in further and more specific normative development.

Unintended consequences

Shell's proactive implementation of its code of conduct has had considerable repercussions and side effects at the structural level. The company imposed enormous peer pressure on its core competitors, Exxon and BP, to catch up and install similar rigid and transparent anticorruption measures. The extractive industry was able to improve and shake off its negative public image to a considerable degree. It seems too early to judge whether Shell contributed to elevating the overall record of business practice or whether it merely provided the less responsible corporations with a shield to hide behind while continuing to do business as usual. Less responsible competitors might have taken up business opportunities, from which Shell abstained because it considered the negative social repercussions to be too high. There may also be a dark side to more transparency: A potential result of Shell's cooperation with civil society actors might be that NGOs invited to become members of Shell's External Review Committee (Shell 2008: 38) may neglect their important role as watchdogs over other, less engaged corporations.

7.2.2   The Wolfsberg principles

Aiming to provide practical guidelines for implementing antimoney laundering measures in the daily business of commercial banks, the Wolfsberg Group represents an extremely ambitious example of a purely private initiative. A group of 12 globally operating banks,[5] with the support of Transparency International and an academic expert, initiated the Wolfsberg Principles. There is no possibility for formal accession by other financial institutions.

Norm commitment

Wolfsberg's effects on norm commitment can be measured in two dimensions: the quality of the normative commitments among the Wolfsberg members and how many companies have actually committed themselves. Member commitments to combating money laundering in their business segments are impressive. In the 8 years since its foundation, the Wolfsberg Group has launched 11 guideline documents and 5 sets of 'Frequently Asked Questions', detailing specific behavioral requirements. Since 2004, the Group has collaborated with the Banker's Almanac[6] to operate a Due Diligence Depository,[7] a web portal gathering detailed information on financial institutions operating worldwide to enable banks to judge the commitment of their peers to antimoney laundering (AML). The data and documents gathered include a detailed questionnaire on AML practices developed by the Wolfsberg Group, which has highly increased its visibility as an AML institution. The 'closed club' principle reinforces member commitments. It strongly advocates a risk based approach by its very nature but does not aim to cover all instances of money laundering, only those judged to be too risky (Pieth and Aiolfi 2003a). Statements usually contain the softest judicially significant language (Hinterseer 2002: 262–82).

The impossibility of accession and the ensuing lack of ownership by the rest of the industry, although it is encouraged to abide by the principles (Pieth 2006: 6; KPMG 2004: 31), leaves considerably less incentive to commit for outsiders. Nevertheless, the creation of the annual Wolfsberg Forum in 2003, where a large number of companies from the finance sector are invited to discuss new standards, allows other banks to support the principles without being members. Approximately 50 financial institutions have participated in the forum every year (Pieth 2007: 101). The Due Diligence Repository reaches beyond the Wolfsberg members and asks banks worldwide to provide information on their internal AML policies. 3783 international banks have provided documents and 2142 used the Wolfsberg questionnaire. However, whether this can be regarded as fostering normative commitment is doubtful since the information is solicited through market pressure.

Wolfsberg members and other banks increasingly underscore their commitment with internal activities such as staff training and establishing AML policies and departments. According to two surveys by KPMG, 85 percent of internationally active banks had a global AML policy in place by 2007, and 218 (out of 224) banks reported that they provide AML training to staff. While it may be difficult to trace these efforts back to Wolfsberg, the same surveys also found significantly more than the member banks acknowledging that they are heavily influenced by the group's standards (KPMG 2004: 32; KPMG 2007: 44).[8] In summary, Wolfsberg has contributed to triggering a significant amount of norm commitment but the quality of commitment varies between members and nonmembers.

Change of behavior

Reliable judgment of changes in behavior is rendered difficult by the general characteristics of the banking industry – an environment of legally protected lack of transparency. The Wolfsberg Group has not implemented any mechanisms for ensuring that the outcomes of the initiative are transparent to or accessible by the public and no reporting requirements exist. Measuring the level of compliance with the principles is possible only to a limited degree, by drawing on external sources. Since Wolfsberg prescribes suspicious transaction reporting (among other things), detailed statistics from the Money Laundering Reporting Office Switzerland (MROS)[9] are used as an indicator. Table 7.3 illustrates these from 1998 to 2008. All interpretations of the results have to be made with great care as it is neither possible to establish factual causation between Wolfsberg and changes in the relevant numbers nor establish whether changes in reporting are attributable to unknown fluctuations in amounts of money laundered.[10] The table includes number of reports per year and reports by all banking institutions in aggregate as well as by the subgroup of major banks – to which the two Swiss Wolfsberg members, Credit Suisse and UBS, belong.

Table 7.3   Suspicious transactions reported in Switzerland

Year	1998[a]	1999	2000	2001	2002	2003	2004	2005	2006	2007	2008
Number of reports	160	303	311	417	652	863	821	729	619	795	851
Reports by banks (absolute/ percent)	128 (80)	260 (86)	234 (75)	255 (61)	271 (42)	302 (35)	340 (41)	293 (40)	359 (58)	492 (62)	572 (67)
Reports by major banks (absolute/ percent)	n/a	58 (22)	92 (39)	73 (29)	59 (22)	54 (18)	46 (13)	44 (15)	143 (39)	213 (43)	196 (34)

[a] The first two MROS annual reports covered a business year beginning 1 April and ending 31 March of the following year. Reporting periods were adjusted in 2000 to cover the period from 1 January to 31 December. The adjusted data were incorporated in this analysis.

Although it might be tempting to attribute the 25 percent rise in total reports in 2001 to Wolfsberg, the number of reports by the major banks significantly fell during the same period. In contrast, reports by private banks rose from 25 to 69, that is, by more than 100 percent. It is likely that these banks, although not being Wolfsberg members, were highly influenced by the release of the first set of principles. The same trends continued in 2002: Total reports rose more than 50 percent, with those of major banks decreasing and those of private banks increasing by 30 percent. MROS suspects this change in the origin of reports is assets laundered being shifted to smaller institutions or heightened diligence on the part of the latter. Both possibilities could potentially be affected by Wolfsberg because criminals might avoid the heightened diligence procedures of the member banks and non-member banks might be under pressure to live up to the same standards. No significant increase in reports by the relevant banks seems to have taken place because of Wolfsberg's inception.

A substantial change occurred in 2006, when reports by major banks tripled and then increased again by 70 percent in 2007. This is especially remarkable since the largest part of these increases can be attributed to additional voluntary, not mandatory, reports in accordance with the Swiss AML law (MROS 2008: 28). Since, in total, three new Wolfsberg documents came into force in this period, among them the highly important overarching frameworks, there is reason to assume that Wolfsberg effects did come into play. The MROS refers to 'the preventive measures implemented and the detection of risks by the compliance services of banks' but does not explicitly name the Wolfsberg Group to explain the increases (MROS 2006: 7).[11] This might have shed a more positive light on the effects of Wolfsberg but neither low nor high reporting can adequately capture whether banks have or have not reduced their involvement in money-laundering; low numbers might stem from low instances of money laundered and high numbers of reports might not include the most relevant transactions. Indeed, a recent analysis by Global Witness found that six of the 11 Wolfsberg members are involved in business with corrupt states and so contribute to state looting. The report also shows that banks might report a suspicious customer but state authorities still permit the transaction. It concludes that the Wolfsberg Principles 'are little more than a statement of intent and have no real power to prevent banks doing business with dubious customers' (Global Witness 2009: 9). There are no public records available on how much the Wolfsberg Principles have actually been implemented; there are some indications that effects on bank behavior have not been widespread.

Identity shift

Wolfsberg's triggering of identity shifts seems highly important: by comprehensively supporting the fight against money laundering, the Wolfsberg banks have taken responsibility for issues far beyond their narrowly defined business interests – and to a certain extent even contravene them. This is highly remarkable, considering that banks have been very reluctant to take part in CSR discourse. In fact, a central claim of the CSR agenda – that business should be more transparent – has traditionally been understood as opposing banker ethics, which were based on legally protected secrecy and confidentiality. Again, this effect might be supported by the limited membership. Empirical constructivist research finds that changes in identity are facilitated by closed-door settings that offer a small number of participants room to openly deliberate, and build trust and shared understandings (Checkel 2001). Nevertheless, the small number of members offers little to no opportunity for other banks to also engage in potentially identity changing discourse. It could be argued that the Wolfsberg members are aware of these limitations, considering that measures focused toward external actors – such as the Due Diligence Repository – do not employ moral or normative terminology but emphasize the business case to motivate others to comply. 'Reduce your compliance burden' is the central motto of the Repository. Potential identity shifts should not be overestimated given that the activities of Wolfsberg members are restricted to one highly specific issue area within banks, often within only a few specialized departments.

Goal attainment

In terms of the actual value of the prevention of money laundering and the supposedly ensuing reduction in crime rates, it must be acknowledged that it is extremely difficult to produce reliable data on such a highly secretive phenomenon. The figures most prominently stated are between U.S.$1 trillion (KPMG 2007) and U.S.$1.5 trillion (UNDP 1999), and no credible source has estimated a decrease to any significant degree. Nevertheless, a general shortcoming that reduces Wolfsberg's problem-solving potential is that the standards refer to increasing numbers of business segments but still do not extend to retail banking – the area where presumably the largest amount of money is laundered.

Contribution to normative order

The Wolfsberg members have influence on the formation of normative order through contributing significantly to increasing the awareness of money-laundering. The effects on other normative goals of globalized society might have been less positive. AML is a relatively recent policy concern for national and international regulators. The support of a high profile private sector segment has helped significantly. Wolfsberg has contributed to the substance of AML policies by setting the terms of reference for public policy approaches, firmly establishing the risk-based approach as the ultimate tool for AML (Pieth and Aiolfi 2003a). Even though it cannot be ascertained which of the international law standards on money-laundering most significantly influenced the others, there is clear evidence of convergence of all the standards on the risk-based model, as advocated by the Wolfsberg Group.[12]

The Wolfsberg process is hindering or at least slowing down the process of normative expansion by focusing exclusively on the technical aspects of how to best implement AML in the daily business of various banking segments without regard for the bigger picture of a fair and just financial sector that ensures money being used for society's overall welfare. This is especially significant to corruption and tax crime, attention to which is diverted rather than increased by Wolfsberg.[13] The member banks still largely deny any responsibility or wrongdoing in their purely business-oriented approach to tax evasion or fraud. Singular incidents of changes in practice are achieved not by norms but only through pressure and force – such as in the settlement deal between the United States and UBS in early 2009 (Browning 2009). Similar observations hold true for corruption. The Wolfsberg members seem to have an explicitly narrow understanding of their responsibility – even within the 'Statement against Corruption' issued in 2007.[14]

Unintended consequences

The Wolfsberg Principles suffer from a number of criticisms that are generally applied to all international AML regulations: for example, it is doubtful whether implementing AML should receive the priority currently devoted to it in the financial systems of developing countries. AML procedures are very costly, for public and private actors, and their designs to date have had little potential to fulfill their task in developing country environments. The local financial systems are usually not elaborate enough to be misused by sophisticated financial crime. Consequently, the Wolfsberg Group's ambition imposes significant costs and might hinder development of functional financial sectors while not reaping any substantial benefits (Sharman and Chaikin 2009). Similar problems are associated with measures such as the Due Diligence Repository – the more it is established as a standard reference tool for major banks, the more developing countries are forced to comply with it and divert resources that could be invested more productively.

7.2.3   The Global Compact

The Global Compact is an example of a public-private self-regulatory initiative set up to promote corporate social responsibility and citizenship in the new global market place. It challenges corporations to demonstrate corporate leadership by embracing ten principles in the areas of human rights, labor, environment, and anticorruption and making them an integral component of entrepreneurial activities.

Norm commitment

Corporate commitment to the principles of the Global Compact is measured by the number of participating corporations and what companies have carried out to operationalize their commitments. The number of signatories has increased steadily, from 40 in the year 2000, 2000 in 2004, to more than 5000 in 2008. Most of its members come from Europe and Latin America (UN Global Compact Office 2009: 9). The Global Compact has also made significant progress in attracting the world's largest companies: in 2006, 105 companies from the Financial Times 500 listing were signatories (UN Global Compact 2006). This number reached 164 in May 2009.[15] An endorsement of the Global Compact implies Chief Executive commitment to take action that is necessary for effective organizational changes. More than half of the participating corporations stated that further policies and strategies have been developed at the Board of Directors level. A large majority conducts regular internal evaluations and monitors actions taken (UN Global Compact 2007: 9–10; 2009: 11). Although most CEOs stressed that they were doing more than they did 5 years ago to incorporate environmental, social and governance issues into their strategy and operations, there are a number of internal barriers, such as competing strategic priorities and complexity issues, that keep companies from implementing new CSR-related strategies (McKinsey 2007: 18–19). Organizational changes, such as the introduction of CSR or sustainability policies and departments, demonstrate a minimum degree of institutionalization of the provisions of the initiative.

Change of behavior

The Global Compact Office describes the gap between commitment and action as the 'greatest challenge for the Global Compact to deepen engagement by companies on a continuing basis' (UN Global Compact 2007: 11). Changes of behavior can be identified by looking at the compliance culture of Global Compact signatories. One indicator is the rate of submitted Communications on Progress (CoP) – on the presumption that companies only issue a report if there is progress to be reported.[16] A closer look is taken at the sort of action that companies took to implement the ten principles and whether companies have engaged in partnerships to advance sustainability solutions, which is one of the major goals of the initiative.

The annual submission of a CoP is the only regular activity required of Global Compact signatories. In general, the number of reports is constantly rising, although in 2008, of about 4000 corporate Global Compact participants, only 1800 submitted a CoP (UN Global Compact 2009: 52–3). Even taking into account that newcomers receive a grace period of two years to submit their first report, at least 25 percent of companies are not submitting.[17] A closer look at policy implementation in the various subject areas shows significant 'performance gaps' (McKinsey 2007). There are remarkable differences between activities directed at improving labor and environmental practices and those aimed at human rights and anticorruption. While cleaner and safer products are regularly installed and, in the majority of cases, freedom of assembly is guaranteed even in autocratic countries, transparent and effective human rights assessment and monitoring of suppliers take place in only a small proportion of companies and anticorruption procedures are far from comprehensive (Rieth 2009b). Overall, the reported information focuses more on commitment and management systems than on materiality, performance, and achievements (Fondation Guilé 2009).

Another indicator is corporate engagement in partnerships that advance the development goals of the United Nations. In 2007, 75 percent engaged in cross-sector partnerships, mostly of a local nature and including strategic philanthropy and social investments (UN Global Compact 2007: 42). However, this number sharply declined to 51 percent in 2009 (UN Global Compact 2009). A country case study on German Global Compact participants underlines these poor results and shows that partnership projects have been the exception rather than the rule among participants (Rieth 2009a). In summary, most corporations have started implementing new policies only half-heartedly, focusing on the procedural side only and with significant differences across policy-areas.

Identity shift

From the very beginning, it was the Global Compact's core goal to embed universal principles and values for universal benefit in markets and societies (Kell and Ruggie 1999). This requires at least partial internalization by corporations who need to develop a new understanding of their political role. In corporate language, a shift from shareholder to stakeholder value orientation has to take place. The extent that this has happened can be examined by studying Global Compact participants during the financial crises in 2008–09. If CSR activities were extended even in times of economic recession this is a solid indicator of a shift in the basic understanding of what is appropriate corporate conduct.

The empirical data available paint a mixed picture. In a newspaper survey in November 2008, companies stressed that they would keep up their CSR activities and expenditures at least at the same level or even expand them.[18] The veracity of such 'socially desirable' answers, which are usually given by corporate representatives in open surveys, is questionable. Other surveys got results that display a diametrically opposed view; CSR efforts were significantly delayed due to recession (Booz&Co. 2009). The fact that most companies still justify their consideration of CSR issues by pointing to a potential business case shows that frameworks for establishing appropriateness have not really changed. Many CEOs recognize that they have to maintain or boost their legitimacy record in society to create long-term shareholder value or risk losing institutional image and reputation (McKinsey 2007: 8). Norm-related activities are still seen as a business opportunity, not a moral issue. Consultancies with knowledge of global trends therefore frame CSR-related issues as a business case and in risk management terms and claim that companies committed to corporate sustainability practices are achieving above-average performance in the financial markets, even during this slowdown (AT Kearney 2009).

Through their commitment to the Global Compact principles, companies have started an overhaul of their identity, in which they reflect on their purely profit-related utility function, adding issues that have formerly been denied any value. Their corporate strategies are in a transitory phase from narrow to extended market rationalism and the Global Compact has supported this process. CSR-related measures are high on the corporate agenda and CSR is a well-known subject. Given the leadership commitment to the Global Compact, the question is no longer if, but to what degree a company wants to invest in CSR issues.

Contribution to goal attainment

The initial goal of the Global Compact was 'to make [the former] nine principles part of the strategic vision and operating practices of companies everywhere' and 'catalyze action in support of broader UN goals' (UN Global Compact 2001). As these goals are more like guiding principles or visions that cannot be properly operationalized and directly measured, this section only evaluates trends that might serve as indicators of goal attainment of the Global Compact.

The Global Compact has produced countless 'how to' guides in relevant subject areas. Numerous case studies are on the website but have no systematic ordering principle. Policy dialogues on various themes and learning forums have been organized to bring together business, states actors, and NGOs to exchange experience and start new projects. Local networks have been established in more than 80 countries to stimulate action. Many activities have taken place but no systematic goal attainment evaluation has been conducted (Witte and Reinicke 2005). Initial analysis shows that it is very difficult to achieve impact on the ground, for example, by improving the workplace of employees in factories across different countries (UN Global Compact Regional Learning Forum 2007; UNDP 2007). Consequently, the Global Compact has started theme-related initiatives instead of supporting hundreds of smaller projects, making use of its convening and issue raising power. Examples of new initiatives are the CEO Water Mandate and the Caring for Climate initiative, which 'provides a framework for business leaders to advance practical solutions and help shape public policy as well as public attitudes'.[19]

Despite numerous individual success stories of cross-sector partnerships, the Global Compact has been subject to the same criticism as public-private partnerships: project ideas were chosen with a positive input/output ratio, not based on the biggest need (Witte and Reinicke 2005). Partnerships failed to live up to the equity challenge. For instance, the involvement of the private sector in energy and water projects has led to a commercialization of services, which does not promote poverty reduction nor lead to sustainable solutions (Utting and Zammit 2009). Partnership projects do not always lead to win-win or win-lose outcomes. Both may even exist simultaneously, even for the same stakeholders, depending on which criteria are applied. There might be trade-offs between certain aspects, for example, between the efficiency and sustainability of large and small solutions within partnerships (Lund-Thomsen 2009: 74). The overall goal attainment record is mixed. The Global Compact principles have been widely spread as guiding norms. However, this mainstreaming process has not led to satisfactory results on the ground level because the sheer volume of local projects makes it almost impossible to keep track and coordinate them.

Contribution to normative order

The potential contribution of the Global Compact to a new normative order concerns its impact above all on a new perception and expectations of the role of corporations in global governance. It can be claimed that Kofi Annan's initial proposal actually led to a paradigm shift in the debate on the political role of private actors. Former intergovernmental agreements, such as the OECD Guidelines for Multinational Enterprises or the ILO Tripartite Declaration of Principles concerning Multinational Enterprises and Social Policy, did not significantly further the issue of corporate responsibility and accountability in areas such as human rights and environmental protection. Voluntary nonhierarchical initiatives, like the Global Compact, contributed to change in the relationship among corporations, state actors, and NGOs (Ruggie 2004). In the wake of corporate environmental activities being labeled 'greenwash' (Karliner 1997) and the 'battle of Seattle' at the WTO Ministerial Conference in 1999 (UN Global Compact 2009), the Global Compact laid the foundation for the emergence of a number of new self-regulatory arrangements (Wolfsberg Principles founded in 2000; AccountAbility 1000 in 1999; Fair Labor Association in 1999; Voluntary Principles on Security and Human Rights in 2000) and boosted existing initiatives (Forest Stewardship Council (FSC) founded in 1993; Social Accountability (SA) 8000 in 1997; Global Reporting Initiative (GRI) in 1999). Through its interactive mode of learning and dialogue, the Global Compact was able to change the political climate, satisfying corporations and appeasing NGOs (Rieth 2009c; see critically Ottaway 2001). Although this approach of voluntariness and learning, rather than mandatory rules and sanctions, has often been criticized for preventing actual changes in corporate behavior (Zammit 2003) there can be little doubt that even without any aspiration to be 'binding', the Global Compact has significantly contributed to changes in the normative expectations of corporations.

Being associated with the positive image of the UN as the bearer of public interest and in the midst of an overwhelming array of other, more issue-specific initiatives, the Global Compact influenced perceptions of consumers, shareholders, employees, and opinion leaders. The Corporate Social

Responsibility Monitor, which documents stakeholder views on an annual basis, stated that society's expectations of companies have grown significantly over the past decade in eight of the world's largest economies, as a result of tracking attitudes to CSR from 2001 to 2009 (GlobeScan 2009). The most recent survey shows a particular increase between 2001 and 2005. Demand for CSR remains strong among corporate employees and has started to grow among investors. Over half of the respondents believe it is less risky to invest in socially responsible companies than in socially irresponsible companies. These are strong indicators that companies face internal and external CSR challenges.

During the past 5 years, there has been an increase in the publication of CSR rankings and growing importance placed on sustainability indices at stock exchanges. Signing on to the Global Compact and actively implementing the 10 principles leads to good CSR rankings and sustainability indices (Hellsten and Mallin 2006). A positive corporate identity (Corporate Knights 2009) gets a good assessment from analysts and demonstrates commitment to internationally accepted rules and norms to the wider public. Thus, the Global Compact has fostered demanding public expectations of what constitutes good corporate practice and sets the trend among numerous self-regulatory initiatives.

Unintended consequences

There are a number of unintended consequences of the emergence, high visibility, and impetus of the Global Compact. In the beginning, corporations were accused of taking advantage of the Global Compact to camouflage their poor social and ecological records without any definite commitment (Corpwatch 2000; 2002). Allowing public image campaigns and free riding without enforceable mechanisms (Knight and Smith 2009), the Global Compact seemed to offer a shield for protecting bad corporate practice from scrutiny rather than being a tool for improving it. The Global Compact was suspected to constitute just another facet of corporate globalization, with UN partnership projects only seen as reinforcing and engineering a fundamental shift in state-market relations in the logic of neo-liberalism (Zammit 2003; Utting and Zammit 2009: 46). The new global economic system is thus more and more molded and controlled by global corporations and corporate elites intending to tame rather than listen to civil society voices (Ottaway 2001). This interpretation is supported by the fact that the political activities of corporations are not handled by international organizations with authority and sanctioning power, such as the WTO, but left to a voluntary forum (Paine 2000). As a result, public policy goals are further undermined and corporate power is expanded.

However, Even NGOs who originally opposed the idea of the Global Compact decided that it was better to participate and be part of the discussion than excluded since the Global Compact made real contributions that were not solely at the level of the lowest common denominator, as was expected in the beginning. Corporations committed to the ten principles cannot easily resign without risking major negative publicity. The UN Global Compact has raised global public awareness of CSR and sustainability issues. Even NGOs reframed their argument about government intervention and mandatory regulation on CSR after positive dialogue and learning experiences within the Global Compact (Germanwatch 2007). The Global Compact was re-identified as a subtle step toward mandatory regulation rather than its prevention.

7.2.4   The Global Reporting Initiative (GRI)

The GRI represents a multistakeholder initiative open to participation by various actors, including business, civil society, labor and professional institutions. It aims to develop a globally accepted framework for voluntary reporting on the economic, environmental, and societal activities of organizations. GRI seeks to ensure quality, credibility, and relevance through continual development of the reporting guidelines in a consensus-seeking manner. GRI-based reports typically include a special report appendix (Hedberg and Malmborg 2003) and apply indicators (Willis 2003) explaining corporate behavioral adaptations. By increasing the transparency of company economic, social and environmental activities, the GRI intends to enable report users to better evaluate and compare company sustainability performance.

Norm commitment

Norm commitment within GRI at the individual company level is measured by looking at the total number of reports that use the GRI guidelines and at companies' engagement in transferring GRI reporting guidelines into the corporate organizational structure. Currently, more than 1500 companies, including many of the world's leading brands, have declared their voluntary adoption of the GRI guidelines. According to the GRI data illustrated in Table 7.4, 2159 company reports have been published since the launch of the third version of the guidelines (G3). The decreasing number of G2 reports shows the growing commitment to the newly introduced reporting standard.

Table 7.4   GRI Reports using G2 or G3[20]

Year	2006	2007	2008
Total number of reports	514	684	961
G3	96	554	938
G2	418	130	23

The establishment of new operational procedures to ensure the reporting process can be used as a further indicator of norm commitment. Several companies set up special management systems, including having sustainability managers that coordinate the reporting process, data gathering, data analysis, and structured data publication. Some companies established even more specialized institutions. For instance, Royal Dutch/Shell invited an External Review Committee[21] to assess the content and process of its sustainability report. However, while some companies institutionalized reporting internally, others outsource the whole process to PR agencies.

Change of behavior

Whether corporations declare their will to contribute to transparency and actually change their behavior is a controversial issue. The following analysis uses the rate of corporate reports with high GRI application levels as an indicator and investigates whether companies actively promote the GRI reporting framework externally. The GRI Application Levels system was established to enable GRI reporters to self-declare their level of compliance. There are three levels: beginners, advanced reporters, and those somewhere in between. The letters C, B, and A reflect a low, medium or high extent of application or coverage of the GRI reporting framework. A 'plus' sign designates (C+, B+, A+) whether external assurance was used for the report. Table 7.5 includes the total number of GRI reports, with the level A or A+ as a proxy for change of behavior.

Between 2006 and 2008 there was a total increase in the number of GRI reports and the number of reports with application levels A or A+. More than 25 percent of all registered reports are currently of the highest application level. However, it also has to be noted that the GRI reporters listed are predominantly TNCs. Although some companies have improved the transparency of their supply chain, widespread changes in corporate behavior attributable to the GRI are hard to measure. One example of a far-reaching change of behavior is the joint project of GRI, the German GTZ, Daimler, Otto Group, Puma, and Telefónica Group to convince suppliers of the competitive advantage and reputational gains of GRI sustainability reporting. Small and medium enterprises (SMEs) were invited to engage in sustainability reporting and to follow the GRI reporting guidelines (Global Reporting Initiative 2008). Significant behavior changes were caused by the GRI

Table 7.5 GRI reports with application level A and A+[22]

Year	2006	2007	2008
Total number of reports	514	684	961
Application level A+	23	128	201
Application level A	10	49	73

reporting framework, with more than a quarter of all reporters applying the highest standards and the majority being strongly influenced by the GRI reporting framework.

Identity shift

GRI participants have modified their reporting routine to include information about the social effects of doing business on employees and consumers, neighboring communities and the environment at large. A corporate identity shift from shareholder to stakeholder value is hard to measure and difficult to attribute to GRI. As in the case of the Global Compact, corporate behavior during the financial crises in late 2008–09 is used as an indicator: if the new norms still guide behavior in times of crisis, when the external conditions relevant to strategic decision making based on cost-benefit considerations change, internalization can provide a more likely explanation than rationalist strategy. A clue to the shift in corporate identity may be that companies not only continued to report but actively lobbied governments to introduce policies requiring other companies to address environmental, social and governance factors. The Amsterdam Declaration on Transparency and Reporting, released in early 2009 by GRI's Board, states: 'The root causes of the current economic crisis would have been moderated by a global transparency and accountability system based on the exercise of due diligence and the public reporting of environmental, social and governance (ESG) performance. The profound loss of trust in key institutions is best addressed by the adoption of a global reporting framework that enhances transparency and is informed by the legitimate interest of all key sectors of society. A revitalized and resilient economic system will only be sustained if it accounts for the full costs and value of ESG activity'.[23] At least some companies have turned into strong believers in the value of sustainability reporting, even during financial crisis.

Contribution to goal attainment

The goal attainment of GRI can be measured by how much it has facilitated transparency and accountability to achieve more substantive goals by providing stakeholders with a universally applicable and comparable framework to understand disclosed information. The remarkably steady rise of GRI-based corporate sustainability reporting is largely limited to TNCs. The number of companies who formally declared their use of the GRI guidelines is steadily increasing: in 2007 there were not more than 1500, of which nearly half (745) were based in Europe (McAusland 2007: 1). However, approximately 77,000 transnational corporations currently operate (UNCTAD 2006: 10) and GRI reporting practices are not applied worldwide. In particular, they do not include many SMEs, although GRI provides learning materials, accredits training partners and provides special guidance for them.[24]

Although the GRI reporting guidelines have increased the availability of corporate data on activities and measures, which 'put things in the right perspective and are very likely to reflect actual company achievements' (Kolk 2004: 59), it is still not clear whether increased corporate transparency really leads to more corporate accountability. In sustainability reports, corporations self-declare and rarely provide the raw data on which their conclusions are based. According to a KPMG and SustainAbility survey of 1827 sustainability report readers, 90 percent note that adherence to reporting standards, such as the GRI guidelines, builds trust and improves sustainability reports. However, although readers, in particular NGOs, seem to welcome sustainability reporting in general, they also suspect corporate green-washing of activities and ask for balanced reporting on the good and the not-so-good news to build trust and credibility. Moreover, NGOs rarely refer to sustainability reports themselves. The majority of readers also stressed the need to verify sustainability efforts (KPMG and SustainAbility 2008).

Progress toward improving the quality of reports seems slow when considering how few company reports gained a 'plus' for external verification in Table 7.5. According to KPMG, only 22 percent of sustainability reports used external verification for the entire report (KPMG 2005: 30). Accordingly, whether there has been a notable change in overall corporate practice to compare corporate sustainability is controversial (Palenberg et al. 2006). Corporate sustainability reports still vary in content, reacting to stakeholder demands for specific information. This has become most apparent for companies in the chemicals, oil and mining industries that were increasingly confronted with stakeholder demands for more openness and transparency (Cashore 2002). Critics could come to the conclusion that sustainability reporting, even when in accordance with GRI, is of little additional value because the limited quality and incomplete content lead to corporate action without meaning and to worthless information gathering rather than to meaningful self-assessment processes. From this perspective and because of the lack of verification and comparability, only a medium to low effectiveness could be attributed to GRI goal attainment.

Contribution to normative order

There are several indications that GRI has contributed to the development of normative order by changing the expectations of the public and corporations in their demand for more corporate transparency. In 2007, the Swedish government was the first to introduce GRI sustainability reporting measures as mandatory for all 55 state-owned companies in Sweden. Through its institutional opportunities for companies to propose or lobby for or against changes in the norm development process, the GRI reporting framework created shared corporate value commitments in the business sector to sustainability reporting. This framework has become a generally accepted standard of corporate behavior for more than three-quarters of the G250 and 69 percent of the N100 reporting companies who follow the GRI guidelines (KPMG 2008: 35). GRI has made sustainability reporting an expected best practice for corporations that want to take on CSR. According to Dingwerth, the norm of nonfinancial reporting has even wider implications: 'Discursive shifts induced or, where they already existed, supported by the GRI include the broad acceptance of the importance of nonfinancial reporting, widespread recognition of the relevance of the CSR agenda and a growing acceptance of the notion that not only firms, but also civil society organizations and public agencies should report the consequences of their activities' (Dingwerth 2007: 114–15).

This contribution is probably further reinforced by the link between GRI and the UN Global Compact (Global Reporting Initiative and Global Compact 2007). The GRI reporting guidelines help transfer the general principles of the Global Compact into practical guidance. The G3 reporting guidelines are applicable to the Global Compact's annually required CoPs, reinforcing the normative force of both.

Unintended consequences

Despite the Swedish legislation, a potentially negative consequence of establishing the voluntary GRI reporting framework at the global level may be its contribution to preventing more mandatory reporting by national or international law. Currently, the GRI still lacks any 'shadow of hierarchy' and does not have binding enforcement mechanisms to ensure an even more widespread application of the reporting standards. Its voluntary nature may hinder sustainability reporting and slow down more far-reaching changes in normative expectations about what constitutes good corporate conduct. Another criticism is that GRI achieves the opposite of what it claims: Instead of increasing corporate transparency through providing comprehensive reporting guidelines, the extensiveness might actually result in a new lack of transparency. In the bulk of detailed information, important facts can be hidden. Another potential effect may be that by requiring highly professionalized reporting, GRI reinforces the trend to outsource corporate sustainability reporting and so precludes the desirable learning effects of thorough self-evaluation.

7.3   Comparing the effectiveness of self-regulatory arrangements

The types of self-regulatory arrangements presented in this chapter provided some strong indications that a role shift of corporations has taken place during the past decade, from political objects to ambitious political subjects. The results of the empirical analysis of four new types of self-regulatory arrangements have shown that the introduction of new modes of transnational governance have started off general debates within and among business actors about the relevance of corporate social responsibility in general and, more specifically, of sustainability reporting and other sensitive issues, such as antimoney laundering. Companies have committed to new norms and have taken the first steps in implementing their commitments. As frontrunners, corporate norm-entrepreneurs have made significant contributions to establishing a new normative order that has increased expectations of companies.

Although corporations have made efforts to find new ways of handling new political challenges, they have only changed their actual behavior slightly. As the empirical analysis has shown, there is still a large gap between norm commitment and change of behavior, contributions to a new normative order and progress in goal attainment. An identity shift within companies has been triggered but has not yet fully translated into organizational changes. The line of argument for justifying engaging in responsible business behavior has changed but corporate practice still lags considerably behind.

Based on this analysis, the different types of self-regulatory arrangements are assessed. What kind of governance contributions are they likely to achieve and what kind of governance gaps left by them have to be addressed by other forums within the broader institutional architecture of global governance? Table 7.6 summarizes the results.

The effectiveness of unilateral governance arrangements – company level

As shown by the Shell case study and summarized in Table 7.6, the potential reach of a single company code can be tremendous. Effects were strongest at the actor level and on norm commitment and identity shift. Even at the structural level, the company's policies were influential in the development

Table 7.6 Effectiveness records of self-regulatory arrangements

	Norm commitment	Change of behavior	Identity shift	Contributions to normative order	Contributions to goal attainment	Unintended consequences
Shell General Business Principles and Code of Conduct	High	Medium	High	Medium	No	Medium
Private-Private (Wolfsberg Principles)	High	Low	Medium	High	Low	High
Public Private (Global Compact)	High	Low	Medium	High	Low	Medium
Multistakeholder (GRI)	Medium	Medium	Medium	High	Low	Medium

of the larger normative order and affected an entire industry through the establishment of best practices, and then serving as role models. Although companies might not change their behavior in all issue areas in accordance with their codes, at least some pilot activities have been launched and awareness is being raised among management, employees, and stakeholders. Unsurprisingly, contributions to goal attainment remain necessarily limited since an individual company's behavior is unlikely to provide the solution to large-scale, multicausal, societal problems. This limitation is reinforced by the negative externalities that result when the positive behavior change of one company offers opportunities for free riding to other companies. Nevertheless, the corporate norm-entrepreneur Shell gives the impression that comprehensive and rigid implementation of unilateral self-regulatory arrangements can constitute a useful contribution to effective transnational governance. It will always have limited reliability due to its voluntary nature and possible corporate strategy shifts.

The effectiveness of collective governance arrangements – private-private

Collective but exclusively private self-regulatory arrangements seem to share a lot of the potential and limitations of individual corporate norm-entrepreneurship. As Table 7.6 shows, there are significant shortcomings in achieving changes of behavior and goal attainment. When business actors get together voluntarily and are ready to rethink their concept of responsibility, the collective process is likely to reinforce individual commitments and identity shifts. It is particularly striking that this can also happen in a sector with a traditionally high resistance to taking on responsibility for anything beyond conventional client confidentiality. However, the achievable identity shift is structurally limited in purely private-private constellations. In the Wolfsberg case, this is due to the limited substantive scope of the Wolfsberg Principles, which covers only money laundering, and due to the fact that little external expertise and ideas are brought to the table. Nevertheless, they can have far-reaching impacts on the normative order.

Again, goal attainment and changes in behavior remain limited, the latter scoring even lower than in the individual company case. This might be because of the well-known argument that collective action problems lead to lowest common denominator solutions. A lack of enforcement instruments impairs effectiveness. Without external assistance, it seems difficult to achieve the goals advanced by the corporations alone, even more so because significant negative consequences can emerge.

The effectiveness of collective governance arrangements – public-private

The Global Compact shows the potential strengths of public-private self-regulatory governance arrangements in the areas of norm creation at the structural level and norm commitment at the actor level. The particular institutional quality of governance arrangements that enables new space for discussion among diverse and sometimes even hostile groups of actors carries a distinct normative power. If the public side is represented as visible, strong, international and reputable, as in the case of the Global Compact, the likelihood of normative effects at the actor and structural level is increased. Owing to the broader publicity and the potentially higher (positive or negative) repercussions of the success or failure of public-private initiatives, high-level management involvement and backing by the CEO or a board level representative may guarantee stronger norm commitment. This can translate into organizational change or agenda shift within a company. The generally positive public image of public-private initiatives has a leverage effect on public reception and on other companies that also want to improve their public image. However, strong normative shifts often start by being regarded as add-ons, used in public statements but not in standard operating procedures where 'business as usual' still dominates. This explains the lower record of changes in behavior and goal attainment. The latter may be further inhibited by a vague goal description, another likely result of the problematic consensus-finding process within a public-private undertaking, or the fear that a voluntary initiative might mutate into stricter forms of regulation in the future. Goal attainment in public-private projects, precisely because of their broad normative aspirations, is rarely a straightforward venture but very often involves complicated trade-offs that were underestimated beforehand.

The effectiveness of collective governance arrangements – multistakeholder

Generalizing from the GRI case, multistakeholder initiatives, while generally having only medium effects over most dimensions, can make strong contributions to normative order. In collaboration, state and nonstate actors seem to be particularly able to agree on setting norms and thus determine collective expectations on proper corporate behavior (in this case: transparency) and concrete behavioral standards by which these norms can be applied (here: reporting). However, the positive effects of multistakeholder initiatives at the actor level are not as far-reaching as one might expect. Although there is a trend among companies toward increased norm commitment and adopting the new standards developed in a multistakeholder setting, companies seem to feel obliged to follow the general spirit but not necessarily fully comply with it. This is also reflected in the limited effects on a possible identity shift of companies. The fact that too many actors are involved, applying and interpreting the standards according to their needs, might hinder cognitive reinforcement and limit the potential for goal attainment. As shown, none of the participants was willing to pay high monitoring and enforcement costs. It seems that multistakeholder initiatives require additional qualities to be effective, such as independent verification mechanisms, which are obviously difficult to achieve when no public 'shadow of hierarchy' or a functional equivalent exists.

Limits of private self-regulation – an agenda for governance

The following observations can be made from the far-reaching case studies on the overall potential and limits of governance contributions by the different types of self-regulation involving corporate norm-entrepreneurs for the provision of public goods.

Self-regulation of all types triggers effects on all dimensions of effectiveness – with the single exception of individual company self-regulation, with its particularly limited influence on goal attainment. This result cannot be underestimated as it demonstrates impressively that self-regulation should not be ignored as a potential private contribution to global governance: It is an influential phenomenon that should receive empirical and normative attention. A second observation results from disaggregating the various dimensions of effectiveness. Self-regulation has considerable strengths in certain areas and distinct shortcomings when it comes to achieving changes of corporate behavior and improvements in goal attainment. Significant as both of these limitations might be, it remains unclear whether public or hierarchical types of regulation would be more successful than the voluntary approach. The search is still on for an institutional architecture for governance beyond the state in which the interplay between governance arrangements compensates for the shortcomings in public good provision of each one.

Goal attainment is unlikely to be achieved within single self-regulation efforts. All critical problems in the social world are of a multicausal nature and demand comprehensive, multiangled governance approaches. Self-regulation by corporate norm-entrepreneurs generally follows an opposite functional logic. It usually disaggregates the social world into intra-sectoral, or even intra-business, issues that are then approached via highly precise sectoral rules and standards. A plurality of self-regulating initiatives tackling comparatively isolated aspects of the social world has emerged. Goal attainment – more than other dimensions of effectiveness – will often fail because of limited or nonexisting linkage management between the functional self-regulatory arrangements. Their growth in number leads to growing regulation of issue areas and growing numbers of uncontrolled holes and unmanaged overlaps and externalities. These problems are supported by the unintended consequences that result from disaggregated self-regulation. All of the initiatives under scrutiny here had strong effects on this dimension and manifold negative externalities that remain unaccounted for. Self-regulation does not seem to be able to control the problems it creates.

In terms of the possible strengths of self-regulatory efforts by corporate norm-entrepreneurs, the case studies showed the strongest effects in contributions to the normative order, directly followed by reinforced norm commitment and possible identity shifts. The implication of this finding is remarkable: corporations are increasingly developing a new understanding of their responsibilities in society, their normative frameworks are changing and the process is significantly reinforced through voluntary mechanisms of self-regulation. Self-regulatory arrangements provide guidance to companies when former yardsticks and terms of reference for business decisions are no longer considered appropriate. They can break with an existing tradition of 'business as usual' and reinforce normatively guided solutions as the 'right solutions'.

While hierarchical and mandatory regulatory approaches relying on the 'shadow of hierarchy' provided by statehood may seem more effective in ensuring compliant corporate behavior, functional equivalents can work if comprehensive and extensive monitoring or other forms of – positive and negative – sanctions are in place. In addition, private self-regulatory approaches then also have the ability to contribute to corporate identity shifts.

However, the findings on the effectiveness of private norm-entrepreneurship in different settings have to be weighted carefully: 'Effectiveness' does not necessarily imply good governance contributions in terms of serving the public good. This becomes evident when looking at the influence on the larger normative order. Corporate self-regulation can effect significant changes in normative expectations, as the Wolfsberg Principles, the Global Compact, and GRI have shown. Corporate influence must not be misunderstood as an automatic advancement of the public good. The influence of private actors on norm setting can also result in an infiltration of normative orders by private interests. The new rules might serve the business case more than the public case. Trends in this direction are evident in the Wolfsberg example, where a cost-efficient and risk-based approach to money laundering was promoted by private institutions and is now enshrined in various public rules. An important implication is that private self-regulation, despite its significant potential for positive achievements, always needs to be linked to the public case.

Having devised and developed a number of self-regulatory arrangements, corporations have gained importance as political actors and lost their political innocence. They can no longer hide behind the division of labor between public and private actors and regard themselves as mere rule takers. As rising co-performers of governance functions, they share responsibility for the development and failure of the global governance project. Although they are not expected to take the public case for self-regulation as seriously as the business case, their governance efforts will have to be embedded in an institutional architecture that guarantees the link.

Notes

1. This general differentiation is also taken up in the conceptualization of the effectiveness of transnational public-private partnerships by a research team at Freie Uuniversität Berlin. They added different stages of the policy cycle to the simple performance dimension and discussed potential side effects of self-regulatory frameworks – concrete findings of the project are not yet available (Schäferhoff et al. 2007: 13–23).

2. The following explanatory notes are based mainly on Rieth et al. 2007.
3. See also BBC News 2004: Shell admits fuelling Corruption, http://news.bbc. co.uk/2/hi/business/3796375.stm, date accessed 16 December 2008.
4. http://www.transparency.org/news_room/in_focus/2008/bpi_2008, date accessed 30 December 2008. The situation within host states such as Nigeria gradually improves; the score rose from 1.6 to 2.7, bringing Nigeria from rank 144 to 121 in the annual Transparency International Corruption Perception Index: http:// www.transparency.org/policy_research/surveys_indices/cpi/2004; http://www. transparency.org/policy_research/surveys_indices/cpi/2008, date accessed 3 January 2008.
5. Due to fluctuations within the industry caused by mergers, 11 member banks currently remain.
6. http://www.bankersalmanac.com/default.aspx, date accessed 12 May 2009.
7. http://www.wolfsberg-principles.com/diligence.html and http://www.banker salmanac.com/addcon/products/due-diligence-repository.aspx, date accessed 12 May 2009.
8. To a certain extent, it is possible that this form of heightened expertise within the Wolfsberg institutions has led to decreases in reports to authorities because they no longer report anything mildly suspicious but feel better equipped to judge for themselves what might constitute a crime. This implies that the overall effect of Wolfsberg on the identification of money laundering activities might not be visible from increased or decreased reporting numbers, as procedures might simply have been rendered more efficient. This was the major goal of member banks (Pieth and Aiolfi 2003a).
9. http://www.fedpol.admin.ch/fedpol/en/home/themen/kriminalitaet/geldwae scherei.html, date accessed 12 May 2009.
10. Other potentially significant influence factors include the revision of the FATF recommendations in 2003 and the increased focus on the prevention of the financing of terrorism since 9/11 in 2001. Regarding the significant increase in total reports in the first years, they most likely result from increased awareness and implementation in the follow-up to the Swiss Anti-Money-Laundering Law of 1998, which prescribed mandatory reporting for certain indicators and encouraged voluntary reporting for others.
11. In 2008, it attributes the increases mainly to the Raiffeisen Banks – nonmembers of Wolfsberg (MRO 2008: 7).
12. There was probably considerable mutual influence as, for example, the original Wolfsberg Principles drew heavily on Swiss law as well as on the Swiss bankers' associations self-regulatory codes; the Basel Statement of 2001 further influenced the Wolfsberg review in 2002, which in turn heavily impacted on the FATF 40 recommendations review in 2003.
13. A similar argument – that the very technical approach by the Wolfsberg Group is detrimental to the fight against corruption – is also sometimes made by representatives of Transparency International. Statements to this effect were gathered in participatory observations at conferences such as the 3rd International CSR Conference 'Corporate Responsibility and Governance', 8–10 October 2008, Institute of Management, Humboldt-Universität zu Berlin.
14. Statements such as 'without further information, it is not possible for financial institutions to make a distinction between accounts and transactions associated with corruption, and those accounts and transactions that have a legal and sound commercial basis' and '[T]he primary responsibility to ensure that funds are neither collected nor used for illicit operations, including bribery, must

rest with a financial institution's customer or that customer's representatives' (Wolfsberg Group 2007) seem to imply major steps back in the extent of responsibility assumed in AML measures. They can only be interpreted as hindering the spread of normative orders in the financial sector.

15. UN Global Compact Homepage, date accessed 16 May 2009.

16. The publication of a CoP does not necessarily imply that a company has made progress on the implementation of 1 of the 10 principles. At least a CoP reflects the efforts of a company and describes actions taken. External readers have the chance to question statements made in the CoPs.

17. A company holds an 'active status' if it complies with the CoP policy because it joined the Global Compact within 2 years or has met the annual CoP deadline. Companies that fail to produce a CoP within 2 or 3 years receive the 'noncommunicating' status or are delisted from the Global Compact homepage.

18. Handelsblatt, 24 November 2008, p. 20.

19. UN Global Compact Homepage, date accessed 15 May 2009.

20. Inquiry based on the GRI Reports List; see http://www.globalreporting.org/NR/rdonlyres/E033E311-68E7-41F9-A97F-9F3B94F3FE40/2813/Copyof1999 2009reportslist_6May.xls, date accessed 19 May 2009.

21. For more details about the Shell External Review Committee, see http://sustaina bilityreport.shell.com/2008/measuringourperformance/externalreviewcommittee. html, date accessed 13 May 2009.

22. Inquiry based on the GRI Reports List; see http://www.globalreporting.org/NR/rdonlyres/E033E311-68E7-41F9-A97F-9F3B94F3FE40/2813/Copyof1999 2009reportslist_6May.xls, date accessed 19 May 2009.

23. For the full text of the 'Amsterdam Declaration on Transparency and Reporting', see http://www.globalreporting.org/NewsEventsPress/PressResources/PressRelease_ 10March2009.htm, date accessed 10 June 2009.

24. For more information on the GRI reporting framework and related documents, see http://www.globalreporting.org/AboutGRI/WhatWeDo/, date accessed 19 May 2009.

8
The Legitimacy of Transnational Private Governance

Engaging in norm-entrepreneurship is not something normatively 'good' in the sense of serving or aiming to serve the public interest. Therefore, corporate norm-entrepreneurship does not answer but raises the question of its potential to increase or even harm the legitimacy of governance beyond the state in a postnational constellation. The answer to this question is of paramount significance for any attempts at designing a future institutional architecture for global governance that reconciles the demands of effective public goods provision raised by policy research with the legitimacy demands normative political theory addresses to decision making processes and the institutions through which they are provided. In other words, what can be the role of corporate norm-entrepreneurship? What kind of transnational private governance contributions should be promoted or ruled out for normative reasons?

Applying these questions to individual and collective self-regulatory arrangements in which corporations set and implement norms is not a self evident exercise but should be based on certain explicit premises. The first and foremost of these premises is that we have to subscribe to the view that transnational private governance and the norm generating and implementing activities performed by corporations in this conduct qualify as *political* activities and thus create certain responsibilities. This assumption is far from Milton Friedman's (1970) classical doctrine that 'the social responsibility of business is to increase its profits'. Corporations' participation in the 'co-performance of governance' (Schuppert 2008) calls for a rigorous reassessment of Friedman's statement as it does not reflect the privatization of governance and how public and private actors are redefining their political roles (Florin 2000; Fuchs 2005; Wolf 2008). The newly emerging governance patterns include private actors who have taken on authoritative roles and regulatory functions (Cutler et al. 1999a; Hall and Biersteker 2002). Compliance basically relies on the use of 'soft power' (Nye 1990), that is on creating 'a sense of obligation rather than coercion' (Cutler et al. 1999c: 359), as in the case of best practice. But each company code that governs supply chains, for example, interferes with the addressees' right to self-rule or self-determination on the norms they promote, even if it may not involve the exercise of power in a formal sense and although it may be voluntary and lack legally binding enforcement mechanisms. Obviously, corporate norm-entrepreneurs claim authority for making decisions about setting and implementing collectively binding rules and norms and may even seek compliance by de facto coercion, using the structural power they have at their disposal. There can thus be little controversy over the legitimacy demands raised by the involvement of private actors in norm setting and norm implementation because it implies exercise of private authority, by setting binding normative standards, with the aim of governing behavior.

The following normative considerations do indeed start out from the above mentioned premise that individual and collective self-regulatory arrangements in which corporations set and implement norms are of a genuine political nature. Therefore, like any *public* governance activities conducted by governments or international organizations which aim at establishing collectively binding rules of behavior, they raise and have to meet certain legitimacy demands. However, before the legitimacy potential of the highly varied types of transnational private governance initiatives can be measured, normative standards are required, against which transnational private governance can be adequately measured. Such a normative framework should be as open as possible in order to help find legitimacy *potential*. It should extend the range of legitimacy demands beyond output effectiveness and also include the input and throughput dimensions of legitimacy that are essential to democratic self-government and refer to legitimization through participation and accountability (Scharpf 2000b: 102). Last but not least, such a framework should also take into account the fundamental differences between governance by, with, and without the state.

8.1 A governance perspective on the legitimacy of corporate norm-entrepreneurship

The new regulatory state is less keen on running things 'from above' than on enabling, regulating and monitoring self-regulation which relies heavily on the participation of nonstate actors. If we subscribe to the view that statehood is in transition because of the insufficiency of the model of hierarchical governance by and within the state, a concept of legitimacy has to be developed which is applicable to the emerging postnational governance patterns. Conceptualizing such postnational legitimacy criteria for private contributions to governance can only work within a paradigm that dissociates political legitimacy from what the state does or fails to do and addresses the issue of legitimacy in the absence of the legal authority of the state (or its supranational equivalent). After all, only a small part of transnational private governance activities occur in a context where private participation is the result of any public authorization; self-authorized and nonelected forms of representation are the rule.

The governance paradigm offers a conceptual framework which is open to the multilevel, multiactor, and multimode reality of transnational governance processes. In contrast to a state centered perspective on legitimacy, it allows us to go beyond the notion 'that legitimacy for these institutions requires the same democratic standards that are now applied to states' (Buchanan and Keohane 2006: 405). This does not render input legitimation with its demands for participation and self-determination, nor throughput legitimation with its demands for accountability and power control superfluous. However, while such basic normative criteria remain valid, neither the governance paradigm nor normative political theory can so far offer an operational set of concrete standards for measuring legitimate governance in the postnational constellation as coherent as the one employed when dealing with the territorial state majority democracy.

This lack of a coherent understanding of how democratic governance can look like in the emerging postnational constellation may be partially explained by deformalized and deinstitutionalized politics which has shifted the emphasis from the institutional to the procedural dimension of politics. While accustomed concepts of legitimacy are closely related to the existence of certain institutions – first and foremost those of the (democratic) state – here the legitimacy issue is analyzed in a highly fragmented landscape of very different governance arrangements in which horizontal governance modes involving nonstate actors have gained more and more prominence. However, deformalization does not mean that legitimacy demands on the institutional and procedural environment in which corporate norm-entrepreneurship is embedded lose any of their importance. Given the widespread suspicion that private actors, in particular, are not automatically geared toward the general interest when they set and implement norms, the opposite is the case. However, institutional demands for legitimacy in transnational private governance arrangements have to take into account the fact that such initiatives no longer take place within institutional settings that are comparable with those we know from the state and therefore cannot be checked and balanced by the mechanisms available in the domestic political setting.

As long as there is no single and undisputed model of legitimate private governance, it seems reasonable to proceed by putting together a tool kit of criteria derived from normative political theory which, applied in combination, can provide a comprehensive evaluation of the legitimacy of corporate governance contributions from as many different angles as possible. This tool kit is based on the following normative principles: *responsiveness* is the normative complement to the effectiveness criteria used in Chapter 7 for evaluating the output legitimacy of corporate norm-entrepreneurship. Input legitimation through *participation* serves the basic right of self-determination. Public *accountability* refers to the control of the abuse of power and to the throughput dimension of legitimacy. It depends on a minimum level of transparency as a prerequisite for evaluating the performance of self-regulatory arrangements. While these criteria address the normative qualities of governance institutions and procedures, *authority* is added as a normative criterion to identify and evaluate the additional legitimacy potential that originates from characteristics of the different public and private actors themselves.

Using these output, input, and throughput related legitimacy concepts, all of which are important in evaluating private contributions to governance, allows a broad range of normative concerns to be covered that make up the rational and democratic qualities of political processes. The criteria measure whether corporate governance contributions are guaranteed reliable responses to collective action problems and address concerns in the public interest (*responsiveness*). They seek the extent to which the addressees of corporate governance contributions have a say in the decision making process (*participation*), and whether and how far corporate actors can be controlled and made accountable for their performance (*accountability*). Finally, at the actors' level, the criteria address the sources of authority with which corporations can justify the legitimacy of their claim to take on political roles (*authority*).

Although all four criteria establish distinct normative yardsticks, contextualization makes their interconnectedness obvious: Processes of norm setting and norm implementation can differ in content. They can concern general standards of appropriate behavior, the establishment of institutional settings for the distribution and control of power or technical standards. At each of these levels of governing, the sources from which different types of actors derive their claim to set norms can provide more or less valuable entry tickets.

The value of the authority currency at the disposal of different actors depends on the mode of governance which may be based on 'vote' or 'voice'. Legitimacy problems concerning self-rule and the control of power are mitigated or enhanced depending on how decisions are made, ranging from voluntary self-commitments to committing others to legally binding rules. Finally, legitimacy demands depend on the scope of the governance arrangements in which corporate norm-entrepreneurship is embedded and may have an inward or outward focus.

8.1.1 Responsiveness – the normative complement to effectiveness for measuring output legitimacy

Raising the question of legitimacy within the governance paradigm has often given rise to skepticism. At the heart of this is the supposed shift in understanding politics not in terms of the use and control of power but, rather, in terms of acting in the public interest and solving problems in a society

(Mayntz 2005: 12). Indeed, when one of the most prominent political advocates of global governance, Kofi Annan, first addressed the issue of inclusion and called upon 'partnerships involving governments, international organizations, the business community and civil society' (Annan 1998) at the World Economic Forum in January 1998, the underlying notion of 'participatory governance' had an output biased core. It is primarily guided by the expectation that more participation will result in more effective problem solving and in better compliance by those included in governance processes beyond the state. Participation thus becomes a rational choice as a means to reach certain ends: more effective governance by mobilizing additional, nonstate problem solving resources. This is far from ascribing 'more citizen participation' a value in its own right. When it comes to defining legitimacy criteria for corporate contributions to governance, this output bias of the governance debate needs to be addressed and balanced. This does not mean skipping output concerns about legitimacy altogether. The usually voluntary nature of private actors' policies and activities sheds light on a particular aspect of output legitimacy: the responsiveness and reliability of private governance contributions. There are some objections to the criticism that private actors, unlike governments, act voluntarily and are not obliged to act in the public interest. After all, in the international sphere, the governments of individual states do not have any obligation either to act in anything more than their national, that is, 'private', interest. In both cases, public and private actors alike, the 'public interest' proof ultimately lies in the quality of the norms they advocate.

Corporations are not legally obliged to respond to collective action problems in the public interest. The voluntary nature of private self-regulation implies that private actors may decide to self-regulate, but they may also (and have the power to) opt for nonregulation. Furthermore, the reliability of private governance contributions is further diminished by the fact that private norm-entrepreneurs usually mandate themselves. This raises questions of responsiveness: How can it be assured that private self-regulation is regardful of peoples' demands and that action deemed necessary by the public is taken? The responsiveness of private norm-entrepreneurship must therefore be guaranteed by further conditions to ensure that corporate contributions to setting and developing norms are close to peoples' demands and that the necessary action is taken.

8.1.2   Participation and accountability: the input and throughput dimensions of legitimacy

Despite the inapplicable institutional and procedural answers that the territorial state majority-democracy model has to offer when dealing with input and throughput demands on governance beyond the state, the basic normative challenges still apply within the context of more informal transnational governance arrangements. In this realm, authentic participation and

effective accountability mechanisms still remain two fundamental normative standards for evaluating whether a fair chance of access is ensured for
those who are affected by the decisions and to what extent the addressees of
private governance contributions have a say in the decision making process.
General claims for more direct citizen participation in order to meet these
input demands of legitimacy and protect the right of self-determination
have raised critical questions: Given the participatory potential of opening
governance arrangements to all kinds of nonstate stakeholders, can it be
assumed that more privatization and deformalization, which are only two
ways to circumscribe this change, will make governance beyond the state
any better in a democratic sense?

A standard criticism fuelled by such trends toward privatization and
informalization is the lack of accountability in governance beyond the state
(Koenig-Archibugi 2004). This criticism underlines the importance of procedural legitimacy demands which guarantee transparency, and checks and
balances to control the use of de facto power of private actors making governance contributions as norm-entrepreneurs. Although in the domestic
and transnational realms the same standards of accountability should be
applied to whether and how far those who govern can be made accountable by those governed, it would be misleading to assume that the same
mechanisms for ensuring accountability are applicable in both spheres. The
domestic model of democratic accountability guaranteed by the state with
legally binding sanctions can only work in the 'shadow of hierarchy'. As
long as the transnational sphere is characterized by a 'shadow of anarchy',
this underlines the need for more specific procedural mechanisms that
increase the accountability of private norm-entrepreneurs under conditions
fundamentally different from those within the state.

Accountability mechanisms are required that are functionally equivalent (see Rosenau 1998; Buchanan and Keohane 2006) to the democratic,
state provided accountability mechanisms of institutionalized checks and
balances which hold public actors responsible and ensure effective power
control via electoral processes. Nonstate actors are usually not accountable to any electoral constituency, only to their supporters, members, or
shareholders. How can responsible actors be identified (criteria of transparency and information) and rewarded or punished (criterion of sanctions)?
In search of such functional equivalents the lack of legal (or democratic)
accountability measures in the transnational sphere may – at least to some
extent – be compensated by social (or reputational) and market mechanisms
of accountability. Even within governance contexts where the authority
of private actors does not rest on public authorization – and that may be
withdrawn when they abuse their power – their regulatory competencies
need the approval of professional peers or the wider public, depending on
whether their claims to norm setting are based on their own moral or professional authority.

In each case, and similarly to elected politicians who can be discharged in the domestic context of a majority democracy, private actors may be held responsible for their governance contributions: formal entitlement may be withdrawn and legal action may be taken against them when private norm-entrepreneurship has been mandated by the state; the credibility of their moral and professional authority may be lost, and subsequently their public acceptance, financial support or peer reputation, when reporting require-ments are not met or peer reviews are negative. All these market based and reputational checks can be regarded as accountability mechanisms func-tionally equivalent to those within the political system of the democratic state. Of course, they require a functioning market, an open public, and – above all – robust commitments to accountability standards. The commit-ments are reflected in the existence of concrete accountability measures that form part of the institutional design of a public-private or multistakeholder governance arrangement, such as reporting requirements or independent review procedures.

8.1.3   Actor-related legitimacy criteria based on sources of authority

Legitimacy criteria may refer to institutions and governance arrangements and to actors' characteristics. Actors, such as governments, parliaments, international or supranational organizations, NGOs and business corpo-rations, can contribute to the legitimacy of governance in different ways, depending on the sources of legitimacy relevant authority that are avail-able to them as public or as private actors. Normative objections to a more direct involvement of private actors in the decision making phases of gov-ernance processes are usual because of the lack of democratic legitimacy in nongovernmental actors. In fact, many NGOs and all business corpora-tions are not organized in a democratic fashion, but are usually hierarch-ical (this applies to NGOs such as Greenpeace and to business corporations alike).[1] Nonstate actors may indeed lack basic qualifications for government functions. However, this deficit has to take into account that the modes of governance that prevail in transnational private governance arrangements differ from those within the democratic state. This implies that the qualifi-cations required of those who want to participate may be different as well. What this means in terms of adequate normative assessment of private norm-entrepreneurship is discussed later in the introduction to the different sources of authority that different types of actors have at their disposal.

In the context of the state, political authority is traditionally regarded as legitimate if it is held by a legally authorized body. This concept of legitim-acy is reflected in the general recognition of the state as the only political actor with an authorized claim on the legitimate use of physical power. The notion of 'private' authority would be the prototype of a *contradictio in adiecto* if an approach to understanding the concept of authority was chosen which started out from the assumption that private actors are in principle 'not entitled to prescribe behavior' (Friedman 1970: 58, 79). The authorization of private governance claims would only be conceivable via an explicit delegation of competencies by the only body with the authoritative competence to allocate competencies – the state.

However, this way of founding the legitimacy of nonstate ('private') regulatory activities on a formal ('public') authorization by the state becomes highly problematic at the international level. There are two reasons for this. Firstly, the boundaries between 'public' and 'private' are much less clear in the political space beyond the state. As indicated earlier, national governments follow 'private' purposes ('the national interest'), and private actors are often the only protagonists of what is generally perceived as the common good. Secondly, authorization by an intergovernmental delegation cannot provide the same legitimacy as authorization by the state in the domestic context. In the sphere beyond the state all governance contributions, no matter by which actors (including national governments), take place in the absence of government institutions. There is no international public authority above states with a legitimate claim on competence delegation and the monopoly of legitimate power. Once again, public and private actors turn out to be surprisingly like units in the international sphere.

In ideal terms, the legitimacy of corporate contributions to governance can only be derived from the sources of authority they themselves claim to possess or that are attributed to them by others. In fact, a private actor may (or may not) have substantial authority independent of formal authorization. Their claim of contributing to governance may be based, for example, on a credible commitment to universally accepted basic norms, general welfare, knowledge-based professional expertise, or more general problem solving resources. These assets are 'the last resort' when it comes to justifying the legitimacy of private actors' governance contributions. They are inherent in the attitude and the integrity of the conduct of actors, and they live on the general or, at least, widespread recognition of the appropriateness of their goals. Input legitimacy based on them results from the power of the moral and professional authority of private actors. It unfolds its impact primarily in deliberative processes. It is inherent in the attitude and the integrity of the conduct of actors, and it lives on the general or, at least, widespread recognition of the appropriateness of their programmatic goals.

Cutler, Haufler and Porter (1999c) describe the authority of public actors as being elected 'in authority' in contrast to nonstate actors being regarded as 'an authority'. For example, the constitutionally institutionalized delegation of competencies by democratic procedures provides the state with the legal authority to use coercive measures to secure compliance with legally binding norms. Civil society actors can exercise moral authority based on the credibility with which they pursue goals in the public interest (see also Lipschutz and Fogel 2002: 125). Epistemic communities are often considered to exercise authority only by virtue of being credible providers of technical expertise or information.

In a similar way, the legitimacy of private norm-entrepreneurship rests on the promise of more rational outcomes by bringing in knowledge-based expertise and substantial problem solving resources, such as technical know-how or financial means. Leaving aside for a moment the question whether a claim is rightfully made, this source of legitimacy becomes significant only in the context of certain modes of governance and at certain levels of governing. However, for groups of potential norm-entrepreneurs, such as states, civil society, epistemic communities, and corporations, these conceptual arguments in favor of their engagement do not imply that they are valid or supported by actual behavior at the empirical level. In each case it remains an open question of how far and under which circumstances norm-entrepreneurship actually fosters norm emergence that is in the public interest.

8.1.4   Context dependency of the legitimacy value of actors' authority sources

The legitimacy potential of corporate norm-entrepreneurship cannot be sufficiently evaluated by only looking at the actors' level sources of authority. It has to take into account the context within which corporations act as norm-entrepreneurs. The value of the authority 'currencies' at the disposal of actors varies according to (a) the mode of governance, (b) the contents of norms at different levels of governing, and (c) the scope of norm-entrepreneurship (inward- or outward-focused).

Depending on the mode of governance, normative commitments may be invited or imposed. As in the case of moral authority, the recognition of knowledge-based authority only provides a sufficient source of legitimacy for corporate actors in the context of soft modes of governance, such as voluntary self-regulation. The more coercive subordination is involved, the more legal (public) authority would be needed and the less the specific authority claims of corporate actors can count as legitimate. On the other hand, corporate governance contributions carry a high legitimacy potential in contexts of horizontal, consensus seeking and learning oriented processes of norm emergence. In the terminology of deliberative democratic theory which emphasizes the legitimacy of the public use of reason, corporate norm-entrepreneurs could at least claim that their factual expertise strengthens the rationality of norm setting and the effectiveness of norm implementation (Niesen 2008: 249).

The content of corporate norm-entrepreneurship may refer to establishing and implementing general normative principles, such as the prohibition of child labor and to technical standards, such as the specific indicators included in sustainability reports. These norm contents also have an impact on the value of the legitimacy resources available to a group of actors. The significance of norm contents can be addressed more systematically with Kooiman's three levels or 'orders' of governing (Kooiman 2000). They allow specification of the concrete governance contributions when corporations engage in norm-entrepreneurship, and the evaluation of the legitimacy of their claims to do so. At the most general level of norm-entrepreneurship, *meta-governing*, the creation of normative standards of appropriateness favors legitimacy claims based on moral authority and the willingness to engage in impartial moral reasoning. Since participation relies on 'voice' rather than 'vote', meta-governing draws its legitimacy primarily from the deliberative rather than the democratic quality of decision making. In contrast, *second-order governing*, which deals with the shaping of institutional settings, is concerned with authorization and represents the 'constitutional moment' in norm emergence. It is the constitutional authorization of competences or the guarantee of discursive and decision-making settings which allows equal representation of all relevant perspectives. It requires hierarchical if not coercive mechanisms for compliance and favors authority based on democratic 'vote' which privileges the regulatory claims of the state as the only actor capable of legitimizing coercion. *First-order governing*, finally, is not normative in a strong sense, nor is it constitutional in purpose, but primarily responds to factual knowledge problems. It 'aims to solve problems directly' (Kooiman 2000: 154). Corporate norm-entrepreneurship that engages in such issue specific practical solutions to implement general norms could derive its justification from the knowledge-based quality of norm emergence. Disregarding the legitimacy providing – or reducing – characteristics of the larger institutional and procedural settings in which corporate norm-entrepreneurship may be embedded, the sources of corporate authority have the highest legitimacy potential in inward-focused, consensus-oriented processes of norm emergence at the level of first-order governing.

Finally, in the scope of corporations' activities as norm-entrepreneurs, norm setting, and norm development aim at self-commitments or commitments in a group of norm-entrepreneurs, or it may have an external focus by addressing norm consumers outside this group. By also taking into account the mode of governance that is employed in a given case and that may range from offering best practice to exerting de facto power, committing third parties as rule takers raises higher legitimacy demands for the right to self-determination than mutual self-commitments where the entrepreneurs are also the only norm-consumers.

8.2 The legitimacy potential of different types of corporate norm-entrepreneurship

In the following section the legitimacy criteria are applied to the different types of individual and collective self-regulatory arrangements in which corporate norm-entrepreneurship can take place in order to gain some more insight into their legitimacy potential. The same empirical cases as in Chapter 7 were selected again: Shell, representing corporate norm-entrepreneurship in individual company codes; the Wolfsberg Group, representing collective corporate norm-entrepreneurship embedded in a private-private self-regulatory initiative; the Global Reporting Initiative, representing a multistakeholder initiative; and the Global Compact, representing a public-private governance arrangement. As each of these case studies combines elements of inward and outward focused governance activities, they allow a separate look at the extent to which legitimacy demands are observed in each case. As empirical representatives of each type, they are regarded as having a high legitimacy potential and therefore also get as close as possible to the potential limits of private transnational governance contributions.

8.2.1   Unilateral corporate norm-entrepreneurship: Shell

In 2006, Shell introduced its first company-wide Code of Conduct (Shell 2006a), intended to put into practice the eight Shell General Business Principles (Shell 2005). The company has its own Code of Ethics for Executive Directors and Senior Financial Officers of the Shell group. These policies are instructive examples of unilateral norm setting and development. They commit Shell's business activities to three core values ('honesty, integrity and respect'), identify various areas of corporate responsibility, formulate general principles, and provide practical guidelines to put them into practice. Shell's decision to withdraw from the Global Climate Coalition in the 1990s (after the activities of the business initiative were deemed incompatible with the company's own views on sustainability, responsibility, and climate change) is often regarded as an indication of the company's seriousness as a norm-entrepreneur.

(1) Shell's inward focused norm-entrepreneurship. From the findings on the causes of corporate norm-entrepreneurship (analyzed in Part II), Shell is regarded as one of the forerunners of unilateral corporate norm-entrepreneur. Shell established their General Business Principles in 1976 as one of the first global companies. The company-wide Code of Conduct of 2006 contains normative standards on antitrust and competition, health, safety, security and environment, personal and business integrity (in particular, bribery and corruption), financial and asset protection (including anti-money-laundering practices), and people (for example, equal opportunity, harassment).

Today, Shell's role as a leading corporate norm-entrepreneur is perhaps most apparent in its norm developing activities to prevent bribery and corruption. This field is still characterized by a lack of effective state regulation, despite the existence of the United Nations Convention against Corruption since December 2003, the OECD Guidelines for Multinational Enterprises,

Transparency International's Business Principles for Countering Bribery, and the inclusion of a tenth principle against corruption in the United Nations Global Compact in 2005. Against this background, Shell took on the challenge of developing policies and concrete programs to address corruption. The company became pro-active by joining the Extractive Industries Transparency Initiative (EITI), by adding Principle 3 on bribery and corruption to its General Business Principles (Shell 2005) and by having a central self-commitment in its company Code of Conduct (Shell 2006a). By doing this and including a more systematic policy banning bribes in its corporate strategy, Shell has acknowledged the blurred dividing line between the responsibilities of corporations and host country governments (Shell 2006b: 20).

Following its general commitment to fostering internationally recognized anticorruption standards at company and multilateral levels, and in order to allow for a more structured response to bribery and corruption issues, the company has developed a policy that goes far beyond standard business practices of not violating existing norms. It includes internal measures to promote Shell's corruption prevention approach, through awareness and training programs for staff in regions where this policy runs counter to common practice. A global help line and website was introduced in 2005 for employees to seek advice and report concerns and violations. An internal Audit Committee of the Board of Royal/Dutch Shell manages the monitoring and implementation of the code. As a result of violations staff can and have been – in over 100 incidents – fired.

Shell's internally focused norm-entrepreneurship is a typical example of norm setting and development in several ways: In the case of its antibribery activities, the company has developed detailed guidelines to expand the reach of the norm to parts of the world where it is not generally accepted and lived by. The company has acted as a norm-entrepreneur in its commitments to human rights in the sense of contributing to a new commitment to an internationally recognized norm for appropriate *corporate* behavior.

(2) Shell's outward focused norm-entrepreneurship. In addition to committing all employees in all branches of the company in over 100 countries worldwide, Shell's General Business Principles and the Code of Conduct (which serves to provide more detailed guidance on behavior required) also have a clear outward focus: in the General Business Principles the company's responsibilities are explicitly extended to contractors, suppliers, and partners in joint ventures in over 100 countries: 'The ability to promote these principles effectively will be an important factor in the decision to enter into or remain in such relationships.' All contractors to Shell are expected to comply with the principles. While those with whom Shell does business were not involved in the setting of the norms they are expected to comply with them. Shell offers assistance to contractors 'to help to understand them' by extensive training and monitoring (Shell 2006b: 20) and 'encourages' business partners to live by them. This 'encouragement' is, however,

not to be mistaken for an outward focused norm-entrepreneurship by best practice but operates with reporting and sanctions.

Taking the integrity measures as an example again, Shell concedes that 'in some parts of the world our policy banning bribes runs counter to common practice' (Shell 2006b: 20). If business partners fail to comply, their relationship with Shell is reviewed and may be cancelled on the basis of reports from senior Shell country representatives. According to the company's own accounts, over 40 contracts were cancelled in 2006 in countries such as Brazil, Canada, Nigeria, Trinidad and Tobago, and the United States (Shell 2006b: 20).

(3) The legitimacy of Shell's norm setting activities. A normative evaluation of Shell's legitimacy as a corporate norm-entrepreneur and the potential of individual corporate norm-entrepreneurship as part of the future global governance architecture demonstrates that Shell – like any other company – cannot derive its norm setting competence from the direct or indirect democratic legitimacy provided by being elected or publicly mandated. The company has instead mandated itself as a norm-entrepreneur on the basis of its de facto power to commit its employees and its business partners to comply with certain standards as normative guidelines for business practices. Its *authority* as a political actor is therefore not a legal one but is fairly substantial, based on professional expertise and on the moral weight that is conveyed by the general acceptance of the norms in question. However, this claim of general acceptance of the norms concerning bribery has to be viewed with some caution in the case of bribery which is still common practice in most countries and not regarded as a crime in some.

Given that Shell does not generate any new norms but uses already existing and widely accepted ones as standards of appropriateness for its own corporate behavior, the company's governance contribution as a norm-entrepreneur is mainly one of translation and of further developing existing norms into practical guidelines for the conduct of business. At this (first-order) level of governing, the company's factual, knowledge-based professional authority is a viably source of legitimacy. The value of this legitimacy 'currency' decreases, however, when we look at the *mode* and *scope* of Shell's governance activities. As we have seen, Shell governs by the use of coercive practices to assure compliance, and even uses its de facto power over third party business partners, such as contractors and suppliers, who have not had a say in the making of the norms they are expected to comply with. Although information and assistance play a certain legitimacy providing role as discursive and inclusive means of making the rule takers follow the rules, their compliance is ultimately assured by sanctions such as ending relationships. These instances of coercion and of the incongruence in norm-entrepreneurship and norm-consumership also cast a shadow on the legitimacy performance in self-determination through *participation*.

As far as the criteria *responsiveness* and *accountability* are concerned, the record of Shell as a unilateral norm-entrepreneur is less problematic. The broad range of self-commitments in several areas shows a reliable response to regulatory issues that are in the general interest. In addition, and given the high level of public awareness of Shell's conduct in particular (the Brent Spar case has become part of the collective memory of a whole generation), mechanisms of social and reputational accountability based on transparency and reporting requirements seem to work well as functional equivalents to missing legal accountability mechanisms in this case.

8.2.2 Collective corporate norm-entrepreneurship in private-private governance: the Wolfsberg Group

The Wolfsberg Group, named after a conference center in Switzerland, is a collective, private-private, self-regulatory initiative of 12 of the world's largest banks (Wolfsberg Group 2000: 1).[2] Wolfsberg's emergence is closely related to the structure of the global banking sector and the lack of legal standards on preventing corporate money-laundering. Banking has always been one of the most highly visible but poorly regulated business sectors, as the global financial crisis of 2008 demonstrated. The group's main goal is to set standards of behavior for the participating banks to prevent money-laundering, corruption, and the financing of terrorism. The group also provides guidance and best practice for nonmembers on how to design banking operations. It is therefore an instructive example of a purely private collective norm-entrepreneurship that is primarily inward-focused and simultaneously outward-oriented. These two foci are described separately to allow for a differentiating normative evaluation according to the legitimacy criteria introduced in the previous section.

(1) Inward focus: Wolfsberg as a collective, private, self-regulatory initiative. Regulation to prevent money-laundering has only recently come into existence (Pieth and Aiolfi 2003a: 6; Pieth and Aiolfi 2003b, 2004). Previously, the few regulatory activities mainly dealt with enforcement; prevention mechanisms in banking processes were only addressed in a vague manner. Against this background, the norm-entrepreneurship undertaken by the Wolfsberg Group occurred at an early stage of norm emergence when no clear standards on corporate behavior to prevent money-laundering existed. In the year 2000 the group collectively agreed on a new set of comprehensive principles to prevent money-laundering in private banking operations. The first Wolfsberg document, the Global AntiMoney-Laundering Guidelines for Private Banking (AML) (revised in May 2002) was the result of a close collaboration with international experts. It introduced detailed technical standards on 'customer due diligence' and 'know your customer' procedures which contributed to a paradigm shift in the mechanism of money-laundering prevention: from a rule-based to a risk-based approach (Pieth and Aiolfi 2003a: 5). Today, the Wolfsberg Principles include common due diligence procedures for opening and monitoring accounts, especially those

identified as belonging to politically exposed persons who are suspected of combining corruption with drug money-laundering and even financing terrorism (Campos and Pradhan 2007: 401).

In the first standards document (Wolfsberg Group 2000) the group advocated new norms regarding the prevention of money-laundering. They also accepted and implemented the principles in their operations by introducing sophisticated models of risk management, including ongoing transaction monitoring and improved initial customer identification. With this change of practice the Wolfsberg members substantially supported the reframing process – a clear indicator of corporate norm-entrepreneurship. Since 2000, the group has further specified the introduced norms through continuous norm development processes, periodic discussions and through publishing a series of related documents. In this way, the Wolfsberg members developed detailed guidance on anti-money-laundering procedures for banking segments that had never before been clearly addressed by any regulatory standards, such as correspondent banking or mutual funds. These standards provide assistance to industry participants and regulatory bodies to form policies on preventing money-laundering.[3] The group published the 'Statement on the Suppression of the Financing of Terrorism' in 2002 and the 'Statement against Corruption' in 2007. The group worked on further specifying its principles about accounts and transaction monitoring as well as on implementing 'smart sanctions'. This led to the 'Statement on Monitoring, Screening and Searching' in 2003. The scope of obligations created by the norm-entrepreneurship formally applies only to the members of the group. It should also be noted that Wolfsberg does not strive to monitor or enforce compliance with these obligations. This soft mode of collective self-regulation is reflected in the relatively informal style of cooperation among the participating banks. There are no formal rules of procedure based on any explicit statute.

(2) Outward focus: the Wolfsberg Principles as best practice. By changing their individual private banking practices the Wolfsberg members initiated a paradigm shift which implicitly also addressed norm-consumers outside the small circle of the twelve member banks (Bauer and Peter 2002: 70). As a standard of best practice in the banking sector, the Wolfsberg Principles have strongly influenced the behavior of other actors in the field. Although having no formal possibility of joining the group,[4] in 2007, 37 nonmember banks from all over the world participated in the annual Wolfsberg Forum, a platform which aims to bring together the whole banking sector to proliferate the principles. Even if the adoption of the Wolfsberg Principles is voluntary, there are strong commercial and regulatory reasons for all institutions undertaking private banking to adhere to the principles wherever possible as part of their risk management strategies (Von Doug 2006: 14). Many actors outside the group quite voluntarily base their anti-money-laundering procedures on the Wolfsberg Principles. In a survey by KPMG,[5]

209 banks in the world rated the impact of the Wolfsberg Principles on their business as 2.89 on a scale of 1 to 5 with 5 marking the highest impact possible (KPMG 2004).'

Another indicator of this enormous impact was that soon after the publication of the first Wolfsberg Principles, the Basel Committee and the FATF (Financial Action Task Force on Money Laundering), representing the two public law regulators in the field, also revised their recommendations to include more detailed information on the responsibility of the private sector in anti-money-laundering. Wolfsberg concepts and terminology were introduced into the intergovernmental standards (such as 'due diligence', 'beneficial owner', 'politically exposed person'), and the shift from a rule to a risk-based approach was completed. Although further research would have to prove this, it can be safely assumed that this regulatory convergence is a result of the Wolfsberg process. It is very likely that the participating banks triggered this paradigm shift and advocated for it when consulted by the public regulators. It can therefore be concluded that even though the Wolfsberg Group appears as a 'closed club' its outreach as corporate norm-entrepreneurs goes far beyond the member banks. The standards set by the group as best practice have guided and heavily influenced other banks and regulators in the banking sector.

(3) The legitimacy of the Wolfsberg initiative. What can we learn from the Wolfsberg case for a general evaluation of the legitimacy potential of collective private-private transnational governance arrangements? Louis Pauly's (1997) often quoted 'Who elected the bankers?', questions the democratic authority of transnational private governance and could be directly addressed to the Wolfsberg Group's activities as norm-entrepreneurs. This is a clear case of self-authorized and nonelected professional *authority* in a group of private regulators with a primarily inward focus, regulating the behavior of the regulators themselves, with an additional external side of the coin. For *participation*, Wolfsberg can claim to be in accordance with the principle of congruence. Only in so far as the group's norm-entrepreneurship also guides the behavior of nonmembers this criterion of self-determination is violated – a normative deficit that is somewhat mitigated by the soft *mode of governance* which lacks any attempts to enforce the standards of the group on others.

While the group's record in self-determination is thus satisfactory (mainly because of its predominantly inward focus), it is more difficult to assess how far the procedural normative demands that should be in place to ensure *accountability* are met. Obviously, power control is not a very critical issue, given the above mentioned lack of coercive enforcement. But there are no independent monitoring or peer review procedures in effect either. The Wolfsberg initiative also lacks formal rules and – ultimately – transparency. This deficit could only be outweighed by pointing to the quality of the norms and basic principles that are generally accepted as being in the general interest – a claim that is supported by international agreements on the basis of this norm and, more recently, its inclusion in the catalogue of principles of the UN Global Compact (see later in this chapter). However, this barely compensates for the lack of institutional checks and balances which should exist to ensure that this is not left to the discretion of private regulators and that, as norm entrepreneurs, they address regulatory deficits by *responding* reliably to concerns of the public and improve standards and implementation mechanisms when they turn out to be too weak to achieve their goals.

The Wolfsberg Principles generate new and original norms rather than transforming existing ones into guidelines for appropriate corporate behavior. As far as the *contents* of these new norms is concerned, the initiative's fight against money-laundering, financial crime, and terrorist financing concerns all three levels of governing, but with a clear emphasis on norm setting at the level of first-order governing. At the utmost, in terms of second-order governing, their annual meeting provides a favorable environment and creates opportunities for the exchange of best practices. The focus of its norm setting lies in detailed practical guidance on anti-money-laundering procedures. The lack of regulation at the meta and second-order levels of governing, the voluntary nature of the initiative, the external focus being limited to best practices, the renunciation of any hierarchical enforcement in favor of horizontal discursive decision making, and the limiting of norm setting to practical matters of first-order governing render this collective self-regulatory initiative far more compatible with the primarily professional authority of business corporations than, for example, the Global Compact with its focus on meta-governing (see later in this chapter).

As a consequence of these relatively weak demands on the democratic side of legitimacy posed by the technical contents of the group's norm setting, and the strong demands on the deliberative and knowledge-based side of legitimacy, the legitimacy record of the Wolfsberg initiative is relatively good. On the one hand, the 'currency' of knowledge-based expertise brought in by the participating banks legitimizes their governance contributions at the level of first-order governing. In addition, and because the 'coercive' element is weak, there is no illegitimate use of power involved in the 'assumption of self-disciplinary responsibilities' (Schuppert 2008: 33; Streeck and Schmitter 1985: 20).

The Wolfsberg case study shows that the legitimacy potential of a private-private self-regulatory initiative is highest as long as the norm-entrepreneurs are the norm-consumers. When the two roles fall apart and, as Wolfsberg exemplifies as well, collective norm-entrepreneurship operates as a collective best practice initiative for the external addressees, in this case the banking sector at large, legitimacy can only be kept up as long as those who are not allowed to join the club are not in any formal sense obliged to apply the group's normative standards. In this case, the condition is met: Third parties are only 'invited' to follow the voluntary best practice model of the group. Going beyond this formal way of looking at the group's external impact there is a more critical view of the legitimacy of Wolfsberg norm-entrepreneurship: the obvious influence of the norms set by the group on subsequent public regulatory efforts, such as the intergovernmental Basel regulations, raises concerns about a potential 'capture' of public regulators by private norm-entrepreneurs (Majone 1996: 18; Stigler 1971). The subsequent imposition of norms originally set by the Wolfsberg Group on a wider range of actors via the coercive means of public regulators can no longer be legitimized by the Wolfsberg members' claimed expert authority alone.

The Wolfsberg initiative also shows that the legitimacy of a purely private-private collective governance initiative would further decline if the focus of its members' norm-entrepreneurship shifted to second-order or meta-governing. In the case of Wolfsberg, this would necessitate fundamental institutional changes to include actors from civil society or public actors who have authority sources other than knowledge-based expertise at their disposal. So far, the 'constitutional moment', for example access procedures or compliance mechanisms at the level of second-order governing, is clearly underdeveloped in the Wolfsberg initiative, where it remains at the exclusive discretion of the club members. With these qualifications added, the Wolfsberg initiative almost fully reaches the legitimacy potential of corporate norm-entrepreneurship in collective private-private governance arrangements, mainly due to its self-restraint in setting meta norms or employing coercive means.

8.2.3   Collective corporate norm-entrepreneurship in multistakeholder governance: the Global Reporting Initiative (GRI)

The Global Reporting Initiative (GRI) is a multistakeholder governance arrangement to improve corporate responsibility through sustainability reporting and transparency about organizational performance. Participants are TNCs, accountancy organizations, human rights and environmental NGOs, labor organizations, and government representatives. Global Reporting Initiative's mission is to enhance the comparability and credibility of sustainability reporting practices worldwide (Global Reporting Initiative 2002). Global Reporting Initiative has been successful in establishing itself as the world's most widely used, self-regulatory, voluntary sustainability reporting of the economic, environmental, and social impacts of public and mainly private organizations (Kolk 2003, 2004).[6]

(1) The Global Reporting Initiative as an inclusive, inward focused self-regulatory initiative. As opposed to the Wolfsberg Group, the Global Reporting Initiative is not a project of an exclusive club but an open invitation to all different kinds of stakeholder groups to participate in norm setting and norm development, which is much more important in the practical day to day routine of

the initiative. Together with other stakeholder groups, corporations engage in norm development by either participating in one of the Global Reporting Initiative governance bodies or by submitting their input, comments, and suggestions on the content of the reporting guidelines in a formal three phase norm development process. These formalized institutional and procedural arrangements, another characteristic which distinguishes the Global Reporting Initiative from the Wolfsberg Group, deserve closer examination. The Global Reporting Initiative consists of a series of governance bodies, the Board of Directors, the Stakeholder Council, and the Technical Advisory Committee, which coordinate the formal components of the initiative. All institutions and procedures of the Global Reporting Initiative governance structure provide opportunities for firms to propose or lobby for or against changes in the norm development process. Within the main governing body, the Board of Directors, business corporations and other actors share ultimate decision making power and fiduciary, financial, and legal responsibility for Global Reporting Initiative, including organizational strategy and final authority on reporting framework development. In the Stakeholder Council, the formal stakeholder policy forum of the Global Reporting Initiative, the various stakeholder groups, including corporations, debate key strategic and policy issues and provide advice to the Board. Corporations also play a significant role in the Technical Advisory Committee. This committee consists of twelve international experts who steer the quality and coherence of the reporting framework and provide technical advice and expertise to the Board. In addition to the internal opportunities for corporate contributions to norm development within the various institutional settings of the GRI governance framework, TNCs can also engage externally by participating in the revision cycles of the reporting guidelines (Gee and Slater 2005). Even companies that are not represented in the governing bodies of GRI can engage in the development procedure of the reporting guidelines. In the first phase of the procedure (review cycle) they comment on a draft document of the reporting guidelines during a 90-day Public Comment Period (phase 1). The corporate feedback is reviewed by the GRI Technical Advisory Committee and results in a new pilot version of the reporting guidelines (phase 2). In this phase participating corporations can test the pilot version of the reporting guidelines for one year as the basis for their sustainability reporting. After the pilot version has been available for use, GRI establishes a Structured Feedback Process (SFP, phase 3). In this phase of further refining the reporting guidelines, corporations can give input on the basis of their individual experience with the pilot version. Based on the results from the SFP, the Technical Advisory Committee, the Board of Directors, and the Stakeholder Council release a new version of the reporting guidelines which enters a new cycle of review.

(2)   Outward   focused   norm-entrepreneurship   in   the   Global   Reporting Initiative. Apart from being an open invitation to all kinds of stakeholders

to participate in its norm setting activities, the GRI affects the behavior of nonparticipants in a number of ways. According to the KPMG International Survey of Responsibility Reporting, the GRI Sustainability Guidelines have become the most influential international reporting standard: 'More than three-quarters (77 percent) of the G250 and 69 percent of the N100 reporting companies follow the Global Reporting Initiative's (GRI) Sustainability Reporting Guidelines. About 20 percent of both cohorts use internally developed company frameworks as the basis for reporting. [...] Even fewer use national standards, although the figure is slightly higher among the G250. This is perhaps counterintuitive since most of these are multinational organizations, and it is somewhat surprising that a higher number of N100 companies do not use national standards for reporting. Instead, like their global counterparts, most look to the international GRI standard' (KPMG 2008: 35). The worldwide impact of the GRI reporting standards for corporate sustainability reporting puts most companies under reputational pressure to adapt these standards. This steady rise of corporate responsibility reporting among the largest 250 companies worldwide (Global 250) and the largest 100 companies (National 100) in 22 countries (KPMG 2008: 13) is a remarkable indication of the GRI's outward orientation.

A further example strengthens the impression of GRI's strong impact on norm-consumers who are not part of the norm development processes within the initiative. In the joint 'Transparency in the Supply Chain' project, the GRI and the German GTZ, which is implementing the PPP for the German Federal Ministry for Economic Cooperation (BMZ), actively encouraged Small and Medium Enterprise (SME) suppliers of TNCs to engage in sustainability reporting (Global Reporting Initiaive 2008). Initiated and supervised by the GRI and GTZ, four TNCs who are generally regarded as leaders in the sustainability reporting practice (Daimler, Otto Group, Puma, and Telefónica Group) and who share a common interest in the transparency of their supply chain[7] invited three of their suppliers to take part. Workshops, individual consultations, and mentoring partnerships were established to create an understanding of the business case for reporting and convince suppliers of the competitive advantage and reputational gains they could achieve by engaging in sustainability reporting. Building on the success of the recently completed GRI/GTZ project, the GRI institutionalized the Global Action Network for Transparency in the Supply Chain in October 2008 as a new major GRI program, inviting all companies concerned about the sustainability reporting practices of their supply chain to participate.

(3) The legitimacy of the Global Reporting Initiative. The GRI is an exemplary case that demonstrates the high legitimacy potential of a highly institutionalized and consensus based transnational multistakeholder initiative in which corporations act as norm-entrepreneurs. Looking at the inward focus first, *participation* demands are met by all stakeholders having the opportunity to have a say in the norm setting and norm development processes. With

regard to *responsiveness*, the likelihood of the reporting standards reliably taking up regulatory issues that are in the general interest is high, given the fact that all kinds of interest groups with different needs can contribute to the agenda of defining and extending these norms. It was further enhanced by the association with the United Nations Environmental Programme (UNEP) and the additional publicity provided by the Global Platform which was established together. This positive record also holds true for GRI's outward focus. Again, the practice of public-private partnership, as in the case of the joint GRI/GTZ projects, provides some additional guarantees of reliability and general interest orientation.

Regarding the *mode of governance*, GRI exerts, at the utmost, only very weak power on norm-consumers. Its horizontal character as a network governance arrangement does not include any formal enforcement mechanisms. The application of the GRI sustainability guidelines is entirely voluntary. Therefore, the abuse of power is not a critical issue. The decision making procedures are transparent and highly formalized, and the discursive, inclusive and consensus seeking mode of governance ensures that no single stakeholder group is structurally discriminated against. The self-authorized and nonelective mode of representation does not provide for democratic *accountability*. This is, however, tolerable since members primarily take part on the basis of professional expertise and with (deliberative) 'voice' rather than (majority) 'vote'. In addition to the internal peer review accountability relationships between the various GRI institutions, the high transparency of GRI allows the general public to observe how far the norm development commits to the continuous improvement of sustainability standards. This adds elements of professional and reputational accountability to corporate norm-entrepreneurship in the GRI.

While GRI's soft mode of governance helps meet the normative demand for the control of the use of power, it at the same time causes some problems in terms of reliability: Although the number of reporting corporations has dramatically increased from 20 in the year 1999 to 800 in the year 2006, the voluntary nature of the initiative does not entail binding enforcement mechanisms to ensure an even more widespread application of the reporting standards. This lack of any 'shadow of hierarchy', which could only be provided by state participation,[8] puts the burden on GRI's professional and reputational authority as incentives for corporations to adopt and follow the guidelines.

The correspondence between the authority sources that the different members of the initiative contribute and the legitimacy demands raised by the *contents* of the norms that are set and developed by GRI further supports the overall positive legitimacy record of the GRI. In Kooiman's terminology, the GRI is primarily operating at the levels of first- and second-order governing. As already mentioned in the Wolfsberg case, the engagement of corporations as norm entrepreneurs is least problematic from a normative perspective when norm setting and norm development occur at the first-order level of governance. Here they can claim to contribute legitimately to the process of norm development on the basis of their authority as norm takers with knowledge-based professional expertise. Private norm-entrepreneurship at the level of second-order governing would pose a severe legitimacy problem for GRI if it solely rested on the shoulders of one group of actors, for instance business corporations, who could shape the decision making procedures to their advantage. However, the institutional architecture of the GRI fulfills the additional legitimacy demands raised by norm setting at the level of second-order governing with its multistakeholder composition and its transparent, highly institutionalized, and formalized review procedure in which different stakeholder groups can interact in a consensus seeking mode of decision making. For example, each organizational stakeholder can be elected to the Stakeholder Council. Second-order governing within GRI has resulted in a transparent governance framework. This framework was established as a result of a multistakeholder process open to all groups of actors with expertise in sustainability reporting. As a consequence, the rules according to which the actors participating in the various governing bodies interact and come to decisions are regarded as fair by the whole range of stakeholders.

It is perhaps most remarkable that the GRI holds up its high legitimacy standard even in its outward norm-entrepreneurship. The joint GRI/GTZ project, in particular, shows that norm-consumers who do not simultaneously act as norm-entrepreneurs, for example small and medium enterprises in the supply chain, are not forced into compliance by any coercive means. In contrast to Shell, soft and inclusive modes of governance prevail, based on invitation, arguing and learning processes. In summary, the GRI, through the involvement of a broad range of relevant stakeholder groups, including actors from civil society and governmental agencies as partners, exemplifies that a high level of legitimacy in all four criteria can be achieved.

8.2.4 Collective corporate norm-entrepreneurship in public-private governance arrangements: the UN Global Compact[9]

The UN Global Compact is the most important and well-known CSR self-regulatory initiative worldwide (Kell and Levin 2003; Schorlemer 2003; Rieth 2004).[10] It was initiated by the former Secretary General of the United Nations, Kofi Annan, at the Davos World Economic Forum in January 1999, as an invitation to the international business community 'individually through your firms, and collectively through your business associations – to embrace, support and enact a set of core values in the areas of human rights, labor standards, and environmental practices [...] because they are all areas where you, as businessmen and women, can make a real difference' (Annan 1999). Later, anticorruption was added to the list of the original nine universal principles.

Since its official launch in July 2000, the Global Compact has grown to more than 6200 participants, including over 4700 businesses in 120 countries.[11] Participants include all relevant social actors: companies, labor organizations, civil society, academia, several UN agencies, public sector organizations, and cities. The United Nations perceives its function as that of 'an authoritative convener and facilitator' – in striking accordance with the self-description of the new cooperative and enabling state of the post–golden age era.

(1) Inward focus: the Global Compact as a learning network. A company becomes a participant by sending a letter to the Secretary General of the United Nations, expressing support for the Global Compact's ten principles. It is then expected to demonstrate its commitment to these basic normative standards in the fields of human rights, labor standards, the environment and anticorruption by providing regular reports (Communication on Progress, CoP) in which it describes the ways it has implemented the ten principles in its business activities. As long as this basic reporting requirement is fulfilled, a company can call itself an active participant.

In addition, companies are invited to take part in the Global Compact Learning Forum where participants share their experiences of good practices by exchanging practical actions they have taken on the Global Compact's principles (Kell 2003). Nonbusiness participants can get involved as equal partners. For instance, annual 'Policy Dialogues' are open to all Global Compact stakeholders and serve the function of identifying innovative and practical solutions. At the state level, the Global Compact is supported by numerous national networks. Their key task is to provide an internal exchange forum for national Global Compact participants and to promote the initiative within their countries. Networks are also expected to assist companies in the implementation of the principles and to report country-specific implementation models that could be replicated globally to the Global Compact Office.

The Global Compact is not a code of conduct, and explicitly refrains from policing, enforcing or (at least in its first phase) judging the behavior of companies. As an open and voluntary corporate citizenship initiative the Global Compact aims at committing the private sector – in partnership with other social actors – to deliberative processes through which experiences and good practices can be shared. Although celebrating the initiative as 'the largest voluntary corporate citizenship network of its kind' that 'exerts a surprisingly powerful influence on companies and within the UN', an impact evaluation undertaken by McKinsey in 2004 also registered 'inconsistent participation and divergent and unmet expectations' that 'threaten the Compact's long-term credibility' (McKinsey 2004). As a consequence, learning (as the original prevailing mode of governance) was increasingly complemented by measures that went beyond the 'best practice' and 'capacity building' approach of the first years. Integrity measures now include standardized indicators for reporting. Companies are required to communicate annually to their stakeholders on progress made implementing the ten principles. Since 2004, corporations can be publicly listed as 'noncommunicating' or even 'inactive' business participants if they fail to submit a CoP by a relevant deadline, or refuse to engage in dialogue.[12] This silent mutation from a learning network to a transnational regulatory regime is further underlined by the establishment of the Global Compact Leaders Summit as the new plenary organ, which meets every 3 years to review progress and provide overall strategic direction.

(2) Outward focus: the Global Compact as best practice. Although the Global Compact is designed as a global self-regulatory initiative and despite the remarkable number of participants, it is still a voluntary project that does not include all potential stakeholders from business, civil society, and other groups. However, this does not mean that its influence does not go beyond its members. Rather, the question 'Is your firm a participant?' has strong reputational repercussions for companies that have chosen to stay outside. Besides these potential immaterial costs of being 'named and shamed' in the eyes of the global public, customers, investors or shareholders, the Global Compact Office cannot exert any pressure on outsiders to commit themselves to the principles of the compact. At the utmost, its influence may lie in the spread of practical policy solutions about how certain normative demands can be met efficiently.

Apart from its normative appeal that may attract outsiders to join either because they want to be regarded as a 'member of the family' for strategic reasons, or because they have become convinced that the principles of the Global Compact provide appropriate guidelines for their own behavior, the Global Compact casts its shadow on the outside world in a number of additional ways. At the level of meta-governing, reference to 1 or more of the 10 principles is employed as an authority resource provider by many other initiatives. The same is true for the Global Compact as a reference model of best practice for its discursive and learning based mode of governance. Taking these two effects together, one could rightfully claim that the Global Compact contributes to the development of normative order in the context of global governance at large.

(3) The legitimacy of the Global Compact. In terms of the *participatory* demands of self-determination, initial norm setting occurred in a 'top-down' manner and with little transparency about why certain principles were included in the original list of nine and others were not. The Global Compact also follows a nonelective mode of representation. However, as far as norm development is concerned, it has broad stakeholder participation on the basis of an inclusive participatory model without entry barriers. This consensual and partnership oriented approach to governance complies with the demands of

self-determination because in principle it offers all stakeholder groups the opportunity to take part in the dialog. In practice, however, some doubts still rise over the bottom up or top down character of changes in substance and procedures introduced when the Global Compact entered its second phase. The addition of principle ten on anticorruption as well as the creeping identity shift from a learning network to a transnational regulatory regime still appears to be more the result of top down initiatives than as the fruit of extensive deliberation among the participants.

Accountability is in flux because of the introduction of new organs, such as the Leaders Summit, and new enforcement instruments, such as the integrity measures. The emerging institutional 'checks and balance' structure is still somewhat unclear and less transparent for outsiders than it used to be in the 'learning network' phase of the Global Compact when it basically relied on the transparency of the exchange of good practices (and the observable refusal to take part in it). These relatively weak mechanisms were in full accordance with the soft externalities produced by the Global Compact as a nonregulatory governance initiative. Sanctions on powerful corporations are a different matter. They were virtually nonexistent, and they are still relatively weak today, too weak to create binding obligations and reliable norm implementation.

This implementation deficit also weakens the generally high degree of *responsiveness* in the Global Compact. On the one hand, the Global Compact seeks to react to the less than satisfactory implementation of international human rights and social norms by states through incentives for voluntary action by companies. On the other hand, the normative guidelines manifested in the ten principles are extremely vague and leave companies wide room for interpretation. The participating companies do not produce standards themselves, but take part in further developing international norms that have been institutionalized in the UN context in order to translate them into corporate activities. The corporate norm-entrepreneurs are virtually free to decide how they want to address environmental standards, anticorruption, and social and human rights norms. The Global Compact Office originally deliberately refrained from assessing the overall performance of companies and did not seek to prescribe a certain standard of behavior. Companies did not have to fear any sanctions when they chose to selectively promote the principles in some areas of their activities but violate them in others, about which they did not have to report. This has changed substantially with the introduction of the integrity measures as an instrument to enhance the *accountability* and thus the credibility of the initiative. By complementing its classical deliberative and learning oriented governance modes, such as best practices and the Global Compact Policy Dialogue, with the introduction of cost-benefit inspired integrity measures, the Global Compact has added the first sticks to the original carrots. Although this ongoing change is a clear indication that its initiators have grasped the still untapped potential of judging and enforcing the behavior of member companies, from the normative perspective it has to be balanced by establishing decision making procedures at the level of second-order governing that are able to conserve the previous horizontal and consensual mode of governance.

In so far as responsiveness refers to addressing concerns in the general interest, the quality of the norms endorsed by the Global Compact fully meets the legitimacy demands: All ten principles are either explicitly derived from universally accepted norms as embodied in the Universal Declaration of Human Rights or core ILO conventions, or they are, like principle 10 on anticorruption, the result of broad consultation exercises with civil society and the business world. However, with regard to the reliability with which important concerns are taken up, there is a mixed legitimacy record: On the one hand, the learning forums are open to civil society input; on the other hand, the implementation of any of the ten principles is completely up to individual companies. Again, the entirely voluntary nature of this initiative cannot ensure that responsiveness in norm setting and development is also achieved in terms of reliability of norm implementation.

Authority is high and in full correspondence with the authority sources that the various members contribute and the soft mode of governance, the basically inward focus and the legitimacy demands raised by the contents of the norms to which the participating corporations commit themselves.

8.2.5 Conclusions

The most important finding of this section is that, judged from a normative point of view, each of the four types of self-regulatory arrangements in which corporate norm-entrepreneurship can take place has the potential to make substantial governance contributions within the context of wider institutional global governance architecture (see Table 8.1). However, in order to fully exhaust but not overstretch the remarkable legitimacy potential, some restraint may be necessary in corporate norm-entrepreneurship for outward focused, hierarchical modes of governance and governance contributions at the levels of second-order and meta-governing. As the Shell and Wolfsberg case studies show, purely private unilateral, or private-private collective norm-entrepreneurship can unfold its legitimacy potential best when the focus remains on first-order self-regulation and is inward oriented only. To the extent that corporate norm-entrepreneurship tries to bind parties, extends to second-order and meta-governing, or employs coercive enforcement mechanisms, the sources of authority available to corporate norm-entrepreneurs do not suffice. In these cases, other actor configurations are needed that bring together additional authority resources to meet the specific legitimacy demands that are raised by developing standards of appropriateness or political order (the 'constitutional moment' of norm-entrepreneurship).

As the case of the Global Reporting Initiative demonstrates, a high level of legitimacy in practically all criteria can be achieved by involving a broad

Table 8.1 The legitimacy potential of different types of corporate norm-entrepreneurship[13]

Type Criteria	Unilateral corporate norm-entrepreneurship (Shell)	Private-private governance arrangements (Wolfsberg)	Multistakeholder governance arrangements (GRI)	Public-private governance arrangements (Global Compact)
Participation	*Medium:* inward focused, self mandated norm-entrepreneurship; top down relationship with contractors; but discursive inclusion	*High:* regarding inward focus, congruence principle is met; only soft governance toward outsiders (best practice); but: prejudicing influence on public regulation?	*High:* inclusive formalized participatory model, even in outward focus; no entry barriers; stakeholders have the opportunity to participate effectively in norm setting and norm development.	*High to medium:* inclusive participatory model of norm development but not transparent norm setting; no entry barriers; top down governance elements
Accountability	*Medium:* nonelected norm-entrepreneurship; social and reputational accountability based	*Low to medium:* self-authorized, nonelected professional peer accountability; not transparent, no formal rules;	*High:* decision making procedures transparent and highly formalized; inclusive and consensus	*Medium:* norm development and institutional reform relatively intransparent to outsiders

	on transparency and reporting	no sanctions; conduct of individual companies hard to identify	seeking mode of governance; professional and reputational accountability	*High:* open to multistakeholder input; amendments possible; principles take up broad range of public concerns;
Responsiveness	*High:* broad range of self-commitments speaks in favor of reliable response	*Medium:* commitment to anticorruption as a generally shared norm, but selective agenda; only selective consultation with stakeholders	*High:* all kinds of interest groups with different needs can contribute to defining norms; PPPs increase reliability and general interest orientation	*High:* broad stakeholder participation provides full range of moral, professional and legal authority sources
Authority	*High to medium:* compatibility of professional authority with first-order governing moral authority by reference to general accepted norms; but lack of legal authority for coercive measures in outward focus	*High:* compatibility of professional authority with soft mode of governance and governing limited to first-order level	*High:* scope and procedures of participation fulfill legitimacy demands raised by second-order governing; reference to commonly shared norm	

range of relevant stakeholders beyond business, and including actors from civil society and governmental agencies as partners. To some perhaps unexpected extent, the Wolfsberg initiative also basically exhausts the legitimacy potential of the collective and purely business based corporate norm-entrepreneurship it represents. The Global Compact, although a good performer in the other criteria, however, clearly remains below the mark of what would be possible in terms of self-determination. Its ongoing search for the right balance between being a top down and bottom up initiative and being a mere learning forum and an initiative 'with teeth', shows that these different demands on legitimacy may not be easily achieved simultaneously – as in fact also demonstrated by Shell's policies of extending the company's General Business Principles toward its suppliers and other contractors. Again, the Global Reporting Initiative demonstrates that both aims are not incompatible and can go together if appropriate means of inclusive, discursive, and noncoercive compliance incentives are employed.

The application of the normative criteria of participation, accountability, responsiveness and authority, for evaluating the legitimacy of four contexts of corporate norm-entrepreneurship underlines that an inward or outward focus, the actors' configurations, modes of governance employed, and content of the normative standards that are to be set or developed all determine how far legitimacy demands arise and can be met. As a consequence, there is no better answer concerning the desirability of corporate norm-entrepreneurship than 'it depends'. Corporate norm-entrepreneurship in multistakeholder governance arrangements such as the Global Reporting Initiative may design institutions and procedures that fulfill almost all criteria and thus represent a prototype of the high legitimacy potential of corporate norm-entrepreneurship in transnational multistakeholder arrangements. However, even a purely private-private governance arrangement, such as the Wolfsberg initiative, can have its merits according to the compatibility between the authority sources that are available to their members, the scope of normative obligations they want to create, and the contents of the norms they seek to promote.

One general conclusion to be drawn from this chapter seems to be, however, that in order to prevent norm setting and norm implementation in the sphere beyond the state from losing sight of the public interest, corporate norm-entrepreneurship should be embedded in some kind of accountability setting. Such a setting may be achieved by professional peer review mechanisms within private-private arrangements as long as norm-entrepreneurship remains within the limits of first-order governing and only employs soft and inclusive governance modes. As soon as these two conditions are transcended, more comprehensive checks and balance mechanisms are needed to ensure accountability. They require the participation of additional types of actors but do not necessarily have to consist of public policing and enforcement under the 'shadow of hierarchy'. Market-based or reputational accountability mechanisms may be acceptable functional equivalents as long as there is sufficient information and transparency to allow for independent monitoring and the mobilization of market forces.

Notes

1. The same objection about lack of democratic legitimacy can be raised about the majority of governments that are allowed to take part in intergovernmental governance systems.
2. See also http://www.wolfsberg-principles.com, accessed 23 June 2009.
3. These documents are the Guidance on a Risk Based Approach for Managing Money Laundering Risks, AML Guidance for Mutual Funds and Other Pooled Investment Vehicles, FAQs on AML issues in the Context of Investment and Commercial Banking and FAQs on Correspondent Banking.
4. According to some Wolfsberg members, the goal of the 'closed club principle' is to ensure that processes of negotiation for new standards run smoothly and efficiently.
5. KPMG (the firm's name is the initials of its founders) is a leading provider of audit, tax, and advisory services.
6. For more detailed information about the institutional structure and decision making procedures of the Global Reporting Initiative, see http://www.global reporting.org, accessed 23 June 2009.
7. 'The identification of suitable participating European companies by the Global Reporting Initiative formed the first step of the project. Daimler AG (formerly DaimlerChrysler), Otto Group and Telefónica SA committed in December 2006. Puma AG joined in March 2007. The companies committed themselves to contribute additional funding to the project and to go through one cycle of sustainability reporting with their SME suppliers in emerging economies. Suppliers were invited by their clients to join the project at the start of 2007' (Global Reporting Initiative 2008: 9).
8. Although the Global Reporting Initiative set up a working group on government involvement in 2007 aiming to look at the potential future role of national governments in the Global Reporting Initiative framework, it is still not clear which role public actors will have to play and if this kind of participation will exert a 'shadow of hierarchy' on corporate behavior.
9. The following description and normative assessment follows and elaborates on an earlier publication, see Conzelmann and Wolf (2007a, 2007b).
10. For basic information about the UN Global Compact, see http://www.unglobal compact.org, accessed 23 June 2009.
11. See http://www.unglobalcompact.org/ParticipantsAndStakeholders/index.html, accessed 23 June 2009.
12. By June 2008, 630 companies had been delisted as part of the new Global Compact integrity measures for failure to communicate progress (http://www.unglobal compact.org/newsandevents/news_archives/2008_06_25.html, accessed 03 July 2009).
13. This table is based on Conzelmann and Wolf (2007a, 2007b).

9
A New Architecture for Global Governance

The most relevant conditions under which corporations are likely to act as norm-entrepreneurs have been identified and the effectiveness and legitimacy potential of different types of individual and collective self-regulatory arrangements were evaluated. In this final chapter, the current polity of global governance is examined to derive policy recommendations for embedding corporate governance contributions in an institutional architecture that encourages corporate norm-entrepreneurs and ensures that they serve the public interest. The empirical evidence that corporate norm-entrepreneurship can provide meaningful contributions to global governance under certain conditions justifies taking stock of the gap between corporate norm production as it is currently known and normative demands, as described in Chapters 7 and 8. Against the background of the identified shortcomings, policy goals are identified that specify *what* could be done to develop the full potential of corporate norm-entrepreneurship as a meaningful private contribution to global governance in the future. An institutional approach to private governance contributions is followed (see also Pattberg 2007: 49–56) where the focus is on corporate norm-entrepreneurship within governance systems. Although individual company codes of conduct may stimulate collective norm-related processes, the different types of *collective* regulatory arrangements are more relevant here.

Policy recommendations should address agents that have the legal or factual competence or authority to implement them. To keep them as close as possible to the present state of the 'global polity', the envisaged agents of such measures to stimulate meaningful corporate norm-entrepreneurship are home states, host states, international organizations, and transnational civil society. This choice presumes a certain understanding of the 'constitutionability' (Dobner 2009) of societal self-regulation within the broader institutional architecture of global governance. In contrast to heterarchical and supranational approaches, a neo-Westphalian understanding of the constitutive rules that hold this global institutional architecture together forms the basis. Against this background, general policy guidelines and more concrete policy measures are suggested referring to *how* and *by whom* the conditions facilitating corporate norm-entrepreneurship could be strengthened and how corporate engagement could be channeled into the types of transnational governance arrangements that come closest to meeting the normative standards set out. Ultimately, the recommendations aim to reconcile the prevalent 'business case' with the 'public case' for private norm production and rule making by establishing a political and institutional setting providing constitutive rules for 'embedded norm-entrepreneurship' within a newly emerging global public domain (Ruggie 2004).

9.1   The gap between likely and meaningful corporate contributions to norm setting and norm development

When comparing the findings on the factors that facilitate corporate norm-entrepreneurship with the evaluation of the different types of collective self-regulatory arrangements, there is an obvious gap between what exists or is likely to occur in the future, and what is desirable and may be encouraged by changing incentives and manipulating relevant *push* or *pull* factors. Although some necessary and additional factors that *push* companies toward becoming norm-entrepreneurs and can pull them further to act as collective norm-entrepreneurs were identified, the types of transnational governance arrangements that are likely to occur still differ from 'meaningful' corporate norm-entrepreneurship, from the normative perspective of the effectiveness and legitimacy criteria applied in Chapters 7 and 8.

The findings on corporate norm-entrepreneurs' contributions to global governance revealed systematic shortcomings of effectiveness criteria in all types of individual and collective self-regulatory arrangements, particularly in 'change of behavior', 'goal attainment' and 'unintended consequences' (Chapter 7). Expectations of goal attainment should take into account that problem solving is unlikely to be achieved within any single regulatory effort because the most critical problems in the social world are of a multicausal nature and therefore demand many-pronged governance approaches. However, the often disaggregated nature of private self-regulatory initiatives – due to the predominance of the business case over the public case – contributes to these failures because negative externalities result from the unmanaged overlaps of numerous disaggregated forms of self-regulation. Therefore, there is a need for independent verification mechanisms that evaluate the degree of goal attainment and elaborate management of the links between the different functional self-regulatory arrangements that tie private norm production back to the public interest.

The observed lack of change of behavior shows effectiveness gaps caused by the voluntary nature and often nonexisting enforcement mechanisms of self-regulatory arrangements. Corporate norm-entrepreneurs may take up regulatory gaps and contribute to filling them by adding new normative claims by which they commit themselves to certain norms. Due to the voluntary nature, they cannot guarantee that the new standards are universally applied, and they may not even be willing to implement them. This deficit points to the need for a shadow of hierarchy, or a functional equivalent, to improve the still poor record of norm implementation and compliance to prompt a factual change of corporate behavior.

Concerning participation, accountability, responsiveness, and authority, the findings in Chapter 8 suggest that collective self-regulatory arrangements have the potential to meet these legitimacy demands and can, in principle, contribute in a meaningful way to governance beyond the state. Problems arise when the initiatives are outwardly focused, noninclusive, employ hierarchical modes of governance, or stray beyond first-order governing by also engaging in meta-governing and second-order governing, that is, in setting constitutive rules and standards of appropriateness. Indeed the empirical findings suggest that corporations prefer to collaborate as norm-entrepreneurs within informal, noninclusive, and nontransparent institutional settings that leave them as much autonomy as possible and allow only minimal external control or limited independent accountability mechanisms. In these types of collective self-regulatory arrangements, the role of regulator seems to go together particularly well with what corporate norm-entrepreneurs may regard as the 'business case' in self-regulation. However, from the broader perspective of global governance, the 'public case' interests most. If there was an irreconcilable gap between the two cases, one policy option could be to turn back the clock and reallocate regulatory competencies from the private to the public sector. This would not only ignore the great potential of corporate norm-entrepreneurship as a meaningful complement to public regulation but also ignore that state failure was the very starting point for considerations about involving nonstate actors in new modes of governance. Hence, the suggestions follow a different course: How can corporate contributions to governance beyond the state be embedded in an institutional architecture that can guarantee that they serve the business and public interests and by whom? The findings of Parts II and III are brought together in Figure 9.1 to illustrate the starting point for further considerations about how the gap between the business case and the public case could be bridged.

General policy goals

When thinking about how to overcome the discrepancy between the extent and forms of corporate norm-entrepreneurship that are likely to occur and those that are desirable from the perspective of the 'public case', not all factors identified in Chapter 6 as necessary or highly significant for corporations' decisions to engage as norm-entrepreneurs can be addressed by concrete policy recommendations. Among the *push* factors, transnational

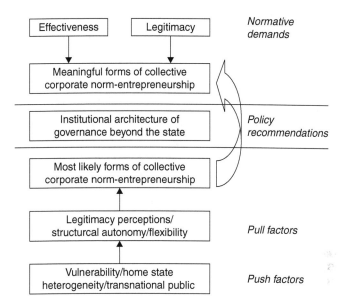

Figure 9.1 Bridging the gap between the business case and the public case in corporate norm-entrepreneurship

public pressure, home state socialization, corporate culture, heterogeneity of the regulatory environment, and vulnerability, only the first two could be strengthened and are open to political interference. Vulnerability and corporate culture are characteristics of a company that cannot be changed from the outside, at least not easily. The same is true for the heterogeneity of the regulatory environments to which potential norm-entrepreneurs are exposed. In practical terms, it would not make much sense to appeal to states to create more of this heterogeneity to mobilize more corporate norm-entrepreneurship. Against this background, policy measures to increase the level of corporate norm-entrepreneurship have to focus on strengthening transnational public pressure and on fostering home state socialization that enables cooperative relationships between state and market actors.

Policy recommendations should contain goals that aim to reach beyond mobilizing corporate norm-entrepreneurship in all its possible manifestations. To bridge the gap illustrated in Figure 9.1, corporate norm-entrepreneurship should be increased and channeled into collective self-regulatory arrangements that meet the normative demands of effectiveness and legitimacy. Otherwise, more corporate norm-entrepreneurship could result in more transnational governance arrangements of the informal, noninclusive, and nontransparent kind that only serve company interests of a high degree of autonomy and weak accountability mechanisms. To counter the 'natural' appeal of collective arrangements with institutional flexibility and structural autonomy, incentives for corporate norm-entrepreneurs should be provided that help to change corporate legitimacy perceptions and increase the attractiveness of inclusive, discursive and noncoercive governance arrangements. These institutions could potentially enhance the reliability of corporate responses to public concerns while having broad stakeholder inclusion. Moreover, they should hold private regulators accountable and limit the substance and mode of regulation to what is legitimately in the authority of the respective regulators. Finally, with reference to the output related shortcomings identified in Chapter 7, the list of policy goals should also include compliance and the avoidance of negative externalities.

9.2   The constitutional background of policy recommendations

The global financial crisis was not necessary to demonstrate that private global norm production within corporate self-regulatory or transnational private governance networks cannot fully substitute public regulation without the risk of falling short of providing public goods or, in this case, even 'bads'. This crisis could be regarded as a mere coincidence. However, failure and crisis are the logical consequence of globalized private self-regulation in an underconstitutionalized global polity. Globalization has broken the historical unity of law and state. The political sphere beyond the state is still characterized by forms of regulation and legalization which, even though states take part as co-regulators, lack fundamental governmental competencies, above all the competence to allocate competencies, as traditionally held by the state in the domestic realm (Habermas 2005: 328). Although business actors increasingly carry a public role (Haufler 2001), market-based private self-regulation systematically lacks the mechanisms that can safeguard its orientation toward what is in the public interest. Leaving norm-related authority to business corporations, based on their claimed expert knowledge, seems to honor the rationality of professional expertise – and market interests – over that of democratic checks and balances when it comes to defining standards of appropriate behavior. The more exclusive and self-referential private self-regulation is, the more likely it will loose sight of the public interest. Even professional first-order self-governing may not be founded on a sufficiently broad knowledge base and normative orientation that would include all stakeholder interests and expectations. Hence, there seems to be a particular necessity to link the often informal self-regulatory and self-referential norm production of private actors back to standards of appropriateness that are generally accepted as serving the public interest, and to some kind of democratically legitimized political authority or public monitoring that can guarantee a broader general interest orientation and hold them accountable when they loose sight of 'the public case' or abuse their regulatory power.

Although the recent financial crisis makes it easy to have the view that governance beyond the state needs some kind of 'government' or 'statehood', who should have or be conferred (by whom and on what grounds?) the legal authority to define general normative standards for appropriateness, allocate basic rights of norm addressees and obligations to norm-entrepreneurs and to guarantee the rule of law is under dispute. What could and should be the role of governments and that of other stakeholders in this context? Does the constitutional order in which governance beyond the state is currently taking place provide an institutional core for the guaranteed checks and balances that seem to be necessary to prevent self-regulation within public-private or purely private governance networks from loosing its links with public interest?

Policy recommendations for closing the gap between the most likely and the more meaningful forms of collective private norm production can only be incremental. It remains unclear if they are legitimate or can be implemented with at least some prospect of success unless they also reflect the status of the agents and the addressees of these measures, as conferred on them by the constitutional setting in which they interact or claim regulatory authority. To develop a sufficiently realistic and forward thinking understanding about the future interplay between the public and the private sectors in the postnational constellation requires an understanding of the constitutive rules of the present political organization of (world) society – that is the way institutions are set up, how competencies are conferred and how the status and basic rights of individuals are to be guaranteed within the broader constitutional frame of a global 'polity'. Whether certain policy recommendations can contribute to making corporate norm-entrepreneurship a more useful component of global governance depends on the constitutional setting in which such recommendations are to be implemented.

9.2.1   Three approaches to the constitutionalization of societal self-regulation

Three conceptual approaches can be distinguished in the academic debate about the constitutionalization and constitutionability of governance beyond the state: two from the periphery and one from the center of the current international political order.

The heterarchical approach to constitutionalizing self-regulation

In the first approach, the heterarchical approach, the spread of transnational self-regulatory activities in a growing number of issue areas is the key for understanding the future political constitution of global governance and its drivers (Willke 1996). Rather than coming from a central agency at the top, the new legal frame is supposed to emerge from the periphery. Global governance develops its constitutional shape in a spontaneous process, during which – independent from a legally binding regulatory frame provided by the state or states – autonomous self-regulators are the authors of the legal constitution of the 'law-free' governance processes in which they are involved. This idea of an emerging 'legal pluralism in an emerging world society' (Teubner 1997b: xiii) within 'a multitude of decentered law-making processes in various sectors of civil society' assumes a multitude of sectoral 'private governments' on a global scale who – in an 'act of self-validation' make their own legal regimes. This approach breaks with the traditional doctrine of legal sources. Teubner justifies this break by referring to the pressures of globalization: 'When the frame of rule hierarchy, with constitutionally legitimated political legislation at its top breaks under the pressures of globalization, then the new frame which replaces it can only be heterarchical. It decenters political law-making, moves it away from its privileged place at the top of the norm-hierarchy and puts it on an equal footing with other types of social law-making' (Teubner 1997b: xiv). The emerging pluralism of constitutional setting reflects constitutionalization in the true sense of the word, namely as a dynamic and open-ended process.

The new heterarchical political constitution that is supposed to be emerging from the decentralized and horizontal self-constitutionalization of functional self-regulators is the result of the fact 'that the politics of sovereign states has lost its controlling potential' (Teubner 1997b: xiv). Its further development is therefore not in the hands of the state but has 'close dependency on other globalized social processes' (Teubner 1997b: xiv), which have to provide a functional equivalent to the guarantees of basic rights and the rule of law of which the state (or states) is no longer assumed to be capable.

The supranational approach to constitutionalizing self-regulation

Another starting point for framing the political constitution of private transnational norm production is Habermas' legal supranationalism. This approach is similar to Teubner's in at least one respect: Habermas, too, is 'de-coupling the concept of "constitution" from the nation-state and revitalizing it in the postnational shape of a politically constituted world society' (Habermas 2005: 345).[1] Without a world government, world citizens constitute a global law of peoples (see also Rawls 1993), instead of states constituting an international legal order. The understanding of the international system as a system of states is transcended by Habermas' distinction between three arenas where different types of collective actors interact: at the supranational level, a 'world organization' as the only actor, responsible for the *legal* protection of human rights and international security, not as a world government but equipped by the international community with the right to impose *political* sanctions; at an intermediate level, functional transnational networks that deal with the solution of technical problems but without legal competence; and, finally, the level of the national states, which still hold the monopoly of power and the primary responsibility to guarantee internal self-determination (Habermas 2005: 336–7).[2]

While the heterarchical approach rightly points to the spread of non-state self-regulation and the lack of a state-based hierarchical constitutional frame for keeping private transnational norm production from going astray, his subsequent reliance on 'other socialized global processes' to make up for this constitutional deficit is less convincing. It overestimates the controlling potential already inherent in a decentered and grossly underconstitutional-ized world society. A related critical point, which will be taken up again later, should also be mentioned here; Teubner also overstates the loss of controlling potential of the state. Habermas seems to share this skepticism regarding the potential of a societal constitution 'from the periphery' to actually guarantee the rule of law or intervene effectively in cases of private norm-production where asymmetries of power and unequal opportunities for effective participation can be discerned. His answer to the question of how much and what kind of government is needed for the constitutional framing of self-regulatory private global norm production transfers the nor-mative content of constitution as a concept away from the state and into the context of a politically constituted world society without a world gov-ernment. Although he claims this to be more than a philosophical thought experiment (Habermas 2005: 345–6), this approach loses some of its persua-sive power when looking for empirical links to the existing world. Habermas seems to regard the development of international law as the embryonic stage of a new kind of constitutionalization that has a new focus, away from strengthening the security and basic rights provided by the state, and toward strengthening the legal status of individuals, making them subjects of an international law of peoples and members of a society of world citi-zens. This view certainly captures the essence of recent – and still ongoing – developments in international law that aim to restrict the sovereign rights of states and highlighting their responsibilities for individuals, including the emergence of new norms and principles such as 'humanitarian inter-vention' or 'responsibility to protect'. However, these principles and rights-in-the-making strengthen the political role of nonstate addressees and still have to be guaranteed by states – which, due to the fact that more than half of them are not democracies, are reluctant to change sovereignty preserving international law standards.

What can be learned from Teubner's heterarchical and Habermas' supra-national approaches to the political constitutionalization of global private norm production? Both subscribe to the view that the historical unity of law and state is fading with the end of the golden age nation state and thus offer a postnational concept of constitutionalization: Not only states can have a constitution; there can also be other sites of public authority within a global constitutional system. Although their relative significance as future functional equivalents to the hierarchical frame of a national constitution may be controversial, there are different levels – or arenas – coexisting in the political sphere beyond the state (see also Rosenau 2002). In each of these, some sort of governing takes place in connection with some kind of private or supranational government. For Habermas, new general obligations for appropriate state behavior are emerging at the supranational level. Governments have to lend their monopoly of power for collective action to protect such fundamental rights when they are violated at the international level, and nonstate actors interact in networks of sectoral self-regulation at the transnational level. Teubner's heterarchical understanding of the role of these arenas and their functional links is much more horizontal and in general less 'orderly', in a way closer to thinking in terms of common law than civil law tradition (Teubner 1997a). Both approaches point to important changes and new developments in the production of norms in a postnational constellation, despite their different starting points. Yet both also share an implicit understanding that the global polity is on its way to constitutionalization rather than already constitutionalized.

The neo-Westphalian approach to constitutionalizing self-regulation

The last distinction separates the third perspective from the previous two. It is simultaneously postnational and state-centered in framing the political constitution in which corporate transnational norm production takes place and is labeled 'neo-Westphalian' to distinguish it from the 'heterarchic' and 'supranational' perspectives. This approach views the current international political and legal order as already constitutionalized on the foundation of the basic principles of an international society in the tradition of the Westphalian world of sovereign nation-states. The emergence of new modes of governance in transnational regulatory networks is usually described as reflecting the transition from an international society of states regulating itself in the frame of 'international governance' to a world society in which all kinds of public and private co-regulators produce norms within the much more complex frame of 'global governance'. While in general subscribing to this description, the neo-Westphalian perspective would claim that the emergence of these new 'political complexes' (Dobner 2009), including the collective arrangements in which corporations act as norm-entrepreneurs, has multiplied the sites and agents of norm production, but does not represent a fundamental challenge to the notion of a still state centered international legal order.

To clarify this distinction between a fundamental change of the global political constitution, and changes within this constitution, it is again helpful to refer to Kooiman's typology of meta, first- and second-order governing (Chapter 8). The existing order, in which states are the only actors who have or can confer legal authority, still provides the political constitution for guaranteeing the rule of law and basic rights. The new forms of transnational nonstate norm production are usually taking place at the levels of meta and first-order governing. Norm setting and norm development take place in the shadow of the legal authority of states, and states allocate and withdraw regulatory competencies to new sites and norm-entrepreneurs.

From this perspective, transnational private governance activities, including corporations that act as norm-entrepreneurs, do not have to invent their own political constitution because they already operate in the shadow of public second-order governing. The activities of nonstate norm production already take place – and can only take place – because they have been invited or because the masters of the game, the states, do not hinder them. If states are overlooked, this does not mean that they were absent but that there was no need, perceived or otherwise, for intervention. In this sense, what in Teubner's view seems to have emerged 'naturally' did not emerge within the context of a preconstitutional state of nature but within a state of deliberate or conscious governmental restraint. The state – or states cooperating in an international organization – could have stepped in at any time and would then have had the legal competence to overrule the results of private regulatory activities, as recent developments in the financial sector have shown where banks were fully or partially nationalized. A state preference for noninterference should not be misinterpreted as the disappearance of the state. In other words, a governing authority can decide on nonaction. Procedurally or structurally, states are still the governors even if, substantially, this leads to nongovernance. It is important to keep this 'shadow existence' of the state in mind; the existing embedding of private norm-entrepreneurship in an existing but perhaps not always visible, neo-Westphalian, constitutional context.

A critical comparison of the three approaches

The criticisms of both Teubner and Habermas of the states' loss of controlling potential and the subsequent need to reestablish government functions somewhere else is met by the argument that the states have long taken up this challenge by changing their roles, acting in different functions at different levels of governing. Within this new setting, their core responsibility is focused on second-order governing. From here, states, as the only actors equipped with the legal authority and competence-competence to do so, set the rules of the game, act as guarantors and have the responsibility to step in when the rule of law or basic rights are violated in norm production processes at the other two levels of governing. States may refrain from enforcing legally binding regulation themselves, sharing or granting regulatory competencies to other actors, and participate as 'activating', 'moderating', or 'enabling' partners in governance. In meta-governing, they can play the role of conveners and moderators and guarantee that all relevant views can be articulated and a broad range of relevant stakeholders can deliberate without coercion about what general moral standards of appropriateness should guide concrete regulatory activities. In first-order governing, they can activate or license nonstate norm-entrepreneurs, set benchmarks, evaluate goal achievement, and, if deemed necessary, reintroduce (inter) state regulation. By changing its role in the described ways, its controlling potential is only needed in the core governance functions. Beyond these, the 'new' state employs new instruments, such as 'context steering', benchmarking or goal-agreements with private self-regulators by which it can make up for much of its loss of control (Héritier 2002).

This conceptual approach is less radical than the previous two. Although taking the transition from international governance to global governance seriously, it also relies on the continuing significance of an already existing, underestimated, unspectacular, and therefore sometimes overlooked constitutional setting that is rooted in 'international governance', as, in ideal analytical terms, the site from where global governance is still directed in terms of constitutional norm setting and norm implementation. In the terminology of Kooiman, 'international governance' is still responsible for the second-order governing layer – or 'the constitutional moment' – within the broader context of an overarching global governance architecture of creating and maintaining the institutional foundations of basic rights of participation, control of power, and self-determination. Within this setting, states are the only legitimate agents with the legal authority to allocate specific competencies to other actors.

This perspective, which is simultaneously neo-Westphalian and postnational, has some merits and some shortcomings that should be mentioned before it is used as the conceptual starting point for policy recommendations to optimize private contributions to global governance. Merits clearly relate to its proximity to the existing world. The reality of transnational regulatory networks is not denied, nor their usefulness as co-providers of certain collective goods, the provision of which has become too burdensome for some governments and which can be provided more effectively by knowledge based expertise rather than legal authority. Nor does it have to deny that the emergence of international law takes place in the teleological view of the Habermasian vision of a law of peoples of a global civil society. This perspective maintains the view that the constitutional project of developing a legal framework for establishing the rule of law in horizontal relationships between different types of actors does not necessarily have to lead to the supremacy of supranationalism. It can be managed within the context of a society of states but only at the expense of the new interplay between the actors, demanding an identity shift by all of them. This implies that further development of the already existing elements of this neo-Westphalian constitutionalization of global governance is required to meet the new regulatory challenges.

Like its merits, the shortcomings of this neo-Westphalian approach to the constitutionalization of societal self-regulation also relate to its proximity to the reality of the existing society of states. International law, as the constitutional framework for establishing the rule of law in horizontal relationships, is still underdeveloped and often violated. Whether it fulfils or is capable of fulfilling its function at all is often disputed. Shortcomings are identified in the international legal order and within its constitutive parts: The majority of states are autocratic or failing states that can either not justify or not use their exclusive formal authority effectively to impose legally binding or even coercive regulation. Thus, the quality of the state system suffers from that of its members. In norm setting and norm implementation, there is an obvious discrepancy between states being 'in charge' on the one hand and being unwilling or unable on the other. Transnational public pressure from civil society thus becomes an indispensable driver for governments to exert influence on transnational self-regulation. All this adds to the empirical criticism that the society of states often fails to meet its second-order governing responsibilities. In principle, states are the only legitimate agents with the legal authority to allocate specific competencies to nonstate actors and to provide the legal-constitutional framework that can guarantee the rule of law. This is the basis for democratic and transparent decision making in transnational sectoral policy networks, including the collective initiatives in which corporations act as norm-entrepreneurs, at the other two levels of governing. Because second-order governing is the prime responsibility of states in this neo-Westphalian understanding, the most critical incidents are those where states fail to address this responsibility or leave it – unjustifiably – to other actors. For this reason, governments and international organizations are the main agents for the implementation of policy recommendations that refer to setting and maintaining the institutional architecture within which private norm production can be a meaningful contribution to global governance.

The differences between the three views may not be as fundamental as they appear. In the end, they can be narrowed down to different estimates of the relative weight and regulatory potential ascribed to developments and actors at the transnational, supranational and international levels. No doubt, the changes depicted from each perspective are taking place at all of these levels, and, in this respect, the different views may even be complementary in depicting a three-dimensional picture of the whole.

9.3   General policy guidelines

None of the existing transnational private governance arrangements, no matter how well or badly they perform in legitimacy or effectiveness, created and maintained the conditions under which they could come into existence by themselves. They were made possible by a constitutional setting that allowed for a configuration of factors that encouraged corporate norm-entrepreneurship and that may have been instrumental in transforming it into meaningful governance contributions by creating incentives for corporate norm-entrepreneurs to choose certain types of self-regulatory arrangements. Contrary to talk of their presumed 'retreat', states are still the only actors who can – and do – provide such constitutional settings. The rules that states define at the level of second-order governing for enabling, limiting or preventing societal self-regulation may differ. Nevertheless, they have the competence to set conditions that can facilitate corporate norm-entrepreneurship, such as strengthening transnational public pressure or fostering home state socialization under which cooperative relationships between state and market actors can emerge. They can provide incentives to enhance the effectiveness and legitimacy of corporate norm-entrepreneurship, for example, with measures that increase compliance, reduce negative externalities, or strengthen stakeholder participation and accountability.

Different configurations of these *push* and *pull* factors can lead to the same end, depending on whether they primarily work through rationalist or constructivist causal mechanisms. This leaves two options in the search for policy recommendations to bridge the gap between corporate norm-entrepreneurship as it is likely to occur and as it would contribute to global governance in a meaningful way, given the various demands for effectiveness and legitimacy: one option appealing to corporations as rational market actors, and the other one appealing to them as good corporate citizens.

9.3.1   Appealing to corporate norm-entrepreneurs as rational market actors

Appealing to the rationalist part of the identity of corporate norm-entrepreneurs, the conditions for continuing public pressure on companies to engage in norm setting and norm development should be protected, improved, or, created where they are nonexistent, as in non-OECD countries that leave little room for an autonomous civil society. In strengthening the business case for making corporate norm-entrepreneurship a more meaningful contribution to global governance, the cost-benefit calculations on which corporate preferences for informal, noninclusive, and nontransparent institutional designs of the collective initiatives rest would have to be changed in a way that makes it more attractive to them to include other stakeholders, to formalize their decision making procedures and to make them more transparent. This general policy recommendation has to be viewed cautiously because corporations seem to have attached great importance to being as autonomous and unaccountable as possible within existing initiatives. Overdoing it might have the unintended consequences of companies shying away from collective norm-entrepreneurship altogether.

Even with the expertise of corporate actors that could be of practical use in norm setting and norm development, such as technical standards, there is no guarantee that these activities are in the public interest. They may primarily serve the interest of those who have the de facto power to impose their preferences on others. Even private self-regulation at the level of first-order governing has to be linked to a transnational public that can judge whether corporate norm-entrepreneurship is geared toward generally accepted notions of what is in the public interest and serves the 'public case'. The link between the 'business case' and the 'public case' depends on two conditions: the openness and transparency of self-regulatory arrangements, and a functioning transnational public.

Both conditions refer to the role of government in transnational private governance. Transparent, private, self-regulatory arrangements, and a functioning transnational public may emerge naturally, reproduce, and put themselves under (private) constitutional rule in reflexive horizontal interaction without further external incentives. As long as this is the case, there is no need for the involvement of 'governments in governance'. Existing social (power) asymmetries can cause unequal opportunities of participation, nontransparency and a lack of effective accountability mechanisms. In this case, the constitutional setting must guarantee that the 'public case' does not suffer from a lack of formality and that private regulatory arrangements remain in the public interest. This requires a political authority that can effectively guarantee the rule of law, accountability, and basic participatory rights.

9.3.2 Appealing to corporate norm-entrepreneurs as good corporate citizens

Policy recommendations could also address the social rather than the economic identity of corporate norm-entrepreneurs or norm-consumers. This may be the longer road to success but is perhaps the more sustainable. The causal analysis concluded with two options for socializing corporations into changing beliefs and, ultimately, into taking on a new role as (collective) norm-entrepreneurs: First, corporations can be habitualized into a new general understanding of their role and responsibilities in business-government relationships as part of the home state socialization. This implies that state actors regard and treat corporations as partners instead of pure norm and rule addressees. Public actors have to concede that business actors are willing to act responsibly and therefore deserve to carry out political tasks. Second, changing corporate beliefs of normative criteria that lead them to perceive an institutional design of an initiative as legitimate. Intensive dialogue and interaction with corporations might increase the acceptance of formal agreements, inclusion of relevant stakeholders and meaningful accountability mechanisms.

This second set of general policy guidelines differs fundamentally from the previous one in the means employed to change corporate behavior and thinking. While the former needs pressure and sanctions, that is, hierarchical instruments of political steering, to be successful, the latter relies on soft modes, such as identity shift by learning and persuasion. These tools may render the strategic options incompatible to some extent because the need for trust and the effect of mistrust do not go together well. The Global

Compact serves as an example of how to avoid this dilemma: This initiative fostered corporate norm-entrepreneurship by employing *pull* factors such as informality and autonomy, only to gradually introduce soft sanctioning mechanisms, relying on normative self-entrapment that would increase the costs to corporations that might want to exit.

9.3.3   Stages of public intervention

Publicly embedded private self-regulation can rest on very different kinds of involvement by 'governments in governance'. These kinds of involvement can have different purposes, ranging from encouraging corporate norm-entrepreneurship at the bottom level of public involvement, to steering it proactively into a meaningful reconciliation of the 'business case' with the 'public case'. Within the political organization of world society previously identified as neo-Westphalian, a shadow of hierarchy can be cast on business self-regulation by individual states and international institutions that use their exclusive right to allow or prohibit private norm production. In principle, national and international law can enforce legally binding regulation on business actors, although individual states may be reluctant to accept strong international regulation and, rather, want to protect 'their' companies.

To give a general conceptual framework to the policy recommendations discussed in the following section, it is useful to take a closer look at the 'ladder of public intervention' in societal self-regulation. At the bottom level of public involvement in private self-regulation, only constitutional governance contributions by public regulators take place. Their main (or only) purpose is to provide a legal framework for allocating rights and responsibilities without prejudicing the future role that the actors who are authorized to provide and change this frame – namely the state in the national context and international organizations in the sphere beyond the state – will actually play within this frame.

Governments and international organizations can exercise their powers to encourage self-regulation or to steer it in a certain direction. The softest instrument for keeping potential corporate norm-entrepreneurs in line with the 'public case' consists of providing incentives that encourage or discourage certain forms of voluntary private governance contributions by manipulating the cost-benefit calculations of corporations. State influence on private norm-entrepreneurs would only provide the constitutional setting – including the state's formal competence to intervene if the constitutional rules of the game are violated – and would refrain from using its competence to intervene in substantive policy making. Private regulators are considered primarily as co-providers of governance functions and norm producers rather than rule takers. The role of the state or of international organizations would thus be limited to activating, enabling, and guaranteeing self-regulation by providing a legal framework; in Kooiman's terminology, they are limited to performing functions at the level of second order governing. However, this is far from a complete retreat because the state remains the master of the constitutive and procedural rules of the game. Given the interest of companies' home states in avoiding more binding external constraints on 'their' companies, second-order governing may in fact be the main contribution of international organizations to regulating self-regulation, for example, by providing space and communication forums for substantive norm production, including NGOs and corporations, at the levels of meta and first-order governing.

Mere encouragement would be confined to public regulatory activities at the level of second-order governing. Steering may go further when its purpose is expanded to ensuring that corporate norm-entrepreneurship in self-regulatory arrangements also serves the public interest. Hence, at the next step on the ladder of public intervention tougher forms of public involvement in self-regulatory arrangements change the interplay between public and private regulators. Constitutional guarantees, encouragement, and incentives are now complemented by instruments such as benchmarking, accreditation, or licensing. These are still instrumental in activating voluntary self-regulation rather than imposing legal obligations. The state or international organizations slip into the role of co-regulators who actively take on (or take part in) meta-governing functions by prescribing goals to be achieved by self-regulatory arrangements or monitoring and evaluating their performance. Self-regulatory initiatives have to follow these procedures if they want to avoid the risk of losing their reputation, legitimacy, or their legal foundation because of waning political support. At this step on the ladder, the shadow of hierarchy, that was present but inactive, reappears. This reappearance is not as hierarchical legally binding intervention, but as the whip that makes private regulators anticipate the 'public case' as a guide for their regulating activities if they do not want to be overruled by legally binding intervention. While these concrete instruments for influencing corporate norm production in self-regulatory arrangements are only available to the state and international organizations, NGOs can use an effective functional equivalent. By monitoring, shaming and blaming or threatening to withdraw its public approval they, too, can make corporate norm-entrepreneurs anticipate public concerns.

At the top of the ladder, the threat of hierarchical intervention by the state or international organizations through legally binding regulation at the level of first-order governing is a tough mode of guaranteeing the 'public case'. State or international organization intervention in private self-regulatory practices would now be more prohibitive than withdrawing the often implicit and tacit, but only borrowed authority to self-regulate. The right to self-regulation may be overruled and the existing legal vacuum will thus turn into a legally grounded obligation or responsibility. At this stage, voluntary but unsuccessful corporate norm-entrepreneurship in public normative demands would give way to obligatory compliance with the law. However, public regulators have to be careful in moving to the top of the ladder. It may have unintended consequences, including the risk of discouraging norm-entrepreneurs altogether and letting corporations fall back into their former role of lobbyists and norm-consumers rather than co-performers of governance functions.

9.4   Policy recommendations

How can these general policy goals translate into concrete measures to bridge the gap between likely and desirable corporate contributions to transnational governance? Who are the agents that could implement such measures? In the previous chapters, the case was made in favor of a functional division of labor between arenas and configurations of actors, and in accordance with the sources of authority that they possess to improve the effectiveness and legitimacy of transnational governance. Policy recommendations can refer to the constitutive rules of the political order in which transnational norm production takes place. In Kooiman's terminology, basic polity-related measures primarily call for public agency to allow or overrule with legally binding state regulation certain forms of self-regulation, to allocate specific competencies to certain regulatory arrangements and specific rights and obligations to certain actors. These policy recommendations should simultaneously aim to encourage corporate norm-entrepreneurship and to channel it toward the normatively desirable variants identified in Chapter 7 and 8 by directly addressing the factors identified as important influences on corporate behavior. Transnational public pressure and home state socialization are the most significant among these factors to encourage norm-entrepreneurship. Compliance should be increased, negative externalities minimized and the legitimacy of self-regulation enhanced to turn norm-entrepreneurship into meaningful contributions to global governance.

Governments, international organizations, and NGOs are therefore all important addressees of complementary policy measures. When states are unwilling or unable to provide adequate regulation for self-regulation, and stand in the way of regulation in international organizations, transnational public pressure may be the only available policy option. As a powerful influence on corporate behavior, transnational public pressure from civil society organizations can be an effective functional equivalent to measures undertaken by states or international organizations. In case both of the latter fail to make use of their legal regulatory competence, either because they are unwilling or unable to exert effective influence on corporations, civil society may even be the only agent left. Yet civil society activists may be unable to exert pressure if they are not allowed to organize themselves in their host country, or because the stakeholders addressed by them, such as customers, investors, shareholders, or the media, are not responsive to their campaigns.

Here again, states and international organizations could play an important role by spreading fundamental civil and political rights to guarantee self-determination and control of the abuse of power. The following recommendations therefore include measures that could be taken by states, international organizations, and NGOs. They follow the policy goals identified in Section 9.3, addressing the conditions that encourage corporate norm-entrepreneurship as well as those that can be instrumental in improving the effectiveness and legitimacy of collective self-regulatory arrangements.

9.4.1 Addressing conditions that facilitate corporate norm-entrepreneurship

Two main conditions required for the spread of corporate norm-entrepreneurship have been identified in this study: an active transnational public that can put pressure on corporations, and a specific type of home state socialization that encourages corporations to take on political responsibility and engage in rule setting and development.

(1) Enabling transnational public pressure

Transnational public pressure is neither a static object nor a fait accompli. Therefore, states should adopt legislation and incorporate strategies at the national level to institutionalize opportunities for civil society formation and involvement. NGOs should be guaranteed the rights of organization, articulation, and participation in national and international governance processes. This includes an enabling environment and supportive institutional opportunities for social movements and networks of civil society groups to organize across borders. Such support might stimulate the often informally structured processes of agenda setting, public opinion formation, and transnational pressure, which trigger and facilitate corporate norm-entrepreneurship.

However, it has to be acknowledged that civil society starts from varying maturity levels and differing points of access to the policy process depending on the country of origin and operation. This might be prejudicial to the further development of a transnational public in certain states. In open societies, governments should start policy dialogues, providing additional voice opportunities for civil society organizations, and invite them to participate in deliberative forums and councils. For countries that are less willing or capable of stimulating the emergence and activities of civil society, the involvement of international organizations becomes particularly important. International organizations can take steps to reform their accreditation systems in a way that allows for institutionalized consultation and inclusion of civil society actors. Some international organizations, such as the United Nations Economic and Social Council (ECOSOC), grant a formal consultative status to NGOs that allows them to participate in the work of the United Nations in many ways. Other organizations, such as the World

Trade Organization (WTO), are reluctantly opening themselves up to NGOs. The WTO has adopted guidelines that state that it 'recognizes the role NGOs can play to increase the awareness of the public in respect of WTO activities'.[3] Civil society actors are still granted only limited access to negotiations, and their right to distribute papers is constrained. There is still a long way to go to enact the commitments articulated by former UN Secretary General Kofi Annan or World Bank President James D. Wolfensohn to 'partnerships involving Governments, international organizations, the business community and civil society' (Annan 1998) or to the need 'to build coalitions for change' (Wolfensohn 1999). International organizations could further improve the provision of supportive measures to allow for more access and ensure a better balance between NGOs from the industrialized and the non-OECD world.

In addition to supporting the empowerment of NGOs, international organizations could also do a lot to improve opportunities for genuine dialogue between stakeholder groups. Following the model of the overarching Global Compact system, the United Nations could establish tripartite or stakeholder consultations in more issue areas, not just in implementation partnerships – as is already aspired to within the Millennium Development Goals framework – but also in discussion boards, roundtables, and other forms of standard setting institutions.

Finally, transnational NGOs or pressure groups could improve their campaigning strategies by not only attacking the 'usual suspects' but also considering companies that have not been in the spotlight of media attention. NGOs and their networks tend to target the same few companies and to apply their naming and shaming strategies to only a few sectors, often focusing on 'business-to-consumer' companies or on those sectors that are known for their doubtful practices, such as the extractive industries. Corporate norm-entrepreneurship and the role shift required for meaningful collaboration in global governance could be extended to large corporations from other sectors, from outside the OECD world and small and medium companies. To achieve this extension, transnational NGOs could focus more on facilitating and empowering smaller civil society groups from other parts of the world who could then engage in more direct pressure and appropriate dialogue in their countries and regions.

(2) Fostering home state socialization

States can foster processes of corporate socialization by creating forums for regular dialogue among national stakeholder groups. In this context, corporations should be asked to share their political views on governance issues and communicate how they can and want to contribute to the provision of public goods. More generally, an open discourse on the political role of companies should help to reduce prejudices and unlock corporate regulatory potential. Governments can encourage corporate norm-related behavior at the national and international level by promoting self-regulatory initiatives and innovative public-private partnerships. Furthermore, states can invite business actors to participate in working groups and national roundtables to raise awareness and invoke learning processes among corporate actors. States can introduce frameworks for action and share regulatory competencies to set the context for corporate norm-entrepreneurship.

Not just home states can socialize corporations into a new self-perception of their political role and responsibility as good corporate citizens. International organizations may also engage in this 'education' process and, particularly in the case of unwilling or unable national governments, provide institutional substitutes for national socialization. International organizations should allow for corporate consultation and inclusion in regulatory discussions far beyond the Global Compact.

Civil society actors, in addition to their roles as watchdogs and in pressure groups, also have a role to play, just like states or international organizations, in the educational and social interaction process that is required for challenging traditional role perceptions. For example, they could lend their expertise to business schools as powerful multipliers of business ideas that shape the mind-sets of future business leaders. Initial steps were undertaken in this direction when the United Nations launched the 'Principles for Responsible Management Education' in April 2008 under the patronage of Secretary-General Ban Ki-moon. Generally, to foster socialization processes in good faith, NGOs have to undergo a role shift themselves – at least under certain circumstances and in certain settings – and understand themselves as discussion partners rather than as opponents of corporations.

9.4.2 Addressing the effectiveness and legitimacy of corporate norm-entrepreneurship

While policy recommendations so far referred to strengthening the influence of factors important to corporate decisions to engage in norm-entrepreneurship, the following recommendations address the shortcomings of self-regulatory arrangements, namely in effectiveness and legitimacy demands. Regarding effectiveness, policy measures should tackle the lack of compliance and should strive to control negative externalities. Legitimacy deficits concern the reliability of responses to public concerns, broader stakeholder participation, instruments of transparency that can hold private regulators accountable, and policies to limit the substance and mode of regulation to what is legitimate under the authority of the private regulators.

(3) Increasing compliance

To increase compliance with the norms and rules set out in self-regulatory arrangements, governments and international organizations have a whole range of measures at their disposal, from the lowest to the highest steps on the ladder of intervention. Among the soft modes of influencing compliance could be incentive structures, such as granting export credits or preferential treatment in public procurement programs to complying corporations. In framing the rules under which self-regulatory arrangements can operate, states or international organizations could allocate self-regulatory competencies – for example, through registration or accreditation – only if effective compliance mechanisms are foreseen as part of the institutional structure of a proposed initiative.

Should self-regulation continue failing to ensure compliance and should cooperative or soft steering instruments not lead to improvement, tougher legal and enforcement mechanisms can be adopted. For example, states could set binding targets to be achieved by self-regulatory initiatives. They could impose financial sanctions when targets are not met. By increasing their commitment to international negotiations, states might foster the emergence of binding international law, which in turn could put further pressure on national executive and legislative bodies to make use of available tools and instruments for regulating self-regulation.

Perhaps most importantly, states could combine the effectiveness of self-regulation in rule-setting with their own responsibility for providing enforcement institutions that are difficult to maintain by nonpublic actors. Monitoring procedures and dispute resolution mechanisms could be fulfilled by or tied to public authorities so that actors who have a public mandate and the necessary resources, expertise, and – above all – authority for such functions guarantee rule compliance and redress for rule violations. At the same time, the substance of the rules would still incorporate business expertise and interests in efficient rules.

The particular role of international organizations in this could be to contribute to a level playing field. They are comparatively free from the suspicion of pursuing political or economic interests when monitoring and judging corporations from different countries, and could establish an international complaint procedure for noncompliance with various self-regulatory arrangements. This could significantly improve the compliance record even if it only resulted in nonbinding recommendations for either compensation to be paid by the corporation or for implementation steps to be taken by national governments. In addition to such a procedure aimed at providing redress, 'compliance committees' could be established at the level of international organizations, with the mandate to collect and verify information and to screen corporate behavior for norm compliance.

International organizations could develop a model for procedures to handle corporate noncompliance, which could include supportive measures to tackle the causes for noncompliance systematically, such as assisting companies that have trouble in meeting their obligations. Where environmental and social impact assessment is required of corporations with no planned production sites, international organizations could undertake these instead of business advisers. They could also play an important role as neutral conveners of the required consultations.

Civil society actors, finally, could also contribute to increasing compliance by engaging in institutionalized monitoring of corporate behavior. This could take place in corporation with the companies or with international organizations. Cooperative rather than confrontational efforts to increase compliance would reflect that failure to comply might be caused by a lack of knowledge and capacity. In that case, exerting public pressure would be less effective than providing policy support and information. Again, a role shift would be required of NGOs as well. If states and international organizations remain unwilling or unable to install an international accreditation and enforcement mechanism for self-regulatory arrangements, NGOs might have to step in and provide a substitute, perhaps even in collaboration with international business and trade-union associations.

(4) Minimizing unintended consequences

Although all of the addressees of these policy recommendations can contribute to avoiding or limiting unwanted side effects of corporate norm-entrepreneurship and self-regulatory arrangements, effective intersectoral externality management can only be established at the level of international organizations and with the participation of governments, business, and civil society.

The shortcomings tackled by an externality management system are mainly the result of the widely uncoordinated proliferation of countless self-regulatory arrangements across the whole range of policy fields, and of overlaps among often competing normative orders with different levels of regulation. To avoid the negative externalities that emerge from these complex, multilayered and multistandard policy areas, states and international organizations can pool their resources to improve the knowledge base necessary for overseeing the self-regulatory world. Only on the grounds of comprehensive information can adequate mechanisms be established for reacting to instances where, for example, new standards fall behind existing ones, or where problems, such as scarcity of resources, are shifted to other areas. Public actors could regularly publish data on such instances, set guidelines and goals for addressing the shortcomings, and provide financial or personal resources to manage interface problems in accordance with publicly set timelines. Generally, states and international organizations should aim to set overarching policy goals for all self-regulatory arrangements. They should act as conveners of open communication forums in which overlap problems could be identified and action plans developed. Finally, and again at the international level, dispute resolution mechanisms are needed to resolve cases of regulatory collisions. The role of civil society actors would primarily consist in providing information about negative externalities and clashes between the 'business case' and the 'public case'.

(5) Improving the legitimacy of self-regulatory arrangements

States and international organizations should provide incentives for corporate norm-entrepreneurs to cooperate in inclusive, discursive, and non-coercive governance arrangements that would enhance the reliability of responses to public concerns, foresee broad stakeholder participation, hold private regulators accountable, and limit the substance and mode of regulation to what is legitimate under the authority of regulators. States can encourage or discourage certain types of self-regulatory arrangements. They can support these initiatives as role models and offer them preferential treatment in national procurement laws. More specifically, such as in the case of the Global Reporting Initiative, states could require – or at least recommend – that company annual reports have to be in line with the GRI guidelines and thus make the content of a voluntary initiative a standard for the implementation of national law. If incentives fail to have the desired effects, states could consider sanctions such as withdrawing accreditation or license to operate, or by replacing voluntary standards with mandatory law, thus demonstrating that the metaphorical whip is a serious policy option that they are capable and willing to use.

Before resorting to this, states should directly address companies and possibly involve other stakeholders in deliberations over the requirements of legitimate self-regulation, such as transparency, inclusiveness, and effective accountability mechanisms as general standards of appropriateness to keep corporate self-regulation in line with the public interest. Again, individual governments can also take the lead by acting as role models in public procurement. They can set incentives by privileging companies that engage in inclusive and accountable self-regulatory initiatives or by blacklisting irresponsible companies and self-regulatory initiatives.

International organizations would have to play a key role in regulating collective self-regulation by serving as registering, accreditation, and licensing bodies for initiatives. Their seal of approval would only be granted to the self-regulatory initiatives that take institutional and procedural precautions to meet the above-mentioned legitimacy demands. The accreditation of self-regulatory initiatives would depend on criteria such as broad stakeholder participation and transparent accountability mechanisms. Registration, accreditation, or licensing may also require the acceptance of fundamental governance goals, such as the 10 principles of the Global Compact. This example shows that international organizations, in addition to acting as 'chartering' bodies for self-regulatory initiatives, can also play an important role in the embedding of self-regulation by convening public forums in which the threshold for acceptable standards can be identified. The standards could concern the recognition of basic rights of norm-addressees, particularly when self-regulation is outwardly focused, or the participation of stakeholders and basic obligations for corporate norm-entrepreneurs to act in the public interest.

International registration, accreditation, and licensing could require mandatory or optional acceptance of a transnational court of appeal dealing with violations of rights and obligations in self-regulatory initiatives. Sanctions could include the withdrawal of accreditation or even the license to self-regulation, and ultimately an appeal to public regulators to step in.

9.4.3   Concluding remarks

To reconcile the 'business case' with the 'public case' measures for regulating self-regulation are necessary at the level of second-order governing or meta-governing at a minimum, or even first-order governing if unavoidable. However, turning corporate norm-entrepreneurship into a meaningful component of transnational governance using 'embedded self-regulation' not only requires a role shift by international organizations, states, and civil society actors. It also calls on corporations to accept and live the role-shift necessary to take on responsibility for the provision of public goods. Corporate decisions to engage as norm-entrepreneurs might be institutionally stimulated to some extent but it ultimately depends on corporate willingness to break new public ground. As John Ruggie, UN Special Representative of the Secretary-General for Business and Human Rights, emphasized on 2 June 2009: 'The solutions for the economic crisis and for business and human rights point to the same direction: governments adopting policies that induce more responsible corporate behavior, and companies adopting strategies that reflect the inescapable fact that their own long-term prospects are tightly coupled with society's well-being'.[4]

Notes

1. Authors' translation.
2. Other authors have analyzed similar issues but have primarily looked at the emergence of new empirical phenomena, such as global public policy networks (Reinicke 1998) or the increasing importance of government networks (Slaughter 2004).
3. http://www.wto.org/english/forums_e/ngo_e/ngo_e.htm, date accessed 10 July 2008.
4. John G. Ruggie, cited in 'Business and human rights matter more than ever, expert tells UN council', UN Press Release, UN Press Center, 2 June 2009; http://www.business-humanrights.org/Links/Repository/370988, date accessed 11 July 2009.

Bibliography

Abbott, Frederick M. (2000) 'The North American Integration Regime and Its Implications for the World Trading System' in Joseph H. H. Weiler (ed.) *The EU, the WTO and the NAFTA. Towards a Common Law of International Trade*, Oxford: Oxford University Press, pp. 169–200.

Abdelal, Rawi, Rose McDermott, Yoshiko M. Herrera and Alastair Iain Johnston (2006) 'Identity as a Variable', *Perspective on Politics*, 4: 4, 695–711.

AccountAbility (2008) *Governing Collaboration, Making Partnership Accountable for Delivering Development*, AccountAbility: http://www.accountability21.net/uploadedFiles/Conference/Governing%20Collaboration_Full%20report.pdf, date accessed 20 May 2009.

Alchian, Armen A. and Harold Demsetz (1972) 'Production, Information Costs, and Economic Organization', *American Economic Review*, LXII: 5, 777–95.

Alsop, Ronald J. (2004) *The 18 Immutable Laws of Corporate Reputation: Creating, Protecting, and Repairing Your Most Valuable Asset*, Washington, DC: Free Press.

Amnesty International, Lawyers Committee for Human Rights, Oxfam and Human Rights Watch (2003) *Open Letter to Ms Louise Fréchette, Deputy Secretary-General of the United Nations*: http://www.humanrightsfirst.org/workers_rights/issues/gc/pdf/joint_ltr_UN_040703.pdf, date accessed 10 October 2008.

Andonova, Liliana B. (2006) 'Globalization, Agency, and Institutional Innovation: The Rise of Public-Private Partnerships in Global Governance', *Goldfarb Center for Public Affairs and Civic Engagement Working Paper* 4, Waterville, ME: Colby College.

Andreasson, Stefan (2007) 'The Political Economy of Corporate Governance in South Africa', *Working Paper*, Belfast: Queen's University.

Annan, Kofi (1999) *Secretary-General Proposes Global Compact on Human Rights, Labour, Environment, in Address to World Economic Forum in Davos*, UN: www.un.org/News/Press/docs/1999/19990201.sgsm6881.html, date accessed 13 May 2009.

Annan, Kofi (1998) *The Secretary-General's Address to the World Economic Forum: Markets For a Better World*, UN Press Release SG/SM/98/16: http://www.un.org/News/Press/docs/1998/19980130.SGSM6448.html, date accessed 13 May 2009.

Argandona, Antonio (1999) 'Business Ethics in Spain', *Journal of Business Ethics*, 22: 3, 155–73.

Argyris, Chris and Donald A. Schön (1996) *Organizational Learning II. Theory, Method, and Practice*, Reading, MA: Addison-Wesley.

Argyris, Chris and Donald A. Schön (1978) *Organizational Learning: A Theory of Action Perspective*, Reading, MA: Addison-Wesley.

Armingeon, Klaus (1997) 'Swiss Corporatism in Comparative Perspective', *West European Politics*, 20: 4, 164–79.

Arts, Bas (1998) *The Political Influence of Global NGOs. Case Studies on the Climate and Biodiversity Conventions*, Utrecht: International Books.

AT Kearney (2009) *Green Winners – The Performance of Sustainability-Focused Companies During the Financial Crises*, AT Kearney: http://www.atkearney.com/images/global/pdf/Green_winners.pdf, date accessed 1 July 2009.

BankTrack (2005) *Unproven Equator Principles. The Equator Principles at year two*, Banktrack: http://www.banktrack.org/show/focus/the_equator_principles, date accessed 20 May 2009.

Barnea, Amir, and Amir Rubin (2006) 'Corporate Social Responsibility as a Conflict between Shareholders', *Zurich Meetings*, Zurich: EFA.

Barnett, Michael L., John M. Jermier and Barbara A. Lafferty (2006) 'Corporate Reputation: The Definitional Landscape', *Corporate Reputation Review*, 9: 1, 26–38.

Bauer, Hans-Peter and Martin Peter (2002) 'Global Standards for Money Laundering Prevention', *Journal of Financial Crime*, 10: 1, 69–72.

Beisheim, Marianne and Klaus Dingwerth (2008) 'Procedural Legitimacy and Democratic Legitimacy: Are the Good Ones Doing Better?', *SFB Governance Working Paper Series* 14, Berlin: Freie Universität.

Bengtsson, Elias (2007) 'A History of Scandinavian Socially Responsible Investing', *Journal of Business Ethics*, 82: 1, 969–83.

Benner, Thorsten, Wolfgang Reinicke and Jan Martin Witte (2004) 'Multisectoral Networks in Global Governance. Towards a Pluralistic System of Accountability?', *Government and Opposition*, 39: 2, 191–210.

Bennett, Roger and Rita Kottasz (2000) 'Practitioner Perceptions of Corporate Reputation: An Empirical Investigation', *Corporate Communication: An International Journal*, 5: 4, 224–34.

Benz, Arthur (2004) 'Multilevel Governance – Governance in Mehrebenensystemen' in Arthur Benz (ed.) *Governance – Regieren in komplexen Regelsystemen*, Wiesbaden: VS Verlag für Sozialwissenschaften, pp. 125–46.

Berman, Shawn L., Andrew C. Wicks, Suresh Kotha and Thomas M. Jones (1999) 'Does Stakeholder Orientation Matter? The Relationship between Stakeholder Management Models and Firm Financial Performance', *Academy of Management Journal*, 42: 5, 488–506.

Bertelsmann Stiftung (2007) *The CSR Navigator – Public Policies in Africa, the Americas, Asia and Europe*, Gütersloh: Bertelsmann Stiftung.

Bhattacharya, C.B., Daniel Korschun and Sankar Sen (2009) 'Strengthening Stakeholder-Company Relationships through Mutually Beneficial Corporate Social Responsibility Initiatives', *Journal of Business Ethics*, 85, Supplement 2, 257–72.

Blasco, Maribel and Mette Zolner (2008) 'Corporate Social Responsibility in Mexico and France: Exploring the Role of Normative Institutions', *Business & Society*, 30 January 2008.

Boeri, Tito, Giuseppe Nicoletti and Stefano Scarpetta (1999) 'Regulation and Labour Market Performance', *IGIER Working Paper* 158, Bocconi University.

Bomann-Larsen, Lene and Oddny Wiggen (eds) (2004) *Responsibility in World Business: Managing Harmful Side-Effects of Corporate Activity*, New York, NY: UNU Press.

Booz&Co. (2009) *Recession Response: Why Companies Are Making the Wrong Moves*, Booz&Co.: http://www.booz.com/media/uploads/Recession_Response.pdf, date accessed 27 May 2009.

Börsch, Alexander (2007) *Global Pressure, National System: How German Corporate Governance is Changing*, Ithaca, NY: Cornell University Press.

Börzel, Tanja A. and Thomas Risse (2005) 'Public Private Partnerships: Effective and Legitimate Tools of Transnational Governance?' in Grande Edgar and Louis W. Pauly (eds) *Complex Sovereignty. Reconstituting Political Authority in the Twenty-First Century*, Toronto: University of Toronto Press, pp. 195–216.

Börzel, Tanja A. and Thomas Risse (2002) 'Die Wirkung internationaler Institutionen. Von der Normanerkennung zur Normeinhaltung' in Markus Jachtenfuchs and Michèle Knodt (eds) *Regieren in internationalen Institutionen*, Opladen: Leske + Budrich, pp. 141–81.

BP (2008) *The Environment: A Growing Concern*, BP: http://www.bp.com/sectiongeneric article.do?categoryId=9014511&contentId=7027672, date accessed 4 March 2008.

BP (1982) 'Briefing Paper: BP and Society in the United Kingdom' in Malcolm McIntosh and Ruth Thomas (eds) (2001) *Global Companies in the Twentieth Century: Selected Archival Histories. Volume IV BP*, London: Routledge, 54.

BP (1979) 'Briefing Paper: Energy Conservation and BP' in Malcolm McIntosh and Ruth Thomas (eds) (2001) *Global Companies in the Twentieth Century: Selected Archival Histories. Volume IV BP*, London: Routledge, 52.

BP (1977) 'Review: New Activities' in Malcolm McIntosh and Ruth Thomas (eds) (2001) *Global Companies in the Twentieth Century: Selected Archival Histories, Volume IV BP*, London: Routledge, 49.

Braithwaite, John and Peter Drahos (2000) *Global Business Regulation*, Cambridge, MA: Cambridge University Press.

Breitmeier, Helmut and Klaus Dieter Wolf (1993) 'Analysing Regime Consequences' in Volker Rittberger (ed.) *Regime Theory and International Relations*, Oxford: Clarendon Press, pp. 339–60.

Briskey, Joseph A., Klaus J. Schulz, John P. Mosesso, Lief R. Horwitz and Charles G. Cunningham (2001) 'It's Time to Know the Planet's Mineral Resources', *Geotimes*, March 2001.

Brown, Halina Szejnwald, Martin De Jong and Teodorina Lessidrenska (2007) 'The Rise of the Global Reporting Initiative (GRI) as a Case of Institutional Entrepreneurship', *Corporate Social Responsibility Initiative Working Papers* 36, Cambridge, MA: John F. Kennedy School of Government.

Browne, John (1997) 'Corporate Responsibility in an International Context' in Malcolm McIntosh and Ruth Thomas (eds) (2001) *Global Companies in the Twentieth Century: Selected Archival Histories. Volume IV BP*, 75.

Browning, Lynnley (2009) 'A Swiss Bank Is Set to Open Its Secret Files', *New York Times*, 19 February 2009.

Brühl, Tanja (2003) *Nichtregierungsorganisationen als Akteure internationaler Umweltverhandlungen: Ein Erklärungsmodell auf der Basis der situationsspezifischen Ressourcennachfrage*, Frankfurt a. M.: Campus.

Brühl, Tanja, Thomas Debiel, Brigitte Hamm, Hartwig Hummel and Jens Martens (eds) (2001) *Die Privatisierung der Weltpolitik*, Bonn: Dietz.

Brunsson, Nils and Bengt Jacobsson (2000) *A World of Standards*, Oxford: Oxford University Press.

Buchanan, Allen and Robert O. Keohane (2006) 'The Legitimacy of Global Governance Institutions', *Ethics and International Affairs*, 20: 4, 405–37.

Büschgen, Hans E. (1995) 'Die Deutsche Bank von 1957 bis zur Gegenwart. Aufstieg zum internationalen Finanzdienstleistungskonzern' in Lothar Gall, Gerald D. Feldman, Harold James, Carl-Ludwig Holtfrerich and Hans E. Büschgen (eds) *Die Deutsche Bank 1870–1995*, Munich: Beck, pp. 579–865.

Business Social Compliance Initiative (2007) *BSCI System: Rules and Functioning*, BSCI: http://www.bsci-eu.com/dl.php?id=10217, date accessed 20 May 2009.

Business Social Compliance Initiative (2006) *BSCI Code of Conduct*, BSCI: http://www.bsci-eu.com/dl.php?id=10407, date accessed 20 May 2009.

Business Social Compliance Initiative (2005) *Annual Report 2005*, BSCI: http://www.bsci-eu.com/index.php?id=2035, date accessed 7 July 2009.

Campos, J. Edgardo and Sanjay Pradhan (eds) (2007) *The Many Faces of Corruption: Tracking Vulnerabilities at the Sector Level*, Washington, DC: World Bank.

Carroll, Archie B. (2004) 'Managing Ethically with Global Stakeholders: A Present and Future Challenge', *Academy of Management Executive*, 18: 2, 114–20.

Carroll, Archie B. (1979) 'A Three-Dimensional Conceptual Model of Corporate Social Performance', *Academy of Management Review*, 4: 4, 497–505.

Cashore, Benjamin (2002) 'Legitimacy and the Privatization of Environmental Governance: How Non-State Market-Driven (NSMD) Governance Systems Gain Rule-Making Authority', *Governance*, 15, 502–29.

Cawson, Alan, Peter Holmes and Anne Stevens (1987) 'The Interaction Between Firms and the State in France: The Telecommunications and Consumer Electronics Sectors' in Stephen Wilks and Maurice Wright (eds) *Comparative Government – Industry Relations. Western Europe, the United States, and Japan*, Oxford: Clarendon Press, pp. 10–34.

Chabane, Neo, Andrea Goldstein and Simon Roberts (2006) 'The Changing Face and Strategies of Big Business in South Africa: More than a Decade of Political Democracy', *Industrial and Corporate Change*, 15: 3, 549–77.

Chareonsuk, Chaichan and Chuvej Chansa-Ngavej (2008) 'Intangible Asset Management Framework for Long-Term Financial Performance', *Industrial Management & Data System*, 108: 6, 812–28.

Checkel, Jeffrey T. (2001) 'Why Comply? Social Learning and European Identity Change', *International Organization*, 55: 3, 553–88.

Chen, Maggie Xiaoyang and Aaditya Mattoo (2008) 'Regionalism in Standards: Good or Bad for Trade?', *Canadian Journal of Economics*, 41: 3, 838–63.

Coen, David and Wyn Grant (2006) 'Managing Business and Government Relations' in Michael Stein and John Trent (eds) *Business and Government. Methods and Practice*, Opladen: Barbara Budrich Publishers, pp. 13–32.

Coleman, William D. and Geoffrey R. D. Underhill (1998) *Regionalism and Global Economic Integration: Europe, Asia and the Americas*, London: Routledge.

Collier, Jane and Rafael Esteban (2007) 'Corporate Social Responsibility and Employee Commitment', *Business Ethics: A European Review*, 16: 1, 19–33.

Consolandi, Costanza, Paola Nascenzi and A. Jaiswal-Dale (2006) 'Ownership Concentration and Corporate Social Performance: an Empirical Evidence for European Firms', *Corporate Responsibility Research Conference*, Belfast: Queen's University, 3–5 September 2006.

Conzelmann, Thomas and Klaus Dieter Wolf (2007a) 'The Potential and Limits of Governance by Private Codes of Conduct' in Jean-Christophe Graz and Andreas Nölke (eds) *Transnational Private Governance and its Limits*, London: Routledge, pp. 98–114.

Conzelmann, Thomas and Klaus Dieter Wolf (2007b) 'Doing Good While Doing Well? Potenzial und Grenzen grenzüberschreitender privatwirtschaftlicher Selbstregulierung' in Andreas Hasenclever, Klaus Dieter Wolf and Michael Zürn (eds) *Macht und Ohnmacht internationaler Institutionen*, Frankfurt a. M.: Campus, pp. 145–75.

Corporate Knights (2009) *Global 100-Most Sustainable Corporations in the World*, Global 100: http://www.global100.org/2009/index.asp, date accessed 15 May 2009.

CorpWatch (2002) *Greenwash +10: The UN's Global Compact, Corporate Accountability and the Johannesburg Summit*, CorpWatch: http://www.corpwatch.org/article.php?id=1348, date accessed 27 May 2009.

CorpWatch (2000) *Tangled up in Blue – Corporate Partnerships at the United Nations*, San Francisco, CA: TRAC-Transnational Resource & Action Center.

Crane, Andrew and Dirk Matten (2007) *Business Ethics: Managing Corporate Citizenship and Sustainability in the Age of Globalization*, Oxford: Oxford University Press.

Cravens, Karen, Elizabeth G. Oliver and Sridhar Ramamoorti (2003) 'The Reputation Index: Measuring and Managing Corporate Reputation', *European Management Journal*, 21: 2, 201–12.

Credit Suisse Group (1998a) *Ökobilanz Schweiz 1996/97*, Credit Suisse Group: http://www.credit-suisse.com/investors/doc/csgeco_perform_d_long.pdf, date accessed 27 Febuary 2008.

Credit Suisse Group (1998b) *Umweltbericht 1997/98*, Credit Suisse Group: http://www.credit-suisse.com/investors/doc/ub_ld.pdf, date accessed 27 Febuary 2008.

Crouch, Colin (1993) *Industrial Relations and European State Traditions*, Oxford: Clarendon Press.

Crouch, Collin and Wolfgang Streeck (eds) (1997) *Political Economy of Modern Capitalism*, London: Sage.

Cusimano, Maryann K. (2000) *Beyond Sovereignty: Issues for a Global Agenda*, Boston, MA: St. Martin's Press.

Cutler, A. Claire, Virginia Haufler and Tony Porter (eds) (1999a) *Private Authority and International Affairs*, Albany, NY: State University of New York Press.

Cutler, A. Claire, Virginia Haufler and Tony Porter (1999b) 'Private Authority and International Affairs' in A. Claire Cutler, Virginia Haufler and Tony Porter (eds) *Private Authority and International Affairs*, Albany, NY: State University of New York Press, pp. 3–28.

Cutler, A. Claire, Virginia Haufler and Tony Porter (1999c) 'The Contours and Significance of Private Authority in International Affairs' in A. Claire Cutler, Virginia Haufler and Tony Porter (eds) *Private Authority and International Affairs*, Albany, NY: State University of New York Press, pp. 333–76.

Dahl, Robert A. (1994) 'A Democratic Dilemma: System Effectiveness versus Citizen Participation', *Political Science Quarterly*, 109: 1, 23–34.

De George, Richard T. (1993) *Competing with Integrity in Internal Business*, Oxford: Oxford University Press.

De Groot, Henri L.F., Gert-Jan Linders and Piet Rietveld (2004) 'The Institutional Determinants of Bilateral Trade Patterns', *Kyklos*, 57: 1, 103–24.

Dehejia, Vivek H. and Samy Yiagadeesen (2006) 'Labour Standards and Economic Integration in the European Union. An Empirical Analysis', *CESifo Area Conference on Employment and Social Protection*, Munich: CESifo, 26–27 May 2006.

Deitelhoff, Nicole (2006) *Überzeugung in der Politik: Grundzüge einer Diskurstheorie internationalen Regierens*, Frankfurt a. M.: Suhrkamp.

Deutsche Bank (2008) *Facts and Figures*, Deutsche Bank: http://www.deutsche-bank.de/csr/en/content/facts_and_figures.htm, date accessed 27 April 2009.

Deutsche Bank (2002) *Corporate Cultural Affairs, Bericht 2002*, Deutsche Bank: http://www.upj-online.de/media/upj/downloads/Corporate_Citizenship/Aktuelle_Entwicklungen/Ueber_CCCSR_berichten/DeutscheBank_de.pdf, date accessed 2 January 2008.

DIHR (2006) *Shell highlights cooperation with DIHR in Developing Countries*, Danish Institute for Human Rights http://www.humanrights.dk/news/archive/news+2006/shell+highlights+collaboration+with+dihr, date accessed 10 March 2009.

DiMaggio, Paul J. and Walter W. Powell (1983) 'The Iron Cage Revisited: Institutional Isomorphism and Collective Rationality in Organizational Fields', *American Sociological Review*, 48: 2, 147–60.

Dingwerth, Klaus (2007) *The New Transnationalism: Transnational Governance and Democratic Legitimacy*, Basingstoke: Palgrave Macmillan.

Dingwerth, Klaus (2004) 'Effektivität und Legitimität globaler Politiknetzwerke' in Tanja Brühl, Heidi Feldt, Brigitte Hamm, Hartwig Hummel and Jens Martens (eds) *Unternehmen in der Weltpolitik*, Bonn: Dietz, pp. 74–95.

Dingwerth, Klaus and Philipp H. Pattberg (2009) 'World Politics and Organizational Fields: The Case of Transnational Sustainability Governance', *European Journal of International Relations*: 15, forthcoming.

Dobner, Petra (2009) 'On the Constitutionability of Global Public Policy Networks', *Indiana Journal of Global Legal Studies*, forthcoming.

Doh, Jonathan P. (2008) 'Between Confrontation and Cooperation: Corporate Citizenship and NGOs' in Andreas Georg Scherer and Guido Palazzo (eds) *Handbook of Research on Global Corporate Citizenship*, Cheltenham: Edward Elgar, pp. 273–92.

Doh, Jonathan P. and Hildy Teegen (2003) *Globalization and NGOs. Transforming Business, Government, and Society*, Westport, CT: Praeger.

Donaldson, Thomas (1989) *The Ethics of Business Ethics*, Oxford: Oxford University Press.

Donaldson, Thomas and Thomas W. Dunfee (1999) *Ties that Bind: A Social Contract Approach to Business Ethics*, Boston, MA: Harvard Business School Press.

Donaldson, Thomas and Lee E. Preston (1995) 'The Stakeholder Theory of the Corporation: Concepts, Evidence, and Implications', *Academy of Management Review*, 20: 1, 65–91.

Dore, Ronald (2004) 'Pros and Cons of Insider Governance', *REITI Working Paper*, Tokyo: Tokyo Research Institute of Economy.

Dore, Ronald (1993) 'What Makes Japan Different?' in Colin Crouch and David Marquand (eds) *Ethics and Markets: Cooperation and Competition within Capitalist Economies*, Oxford: Blackwell, pp. 66–79.

Doremus, Paul N., William W. Keller, Louis W. Pauly and Simon Reich (1999) *The Myth of the Global Corporation*, Princeton, NJ: Princeton University Press.

Dowling, Grahame (2001) *Creating Corporate Reputations: Identity, Image, and Performance*, Oxford: Oxford University Press.

Duncan, Val (1967) 'Overseas Investment or Economic Nationalism?' in Malcolm McIntosh and Ruth Thomas (eds) (2001) *Global Companies in the Twentieth Century. Selected Archival Histories. Volume IX. Rio Tinto*, London: Routledge, 17.

Dunning, John H., Changsu Kim and Donghyun Park (2007) 'Old Wine in New Bottles: a Comparison of Emerging Market TNCs Today and Developed Country TNCs Thirty Years Ago', *SLPTMD Working Paper Series* 11, Oxford: University of Oxford.

Dyer, W. Gibb and David A. Whetten (2008) 'Family Firms and Social Responsibility: Preliminary Evidence from the S&P 500', *Entrepreneurship Theory & Practice*, 30: 6, 785–802.

Easton, David (1965) *A Systems Analysis of Political Life*, New York, NY: Wiley.

Egels-Zandén, Niklas and Evelina Wahlqvist (2007) 'Post-Partnership Strategies for Defining Corporate Responsibility: The Business Social Compliance Initiative', *Journal of Business Ethics*, 70: 2, 175–89.

Elgström, Ole (2000) 'Norm Negotiations. The Construction of New Norms Regarding Gender and Development in EU Foreign Aid Policy', *Journal of European Public Policy*, 7: 3, 457–76.

Elkington, John (1998) *Cannibals with Forks: The Triple Bottom Line of 21st Century Business*, Stony Creek, CT: New Society Publishers.

Epstein, Marc J. (2008) *Making Sustainability Work*, San Francisco, CA: Berrett-Koehler.

Esty, Daniel C. and Michael E. Porter (2005) 'National Environmental Performance: An empirical Analysis of Policy Results and Determinants', *Environment and Development Economics*, 10, 391–434.

Esty, Daniel C. and Michael E. Porter (2002) 'Ranking National Environmental Regulation and Performance: A Leading Indicator of Future Competitiveness?'

in World Economic Forum (ed.) *Global Competitiveness Report 2001–2002*, Davos: World Economic Forum.

Evans, Peter B. (1995) *Embedded Economy. States and Industrial Transformations*, Princeton, NJ: Princeton University Press.

Feil, Moira, Susanne Fischer, Andreas Haidvogl and Melanie Zimmer (2008) 'Bad Guys, Good Guys, or Something in Between? Corporate Governance Contributions in Zones of Violent Conflict', *PRIF Reports* 84, Frankfurt a. M.: Peace Research Institute Frankfurt.

Fieseler, Christian (2008) *Die Kommunikation der Nachhaltigkeit: Gesellschaftliche Verantwortung als Inhalt der Kapitalmarktkommunikation*, Wiesbaden: VS Verlag für Sozialwissenschaften.

Finnemore, Martha (1996) 'Norms, Culture and World Politics: Insights from Sociology's Institutionalism', *International Organization*, 50: 2, 325–47.

Finnemore, Martha (1993) 'International Organizations as Teachers of Norms: The United Nations Educational, Scientific, and Cultural Organization and Science Policy', *International Organization*, 47: 4, 565–97.

Finnemore, Martha and Kathryn Sikkink (1998) 'International Norm Dynamics and Political Change', *International Organization*, 52: 4, 887–917.

Flohr, Annegret, Lothar Rieth, Sandra Schwindenhammer and Klaus Dieter Wolf (2008) *The Corporate Gap: Conceptualizing Business Corporations as Norm-Entrepreneurs*, Technische Universität Darmstadt, mimeo.

Flohr, Annegret, Lothar Rieth and Sandra Schwindenhammer (2007) 'Transnational Corporations as Norm-entrepreneurs? A Conceptual Framework', *DACSReview* 1, Darmstadt: Technische Universität Darmstadt.

Florini, Ann M. (2000) 'Who Does What? Collective Action and the Changing Nature of Authority' in Richard A. Higgott, Geoffrey R. D. Underhill and Andreas Bieler (eds) *Non-State Actors and Authority in the Global System*, London: Routledge, pp. 15–31.

Fombrun, Charles J. and Cees B. M. van Riel (1997) 'The Reputational Landscape', *Corporate Reputation Review*, 1: 1–2, 5–13.

Fondation Guilé (2009) *Taking Stock of Disclosure on the UN Global Compact – The 2009 Guilé Communication on Progress Survey*, Boncourt: Fondation Guilé.

Franck, Thomas M. (1990) *The Power of Legitimacy Among Nations*, Oxford: Oxford University Press.

Freeman, R. Edward (ed.) (1991) *Business Ethics: The State of the Art*, Oxford: Oxford University Press.

Freeman, R. Edward (1984) *Strategic Management: A Stakeholder Approach*, Boston, MA: Pitman.

Friedman, Milton (1970) 'The Social Responsibility of Business is to Increase its Profits', *New York Times Magazine*, 13 September 1970.

Frynas, Jedrzej George (2005) 'The False Developmental Promise of Corporate Social Responsibility: Evidence from Multinational Oil Companies', *International Affairs*, 81: 3, 581–98.

Frynas, Jedrzej George (2001) 'Corporate and State Responses to Anti-Oil Protests in the Niger Delta', *African Affairs*, 100: 1, 27–54.

Fuchs, Doris A. (2005) *Understanding Business Power in Global Governance*, Baden-Baden: Nomos.

Fundinguniverse (2008) *Sasol Limited*, Fundinguniverse: http://www.fundinguniverse.com/company-histories/Sasol-Limited-Company-History.html, date accessed 27 April 2009.

Ganslandt, Mattias and James R. Markusen (2001) 'Standards and Regulation in International Trade: A Modeling Approach', *NBER Working Paper* 8346, Cambridge: NBER.

Gavin, Brigid and Luk van Langenhove (2003) 'Trade in World of Regions', in Gary P. Sampson and Simon Woolcock (eds) *Multilateralism, Regionalism and Economic Integration*, Tokyo: UNU Press, pp. 277–314.

Gee, Careesa and Alyson Slater (2005) 'Developing Next-Generation GRI Guidelines', *Corporate Responsibility Management*, 1: 5, 30–3.

Gehring, Thomas (1994) *Dynamic International Regimes. Institutions for International Environmental Governance*, Frankfurt a. M.: Lang.

George, Alexander L. and Andrew Bennett (2005) *Case Studies and Theory Development*, Cambridge, MA: MIT Press.

Gerhards, Jürgen (1994) 'Politische Öffentlichkeit. Ein system- und akteurstheoretischer Bestimmungsversuch' in Friedhelm Neidhardt (ed.) *Öffentlichkeit, öffentliche Meinung, soziale Bewegungen*, Opladen: Westdeutscher Verlag, pp. 77–105.

Germanwatch (2007) *Anmerkungen zur Rolle des Global Compact im Spannungsfeld von freiwilligen Selbstverpflichtungen und staatlicher Regulierung, Positionspapier*, Germanwatch: http://www.germanwatch.org/corp/gc07.htm, date accessed 1 July 2009.

Gerring, John (2004) 'What Is a Case Study and What Is It Good for?', *American Political Science Review*, 98: 2, 341–54.

Gilbert, Dirk U. and Andreas Rasche (2007) 'Discourse Ethics and Social Accountability: The Ethics of SA 8000', *Business Ethics Quarterly*, 17: 2, 187–216.

Gioia, Dennis A. and Peter P. Poole (1984) 'Scripts in Organizational Behavior', *Academy of Management Review*, 9: 3, 449–59.

Gitterman, Daniel P. (2003) 'European Integration and Labour Market Cooperation. A Comparative Regional Analysis', *Journal of European Social Policy*, 13, 99–120.

Global Reporting Initiative (2008) *Small, Smart and Sustainable. Experiences of SME Reporting in Global Supply Chains*, Global Reporting Initiative: http://www.globalreporting.org/NR/rdonlyres/02AF6322-C207-4F79-85B2-EC017826B60F/0/SSSReport.pdf, date accessed 6 May 2009.

Global Reporting Initiative and Global Compact (2007) *Making the Connection. The GRI Guidelines and the UNGC Communication on Progress*, Global Reporting Initiative: http://www.unglobalcompact.org/docs/news_events/8.1/Making_the_Connection.pdf, date accessed 27 May 2009.

Global Reporting Initiative (2003) *Annual Review 2003. Gaining Momentum*, Global Reporting Initiative: http://www.globalreporting.org/NR/rdonlyres/F098CB69-7569-44D7-981D-3AC5FF5DE14B/0/ActivitiesReport2003.pdf, date accessed 6 May 2009.

Global Reporting Initiative (2002) *Sustainability Reporting Guidelines 2002*, Global Reporting Initiative: http://www.globalreporting.org/NR/rdonlyres/B75A56EB-24D9-43FC-B5F7-153687759627/0/2002_Guidelines_DUE.pdf, date accessed 20 May 2009.

Global Witness (2009) *Undue Diligence: How Banks do Business with Corrupt Regimes*, Global Witness: http://www.globalwitness.org/media_library_detail.php/735/en/undue_diligence_how_banks_do_business_with_corrupt, date accessed 1 July 2009.

GlobeScan (2009) *GlobeScan Corporate Social Responsibility Monitor 2009*, GlobeScan: http://www.globescan.com/csrm_overview.htm, date accessed 7 July 2009.

Goergen, Marc and Luc Renneboog (2002) *The Social Responsibility of Major Shareholders*, SSRN: http://ssrn.com/abstract=356920, date accessed 27 May 2009.

Goldman Sachs (2005) 'How Solid are the BRICs?', *Global Economics Paper* 134, New York, NY: Goldman Sachs.

Goldman Sachs (2003) 'Dreaming with BRICs: The Path to 2050', *Global Economics Paper* 99, New York, NY: Goldman Sachs.

Goldstein, Judith and Robert O. Keohane (1993) 'Ideas and Foreign Policy: An Analytical Framework' in Judith Goldstein and Robert O. Keohane (eds) *Ideas and Foreign Policy: Beliefs, Institutions, and Political Change*, Ithaca, NY: Cornell University Press, pp. 3–30.

Gordenker, Leon and Thomas G. Weiss (1996) 'Pluralizing Global Governance: Analytical Approaches and Dimensions' in Thomas G. Weiss und Leon Gordenker (eds) *NGOs, the UN, and Global Governance*, Boulder, CO: Lynne Rienner, pp. 7–47.

Graafland, Johan J. (2002) 'Profits and Principles: Four Perspectives', *Journal of Business Ethics*, 35: 4, 293–305.

Grant, Wyn (2004) 'Pressure Politics. The Changing World of Pressure Groups', *Parliamentary Affairs*, 57: 2, 408–19.

Grant, Wyn (1993) *Business and Politics in Britain*, Basingstoke: Macmillan.

Gunningham, Neil and Joseph Rees (1997) 'Industry Self-Regulation: An Institutional Perspective', *Law & Policy*, 19: 4, 364–414.

Haas, Peter M. (1992) 'Introduction: Epistemic Communities and International Policy Coordination', *International Organization*, 46: 1, 1–35.

Habermas, Jürgen (2005) 'Eine politische Verfassung für die pluralistische Weltgesellschaft' in Jürgen Habermas (ed.) *Zwischen Naturalismus und Religion*, Frankfurt a. M.: Suhrkamp, pp. 324–65.

Habermas, Jürgen (2001) *The Postnational Constellation. Political Essays*, Cambridge, MA: MIT Press.

Habermas, Jürgen (1990) *Strukturwandel der Öffentlichkeit*, Frankfurt a. M.: Suhrkamp.

Habisch, André, Jan Jonker and Rene Schmidtpeter (eds) (2005) *Corporate Social Responsibility Across Europe*, Berlin: Springer.

Hage, Jerald and Jonathon Mote (2008) 'Transformational Organizations and Institutional Change: The Case of the Institut Pasteur and French Science', *Socio-Economic Review*, 6, 313–36.

Hague, Paul (2008) *Brands – How Much Are They Worth?*, B2B International: http://www.b2binternational.com/library/whitepapers/whitepapers16.php, date accessed 16 March 2009.

Hall, Peter A. and David Soskice (2001) *Varieties of Capitalism. The Institutional Foundations of Comparative Advantage*, Oxford: Oxford University Press.

Hall, Peter A. and Rosemary C. R. Taylor (1996) 'Political Science and the Three New Institutionalisms', *MPIFG Discussion Paper* 96/6, Cologne: MPIFG.

Hall, Rodney Bruce and Thomas J. Biersteker (eds) (2002) *The Emergence of Private Authority in Global Governance*, Cambridge: Cambridge University Press.

Hamann, Kerstin (1998) 'Spanish Unions: Institutional Legacy and Responsiveness to Economic and Industrial Change', *Industrial and Labor Relations Review*, 51: 3, 424–44.

Handley, Antoinette (2005) 'Business, Government and Economic Policymaking in the New South Africa 1990–2000', *The Journal of Modern African Studies*, 43: 2, 211–39.

Harshe, Rajen (1993) 'Understanding Transition towards Post-Apartheid South Africa', *Economic and Political Weekly*, 18 September 1993.

Haufler, Virginia (2001) *A Public Role for the Private Sector: Industry Self-Regulation in a Global Economy*, Washington, DC: Carnegie Endowment for International Peace.

Haufler, Virginia (1999) 'Self-Regulation and Business Norms: Political Risk, Political Activism' in A. Claire Cutler, Virginia Haufler and Tony Porter (eds) *Private Authority and International Affairs*, Albany, NY: State University of New York Press, pp. 199–222.

Hedberg, Carl-Johan and Fredrik von Malmborg (2003) 'The Global Reporting Initiative and Corporate Sustainability Reporting in Swedish Companies', *Corporate Social Responsibility and Environmental Management*, 10, 153–64.

Heins, Volker (2005) 'NGOs als Partner und Gegenspieler transnationaler Unternehmen und internationaler Organisationen' in Achim Brunnengräber, Ansgar Klein and Heike Walk (eds) *NGOs im Prozess der Globalisierung: Mächtige Zwerge – Umstrittene Riesen*, Wiesbaden: VS Verlag für Sozialwissenschaften, pp. 172–211.

Heins, Volker (2001) *Der Neue Transnationalismus. Nichtregierungsorganisationen und Firmen im Konflikt um die Rohstoffe der Biotechnologie*, Frankfurt a. M.: Campus.

Held, David (2005) 'Principles of Cosmopolitan Order' in Gillian Brock and Harry Brighouse (eds) *The Political Philosophy of Cosmopolitanism*, Cambridge: Cambridge University Press, pp. 10–27.

Hellsten, Sirkku and Chris Mallin (2006) 'Are "Ethical" or "Socially Responsible" Investments Socially Responsible?', *Journal of Business Ethics*, 66: 4, 393–406.

Henderson, David (2001) *Misguided Virtue: False Notions of Corporate Social Responsibility*, Wellington: New Zealand Business Roundtable.

Héritier, Adrienne (2002) 'New Modes of Governance in Europe: Policy Making without Legislating', *Political Science Series*, 81, Vienna: Institute for Advanced Studies.

Hess, David (2007) 'Public Pensions and the Promise of Shareholder Activism for the Next Frontier of Corporate Governance: Sustainable Economic Development', *Virginia Law & Business Review*, 2: 2, 221–63.

Higgott, Richard A., Geoffrey R. D. Underhill and Andreas Bieler (2000) *Non-State Actors and Authority in the Global System*, London: Routledge.

Hinterseer, Kris (2002) *Criminal Finance. The Political Economy of Money Laundering in a Comparative Legal Context*, The Hague: Kluwer Law International.

Holliday, Charles O., Stephan Schmidheiny and Philip Watts (2002) *Walking the Talk: The Business Case for Sustainable Development*, Sheffield: Greenleaf Publishing.

Hönke, Jana, Nicole Kranz, Tanja A. Börzel and Adrienne Héritier (2008) 'Fostering Environmental Regulation? Corporate Social Responsibility in Countries with Weak Regulatory Capacities: The Case of South Africa', *SFB-Governance Working Paper Series 9*, Berlin: Freie Universität.

Hopkins, Michael (2003) *The Planetary Bargain: Corporate Social Responsibility Matters*, London: Earthscan.

Huckel, Carmen, Lothar Rieth and Melanie Zimmer (2007) 'Die Effektivität von Public-Private Partnerships' in Andreas Hasenclever, Klaus Dieter Wolf and Michael Zürn (eds) *Macht und Ohnmacht internationaler Institutionen*, Frankfurt a. M.: Campus, pp. 115–44.

Hurd, Ian (1999) 'Legitimacy and Authority in International Politics', *International Organization*, 53: 2, 379–408.

ICEM (1997) 'Rio Tinto, Tainted Titan' in Malcolm McIntosh and Ruth Thomas (eds) (2001) *Global Companies in the Twentieth Century: Selected Archival Histories. Volume IX. Rio Tinto*, London: Routledge, 32.

Independent Evaluation Group (2007) *Sourcebook for Evaluating Global and Regional Partnership Programs. Indicative Principles and Standards*, World Bank: http://siteresources.worldbank.org/EXTGLOREGPARPRO/Resources/sourcebook.pdf, date accessed 20 May 2009.

Institute of Directors (1994) *King Report on Corporate Governance*, Johannesburg: Institute of Directors.

International Organization of Employees (2003) *Corporate Social Responsibility. An IOE Approach*, IOE: http://www.ioe-emp.org/fileadmin/user_upload/documents_pdf/ papers/position_papers/english/pos_2003march_csr.pdf, date accessed 20 May 2009.

Jackson, Gregory and Richard Deeg (2006) 'How many Varieties of Capitalism? Comparing the Comparative Institutional Analyses of Capitalist Diversity', *MPIfG Diskussionspapier* 2, Cologne: Max-Planck-Institut für Gesellschaftsforschung.

Jacobsson, Bengt and Kerstin Sahlin-Andersson (2006) 'Dynamics of Soft Regulations' in Marie-Laure Djelic and Kerstin Sahlin-Andersson (eds) *Transnational Governance – Institutional Dynamics of Regulation*, Cambridge: Cambridge University Press, pp. 247–65.

Javorcik, Beata Smarzynska and Mariana Spatareanu (2005) 'Do Foreign Investors Care about Labour Market Regulations?', *Review of World Economics*, 141: 4, 375–403.

Jensen, Michael C. and William H. Meckling (1976) 'Theory of the Firm: Managerial Behavior, Agency Costs and Ownership Structure', *Journal of Financial Economics*, 3: 4, 305–60.

Jepperson, Ronald, Alexander Wendt and Peter J. Katzenstein (1996) 'Norms, Identity, and Culture in National Security' in Peter J. Katzenstein (ed.) *The Culture of National Security: Norms and Identity in World Politics*, New York, NY: Columbia University Press, pp. 33–75.

Jeucken, Marcel (2001) *Sustainable Finance and Banking – The Financial Sector and the Future of the Planet*, London: Earthscan Publications.

Jones, Meredith Marshall and Richard Shelley Mitchell (2007) 'Corporate Social Responsibility and the Management of Labour in Two Australian Mining Industry Companies', *Corporate Governance*, 15: 1, 57 – 67.

Jung, Joseph (2000) *Von der Schweizerischen Kreditanstalt zur Credit Suisse Group*, Zurich: NZZ.

Kagan, Robert A. (1991) 'Adversarial Legalism and American Government', *Journal of Policy Analysis and Management*, 10: 3, 369–406.

Kagan, Robert A. and Lee Axelrad (1997) 'Adversarial Legalism: An International Perspective' in Pietro S. Nivola (ed.) *Comparative Disadvantages? Social Regulations and the Global Economy*, Washington, DC: Brookings Institution Press, pp. 146–202.

Kaptein, Muel and Mark S. Schwartz (2008) 'The Effectiveness of Business Codes: A Critical Examination of Existing Studies and the Development of an Integrated Research Model', *Journal of Business Ethics*, 77: 2, 111–27.

Karliner, Joshua (1997) *The Corporate Planet: Ecology and Politics in the Age of Globalization*, San Francisco, CA: Sierra Club Books.

Katzenstein, Peter J. (1985) *Small States in World Markets*, Ithaca, NY: Cornell University Press.

Keck, Margaret E. and Kathryn Sikkink (1998) *Activists Beyond Borders*, Ithaca, NY: Cornell University Press.

Keizai Doyukai (2003) 'Market Evolution and CSR Management Toward Building Trust and Creating Sustainable Stakeholder Value', *15th Corporate White Paper of the Japan Association of Corporate Executives*, Tokyo.

Kell, Georg (2003) 'The Global Compact: Origins, Operations, Progress, Challenges', *Journal of Corporate Citizenship*, 3: 11, 35–49.

Kell, Georg and David Levin (2003) 'The Global Compact Network: An Historic Experiment in Learning and Action', *Business and Society Review*, 108: 2, 151–81.

Kell, Georg and John G. Ruggie (1999) 'Global Markets and Social Legitimacy: The Case of the Global Compact', *Transnational Corporations*, 8: 3, 101–20.

Keohane, Robert O. and Joseph S. Nye (1977) *Power and Interdependence: World Politics in Transition*, Boston, MA: Little, Brown and Co.

Keohane, Robert O. and Joseph S. Nye (1972) *Transnational Relations and World Politics*, Cambridge, MA: Harvard University Press.

Kersting, Silke (2001) *Amancio Ortega: Der alte Mann mit dem Gespür für junge Mode*, Handelsblatt: http://www.handelsblatt.com/archiv/amancio-ortega-der-alte-mann-mit-dem-gespuer-fuer-junge-mode;423131, date accessed 20 May 2009.

Khagram, Sanjeev, James Riker and Kathryn Sikkink (eds) (2002) *Restructuring World Politics: Transnational Social Movements, Networks, and Norms*, Minneapolis, MN: University of Minnesota Press.

Klein, Naomi (2002) *No Logo! Der Kampf der Global Players um Marktmacht: Ein Spiel mit vielen Verlierern und wenigen Gewinnern*, Munich: Riemann.

Klein, Naomi (2000) *No Space, no Choice, no Jobs, no Logo: Taking Aim at the Brand Bullies*, New York, NY: Picador USA.

Klotz, Audie (1995) *Norms in International Relations: the Struggle Against Apartheid*, Ithaca, NY: Cornell University Press.

Kneller, Richard, Mauro Pisu and Zihong Yu (2008) 'Overseas Business Costs and Firm Export Performance', *Canadian Journal of Economics*, 41: 2, 639–69.

Knight, Graham and Jackie Smith (2009) 'The Global Compact and its Critics: Activism, Power Relations, and Corporate Social Responsibility' in Janie Leatherman (ed.) *Discipline and Punishment in Global Politics: Illusions of Control*, Basingstoke: Palgrave Macmillan.

Koenig-Archibugi, Mathias (2006) 'Introduction: Institutional Diversity in Global Governance' in Mathias Koenig-Archibugi and Michael Zürn (eds) *New Modes of Governance in the Global System: Exploring Publicness, Delegation and Inclusiveness*, Basingstoke: Palgrave, pp. 1–30.

Koenig-Archibugi, Matthias (2004) 'Transnational Corporations and Public Accountability', *Government and Opposition*, 39: 2, 234–59.

Kohler-Koch, Beate, Thomas Conzelmann and Michèle Knodt (2003) *Europäische Integration. Europäisches Regieren*, Wiesbaden: VS Verlag für Sozialwissenschaften.

Köke, F. Jens (1999) 'New Evidence on Ownership Structures in Germany', *ZEW Discussion Paper* 60, Mannheim: Zentrum für Europäische Wirtschaftsforschung.

Kolk, Ans (2004) 'A Decade of Sustainability Reporting: Developments and Significance', *International Journal of the Environment and Sustainable Development*, 3: 1, 51–64.

Kolk, Ans (2003) 'Trends in Sustainability Reporting by the Fortune Global 250', *Business Strategy and the Environment*, 12, 279–91.

Kollmann, Kelly and Aseem Prakash (2001) 'Green by Choice? Cross-National Variations in Firms' Responses to EMS-Based Environmental Regimes', *World Politics*, 53: 3, 399–430.

Kong, Nancy, Oliver Salzmann, Ulrich Steger and Aileen Ionescu-Somers (2002) 'Moving Business/Industry towards Sustainable Consumption. The Role of NGOs', *European Management Journal*, 20: 2, 109–27.

Kooiman, Jan (2000) 'Societal Governance: Levels, Modes, and Orders of Social-Political Interaction' in Jon Pierre (ed.) *Debating Governance – Authority, Steering, and Democracy*, Oxford: Oxford University Press, pp. 138–64.

Koremenos, Barbara, and Charles Lipson (2001) 'The Rational Design of Institutions', *International Organization*, 55: 4, 761–99.

Korten, David C. (1995) *When Corporations Rule the World*, West Hartford, CT: Kumarian Press.

Kox, Henk and Arjan Lejour (2005) 'Regulatory Heterogeneity as Obstacle for International Services Trade', *CPB Working Paper* 49, Den Haag: CPB.

KPMG (2008) *International Survey of Corporate Responsibility Reporting 2008*, KPMG: http://www.kpmg.se/pages/102715.html, date accessed 20 May 2009.

KPMG (2007) *Global Anti-Money Laundering Survey. How Banks are Facing up to the Challenge*, KPMG: http://www.kpmg.com/SiteCollectionDocuments/Global%20 Anti-money%20laundering%20survey%202007.pdf, date accessed 27 May 2009.

KPMG (2005) *International Survey of Corporate Responsibility Reporting 2005*, KPMG: http://www.kpmg.com.au/Portals/0/KPMG%20Survey%202005_3.pdf, date accessed 27 May 2009.

KPMG (2004) *Global Anti-Money Laundering Survey. How Banks are Facing up to the Challenge*, KPMG: http://www.kpmg.se/pages/102715.html, date accessed 27 May 2009.

KPMG (2002) *International Survey of Corporate Sustainability Reporting 2002*, KPMG: http://www.gppi.net/fileadmin/gppi/KPMG2002.pdf, date accessed 20 June 2009.

KPMG and SustainAbility (2008) *Count Me in: The Readers' Take on Sustainability Reporting*, KPMG and SustainAbility: http://www.kpmg.com.au/Portals/0/sas_ count-me-in-survey-report2008.pdf, date accessed 16 May 2009.

Krasner, Stephen D. (1983) 'Structural Causes and Regime Consequences: Regimes as Intervening Variables' in Stephen D. Krasner (ed.) *International Regimes*, Ithaca, NY: Cornell University Press, pp. 1–21.

Kurucz, Elizabeth C., Barry A. Colbert and David Wheeler (2008) 'The Business Case for Corporate Social Responsibility' in Andrew Crane, Abagail McWilliams, Dirk Matten, Jeremy Moon and Donald S. Siegel (eds) *The Oxford Handbook of Corporate Social Responsibility*, Oxford: Oxford University Press, pp. 83–112.

Labitzke, Olaf (2008) *Institutionen, Akteurskonstellationen und wirtschaftliche Leistungsfähigkeit Deutschlands. Eine institutionenökonomische Analyse*, Hamburg: Verlag Dr. Kovac.

Lal, Anil K. and Roland W. Clement (2005) 'Economic Development in India', *Asia-Pacific Development Journal*, 12: 2, 81–99.

Lala, R. M. (1992) *Beyond the Last Blue Mountain. A Life of J.R.D. Tata*, New Delhi: Viking Penguin Books India.

Lamb, Derk (1970) 'A World Fit to Live In' in Malcolm McIntosh and Ruth Thomas (eds) (2001) *Global Companies in the Twentieth Century: Selected Archival Histories, Volume IV BP*, London: Routledge, 41.

Lehmbruch, Gerhard (1982) 'Introduction: Neo-Corporatism in Comparative Perspective' in Gerhard Lehmbruch and Philippe C. Schmitter (eds) *Patterns of Corporatist Policy Making*, London: Sage, pp. 1–28.

Leibfried, Stephan and Michael Zürn (eds) (2005) *Transformations of the State?*, Cambridge: Cambridge University Press.

Leipziger, Deborah (2003) *The Corporate Responsibility Code Book*, Sheffield: Greenleaf Publishing.

Leipziger, Deborah (2001) *SA 8000: The Definitive Guide to the New Social Standard*, London: Financial Times Prentice Hall.

Lev, Baruch (2001) *Intangibles: Management, Measurement, and Reporting*, Washington, DC: Brookings Institution Press.

Levi, Margaret (1987) 'Theories of Historical and Institutional Change', *Political Science and Politics*, 20: 3, 684–8.

Lewin, Arie Y., Tomoaki Sakano, Carroll U. Stephens and Bart Victor (1995) 'Corporate Citizenship in Japan: Survey Results from Japanese Firms', *Journal of Business Ethics*, 14: 2, 83–101.

Lijphart, Arend (1999) *Patterns of Democracy. Government Forms and Performance in Thirty-Six Countries*, New Haven, CT: Yale University Press.

Lipschutz, Ronnie D. and Cathleen Fogel (2002) 'Global Civil Society and the Privatisation of Transnational Regulation' in Rodney Bruce Hall and Thomas J. Biersteker (eds) *The Emergence of Private Authority in Global Governance*, Cambridge: Cambridge University Press, pp. 115–40.

Lund-Thomsen, Peter (2009) 'Assessing the Impact of Public-Private Partnerships in the Global South: The Case of the Kasur Tanneries Pollution Control Project', *Journal of Business Ethics*, 90, Supplement 1, 57–78.

Majone, Giandomenico (1996) 'Regulation and its Modes' in Giandomenico Majone (ed.) *Regulating Europe*, London: Routledge, pp. 9–27.

Manager Magazin (2001) *Amancio Ortega: Die spanische Variante des 'American Dream'*, Manager Magazin: http://www.manager-magazin.de/koepfe/artikel/0,2828, 134240,00.html, date accessed 20 May 2009.

March, James G. and Johan P. Olsen (1998) 'The International Dynamics of International Political Orders', *International Organization*, 52: 4, 943–69.

Mark-Ungericht, Bernhard (2001) 'Business and Newly Emerging Civil Society Actors. Between Conflict and New Forms of Social Dialogue', *Global Business Review*, 2: 1, 55–68.

Mark-Ungericht, Bernhard and Richard Weiskopf (2007) 'Filling the Empty Shell: The Public Debate on CSR in Austria as a Paradigmatic Example of a Political Discourse', *Journal of Business Ethics*, 70: 3, 285–97.

Mathiesen, Henrik (2002) *Managerial Ownership and Financial Performance*, Department of Economy, Ph. D. Thesis, Copenhagen: University of Copenhagen.

Matten, Dirk and Andrew Crane (2005) 'Corporate Citizenship: Towards an Extended Theoretical Conceptualization', *Academy of Management Review*, 30: 1, 166–79.

Mayer, Colin (2003) 'Firm Control' in Joachim Schwalbach (ed.) *Corporate Governance*, Berlin: Berliner Wissenschafts-Verlag, pp. 69–90.

Mayntz, Renate (2008) 'Von der Steuerungstheorie zu Global Governance' in Gunnar Folke Schuppert and Michael Zürn (eds) *Governance in einer sich wandeln-Welt. Special Issue of Politische Vierteljahresschrift 41*, Wiesbaden: VS Verlag für Sozialwissenschaften, pp. 43–60.

Mayntz, Renate (2005) 'Governance Theory als fortentwickelte Steuerungstheorie?' in Gunnar Folke Schuppert (ed.) *Governance-Forschung. Vergewisserung über Stand und Entwicklungslinien*, Baden-Baden: Nomos, pp. 11–20.

Mayntz, Renate (1993) 'Policy-Netzwerke und die Logik von Verhandlungssystemen' in Adrienne Héritier (ed.) *Policy-Analyse. Kritik und Neuorientierung. Special Issue of Politische Vierteljahresschrift 24*, Opladen: Westdeutscher Verlag, pp. 39–57.

McAusland, Scott (2007) *European Sustainability Reporting Association Report from GRI*, GRI: http://www.globalreporting.org/NR/rdonlyres/010AF43C-0717-4F86-9008-792AA600F6A9/0/ESRAMay08.pdf, date accessed 9 June 2009.

McIntosh, Malcolm and Ruth Thomas (2001) 'Introduction' in Malcolm McIntosh and Ruth Thomas (eds) *Global Companies in the Twentieth Century. Selected Archival Histories. Volume IX. Rio Tinto*, London: Routledge, pp. xiii–xxiv.

McKinsey&Company (2007) *Shaping the New Rules of Competition: UN Global Compact Participant Mirror*, UN Global Compact Office: http://www.unglobalcompact.org/docs/news_events/8.1/McKinsey.pdf, date accessed 27 May 2009.

McKinsey&Company (2004) *Assessing the Global Compact's Impact. Report Prepared for the Global Compact Office*, UN Global Compact Office: http://www.unglobal compact.org/docs/news_events/9.1_news_archives/2004_06_09/imp_ass.pdf, date accessed 6 May 2009.

Mercer, Jonathan (1996) *Reputation and International Politics*, Ithaca, NY: Cornell University Press.

MROS (1998–2008) *Annual Report by the Money Laundering Reporting Office Switzerland*, MROS: http://www.fedpol.admin.ch/fedpol/en/home/themen/kriminalitaet/geldwaescherei/jahresberichte.html, date accessed 27 May 2009.

Muchlinski, Peter T. (2007) *Multinational Enterprises and the Law*, Oxford: Oxford University Press.

Mullins, Laurie J. (2005) *Management and Organisational Behaviour*, Essex: Pearson Education Limited.

Nadelmann, Ethan A. (1990) 'Global Prohibition Regimes: The Evolution of Norms in International Society', *International Organization*, 44: 4, 479–526.

Nayar, Baldev Raj (1998) 'Business and India's Economic Policy Reforms', *Economic and Political Weekly*, 33: 38, 2453–68.

Neidhardt, Friedhelm (1994) 'Öffentlichkeit, öffentliche Meinung, soziale Bewegungen' in Friedhelm Neidhardt (ed.) *Öffentlichkeit, öffentliche Meinung, soziale Bewegungen*, Opladen: Westdeutscher Verlag, pp. 7–41.

Niesen, Peter (2008) 'Deliberation ohne Demokratie – Zur Konstruktion von Legitimität jenseits des Nationalstaats' in Regina Kreide and Andreas Niederberger (eds) *Transnationale Verrechtlichung*, Frankfurt a. M.: Campus, pp. 240–59.

Nölke, Andreas and Heather Taylor (2007) 'The Rise of Challenger Companies and its Implications for Global Governance: A Varieties of Capitalism Perspective', *GARNET Workshop on Business and Global Governance*, Copenhagen: Copenhagen Business School, November 2007.

North, Douglass C. (1990) *Institutions, Institutional Change and Economic Performance*, Cambridge: Cambridge University Press.

Nye, Joseph S. (1990) 'Soft Power', *Foreign Policy*, 80, 153–71.

OECD Watch (2009) *OECD Watch Quarterly Case Update Summer 2009*, 4: 1, http://oecdwatch.org/publications-en/Publication_3087/, date accessed 10 July 2009.

Ohmae, Kenichi (1995) *The End of the Nation-State: The Rise of Regional Economics*, New York, NY: The Free Press.

OneWorldTrust (2008) *2008 Global Accountability Report – Accountability Profile*, http://www.oneworldtrust.org/index.php?option=com_docman&task=search_result&Itemid=55, date accessed 15 July 2009.

Ottaway, Marina (2001) 'Corporatism Goes Global. International Organizations, Nongovernmental Organization Networks, and Transnational Business', *Global Governance*, 7: 3, 265–93.

Paine, Ellen (2000) *The Road to the Global Compact: Corporate Power and the Battle over Global Public Policy at the United Nations*, Global Policy Forum: http://www.global policy.org/reform/papers/2000/road.htm, date accessed 22 January 2004.

Paiva, Paulo (2003) 'Mercosur. Past, Present, and Future', *Nova Economia Belo Horizonte*, 13: 2, 115–36.

Palazzo, Guido and Andreas Georg Scherer (2007) 'Organizational Legitimacy as Deliberation' in Rainhart Lang and Annett Schmidt (eds) *Individuum und Organisation: Neue Trends eines organisationswissenschaftlichen Forschungsfelds*, Wiesbaden: DUV, pp. 17–42.

Palenberg, Markus, Wolfgang Reinicke and Jan Martin Witte (2006) *Trends in Non-Financial Reporting*, Berlin: Global Public Policy Institute.

Pandey, S. N. (1989) *Human Side of Tata Steel*, New Delhi: Tata McGraw-Hill.

Parsons, Talcott (1951) *The Social System*, Glencoe, IL: Free Press.

Pattberg, Phillip H. (2007) *Private Institutions and Global Governance. The New Politics of Environmental Sustainability*, Cheltenham: Edward Elgar.

Pattberg, Phillip H. (2005) 'The Forest Stewardship Council: Risk and Potential of Private Forest Governance', *Journal of Environment and Development*, 14: 3, 356–74.

Pauly, Louis W. (1997) *Who Elected the Bankers? Surveillance and Control in the World Economy*, Ithaca, NY: Cornell University Press.

Pfahler, Thomas (2006) *Unternehmenskultur zwischen Markt und Plan in Mittel- und Osteuropa*, Bern: Haupt.

Pierson, Paul (2004) *Politics in Time: History, Institutions and Social Analysis*, Princeton, NJ: Princeton University Press.

Pies, Ingo and Markus Sardison (2006) 'Wirtschaftsethik' in Nikolaus Knoepffler, Peter Kunzmann, Ingo Pies and Anne Siegetsleitner (eds) *Einführung in die Angewandte Ethik*, Freiburg: Verlag Karl Alber, pp. 267–98.

Pieth, Mark (2007) 'The Wolfsberg Process' in Wouter H. Muller, Christian H. Kälin and John G. Goldsworth (eds) *Anti-Money Laundering. International Law and Practice*, West Sussex: John Wiley & Sons, pp. 93–103.

Pieth, Mark (2006) 'Multistakeholder Initiatives to Combat Money Laundering and Bribery', *Working Paper Series*, Basel: Basel Institute on Governance.

Pieth, Mark and Gemma Aiolfi (2004) *A Comparative Guide to Anti-Money Laundering. A Critical Analysis of Systems in Singapore, Switzerland, the UK and the USA*, Cheltenham: Edward Elgar.

Pieth, Mark and Gemma Aiolfi (2003a) 'The Private Sector becomes Active: The Wolfsberg Process', *Journal of Financial Crime*, 11: 4, 359–65.

Pieth, Mark and Gemma Aiolfi (2003b) *Anti-Money Laundering: Levelling the Playing Field*, Basel: Institute on Governance.

Pollack, Mark A. (1997) 'Delegation, Agency, and Agenda Setting in the European Community', *International Organization*, 51: 1, 99–134.

Ponte, Stefano, Simon Roberts and Lance van Sittert (2007) 'Black Economic Empowerment Business and the State in South Africa', *Development and Change*, 38: 5, 933–55.

Porter, Michael E. and Klaus Schwab (2008) *The Global Competitiveness Report 2008–2009*, Geneva: World Economic Forum.

Porter, Toni and Karsten Ronit (2005) 'Self-Regulation as Policy Process: The Multiple and Criss-Crossing Stages of Private Rule-Making', *Policy Sciences*, 39, 41–72.

Power, Michael (1997) *The Audit Society – Rituals of Verification*, Oxford: Oxford University Press.

Preisendörfer, Peter (2005) *Organisationssoziologie – Grundlagen, Theorien, Problemstellungen*, Wiesbaden: VS Verlag für Sozialwissenschaften.

Price, Richard (1998) 'Reversing the Gun Sights: Transnational Civil Society Targets Land Mines ', *International Organization*, 52: 3, 613–44.

Rappaport, Alfred (1986) *Creating Shareholder Value: The new Standard for Business Performance*, New York, NY: Free Press.

Rawls, John (1993) 'The Law of Peoples' in Stephen Shute and Susan Hurley (eds) *On Human Rights. The Oxford Amnesty Lectures*, New York: Basic Books, pp. 41–82.

Reed, Ananya Mukherjee (2002) 'Corporate Governance Reforms in Developing Countries', *Journal of Business Ethics*, 37: 3, 249–68.

Reinicke, Wolfgang H. (1998) *Global Public Policy. Governing without Government?*, Washington, DC: Brookings Institution Press.

Reinicke, Wolfgang H. and Francis Deng (2000) *Critical Choices: The United Nations, Networks, and the Future of Global Governance*, Washington, DC: Brookings Institution Press.

Rhodes, Martin and Oscar Molina (2007) 'The Political Economy of Adjustment in Mixed Market Economies: A Study of Spain and Italy' in Bob Hancké, Martin Rhodes and Mark Thatcher (eds) *Beyond Varieties of Capitalism. Conflict, Contradictions, and Complementarities in the European Economy*, Oxford: Oxford University Press, pp. 223–52.

Riboud, Michelle, Carolina Sánchez-Páramo and Carlos Silva-Jáuregui (2002) 'Does Eurosclerosis Matter? Institutional Reform and Labour Market Performance in Central and Eastern European Countries in the 1990s', *Social Protection Discussion Paper*, New York, NY: World Bank.

Richter, Rudolf and Eirik G. Furubotn (1999) *Neue Institutionenökonomik: Eine Einführung und kritische Würdigung*, Tübingen: Mohr Siebeck.

Rieth, Lothar (2009a) *COP-Projekt II: Deutsche Unternehmen im Global Compact – Allgemeines Bekenntnis und selektive Umsetzung*, TU Darmstadt, UN Global Compact COP-Projekt: http://www.cop-projekt.de/Media/COP_II-Projektbericht.pdf, date accessed 1 July 2009.

Rieth, Lothar (2009b) 'Der Global Compact in der Praxis – Eine Analyse der COPs' in Deutsches Global Compact Netzwerk (ed.) *Jahrbuch 2008*, Berlin: Macondo, pp. 130–5.

Rieth, Lothar (2009c) *Global Governance und Corporate Social Responsibility*, Opladen: Budrich UniPress.

Rieth, Lothar (2004) 'Der VN Global Compact: Was als Experiment begann...', *Die Friedenswarte*, 79: 1–2, 151–70.

Rieth, Lothar and Thorsten Göbel (2005) 'Unternehmen, gesellschaftliche Verantwortung und die Rolle von NGOs', *Zeitschrift für Wirtschafts- und Unternehmensethik*, 6: 2, 244–61.

Rieth, Lothar and Melanie Zimmer (2004) 'Transnational Corporations and Conflict Prevention – The Impact of Norms on Private Actors', *Tübinger Arbeitspapiere zur internationalen Politik und Friedensforschung* 43, Tübingen: Eberhard-Karls-Universität.

Rieth, Lothar, Melanie Zimmer, Ralph Hamann and Jonathan Hanks (2007) 'The UN Global Compact in Sub-Sahara Africa – Decentralization and Effectiveness', *Journal of Corporate Citizenship*, 7: 28, 99–112.

Rio Tinto (1992) 'RTZ: The Global Neighbour' in Malcolm McIntosh and Ruth Thomas (eds) (2001) *Global Companies in the Twentieth Century. Selected Archival Histories. Volume IX. Rio Tinto*, London: Routledge, 31.

Rio Tinto (1987) 'RTZ and South Africa, Company Report' in Malcolm McIntosh and Ruth Thomas (eds) (2001) *Global Companies in the Twentieth Century: Selected Archival Histories. Volume IX. Rio Tinto*, London: Routledge, 26.

Rio Tinto (1973) 'Company Report' in Malcolm McIntosh and Ruth Thomas (eds) (2001) *Global Companies in the Twentieth Century: Selected Archival Histories, Volume IX. Rio Tinto*, London: Routledge, 21.

Risse, Thomas (2004) 'Global Governance and Communicative Action', *Government and Opposition*, 39: 2, 288–313.

Risse, Thomas, Stephen C. Ropp and Kathryn Sikkink (1999) *The Power of Human Rights: International Norms and Domestic Change*, Cambridge: Cambridge University Press.

Risse-Kappen, Thomas (ed.) (1995) *Bringing Transnational Relations Back In: Non-State Actors, Domestic Structures and International Institutions*, Cambridge: Cambridge University Press.

Robson, Peter (1998) *The Economics of International Integration*, London: Routledge.

Rock, Philip (1968) 'Manpower Management' in Malcolm McIntosh and Ruth Thomas (eds) (2001) *Global Companies in the Twentieth Century: Selected Archival Histories, Volume IV BP*, London: Routledge, 39.

Rogge, Peter G. (1997) *Die Dynamik des Wandels. Schweizerischer Bankverein 1872ä 1997: Das fünfte Vierteljahrhundert*, Basel: Reinhardt.

Ronit, Karsten and Volker Schneider (1999) 'Global Governance through Private Organizations', *Governance*, 12: 3, 243–66.

Roselle, James (2005) 'The Triple Bottom Line: Building Shareholder Value' in Ramon Mullerat (ed.) *Corporate Social Responsibility: The Corporate Governance of the 21st Century*, The Hague: Kluwer Law International, pp. 113–39.

Rosenau, James (2002) 'Governance in a New Global Order' in David Held and Anthony McGrew (eds) *Governing Globalization*, Cambridge: Polity, pp. 70–86.

Rosenau, James N. (1998) 'Governance and Democracy in a Globalizing World' in Daniele Archibugi, David Held and Martin Köhler (eds) *Re-imagining Political Community: Studies in Cosmopolitan Democracy*, Cambridge: Cambridge University Press, pp. 28–57.

Rosenau, James N. (1997) *Along the Domestic-Foreign Frontier: Exploring Governance in a Turbulent World*, Cambridge: Cambridge University Press.

Rossouw, Gedeon J. (1997) 'Business Ethics in South Africa', *Journal of Business Ethics*, 16: 14, 1539–47.

Royo, Sebastián (2008) *Varieties of Capitalism in Spain: Remaking the Spanish Economy for the New Century*, New York, NY: Palgrave Macmillan.

Royo, Sebastián (2007) 'Varieties of Capitalism in Spain: Business and the Politics of Coordination', *European Journal of Industrial Relations*, 13: 1, 47–65.

Royo, Sebastián (2004) 'Still Two Models of Capitalism? Economic Adjustment in Spain', *Workingpaper 2004 Annual Meeting*, Chicago, IL: American Political Science Association.

Ruggie, John G. (2004) 'Reconstituting the Global Public Domain – Issues, Actors, and Practices', *European Journal of International Relations*, 10: 4, 499–531.

Ruggie, John G. (2002) 'Corporate Social Responsibility and the Global Compact', *Journal of Corporate Citizenship*, 5, 27–36.

Sako, Mari (1992) *Prices, Quality, and Trust: Inter-firm Relations in Britain and Japan*, Cambridge: Cambridge University Press.

Sampson, Gary P. (2003) 'Introduction' in Gary P. Sampson and Simon Woolcock (eds) *Multilateralism, Regionalism and Economic Integration*, Tokyo: UNU Press, pp. 3–17.

Samuels, Richard J. (1987) *The Business of the Japanese State*, Ithaca, NY: Cornell University Press.

Sasol (1996) 'Sasol Environmental Report 1996', http://www.sasol.com/sasol_internet/frontend/navigation.jsp;jsessionid=4XARMFUCTJAJPG5N4EZSFEQ?navid=17200 010&rootid=4, date accessed 10 July 2009.

Schäferhoff, Marco, Sabine Campe and Christopher Kaan (2007) 'Transnational Public-Private Partnerships in International Relations. Making Sense of Concepts, Research Frameworks and Results', *SFB-Governance Working Paper Series* 6, Berlin: Freie Universität.

Schaltegger, Stefan and Frank Figge (1997) 'Environmental Shareholder Value. Success with Corporate Environmental Management', *Eco-Management and Auditing*, 7: 1, 29–42.

Schaltegger, Stefan and Marcus Wagner (2006) 'Introduction: Managing and Measuring the Business Case for Sustainability' in Stefan Schaltegger and Marcus Wagner (eds) *Managing the Business Case for Sustainability – The Integration of Social, Environmental and Economic Performance*, Sheffield: Greenleaf Publishing, pp. 1–27.

Scharpf, Fritz W. (1999) Governing in Europe. Effective and Democratic?, Oxford: Oxford University Press.

Scharpf, Fritz W. (2000a) *Interaktionsformen. Akteurszentrierter Institutionalismus in der Politikforschung*, Opladen: Leske + Budrich.

Scharpf, Fritz W. (2000b) 'Interdependence and Democratic Legitimation' in Susan J. Pharr and Robert D. Putnam (eds) *Disaffected Democracies: What's Troubling Trilateral Countries?*, Princeton, NJ: Princeton University Press, pp. 101–20.

Schein, Edgar H. (1989) *Organizational Culture and Leadership*, San Francisco, CA: Jossey-Bass.

Scherer, Andreas Georg and Guido Palazzo (eds) (2008) *Handbook of Research on Global Corporate Citizenship*, Cheltenham: Edward Elgar.

Scherer, Georg (2004) 'Zehn Jahre NAFTA. Bilanz und Perspektiven', *SWP Diskussionspapier*, Berlin: SWP.

Schimmelfennig, Frank (2003) 'Internationale Sozialisation. Von einem "erschöpften" zu einem produktiven Forschungsprogramm?' in Gunther Hellmann, Klaus Dieter Wolf and Michael Zürn (eds) *Die neuen Internationalen Beziehungen: Forschungsstand und Perspektiven in Deutschland*, Baden-Baden: Nomos, pp. 401–27.

Schimmelfennig, Frank, Stefan Engert and Heiko Knobel (2003) 'Costs, Commitment, and Compliance. The Impact of EU Democratic Conditionality on Latvia, Slovakia, and Turkey', *Journal of Common Market Studies*, 41: 3, 495–517.

Shleifer, Andrei and Robert W. Vishny (1986) 'Large Shareholders and Corporate Control', *Journal of Political Economy*, 94: 3, 461–89.

Schmidt, Reinhardt (2004) 'Corporate Governance in Germany' in Jan Krahnen and Reinhardt Schmidt (eds) *The German Financial System*, Oxford: Oxford University Press, pp. 386–424.

Schmidt, Vivien A. (2003) 'French Capitalism Transformed, Yet Still a Third Variety of Capitalism', *Economy and Society*, 32: 4, 526–54.

Schmidt, Vivien A. (2002) *The Futures of European Capitalism*, Oxford: Oxford University Press.

Schmidt, Vivien A. (1996) *From State to Market? The Transformation of French Business and Government*, Cambridge: Cambridge University Press.

Schmitter, Philippe and Gerhard Lehmbruch (eds) (1979) *Trends Toward Corporatist Intermediation*, Beverly Hills, CA: Sage.

Schmitter, Philippe C. (1982) 'Reflections on Where the Theory of Neo-Corporatism has Gone and Where the Praxis of Neo-Corporatism May Be Going' in Gerhard Lehmbruch and Philippe C. Schmitter (eds) *Patterns of Corporatist Policy-Making*, London: Sage, pp. 259–79.

Schorlemer, Sabine von (2003) 'Der "Global Compact" der Vereinten Nationen – ein Faustscher Pakt mit der Wirtschaftswelt?' in Sabine von Schorlemer (ed.) *Praxishandbuch UNO: die Vereinten Nationen im Lichte globaler Herausforderungen*, Berlin: Springer, pp. 507–51.

Schranz, Mario (2007) *Wirtschaft zwischen Profit und Moral die gesellschaftliche Verantwortung von Unternehmen im Rahmen der öffentlichen Kommunikation*, Wiesbaden: VS Verlag für Sozialwissenschaften.

Schuler, Douglas A. and David S. Brown (1999) 'Democracy, Regional Market Integration, and Foreign Direct Investments: Lessons from Costa Rica', *Business & Society*, 38: 4, 450–73.

Schuppert, Gunnar Folke (2008) 'Von Ko-Produktion von Staatlichkeit zur Co-Performance of Governance', *SFB-Governance Working Paper Series* 12, Berlin: Freie Universität.

Schwarz, Friedhelm (2003) *Die Deutsche Bank: Riese auf tönernen Füßen*, Frankfurt a. M.: Campus.

Shapiro, Carl, and Robert D. Willig (1990) 'Economic Rationales for the Scope of Privatization' in Ezra N. Suleiman and John Waterbury (eds) *Political Economy of Public Sector Reform*, Boulder, CO: Westview Press, pp. 55–87.

Sharman, Jason C. and David Chaikin (2009) 'Corruption and Anti-Money-Laundering Systems: Putting a Luxury Good to Work', *Governance*, 22: 1, 27–45.

Shell (2009) *Shell Nigeria & the Environment*, Shell: http://www.shell.com/home/content2/nigeria/society_environment/sust_dev/env.html, date accessed 8 July 2009.

Shell (2008) *Responsible Energy – The Shell Sustainability Report 2007*, Shell: http://www.static.shell.com/static/responsible_energy/downloads/sustainability_reports/shell_sustainability_report_2007.pdf, date accessed 27 May 2009.

Shell (2006a) *Shell Code of Conduct*, Shell: http://www-static.shell.com/static/about shell/downloads/who_we_are/code_of_conduct/english.pdf, date accessed 6 May 2009.

Shell (2006b) *The Shell Report 2006: Meeting the Energy Challenge*, Shell, date accessed 27 May 2009.

Shell (2005) *Shell Business Principles*, Shell: http://www-static.shell.com/static/about shell/downloads/who_we_are/sgbps/sgbp_english.pdf, date accessed 6 May 2009.

Shell (1998) *The Shell Report 1998: Profits and Principles – does there have to be a choice?*, Shell: http://www-static.shell.com/static/responsible_energy/downloads/sustainability_reports/shell_report_1997.pdf, date accessed 27 May 2009.

Shell (1997) *Health, Safety and Environment Report*, London.

Shepsle, Kenneth A. (1986) 'Institutional Equilibrium and Equilibrium Institutions' in Herbert F. Weisberg (ed.) *Political Science. The Science of Politics*, New York, NY: Agathon Press, pp. 51–81.

Siaroff, Alan (1999) 'Corporatism in 24 Industrial Democracies: Meaning and Measurement', *European Journal of Political Research*, 36: 2, 175–205.

Sjöström, Emma (2008) 'Shareholder Activism for Corporate Social Responsibility: What Do We Know?', *Sustainable Development*, 16: 3, 141–54.

Slaughter, Anne-Marie (2004) *A New World Order*, Princeton, NJ: Princeton University Press.

Söderbaum, Fredrik and Timothy M. Shaw (2003) *Theories of New Regionalism: A Palgrave Reader*, Basingstoke: Palgrave Macmillan.

Sparkes, Russell and Christopher J. Cowton (2004) 'The Maturing of Socially Responsible Investment: A Review of the Developing Link with Corporate Social Responsibility', *Journal of Business Ethics*, 52: 1, 45–57.

Stadler, Christian (2004) *Unternehmenskultur bei Royal Dutch/Shell, Siemens und DaimlerChrysler*, Stuttgart: Steiner.

Stavrou, Eleni, George Kassinis and Alexis Filotheou (2007) 'Downsizing and Stakeholder Orientation Among the Fortune 500: Does Family Ownership Matter?', *Journal of Business Ethics*, 72: 2, 149–62.

Stevens, Betsy (2008) 'Corporate Ethical Codes: Effective Instruments for Influencing Behavior', *Journal of Business Ethics*, 78: 4, 601–9.

Stigler, George J. (1971) 'The Theory of Economic Regulation', *The Bell Journal of Economics and Management Science*, 2: 1, 3–21.

Stoker, Gerry (1998) 'Governance as Theory: Five Propositions', *International Social Science Journal*, 50: 155, 17–28.

Stopford, John M., Susan Strange and John S. Henley (1991) *Rival States, Rival Firms: Competition for World Market Shares*, Cambridge: Cambridge University Press.

Strange, Susan (1996) *The Retreat of the State: The Diffusion of Power in the World Economy*, Cambridge: Cambridge University Press.

Stratos (2007) *Stratos Sustainability Integration Report Case Study – Royal-Dutch Shell* Ontario.

Streeck, Wolfgang and Philippe C. Schmitter (1985) *Private Interest Government: Beyond Market and State*, London: Sage.

Streeck, Wolfgang and Kozo Yamamura (eds) (2001) *The Origins of Nonliberal Capitalism. Germany and Japan*, Ithaca, NY: Cornell University Press.

Suchman, Mark C. (1995) 'Managing Legitimacy: Strategic and Institutional Approaches', *Academy of Management Review*, 20, 571–610.

SustainAbility and UNEP (2001) *Buried Treasure: Uncovering the Business Case for Corporate Sustainability*, London: SustainAbility.

Svenjar, Jan (2004) 'Labour Market Flexibility in Central and East Europe' in Marek Dabrowski, Ben Slay and Jaroslaw Neneman (eds) *Beyond Transition: Development Perspectives and Dilemma*, Aldershot: Ashgate, pp. 101–18.

Taka, Iwao (1997) 'Business Ethics in Japan', *Journal of Business Ethics*, 16: 14, 1499–508.

Take, Ingo (2002) *NGOs im Wandel: Von der Graswurzel auf das diplomatische Parkett*, Wiesbaden: Westdeutscher Verlag.

Tanimoto, Kanji and Kenji Suzuki (2005) 'Corporate Social Responsibility in Japan: Analyzing the Participating Companies in Global Reporting Initiative', *EIJS Working Papers Series* 208, Stockholm: School of Economics.

Tata Steel (2007) *Setting Sustainability Standards*, Tata Steel: http://www.tatasteel.com/landmarks/default.asp, date accessed 12 December 2007.

Taylor, Rupert (2004) *Creating a Better World: Interpreting Global Civil Society*, Bloomfield, CT: Kumarian Press.

Taylor, Scott D. (2007) *Business and the State in Southern Africa: The Politics of Economic Reform*, London: Lynne Rienner.

Teubner, Gunther (1997a) 'Legal Pluralism in the World Society' in Gunther Teubner (ed.) *Global Law without a State*, Aldershot: Dartmouth, pp. 3–28.

Teubner, Gunther (1997b) 'Foreword: Legal Regimes of Global Non-state Actors' in Gunther Teubner (ed.) *Global Law without a State*, Aldershot: Dartmouth, pp. xiii–xvii.

Thelen, Kathleen A. (2004) *How Institutions Evolve: The Political Economy of Skills in Germany, Britain, the United States, and Japan*, Cambridge: Cambridge University Press.

Thérien, Jean-Philippe and Vincent Pouliot (2006) 'The Global Compact: Shifting the Politics of International Development?', *Global Governance*, 12: 1, 55–75.

Transparency International (2008a) *Business Principles for Countering Bribery. Small and Medium Enterprise (SME) Edition*, Transparency International: http://www.transparency.org/content/download/29197/443933/, date accessed 20 May 2009.

Transparency International (2008b) *Promoting Revenue Transparency. 2008 Report of Revenue Transparency of Oil and Gas Companies*, London: Transparency International.

Transparency International (2005) *Business Principles for Countering Bribery: TI Six-Step Process*, Transparency International: http://www.transparency.org/content/download/570/3480/file/ti_six_step_process_july2005.doc, date accessed 20 May 2009.

Transparency International (2004) *Business Principles for Countering Bribery: Guidance Document*, Transparency International: http://www.transparency.org/content/download/573/3493/file/bpcb_ti_guidance_doc_november_%202004.pdf, date accessed 20 May 2009.

Transparency International (2003) *Business Principles for Countering Bribery*, Transparency International: http://www.asce.org/files/pdf/global/tibusiness_principles2.pdf, date accessed 20 May 2009.

UN Global Compact (2009) *UN Global Compact Annual Review 2008*, UN Global Compact Office: http://www.unglobalcompact.org/docs/news_events/9.1_news_archives/2009_04_08/GC_2008AR_FINAL.pdf, date accessed 27 May 2009.

UN Global Compact (2007) *UN Global Compact Annual Review – 2007 Leaders Summit*, UN Global Compact Office: http://www.unglobalcompact.org/docs/news_events/8.1/GC_Summit_Report_07.pdf, date accessed 27 May 2009.

UN Global Compact (2006) *Impact and Progress of the Global Compact's 105 Largest Companies* http://www.unglobalcompact.org/NewsAndEvents/news_archives/2006_04_26.html, date accessed 1 July 2009.

UN Global Compact (2001) *The Global Compact – Corporate Leadership in the World Economy (Leaflet)*, New York, NY: UN Global Compact.

UN Global Compact Regional Learning Forum (2007) *Survey among Companies in Sub-Saharan Africa, draft version*, UN Global Compact Regional Learning Forum, date accessed 10 January 2008.

UNCTAD (2006) *World Investment Report 2006 – FDI from Developing and Transition Economies: Implications for Development*, Geneva.

Underdal, Arild (2002) 'One Question, Two Answers' in Edward L. Miles, Arild Underdal and Steinar Andresen (eds) *Environmental Regime Effectiveness: Confronting Theory with Evidence*, Cambridge, MA: MIT Press, pp. 3–45.

UNDP (2007) *Baseline Study on CSR Practices in the New EU Member States and Candidate Countries*, UN Development Program: http://www.acceleratingcsr.eu/uploads/docs/BASELINE_STUDY_ON.pdf, date accessed 27 May 2009.

UNDP (1999) *Human Development Report 1999: Globalization with a Human Face*, Washington, DC.

Utting, Peter and Ann Zammit (2009) 'United Nations-Business Partnerships: Good Intentions and Contradictory Agendas', *Journal of Business Ethics*, 90, Supplement 1, 39–56.

Vaillant, Marcel (2005) 'Mercosur. Southern Integration under Construction', *Internationale Politik und Gesellschaft*, 2, 52–71.

Van der Veer, Jeroen (2005) *The Role of the Private Sector in a Changing Africa, Speech at the Business for Africa Summit*, http://www-static.shell.com/static/media/downloads/speeches/jvdv_africa.pdf, date accessed 8 July 2009.

Van Evera, Stephen (1997) *Guide to Methods for Students of Political Science*, Ithaca, NY: Cornell University Press.

Van Rooy, Alison (2004) *The Global Legitimacy Game: Civil Society, Globalization and Protest*, Basingstoke: Palgrave Macmillan.

Varley, Pamela (ed.) (1998) *The Sweatshop Quandary: Corporate Responsibility on the Global Frontier*, Washington, DC: Investor Responsibility Research Center.

Visser, Wayne, Dirk Matten, Manfred Pohl and Nick Tolhurst (2007) *The A to Z of Corporate Social Responsibility*, Hoboken, NJ: Jon Wiley.

Vivo, Laura Albareda and Maria Rosario Balaguer Franch (2009) 'The Challenges of Socially Reponsible Investment Among Institutional Investors: Exploring the Links between Corporate Pension Funds and Corporate Governance', *Journal of Business Ethics*, 114, 31–57.

Vogel, David (1987) 'Government-Industry Relations in the United States: An Overview' in Stephen Wilks and Maurice Wright (eds) *Comparative Government –*

Industry Relations. Western Europe, the United States, and Japan, Oxford: Clarendon Press, pp. 91–116.

Vogel, David (1986) *National Styles of Business Regulation*, Ithaca, NY: Cornell University Press.

Von Doug, Hopton (2006) *Money Laundering: A Concise Guide for All Business*, Aldershot: Gower Publishing.

Waddock, Sandra (2004) 'Creating Corporate Accountability: Foundational Principles to Make Corporate Citizenship Real', *Journal of Business Ethics*, 50, 313–27.

Walters, Peter (1984) 'Employee Involvement in Productive Management' in Malcolm McIntosh and Ruth Thomas (eds) (2001) *Global Companies in the Twentieth Century: Selected Archival Histories. Volume IV BP*, London: Routledge, 58.

Ward, Halina and Craig Smith (2006) 'Corporate Social Responsibility at a Crossroads. Futures for CSR in the UK to 2015', *IIED Workingpaper*, London: International Institute for Environment and Development.

Warleigh, Alex (2002) *Flexible Integration: What Model for the European Union?*, London: Routledge.

Weiss, Thomas G. and Leon Gordenker (eds) (1996) *NGOs, the UN, and Global Governance*, Boulder, CO: Lynne Rienner.

Wessels, Petra (1990) *Crescendo to Success. Sasol 1975–1987*, Cape Town: Human & Rousseau.

Wheeler, David and John Elkington (2001) 'The End of the Corporate Environmental Report? Or the Advent of Cybernetic Sustainability Reporting and Communication', *Business Strategy and the Environment*, 10: 1, 1–14.

Whitley, Richard (2001) 'Business Systems in India' in Gurli Jakobsen and Jens E. Torp (eds) *Understanding Business Systems in Developing Countries*, London: Sage, pp. 42–65.

Wick, Ingeborg (2005) *Workers' Tool or PR Ploy? A Guide to Codes of International Labour Practice*, Bonn: Friedrich-Ebert-Stiftung.

Willets, Peter (ed.) (1996) *The Conscience of the World: The Influence of Non-Governmental Organisations in the UN System*, Washington, DC: The Brookings Institution.

Willis, Alan (2003) 'The Role of the Global Reporting Initiative's Sustainability Reporting Guidelines in the Social Screening of Investments', *Journal of Business Ethics*, 43, 233–7.

Willke, Helmut (1996) *Ironie des Staates: Grundlinien einer Staatstheorie polyzentrischer Gesellschaft*, Frankfurt a. M.: Suhrkamp.

Winston, Morton (2002) 'NGO Strategies for Promoting Corporate Social Responsibility', *Ethics and International Affairs*, 16: 1, 71–87.

Witte, Jan Martin and Wolfgang Reinicke (2005) *Business UNusual: Facilitating United Nations Reform through Partnerships*, New York, NY: UN Publications.

Wolf, Klaus Dieter (2000) *Die Neue Staatsräson: Zwischenstaatliche Kooperation als Demokratieproblem in der Weltgesellschaft*, Baden-Baden: Nomos.

Wolf, Klaus Dieter (2002) 'Contextualizing Normative Standards for Legitimate Governance beyond the State' in Jürgen R. Grote and Bernard Gbikpi (eds) *Participatory Governance: Political and Societal Implications*, Opladen: Leske + Budrich, pp. 35–50.

Wolf, Klaus Dieter (2005) 'Möglichkeiten und Grenzen der Selbststeuerung als gemeinwohlverträglicher politischer Steuerungsform', *Zeitschrift für Wirtschafts- und Unternehmensethik*, 6: 1, 51–69.

Wolf, Klaus Dieter (2006) 'Private Actors and the Legitimacy of Governance beyond the State' in Arthur Benz and Ioannis Papadopoulos (eds) *Governance and Democracy.*

Comparing National, European and International Experiences, London: Routledge, pp. 200–27.

Wolf, Klaus Dieter (2007) 'Output, Outcome, Impact: Focusing the Analytical Lens for Evaluating the Success of Corporate Contributions to Peace-Building and Conflict-Prevention', mimeo.

Wolf, Klaus Dieter (2008) 'Emerging Patterns of Global Governance: The New Interplay between the State, Business and Civil Society' in Andreas Georg Scherer and Guido Palazzo (eds) *Handbook of Research on Global Corporate Citizenship*, Cheltenham: Edward Elgar, pp. 225–48.

Wolf, Klaus Dieter (2010) 'Chartered Companies: Linking Private Security Governance in Early and Post Modernity' in Nicole Deitelhoff and Klaus Dieter Wolf (eds) *Corporate Security Responsibility?*, Basingstoke: Palgrave Macmillan, pp. 154–76.

Wolf, Klaus Dieter, Annegret Flohr, Lothar Rieth and Sandra Schwindenhammer (2010) 'Variations in Corporate Norm-Entrepreneurship: Why the Home State Matters' in Morten Ougaard and Anna Leander (eds) *Business and Global Governance*, London: Routledge, forthcoming.

Wolfensohn, James D. (1999) *Coalitions for Change: Address to the Board of Governors*, Washington, DC: The World Bank Group, 28 September 1999.

Wolfsberg Group (2007) *The Wolfsberg Statement against Corruption*, Wolfsberg: http://www.wolfsberg-principles.com/standards.html, date accessed 6 May 2009.

Wolfsberg Group (2000) *Global Anti-Money-Laundering Guidelines for Private Banking*, Wolfsberg: http://www.wolfsberg-principles.com/standards.html, date accessed 6 May 2009.

Wood, Donna J., Jeanne M. Logsdon, Patsy G. Lewellyn and Kimberly S. Davenport (2006) *Global Business Citizenship: A Transformative Framework for Ethics and Sustainable Capitalism*, Armonk, NY: M.E. Sharpe.

World Society Research Group (2000) 'Introduction: World Society' in Mathias Albert, Lothar Brock and Klaus Dieter Wolf (eds) *Civilizing World Society. Society and Community beyond the State*, Lanham: Rowland and Littlefield, pp. 1–17.

Wright, Roy W. (1968) 'The Policies and Practices of the Rio Tinto-Zinc Corporation Limited' in Malcolm McIntosh and Ruth Thomas (eds) (2001) *Global Companies in the Twentieth Century: Selected Archival Histories, Volume IX. Rio Tinto*, London: Routledge, 18.

Xiaonian, Xu and Wang Yan (1997) 'Ownership Structure, Corporate Governance and Firms': The Case of Chinese Stock Companies', *Working Paper*, Amherst College and The World Bank.

Young, Oran R. (2002) *The Institutional Dimensions of Environmental Change: Fit, Interplay, and Scale*, Cambridge, MA: MIT Press.

Young, Oran R. (1999) *Governance in World Affairs*, Ithaca, NY: Cornell University Press.

Young, Oran R. (1994) *International Governance: Protecting the Environment in a Stateless Society*, Ithaca, NY: Cornell University Press.

Young, Oran R., and Marc. A. Levy (1999) 'The Effectiveness of International Environmental Regimes' in Oran R. Young (ed.) *The Effectiveness of International Environmental Regimes: Causal Connections and Behavioral Mechanisms*, Cambridge, MA: MIT Press, pp. 1–32.

Zadek, Simon and Alex MacGillivray (2007) 'The State of Responsible Competitiveness 2007' in AccountAbility (ed.) *The State of Responsible Competitiveness: Making Sustainable Development Count in Global Markets*, London: AccountAbility, pp. 11–34.

Zahra, Shaker A., James C. Hayton, Donald O. Neubaum, Clay Dibrell and Justin Craig (2008) 'Culture of Family Commitment and Strategic Flexibility: The Moderating Effect of Stewardship', *Entrepreneurship Theory & Practice*, 30: 6, 1035–54.

Zammit, Ann (2003) *Development at Risk: Reconsidering UN-Business Relations*, Geneva: UN Research Institute for Social Development.

Zerk, Jennifer A. (2006) *Multinationals and Corporate Social Responsibility. Limitations and Opportunities in International Law*, Cambridge: Cambridge University Press.

Zürn, Michael (2005) 'Global Governance' in Gunnar Folke Schuppert (ed.) *Governance-Forschung: Vergewisserung über Stand und Entwicklungslinien*, Baden-Baden: Nomos, pp. 121–46.

Index

acceptance 5, 19, 21, 22, 146–8
accountability 15, 24–5, 140, 147–57, 176, 179, 188, 192–3, 203–8, 214–5, 217, 222, 226, 228–30, 235, 244–5, 254
   accountability mechanism 150–2
   accountability relationship 155–6
actors
   configurations of 40, 128–9, 130–2, 175, 194–7
   see also civil-society actors, stakeholders
adversarial legalism 54, 64
appropriateness 21, 82, 84, 86, 112, 164, 186
   see also logic of appropriateness
architecture, global institutional 3, 13–15, 17, 141, 146, 162, 198–9, 214, 227, 232–5
   see also global governance, constitutionalization of
authority 7–8, 52, 57, 153, 208–10, 227, 229, 236–7, 240–1
authorization 204, 207, 209–11
autonomy, structural 34, 36, 40, 126–36, 163–4, 167

best practices 19, 20, 22, 25, 53, 59
brand 34, 84–97, 165
Business case 12, 41, 170, 221, 233–5, 244–6, 253–5
business-government relations 32, 33, 39, 41, 52–66, 88, 165
   adversarial relations 54–5, 57, 60
   cooperative relations 54–5, 57, 59, 60, 61, 62, 64, 65, 66
   corporatist relations 54, 57, 58, 60,
Business Principles Countering Bribery (BPCB) 24, 25, 28, 30, 31, 132–3, 143
Business Social Compliance Initiative (BSCI) 24, 26, 28, 30, 31, 132–3, 143

causal mechanisms 10–12, 33, 42, 45, 50–5, 52, 67, 82, 108, 127, 136, 137–8, 146, 161–7

   see also logic of action
civil society 6, 21, 25, 32, 35, 41–52, 163
   and campaign 6, 12, 39, 42–5, 49, 52, 165, 248
   see also NGOs
code of conduct 10, 19–21, 26, 52, 134, 173, 175–9, 195, 212–5, 224
coercion 10, 14, 44, 129, 134, 227
cognitive frames 19, 44, 51,
cognitive predisposition 108–9, 112, 122, 166
collective initiatives 19–24, 27, 34, 40, 42, 52, 53, 161–7, 174
company characteristics
   corporate culture of 34, 36, 39, 61, 101, 108–122, 164–7
   ownership structure of 33–4, 36, 39, 81, 94–108
   vulnerability of 33–4, 36, 39, 81–94, 81, 163–5
   see also corporate identity
configuration of actors
   see actors
constitutionalization
   see global governance, constitutionalization of
constructivist theory 18, 33, 40, 52, 54–55, 68, 84–5, 108–9, 162–7
consumers 34, 41, 42, 43, 44, 51, 165, 166
   see also customers, stakeholders
coordinated market economies 59, 60
co-regulator 147–8
corporate identity 33–4, 36, 44, 55, 58, 172–3, 177, 182, 186, 192, 199
   see also company characteristics
corporate social responsibility (CSR) 9, 19, 39, 42, 60
corporatism 44, 54, 57,
corruption 7, 8–9, 19, 25, 26,
   see also Business Principles Countering Bribery, Partnering Against Corruption Initiative
cost-benefit calculations
   see rationalist theory